ns to Byzantine History and Culture

Series Editors

Florin Curta
University of Florida, USA

Leonora Neville
University of Wisconsin Madison, USA

Shaun Tougher
Cardiff University, UK

New Approaches to Byzantine History and Culture publishes high-quality scholarship on all aspects of Byzantine culture and society from the fourth to the fifteenth centuries, presenting fresh approaches to key aspects of Byzantine civilization and new studies of unexplored topics to a broad academic audience. The series is a venue for both methodologically innovative work and ground-breaking studies on new topics, seeking to engage medievalists beyond the narrow confines of Byzantine studies. The core of the series is original scholarly monographs on various aspects of Byzantine culture or society, with a particular focus on books that foster the interdisciplinarity and methodological sophistication of Byzantine studies. The series editors are interested in works that combine textual and material sources, that make exemplary use of advanced methods for the analysis of those sources, and that bring theoretical practices of other fields, such as gender theory, subaltern studies, religious studies theory, anthropology, etc. to the study of Byzantine culture and society.

More information about this series at
http://www.springer.com/series/14755

Gerasimos Merianos · George Gotsis

Managing Financial Resources in Late Antiquity

Greek Fathers' Views on Hoarding and Saving

palgrave
macmillan

Gerasimos Merianos
Institute of Historical Research
National Hellenic Research
 Foundation
Athens, Greece

George Gotsis
Department of History and
 Philosophy of Science
National and Kapodistrian University
 of Athens
Athens, Greece

New Approaches to Byzantine History and Culture
ISBN 978-1-137-56408-5   ISBN 978-1-137-56409-2   (eBook)
DOI 10.1057/978-1-137-56409-2

Library of Congress Control Number: 2017947168

© The Editor(s) (if applicable) and The Author(s) 2017
The author(s) has/have asserted their right(s) to be identified as the author(s) of this work in accordance with the Copyright, Designs and Patents Act 1988.
This work is subject to copyright. All rights are solely and exclusively licensed by the Publisher, whether the whole or part of the material is concerned, specifically the rights of translation, reprinting, reuse of illustrations, recitation, broadcasting, reproduction on microfilms or in any other physical way, and transmission or information storage and retrieval, electronic adaptation, computer software, or by similar or dissimilar methodology now known or hereafter developed.
The use of general descriptive names, registered names, trademarks, service marks, etc. in this publication does not imply, even in the absence of a specific statement, that such names are exempt from the relevant protective laws and regulations and therefore free for general use.
The publisher, the authors and the editors are safe to assume that the advice and information in this book are believed to be true and accurate at the date of publication. Neither the publisher nor the authors or the editors give a warranty, express or implied, with respect to the material contained herein or for any errors or omissions that may have been made. The publisher remains neutral with regard to jurisdictional claims in published maps and institutional affiliations.

Cover credit: Gregory of Nazianzus giving alms to the poor (cod. Sin. gr. 339, f. 341^v, twelfth century). Source: G. Galavaris, *Ζωγραφική βυζαντινών χειρογράφων* (Athens: Ekdotike Athenon, 1995), fig. 148, by kind permission of the publisher.

Printed on acid-free paper

This Palgrave Macmillan imprint is published by the registered company Macmillan Publishers Ltd. part of Springer Nature
The registered company address is: The Campus, 4 Crinan Street, London, N1 9XW, United Kingdom

Contents

1 Introduction and Acknowledgements   1

2 Historical Background: Early Christian Conceptions
   of Hoarding   15

3 Justifying Savings but not the Pursuit of Wealth:
   Contradictions, Tensions and Accommodations
   in Early Patristic Texts   43

4 Savings for Redistributive Purposes: Stewardship
   of Wealth in the Teachings of Basil of Caesarea
   and John Chrysostom   73

5 Fifth-Century Patristic Conceptions of Savings and
   Capital: Isidore of Pelusium and Theodoret of Cyrrhus   117

6 Contextualizing Patristic Concepts of Hoarding
   and Saving   159

7 Conclusions   197

Bibliography 207

Index 241

Abbreviations

Old Testament

Ex.	Exodus
Lev.	Leviticus
Num.	Numbers
Deut.	Deuteronomy
Ps.	Psalms
Prov.	Proverbs
Eccl.	Ecclesiastes
Sir.	Sirach
Isa.	Isaiah
Jer.	Jeremiah
Ezek.	Ezekiel
Hos.	Hosea
Am.	Amos
Mic.	Micah
Nah.	Nahum

New Testament

Mt.	Matthew
Mk.	Mark
Lk.	Luke

Acts	Acts of the Apostles
Rom.	Romans
1–2 Cor.	1–2 Corinthians
Gal.	Galatians
Eph.	Ephesians
Phil.	Philippians
Col.	Colossians
1–2 Thess.	1–2 Thessalonians
1–2 Tim.	1–2 Timothy
Tit.	Titus
Philem.	Philemon
Heb.	Hebrews
Jas.	James
1–2 Pet.	1–2 Peter
1 Jn.	1 John
Jud.	Jude
Rev.	Revelation

Patristic Texts

Basil	Basil of Caesarea
Hom. Destr. horr.	*Homilia in illud: "Destruam horrea mea"*
Hom. div.	*Homilia in divites*
Hom. temp. fam.	*Homilia dicta tempore famis et siccitatis*
*HPs.*14b	*Homilia in psalmum* 14b
1–2 Clem.	*1–2 Clement*
Clem. Alex.	Clement of Alexandria
Quis div.	*Quis dives salvetur*
Chrysostom	John Chrysostom
De dec. mill.	*De decem millium talentorum debitore*
De Laz. conc.	*De Lazaro conciones*
De stat. hom.	*De statuis hom.*
In Act. apost. hom.	*In Acta apostolorum hom.*
In Col. hom.	*In epistulam ad Colossenses hom.*
In 1 Cor. hom.	*In epistulam I ad Corinthios hom.*
In 2 Cor. hom.	*In epistulam II ad Corinthios hom.*
In Eph. hom.	*In epistulam ad Ephesios hom.*
In Heb. hom.	*In epistulam ad Hebraeos hom.*
In Ioh. hom.	*In Iohannem hom.*
In Mt. hom.	*In Matthaeum hom.*
In Phil. hom.	*In epistulam ad Philippenses hom.*

ABBREVIATIONS ix

In 1 Thess. hom.	*In epistulam I ad Thessalonicenses hom.*
In 1 Tim. hom.	*In epistulam I ad Timotheum hom.*
In 2 Tim. hom.	*In epistulam II ad Timotheum hom.*
Princ. Act. hom.	*In principium Actorum hom.*
Did.	*Didache*
Greg. Naz.	Gregory of Nazianzus
Test.	*Testamentum*
Greg. Nyss.	Gregory of Nyssa
Paup. 1	*De beneficentia*; vulgo *De pauperibus amandis* 1
Usur.	*Contra usurarios*
SH	*Shepherd of Hermas*
Mand.	*Mandata*
Sim.	*Similitudines*
Vis.	*Visiones*
Theodoret	Theodoret of Cyrrhus
De prov.	*De providentia orationes decem*
Interpr. 2 Cor.	*Interpretatio epistolae II ad Corinthios*
Interpr. Heb.	*Interpretatio epistolae ad Hebraeos*
Interpr. 1 Tim.	*Interpretatio epistolae I ad Timotheum*
Or. de div. et s. char.	*Oratio de divina et sancta charitate*

Legal Texts

CJ	*Codex Justinianus*
CTh	*Codex Theodosianus*
NVal	*Novellae Valentiniani*

Editions and Secondary Sources

ACO   Schwartz, E. et al., ed., Acta Conciliorum Oecumenicorum. Strasbourg: W. de Gruyter, 1914; Berlin and Leipzig: W. de Gruyter, 1924–.

Azéma 1–4   Azéma, Y., ed. and trans., *Théodoret de Cyr, Correspondance*, 4 vols. SC 40, 98, 111, 429. Paris: Les Éditions du Cerf, 1955–1998.

BHG   Halkin, F. *Bibliotheca hagiographica graeca*, 3 vols. in 1. Subsidia Hagiographica, 8a. 3rd edn. Brussels: Société des Bollandistes, 1957.

BHL   [Société des Bollandistes] *Bibliotheca hagiographica latina antiquae et mediae aetatis*, 2 vols. Subsidia Hagiographica, 6. Brussels: Société des Bollandistes, 1898–1901.

BSGRT	Bibliotheca Scriptorum Graecorum et Romanorum Teubneriana
CCS	Cambridge Classical Studies
CS	Variorum Collected Studies Series
ECF	The Early Church Fathers
Ehrman 1–2	Ehrman, B. D., ed. and trans., *The Apostolic Fathers*, 2 vols. LCL, 24–25. Cambridge, MA: Harvard University Press, 2003.
Évieux 1–2	Évieux, P., ed. and trans., *Isidore de Péluse, Lettres*, 2 vols. SC, 422, 454. Paris: Les Éditions du Cerf, 1997–2000.
GCS	Die Griechischen Christlichen Schriftsteller
GCS NF	Die Griechischen Christlichen Schriftsteller, Neue Folge
GNO	Jaeger, W. et al., ed., *Gregorii Nysseni Opera*, vol. 1–. Leiden: Brill, 1952–.
HTSTS	*HTS Teologiese Studies / Theological Studies*
JECS	*Journal of Early Christian Studies*
JSNT	*Journal for the Study of the New Testament*
JSNTSup	Journal for the Study of the New Testament: Supplement Series
Lampe	Lampe, G. W. H., *A Patristic Greek Lexicon*. Oxford: Clarendon Press, 1961.
LCL	Loeb Classical Library
LSJ	Liddell, H. G., Scott, R., and Jones, H. S., *A Greek-English Lexicon*. 9th edn. with revised supplement. Oxford: Clarendon Press, 1996.
NPNF 2	*A Select Library of Nicene and Post-Nicene Fathers of the Christian Church*, 2nd series, ed. P. Schaff and H. Wace. 14 vols. New York: The Christian Literature Company, 1890–1900.
NRSV	New Revised Standard Version
NTS	*New Testament Studies*
ODB	Kazhdan, A.P., ed., *The Oxford Dictionary of Byzantium*, 3 vols. New York and Oxford: Oxford University Press, 1991.
OECS	Oxford Early Christian Studies
PG	Migne, J-P., ed., Patrologiae Cursus Completus. Series Graeca, 161 vols. Paris: Imprimerie Catholique, 1857–1866.
PLRE 1–3	Jones, A.H.M. (vol. 1), Martindale, J.R. (vols. 1–3), and Morris, J. (vol. 1), *The Prosopography of the Later Roman Empire*, 3 vols. Cambridge: Cambridge University Press, 1971–1992.
SC	Sources Chrétiennes
SNT	Supplements to Novum Testamentum
SNTSMS	Society for New Testament Studies: Monograph Series
Sophocles	Sophocles, E.A., *Greek Lexicon of the Roman and Byzantine Periods (from B.C. 146 to A.D. 1100)*. Cambridge, MA: Harvard University Press, 1914.
SP	*Studia Patristica*

SupVC	Supplements to Vigiliae Christianae
TCH	Transformation of the Classical Heritage
VC	*Vigiliae Christianae*
VitMelGr	Gorce, D., ed. and trans., *Vie de sainte Mélanie*. SC, 90. Paris: Les Éditions du Cerf, 1962 (Greek version).
VitMelL	Laurence, P., ed. and trans., *Gérontius, La Vie latine de sainte Mélanie*. Studium Biblicum Franciscanum, Collectio Minor, 41. Jerusalem: Franciscan Printing Press, 2002 (Latin version).
WUNT	Wissenschaftliche Untersuchungen zum Neuen Testament
ZAC	*Zeitschrift für Antikes Christentum*

Other Abbreviations

Ep(p).	*Epistula(e)*
hom.	*homilia, -ae*
Or.	*Oratio*
Serm.	*Sermo*

CHAPTER 1

Introduction and Acknowledgements

Hoarding is a practice akin to accumulating behaviours. In the world of legend and epic, it is often considered to be a feature of monsters and dragons—such as Fafnir in the *Nibelungenlied*—living an isolated and marginal life. In the Old English epic poem *Beowulf*, good leaders are regarded as those who distribute their wealth freely, while the dragon, the great opponent of Beowulf, amasses treasures for self-gratification. The allusion is obvious: hoarding is associated with greed, while wealth accumulation denotes loneliness and social contempt, as in the dragon's case.[1] Although both Beowulf and the dragon collect riches, the first distributes a part of them, while the latter jealously holds on to everything. In certain ethnographic contexts, chiefs may have been subject to the obligation to redistribute part of their takings, suggesting that the degree of appropriation is not left unfettered by community.[2] It seems that the appropriation of vast wealth by "dragons," this supreme expression of greed, opposes community interests and welfare.[3]

Individuals in the past, according to the political and socio-economic context and their status, employed whichever method was handy at a given time to channel their surplus, whether this was storing it in the walls of their houses or storerooms, depositing it in financial institutions, lending at interest or financing entrepreneurial activities, and so on. In the urban centres of the late antique Mediterranean, people were aware of what we characterize as "productive investment" or "rational use of financial resources." Yet their choices were not always "rational" from a modern economics point of view, a fact that stresses the need to define

© The Author(s) 2017
G. Merianos and G. Gotsis, *Managing Financial Resources in Late Antiquity*, New Approaches to Byzantine History and Culture,
DOI 10.1057/978-1-137-56409-2_1

1

what we really mean by using terms like these within an ancient or a medieval context. Some of the alternatives, having their own logic and aiming at social equity and cohesion rather than economic growth, were promoted by the Fathers of the Church.

This book is intended to provide an overview of Greek patristic responses to the problem of management of surplus income and savings in urban economic environments, where poverty, persistent inequality and disparity in the distribution of wealth were endemic. In this respect, we examine the work of Church Fathers who were active in the urban centres of the Eastern Mediterranean (e.g., Alexandria, Pelusium, Antioch, Constantinople) and whose literary output was in Greek. How did, for instance, Clement of Alexandria, John Chrysostom and Isidore of Pelusium face "hoarding dragons" within their societies? How did their views evolve through time, as the setting gradually became "Byzantine"? Are their positions just ethico-religious discourse or do they reflect the impact of contemporary socio-economic phenomena, such as the economic crisis of the third century or the economic expansion and social change from the fourth century onwards?

This critical investigation of patristic views, through the interrelated yet distinct lenses of history of ideas, economic history and history of economic thought, is mainly centred on income acquisition, maintenance of financial resources and their proper use. Thus, we attempt to determine the literal and, where appropriate, the metaphorical meaning of hoarding and saving in patristic thinking, as well as to bring to the existing literature an exploration of these concepts as specific practices embedded in their social and economic contexts. This effort allows for an in-depth evaluation of the respective contributions of Church Fathers to aspects of the economic problem per se (e.g., division of labour and work ethic, parsimonious behaviour, self-centred vs. other-centred economic attitudes, and so on).

For the better understanding and easiest contextualization of patristic views, our survey begins with the related ideas of New Testament authors. As for its end, we chose the late fifth century for several reasons: from a patristic point of view, the respective ideas present a relative cohesion until the fifth century, focusing mainly on the social impact of hoarding and saving conducted in urban milieus. It is notable that hagiography, from the fifth century onwards, presents new or alternative perceptions of these economic practices. The surplus material wealth, often stored miraculously in monasteries, is depicted in a positive way, in sharp contrast to the perception of hoarded wealth by the fourth- and many of the fifth-century Fathers.[4] From a fiscal and monetary point of view, the bronze currency reform in 498 by Anastasius I (491–518) facilitated everyday transactions and inaugurated a series of fiscal measures for the restoration of revenues and prosperity; as a result, his reign poses a turning point in this respect and a plausible limit. In any case, the following period, and particularly the reign of Justinian I (527–565), is such a watershed in Byzantine history that a partial examination could not have done justice to all important facets related to it.

The examination of hoarding and saving, as well as their interrelation and differences, has long been under scrutiny in various scientific fields. The respective approaches cannot be fully taken into consideration in this study, yet a glance at recent bibliography reveals their multiplicity. From an economic psychology perspective, hoarding is viewed as the corollary of corrupt patterns of consumption stemming from certain individual psychological aberrations. Hoarding behaviours are frequently analysed as implying an outright attachment to material possessions that reflects strong compulsive dispositions,[5] being highly harmful to psychic health and overall psychological well-being.[6] The disruptive effects of hoarding attitudes are significantly reinforced in the absence of deeper and genuine relationships with others,[7] and denote identity substitutes that suffocate experiences of sharing,[8] while entailing personality disorders subject to proper medical treatment.[9] In this respect, hoarding impulses are entrenched in abnormal psychological states inimical to healthy behaviours.

Furthermore, economic psychology conceptualizes hoarding as an avoidance behaviour linked with indecisiveness. The hoarder cannot make the required decision to throw something away and cope with emotional reactions that accompany parting with cherished possessions, because of an increased perception of control. Hoarding is defined as a multi-faceted problem stemming from information processing deficits, problems in forming emotional attachments, behavioural avoidance and erroneous beliefs concerning the nature of possessions.[10] Despite the fact that hoarders elaborate various rationales to justify their accumulation habits, attachment to possessions implies a stronger belief that items are integral to emotional well-being.[11] Reluctance to dispose of material possessions provides a sense of security to the owner, yet hoarding as the acquisition of a significant amount of possessions is related to substantial health impairment.[12]

From an economic history point of view, hoarding has been conceptualized as a highly controversial, if not socially detrimental, process.

Matthew J. M. Coomber, for instance, argues that long-held traditions and societal patterns, which underlay outdated economic strategies in eighth-century Judah, were challenged in an environment of rapid economic development. As a result, agrarian societies experienced an abandonment of subsistence practices, land consolidation and the ensuing hoarding of riches among the elites.[13] Exploring an entirely different environment and drawing on early Islamic sources, Ahmad Asad Ibrahim et al. investigate a variety of concepts of hoarding and focus on the challenge that such an economic practice poses the need for greater circulation of accumulated wealth.[14] Hoarding was highly suspected in the Islamic texts. The early Islamic legal schools introduced certain constraints on hoarding activities by commanding the hoarder to sell his commodities at a specified price.[15]

Negative attitudes toward hoarding were not infrequent in medieval and early modern Europe. Surplus from hoarding practices had to be directed to markets to mitigate shortages in commodities' supply. Buchanan Sharp demonstrated that Edward II's (1307–1327) response to the famine of 1315–1317 in England consisted in regulatory measures that involved not only prohibitions imposed on the export of grain dictated by high prices, but also efforts to persuade or even compel those hoarding grain to sell surplus that exceeded the level of self-sufficiency.[16] In a similar vein of reasoning, Randall Nielsen examined early modern English policies for the relief of grain dearth, such as the forced delivery of private stocks, as an effective response to speculative hoarding.[17] Beyond hoarding of commodities, monetary hoarding and luxury spending were two alternative responses to an abrupt augmentation of assets, which affected the circular flow of wealth in mid-fourteenth-century England.[18] Edward III's (1327–1377) debasement of the coinage in the period up to 1351 resulted in monetary hoarding due to, at least in part, the widely held belief that gold coinage should primarily serve the acts of hoarding and noble almsgiving.[19]

Jaco Zuijderduijn and Tine De Moor found that late medieval Dutch households, rather than engaging in hoarding practices, increasingly invested in capital markets as a more productive risk-aversion strategy that served as a means to absorb and neutralize a wide range of external adversities.[20] In this context, elite and middling groups but also poorer households invested their savings in capital markets: thus, they engaged in pro-active, enterprising behaviours and incurred debts through their participation in real estate transactions.[21]

In the cultural setting of the Protestant Reformation, Philipp Robinson Rössner underscores the effect of hoarding monetary assets on the ongoing scarcity of silver. Rössner investigates the monetary origins of Luther's ideas stemming from his conception of *avaritia*, of greedy motives; the latter are associated with unnatural chrematistics, the desire to acquire more than one's fair share.[22] Rössner argues that the development of the money supply in late medieval Germany, as well as the velocity of the circulating coins, were not unimportant for setting the context of Luther's economic discourse. Such debates on indulgences waged by early reformers have been thought of as a part of a long-standing proto-Keynesian tradition in continental economic thought that placed an emphasis on the need to spend or invest money rather than letting it lie in idleness through hoarding practices.[23]

Obviously, the concept of hoarding has been subject to intellectual scrutiny in the field of economics. Mercantilism, for instance, supported policies that protected the quality of coinage and discouraged the hoarding of bullion through regulations that restricted its conversion into jewellery or plate, in view of ensuring sufficient currency to trigger economic activity.[24] Among the late mercantilists, David Hume (1711–1776) endorsed the established belief that hoarding, namely the gathering of large sums into a public treasury that prevented their circulation, was a destructive practice. Yet, in some instances, he favoured the hoarding of gold and silver by a public reserve bank, since an increased money supply entailed higher prices, and, as a consequence, hindered exports and economic growth.[25] Hume had in mind cases such as the massive hoarding by Henry VII (1485–1509), which was offset by the abrupt sinking of the prices of all commodities, thus offering England a competitive advantage in international commerce.[26]

In another vein of reasoning, Sir James Steuart (1713–1780) observed that rich people tend to hoard their wealth, thus inducing a deficiency of demand that may in turn entail higher unemployment rates. This effect of hoarding, if combined with increasing luxury consumption of imported goods, may undermine efforts to maintain prosperity.[27] In the early twentieth century, the eminent economist Thorstein Veblen (1857–1929) employed the term "conspicuous consumption" to denote that acquisition of possessions is invested with a social dimension, involving the need to display one's elevated social status through luxury spending. For Veblen, status-oriented consumption helps to legitimize processes of exclusion and dispossession.[28]

John Maynard Keynes (1883–1946) revisited the mercantilist hoarding theories by arguing that hoarding is responsible for a lack of effective demand, and therefore an equilibrium with unemployment will prevail. In times of crisis, the individuals will not engage in investment or consumption expenditure but will hoard their money, so the propensity to hoard, or the liquidity preference, increases. Monetary policies are thus ineffective in stimulating the level of economic activity because new money is hoarded in a deflationary incident.[29] The liquidity trap argument has fuelled further academic discussion.

Jörg Guido Hülsmann observes that, despite their opposing views, both Keynes and Friedrich August Hayek (1899–1992) shared the belief in the deleterious nature of money hoarding, as well as in the desirability of a flexible money supply to offset changes in money demand.[30] But Nicholas Rowe contends that Keynes failed to draw with precision a demarcation line between hoarding, consisting in savings in the form of money on the one hand, and thrift, comprising savings in means other than money on the other. Concomitantly, according to Rowe, it is rather excessive hoarding, not excessive thrift, that generates a dysfunctional effect that impedes the proper operation of the economic system.[31] Of course, hoarding as a financial practice is entwined with recent developments in the global economy, in the aftermath of the current financial crisis.[32]

The aforementioned indicative references serve to show the diachronic distrust primarily toward private hoarding as an irrational or antisocial practice that withdraws mainly, but not solely, monetary resources from circulation, which could be alternatively utilized in an economically or socially beneficial way. It should be noted that in the context of speculative hoarding in particular, the accumulation of commodities like grain in turbulent times generated considerable profits for hoarders, who often were members of local elites. This points to a necessary clarification. Roughly all social strata could engage in hoarding—and for the poorer it probably represented the only opportunity for financial security—yet it was the volume of hoarded wealth in association with the purpose behind its accumulation that rendered hoarding ethically a more or less reprehensible practice.

Hoards, according to numismatics, comprise one of the three major categories of coin finds, the other two being casual or stray finds and excavation finds. Hoards can be divided into four categories: accidental losses, emergency hoards, savings hoards and abandoned hoards. Savings hoards are the most pertinent to our theme, yet other coin finds, such as accidental losses, can be very informative on the various forms of savings (e.g., the capital of a travelling merchant). Savings hoards consist mainly of coins, as well as occasionally of plate and other valuables, and are very telling about the economic status of their owner: the wealthy saved precious metals, while others saved billon and bronze. One of the differences between emergency and savings hoards is that the latter have a selective character, containing high-value and high-quality coins (i.e. better specimens).[33] This kind of hoard can have a remarkable span of years. However, Philip Grierson observes aptly that "under conditions of peace the vast majority of savings hoards will not have survived to modern times, since in due course they will have been put back into circulation by their owners or inheritors."[34] The precarious nature of savings hoards was evident, and a reason why hoarding is presented as a futile activity in Christian and Byzantine traditions is the belief that people foolishly accumulate assets to be enjoyed by invaders and conquerors.[35]

Hoarding is not the only practice associated with capital accumulation, which is intended to generate profit. Employing a behavioural standpoint, capital accumulation comprises three distinct aspects: hoarding, saving and investing. Differences between these concepts remain subtle yet functional. Hoarding primarily designates a process of withdrawal of money from active circulation by accumulating it, rather than choosing to spend it on consumption or buying fixed assets, thus holding it in private in a "state of idleness." On the contrary, saving is an activity focusing on provision for the future and, as such, is commonly held to be a virtuous aspiration. Whereas saving is related to refraining from spending, investing refers to acts that yield financial returns or benefits and involve a motive for profit.[36] This relationship between saving and investing, typical of a Keynesian context, significantly differs from that of classical and neoclassical economics, in which saving and investment are entwined: in the absence of hoarding, what is saved is invested. In the Keynesian context, a typical definition of saving involves the assumption that current income is not spent on consumption in its entirety in the same time period, thus there is excess income, but individuals do not proceed to rational decisions about how and when to spend it. The idea of a future time horizon (or even life expectancy) as a critical aspect for determining decisions on saving is central to neoclassical approaches.[37] Interestingly, the concept of a propensity to hoard is frequently used by post-Keynesians to account for how households manage their flow of savings, a concept that is controversial in economic literature.[38]

Although the Church Fathers did not use the tripartite distinction between hoarding, saving and investing, this differentiation could be used heuristically in studying their views. Accumulation in the form of hoarding is what Fathers discuss and rebuke the most, yet sometimes the two other concepts are implied or described. Hoarding, especially as an elite practice, was highly suspected in patristic thought and literature, yet there is a paucity of research focusing on how Fathers conceived of the antecedents and consequences of such activities. This book is intended to narrow this gap. A set of research questions around the issues of the justification and social desirability of savings and capital from surplus wealth guides the study.

More specifically, we seek to: (a) identify the origin of legitimate income, according to various notions; (b) explicate the widely held binary distinction between ethical and unethical activities on the one hand, and productive and lucrative engagements on the other; (c) differentiate between conspicuous consumption, denoting the superfluity of riches, and accumulation of resources, which reflect the precarious nature of wealth; (d) illustrate methods of laudable use of surplus (i.e. almsgiving), as reflected in various patristic narratives; (e) underscore the polarity between self-centred and other-centred economic pursuits; (f) demonstrate how Christian appropriation of household management traditions was exemplified in virtuous and socially responsible practices that alleviated the economically worse off, fostered spiritual well-being and reduced societal segmentation; (g) investigate the principles underlying honest stewardship of wealth in general, and financial resources in particular; and (h) study the evolution of the respective ideas, shifting gradually from the late Roman to the early Byzantine milieu.

The book is divided into seven chapters, introduction and conclusions included. We would like to stress that different strategies were employed per chapter in order for us to better present the Greek patristic views on hoarding and saving, as well as their evolution from the late first through the fifth century. This choice was mainly dictated by the fact that the Fathers under discussion have received different degrees of scholarly attention. In this respect, the second and third chapters, which deal with relatively better-examined themes, are written as an overview. The second chapter, in particular, deals with the views of New Testament authors, which serve as the background of early patristic thought, while the third chapter covers the period from the late first to the third century, focusing mainly on the so-called "Apostolic Fathers" and Clement of Alexandria. The fourth chapter discusses the highly influential stance of Basil of Caesarea and John Chrysostom. This is a structural chapter that surveys what is considered to be the "classical" approach to the hoarding and management of financial resources in Greek patristic thinking. The fifth chapter employs Isidore of Pelusium and Theodoret of Cyrrhus as case studies of fifth-century diverse responses to the issue of managing resources. Isidore's views are the least discussed by contemporary research in comparison to those of other Fathers examined in this book. Theodoret's case is also particular, since his theological rather than his socio-economic views have been the subject of detailed scrutiny. Finally, the sixth chapter adopts a mixed structure: it comprises two sections, of which the first is written as an overview, focusing selectively on economic, monetary and social aspects of the period under discussion. The other section employs the *Life* of Melania the Younger as a case study of the way a super-rich person experimented so as to renounce her wealth in conformity to the normative tenets of Christian tradition but also to her elite mentality. Both sections emphasize the need to place patristic views on hoarding and saving in context.

Thus, the study rotates around three axes: the patristic views on hoarding and saving, the moral and social obligations of the elite, and the socio-economic realities of highly urbanized environments in the late antique Eastern Mediterranean. It does not deal systematically with aspects such as monastic attitudes to respective issues or the impact of Classical and Hellenistic philosophy on the development of certain patristic views. Although we do recognize the significance of these and other facets for a comprehensive evaluation of our theme, we have chosen to focus on previously underdeveloped yet significant economic aspects. It is obvious that the book's debt to recent scholarship is great, due to the insightful approaches that have recast our understanding of various aspects upon which this study touches, but also because it has permitted us to build on already conducted fundamental analyses concerning, for example, the role of elites, poverty groups, bishops, monks and saints. A glance at the bibliography suffices to indicate our intellectual loans.

And if our debt to recent scholarship is given, we must also acknowledge those without the assistance of whom the writing of this book would have been a much more difficult task. We would like to thank the Director of the Institute of Historical Research, National Hellenic Research Foundation (IHR, NHRF, Athens), Professor Taxiarchis

Kolias, for supporting the idea of writing this book and facilitating its realization within the Institute. Special thanks are due to Ilias Anagnostakis, Research Director at the IHR, NHRF, for his constant encouragement and also for his critical eye. We are indebted to Telemachos Lounghis, Research Director Emeritus, IHR, NHRF, who has readily provided his expertise. Evi Delli, Marina Koumanoudi, Nikos Livanos and Zisis Melissakis, colleagues and friends in the IHR, NHRF, offered, as always, helpful suggestions with respect to particular aspects at various stages of the book's writing, for which we are grateful. A friend indeed, Yannis Stoyas, Researcher Curator in the KIKPE Numismatic Collection of the Welfare Foundation for Social and Cultural Affairs (Athens), is cordially thanked for helping us clarify matters of his expertise. The tireless efforts of Georgia Karaiskaki, National Documentation Centre, NHRF, to make hard-to-find books and articles accessible are also acknowledged with gratitude.

Gerasimos Merianos in particular wishes to thank his wife, Sandy Sakorrafou, and his daughter, Georgina, for their love, support and patience.

George Gotsis would like to thank his family for encouragement, support and timeless understanding.

Notes

1. See, for instance, L. K. Little, *Religious Poverty and the Profit Economy in Medieval Europe* (Ithaca, NY: Cornell University Press, 1978), 5; H. J. Hummer, *Politics and Power in Early Medieval Europe: Alsace and the Frankish Realm, 600–1000.* Cambridge Studies in Medieval Life and Thought, 4th ser., 65 (Cambridge: Cambridge University Press, 2005), 20. On hoarding in *Beowulf*, see indicatively R. P. Creed, "Beowulf and the Language of Hoarding," in *Medieval Archaeology: Papers of the Seventeenth Annual Conference of the Center for Medieval and Early Renaissance Studies*, ed. C. L. Redman. Medieval and Renaissance Texts and Studies, 60 (Binghamton, NY: Center for Medieval and Early Renaissance Studies, 1989), 155–167.
2. S. Gudeman, *The Anthropology of Economy: Community, Market, and Culture* (Oxford: Blackwell, 2001), 107.
3. See G. Merianos, "Αντιλήψεις περί αποταμιεύσεως στο Βυζάντιο: Πατερικές διδαχές, ψυχωφελείς διηγήσεις και κοσμικές θεωρήσεις," in *Αποταμίευση και διαχείριση χρήματος στην ελληνική ιστορία*, eds. K.

Bouraselis and K. Meidani (Athens: Tachydromiko Tamieutērio Hellados, 2011), 198 n. 97.
4. See D. Caner, "Towards a Miraculous Economy: Christian Gifts and Material 'Blessings' in Late Antiquity," *JECS* 14.3 (2006): 329–377; *idem*, "Wealth, Stewardship, and Charitable 'Blessings' in Early Byzantine Monasticism," in *Wealth and Poverty in Early Church and Society*, ed. S. R. Holman. Holy Cross Studies in Patristic Theology and History (Grand Rapids, MI: Baker Academic, 2008), 221–242.
5. See, for instance, H. Cherrier and T. Ponnor, "A Study of Hoarding Behavior and Attachment to Material Possessions," *Qualitative Market Research* 13.1 (2010): 8–23; D. F. Tolin et al., "The Economic and Social Burden of Compulsive Hoarding," *Psychiatry Research* 160.2 (2008): 200–211.
6. J. L. Lastovicka and L. Anderson, "Loneliness, Material Possession Love, and Consumers' Physical-Well-Being," in *Consumption and Well-Being in the Material World*, ed. M. Tatzel (Dordrecht: Springer, 2014), 63–72.
7. P. A. Caprariello and H. T. Reis, "To Do, to Have, or to Share? Valuing Experiences over Material Possessions Depends on the Involvement of Others," *Journal of Personality and Social Psychology* 104.2 (2013): 199–215.
8. See indicatively L. Claes, A. Müller and K. Luyckx, "Compulsive Buying and Hoarding as Identity Substitutes: The Role of Materialistic Value Endorsement and Depression," *Comprehensive Psychiatry* 68 (2016): 65–71; R. M. Winters, *The Hoarding Impulse: Suffocation of the Soul* (Hove, East Sussex: Routledge, 2015).
9. For further discussion in the abundant literature, see, for instance, V. E. Kress et al., "Hoarding Disorder: Diagnosis, Assessment, and Treatment," *Journal of Counseling and Development* 94.1 (2016): 83–90; M. G. Wheaton, "Understanding and Treating Hoarding Disorder: A Review of Cognitive-Behavioral Models and Treatment," *Journal of Obsessive-Compulsive and Related Disorders* 9 (2016): 43–50.
10. See F. Penzel, "Hoarding in History," in *The Oxford Handbook of Hoarding and Acquiring*, eds. R. O. Frost and G. Steketee. Oxford Library of Psychology (Oxford: Oxford University Press, 2014), 15.
11. P. J. Phung et al., "Emotional Regulation, Attachment to Possessions and Hoarding Symptoms," *Scandinavian Journal of Psychology* 56.5 (2015): 573–581.
12. R. O. Frost et al., "Excessive Acquisition in Hoarding," *Journal of Anxiety Disorders* 23.5 (2009): 632–639.
13. M. J. M. Coomber, "Caught in the Crossfire? Economic Injustice and Prophetic Motivation in Eighth-Century Judah," *Biblical Interpretation* 19.4–5 (2011): 396–432.
14. A. A. Ibrahim, R. J. Elatrash and M. O. Farooq, "Hoarding versus Circulation of Wealth from the Perspective of *maqasid al-Shari'ah*," *International Journal of Islamic and Middle Eastern Finance and Management* 7.1 (2014): 6–21.

15. B. E. Hawk, *Law and Commerce in Pre-Industrial Societies* (Leiden: Brill, 2016), 277–278.
16. B. Sharp, "Royal Paternalism and the Moral Economy in the Reign of Edward II: The Response to the Great Famine," *Economic History Review* 66.2 (2013): 628–647. Modern economists have considered anti-hoarding laws as irrational responses to a non-existent monopoly on the storage of grain. Such anti-hoarding measures, they argue, cannot be directed against a monopolistic storer, for he will always store less, not more, than would be stored under perfect competition. Anti-hoarding laws, however, can be desirable and efficient second-best policies in cases in which excessive private stockholding can induce active market manipulation, implying a perverse economic behaviour that distorts effective operation of market mechanisms. For a detailed discussion, see B. D. Wright and J. C. Williams, "Anti-Hoarding Laws: A Stock Condemnation Reconsidered," *American Journal of Agricultural Economics* 66.4 (1984): 447–455.
17. R. Nielsen, "Storage and English Government Intervention in Early Modern Grain Markets," *Journal of Economic History* 57.1 (1997): 1–33.
18. D. Wood, *Medieval Economic Thought*. Cambridge Medieval Textbooks (Cambridge: Cambridge University Press, 2002), 122.
19. Wood, *Medieval Economic Thought*, 129–131.
20. J. Zuijderduijn and T. De Moor, "Spending, Saving, or Investing? Risk Management in Sixteenth-Century Dutch Households," *Economic History Review* 66.1 (2013): 38–56.
21. T. De Moor and J. Zuijderduijn, "Preferences of the Poor: Market Participation and Asset Management of Poor Households in Sixteenth-Century Holland," *European Review of Economic History* 17.2 (2013): 233–249.
22. P. R. Rössner, "Luther – Ein tüchtiger Ökonom? Über die monetären Ursprünge der Deutschen Reformation," *Zeitschrift für Historische Forschung* 42.1 (2015): 37–74.
23. P. Rössner, "Burying Money? Monetary Origins and Afterlives of Luther's Reformation," *History of Political Economy* 48.2 (2016): 225–263.
24. On mercantilist economic policies, see S. G. Medema, "The Economic Role of Government in the History of Economic Thought," in *A Companion to the History of Economic Thought*, eds. W. J. Samuels, J. E. Biddle and J. B. Davis. Blackwell Companions to Contemporary Economics, 3 (Malden, MA: Blackwell Publishing, 2003), 431. A decrease in the velocity of money due to hoarding was considered a threat to economic growth. To offset hoarding, money should be in circulation even in the form of luxury spending; yet luxury goods should not be imported, because an increase in imports contravened mercantilist principles.

25. M. P. Paganelli, "David Hume on Banking and Hoarding," *Southern Economic Journal* 80.4 (2014): 968–980.
26. T. Hutchison, *Before Adam Smith: The Emergence of Political Economy, 1662–1776* (Oxford: Blackwell: 1988), 207.
27. A. Brewer, "Pre-Classical Economics in Britain," in *A Companion to the History of Economic Thought*, eds. Samuels, Biddle and Davis, 91.
28. M. Watson, "Desperately Seeking Social Approval: Adam Smith, Thorstein Veblen and the Moral Limits of Capitalist Culture," *The British Journal of Sociology* 63.3 (2012): 507.
29. P. Bagus, *In Defense of Deflation*. Financial and Monetary Policy Studies, 41 (Cham: Springer, 2015), 26.
30. J. G. Hülsmann, "Cultural Consequences of Monetary Interventions," *Journal des Économistes et des Études Humaines* 22.1 (2016): 77–98.
31. N. Rowe, "Keynesian Parables of Thrift and Hoarding," *Review of Keynesian Economics* 4.1 (2016): 50–55.
32. See J. Aizenman, Y.-W. Cheung and H. Ito, "International Reserves Before and After the Global Crisis: Is There no End to Hoarding?" *Journal of International Money and Finance* 52 (2015): 102–126.
33. P. Grierson, *Numismatics* (London: Oxford University Press, 1975), 125–136.
34. Grierson, *Numismatics*, 135.
35. Merianos, "Αντιλήψεις περί αποταμιεύσεως," 211 and n. 137.
36. In modern parlance, the relation between saving, investment and growth becomes more complex the more the financial sector is involved in economic activities. For example, in the case of an increasing part of financial funds circulating outside the circular flow of money associated with market activities, these money flows may be viewed as a new kind of financial hoarding which assumes a critical role in modern credit money economies. See, for instance, M. Binswanger, "The Finance Process on a Macroeconomic Level from a Flow Perspective: A New Interpretation of Hoarding," *International Review of Financial Analysis* 6.2 (1997): 107–131.
37. K.-E. Wärneryd, *The Psychology of Saving: A Study on Economic Psychology* (Cheltenham: E. Elgar, 1999), 50–55.
38. T. Andresen, "A Critique of a Post Keynesian Model of Hoarding, and an Alternative Model," *Journal of Economic Behavior and Organization* 60.2 (2006): 230–251.

CHAPTER 2

Historical Background: Early Christian Conceptions of Hoarding

THE NEW TESTAMENT WORLD:
SOCIAL AND ECONOMIC CONTEXT

Early Christian economic ideas emerged and evolved in a specific setting, that of the ancient economy as an inextricable part of processes and structures that shaped socio-economic life. A group of New Testament scholars interested in economic issues adopted a view of the ancient economy as a constitutive, albeit not distinct, element of the overall social system.[1] Douglas E. Oakman, for instance, argues that ancient Roman economy was political in two aspects: first, it was based upon forced extraction of goods through taxation or rents imposed on agricultural resources in the provinces, and second, it encouraged a movement of goods through commercial activities favouring the interests of prosperous elites or their delegates, and denoting an unequal distribution of riches.[2] In contrast to the unprivileged, a small elite minority concentrated, appropriated and controlled a vast amount of resources through hoarding wealth. Accordingly, the economic system was not viewed as an autonomous sphere of social action.[3] Against this background, emerging Christian communities were reflecting experiences that substantially opposed the prevailing arrangements of political economy as akin to an overarching institutional structure. David A. Fiensy observes that, although the economic conditions of the Lower Galilee did not necessarily drive peasants toward poverty and starvation, it was hard for lower strata to survive and harder to thrive in this economic world. Jesus was critical not so much of the economic system as of the dominant and prosperous partners that controlled it.[4]

According to this line of thought, such a kind of domestic economy was embedded in the two-fold institutional sphere of an ancient society. Kinship and politics encompassed economic behaviour in such a way that there was hardly any particular focus on economics apart from these two sub-systems. Bruce J. Malina, for example, deems that the ancient economy did not witness the emergence of economic arrangements detached from such forms of belonging that constrained the scope of markets, while it did favour reciprocities not pertaining to modern economics.[5] Malina highlights the extractive nature of this political economy too. On the one hand, political economy represented one aspect of this subsistence economy in which taxation appeared detrimental to the well-being of lower strata but beneficial to the prosperity of the extremely few.[6] Domestic economy, on the other hand, denoted kinship norms that regulated relationships and determined social stratification and interacting economic partners.

Seán Freyne emphasizes Jesus' appeal to those engaging in fishing enterprises in an area that enabled export of Galilean produce and interregional trade.[7] In so doing, Jesus was challenging the deeper social values on which the Herodian market economy was founded.[8] Being exploitative in nature, this market economy was entwined with a rigid social stratification, contributing to the maintenance of power of those who dominated a wide range of productive activities.[9] Inimical to this political economy was a system based on kinship, the extended family, associated with non-economic values.[10] In this context, unprivileged groups like small farmers, artisans and manual labourers, though not enviable, were deemed essential to the overall welfare.[11] In contrast to these ideals, ostentatious living, reflecting the moral promiscuity of the elite and the concomitant lack of concern for lower strata, penetrated the behavioural patterns of those competing for pre-eminence with a view to controlling the supply of commodities.

In sum, the idea of an embedded economy in Graeco-Roman antiquity is widely held among scholars examining the economic world of the New Testament. Such a stance could be conventionally located on the "primitivist" side of the so-called "primitivist–modernist controversy." This controversy has raged since the late nineteenth century, its main argument being over whether an ancient economy is qualitatively or quantitatively different from a modern one. After Moses I. Finley, the debate has been reformulated into "substantivist–formalist."[12]

However, primitivist and/or substantivist views of Roman economy have been challenged by recent contributions to Roman economic history. These approaches have highlighted issues such as the efficiency of market mechanisms in coordinating economic activities,[13] or the ability of the Roman Empire to provide low-cost security, to effectively enforce a structure of property rights, to secure currency, to reduce transport costs, as well as to entail lower transaction costs as a result of a proper institutional framework.[14] In contrast to the alleged underdevelopment and stagnation of Roman economy, evidence is adduced on innovative economic rationality aiming at profit maximization, the latter underlying elite involvement in trade and manufacture. In this respect, the market was important both for the enrichment of elite mentalities and the orientation of individuals to risky activities rather than mere self-sufficiency.[15]

This kind of argumentation has been variously characterized as "neo-modernist," "moderate modernist" or "anti-primitivist,"[16] yet these labels are of little importance. What really matters for a modern historian is to construe the multi-faceted contexts of ancient societies and economies. A perception of the ancient economy in which rational decision making and self-interested activities coexisted with notions of friendship, virtue and beneficence seems plausible. Contradictions appear less puzzling if we place an equal emphasis on the values and economic attitudes of economic agents without underestimating either side.[17] Otherwise, we will remain attached to highly distorted assessments of Roman aristocracy, for instance, considering it first and foremost as an agrarian class whose income was almost exclusively generated from agriculture.[18] As we shall briefly see, certain New Testament narratives suggest engagement with lending and investment practices on behalf of members of the elite (and, equally important, their agents), but also of other social groups, with a view to maximizing profits in the context of the marketplace.[19] At the same time, long-standing concepts, such as that of household management, were appropriated by New Testament authors.

Intellectual Encounters:
The Greek and Roman Literature
on Household Management

The analytical category of the "household," which permeates a diversity of ancient narratives, could be used heuristically so as to conceive the way in which certain economic themes are formulated in New Testament narratives. This concept, imbued with moral connotations, originates in Xenophon's *Oeconomicus* and is subject to further elaboration in Aristotle's *Politics*[20] as a sort of counsel offered to aristocratic elites on the specific way they should espouse to properly rule wives, children and slaves.[21] The household-management (*oikonomia*) tradition remained an administrative not a market approach to economic phenomena, its prime aim being the efficient management of resources to achieve desired objectives. In respective importance, however, personal competences as conducive to economic efficiency were also taken into consideration.[22]

The concept of *oikonomia* was designating the prudent management of resources, but it could equally be employed in other spheres of human existence. Dotan Leshem advocates an integration of *oikonomia* in the civic community, delineating an *oikonomia* of the self, a cosmological *oikonomia* and an *oikonomia* of the law.[23] In imperial formations, the concept was no more subservient to both politics and philosophy, but it occupied an intermediary space between these two realms. Apart from Xenophon and Aristotle, rich textual evidence on the initial meaning of economy as household management is offered by works from later periods, such as those of Callicratidas, Philodemus of Gadara and Bryson, as well as fragments of texts ascribed to female members of the Pythagorean School.[24] It is notable that the ancient art of economics comprises discourses on both things human (primarily slaves and wives) and inhuman. Concomitantly, the practice of thrift, of stewardship of property and wealth, was not only encouraged but also mandated in administering scant resources.[25] Leshem argues that:

> [...] the ancient philosophers thought of the *oikonomia* as a sphere in which man, confronting abundant means, must acquire an ethical disposition of economic rationality enabling him to meet his needs and generate surplus to be spent outside the boundaries of the economic sphere (that is, in philosophy and politics).[26]

In sum, wealth in ancient economies was defined as anything that satisfies human wants and participates in the generation of surplus that can provide opportunities for leisure, so as to meet human goals external to the economic domain. Wealth was subjectively valued, while excess in economic behaviour was frequently viewed as integral to the human condition, as a part of an "ontology of abundance."[27] Surplus was expected to be used in ways pertinent to the virtue of benevolence through friendship, enabling meditation, participation in manifestations of civic life and financial support of public institutions. Excesses could be harnessed through an ethical choice intended to channel resources outside the boundaries of the economic domain, allowing the head of an *oikos* to demonstrate beneficence, to pursue politics, to engage in philosophy and to sustain institutions.

In this framework, perceptions of "limited good" constrained economic initiatives, because all productive resources were considered finite in number and limited in quantity: given the shortage of supply of all goods, both material (e.g., wealth) and symbolic (e.g., reputation, honour, friendship), wealth accumulation was considered feasible only at the expense of others.[28] This was especially true for individuals who engaged in profit-seeking activities, who were viewed as placing their effort in satisfying insatiable desires through the pursuit of wealth. Not unexpectedly, enrichment reflected greedy motives in an alleged limited good economy: at a near-subsistence level, the interplay between various economic agents often resulted in "zero-sum games," in which any apparent improvement in one's position regarding distribution of wealth was perceived as a substantial threat to the common good.[29]

Conceptualizing Hoarding

The Synoptic Gospels: Hoarding as Endemic to Human Acquisitiveness

A rich variety of economic issues has been assimilated into the parables and other New Testament material. Activities that implied a tendency for enrichment were vehemently denounced in an idealized world of reciprocities as involving fraud that secured economic benefit at the expense of others. Accordingly, the concept of excessive wealth contrasted with traditional views of self-sufficiency, which formed a hierarchical evaluation of riches. Landed property, rather than mercantile and business engagements, was considered a noble occupation, and revenues deriving from agricultural enterprises opposed to dishonest sources of wealth, such as commercial profit and tax extraction.[30] Unlike agricultural pursuits, which responded to this ideal of self-sufficiency as a unique source of honourable income, wage-earning occupations placed a man in a state of dependence upon others, and thus they were deemed as inappropriate to free persons.[31]

Of course, these concepts more often than not stemmed from the ideological pronouncements of the elite literati of the Graeco-Roman world, who typically presented elites as more conservative than they were in practice. Economic ideology reflecting on proper and improper activities was most probably used to set boundaries to anyone outside the elite, not to the elite itself, the members of which would not have left unexploited any opportunity for enrichment, such as engagement (direct or indirect) in "dishonourable" trade or in "despicable" tax collection.

Early Christian economic attitudes were reflective of the social ethic of an agrarian economy, while social values, such as the condemnation of the pursuit of anything more than a modest level of wealth, were entrenched in the mentalities of the era. Jesus' teaching originated in first-century Roman Palestine, an agrarian economy in which production and distribution were controlled by prosperous and influential families.[32] Social antagonisms between, on the one hand, powerful elites that possessed large estates and controlled land, and, on the other, tenants striving for the necessities of life (Mt. 13:24–30; Lk. 12:16–21) or labourers raising agricultural produce and engaging in manufacturing activities, were typical of Roman Palestine's socio-economic structures.[33]

Parable narratives are replete with such economic connotations. It has been suggested that the institution of farm tenancy became an instrument of agricultural exploitation in first-century Palestine, in which the implementation of tenancy affected the structure of labour supply, shaping two distinct groups: the underemployed day labourers and the free tenants.[34] This economic organization, portraying control of land and capital, permeates parable narratives: indebtedness to great landlords was the social corollary of processes of wealth accumulation perceived as highly detrimental to the economically worse off.[35] Resort to violence to collect rents (cf. Mk. 12:1–9) was a common practice of wealthy landlords, who were involved in the leasing of farms for commercial purposes. A landlord's departure provided an opportunity for money lending by retainers who were encouraged to invest their holdings, yet were condemned if they appropriated resources entrusted to them or failed to place monetary assets as bank deposits (Lk. 19:20–23). Honest administration of resources was countenanced (Lk. 16:11). Estate stewards managed considerable monetary funds (Lk. 12:41–48) and manipulated loans to their own benefit.[36] Financial transactions were often operated by slave managers enjoying professional autonomy inconsistent with their legal status.[37]

More specifically, slave managers were profiting from loans to free persons entering into patron–client relationships. For instance, the unjust steward in Luke (16:1–13) secures his welfare by discounting the debts owed to his master. Such stewards were situated within political kinship structures of Roman Galilee.[38] On the contrary, occupational categories such as peasants, artisans and fishers were regarded as insignificant, the non-elites, the deepest needs of whom Jesus addresses.[39] It has been suggested that Jesus came from a middling class of artisans; he was certainly not poor (though his family possessed modest means) and he was experienced in urban culture to the extent that he could serve as a leader of a mass religious movement.[40] In respective importance, the Sayings Gospel Q does not seem to be grounded in either a peasant or an elite milieu, insofar as the text is replete with evidence of social and economic marginality.[41]

The Excesses of Wealth Accumulation

In a cultural context dominated by the traditional value-system of benevolence, hoarding denoted a process disruptive of this socially sanctioned type of economic organization, primarily because of the self-interested motivation perceived as perilous to the perpetuation of social order. Not unexpectedly, social harmony was enfeebled by hoarding behaviours: the rich fool in Luke 12:13–21 is not only implicated in greedy behaviour but also fails to take account of God in his entrepreneurial planning.[42] These attitudes were deemed a by-product of the imprudent aspiration of hoarding of possessions, a theme consistently evoked in, and anticipated by, the Jewish wisdom literature. The sages favoured a level of moderate prosperity, but condemned the excesses of wealth acquired through iniquity.[43] Reliance on ephemeral riches is far from being considered germane to happiness,[44] given that the foolish rich person is abruptly deprived of his alleged security.[45]

Beyond Jewish wisdom moral literature, Philo of Alexandria (d. ca. 50 AD) provides an ethical framework for assessing attitudes to material possessions that is, at least in part, akin to that elaborated by early Christian writers. For Philo, storing up in heaven true wealth (cf. Mt. 6:20), attained through wisdom and godliness, is connected with enjoying the affluence of earthly riches through the providence and care of God.[46] In his view, "neither the possession of wealth nor the willingness to impoverish oneself is a significant factor within ethical discourse regarding issues of wealth and poverty."[47] Philo did not consider ownership of possessions as shameful, insofar as he distinguished between the actual possession of wealth and the morally perilous desire for wealth of which one could not be freed even if dispossessed of everything by choice.[48]

We proceed to frame the main early Christian conceptions of hoarding by employing a tentative taxonomy of their form and content, as they emerge in a variety of New Testament literary works, the theology of which influences the particular type of rhetoric advocated in each of these cases. These distinct yet interrelated and interacting conceptions influenced later developments in economic issues, as we shall explicate in the following chapters.

Framing Early Christian Rhetoric on Hoarding

Hoarding Denounced:
Wealth Employed to Perpetuate Injustice

Jesus opposes the moral foundations of prevailing Galilean economic structures. Kenneth C. Hanson and Douglas E. Oakman argue that God's household was critical of prevailing arrangements based on balanced reciprocities in economic exchanges.[49] In place of the redistributive mechanisms of an economic system perceived as highly exploitative by lower strata, Jesus envisions the possibility of generalized reciprocity, of an unconditional commitment to others' needs. Exchanges are thus permeated by a generalized reciprocity that transcends social status (Mt. 18:23–34; Lk. 6:30, 14:12–14).[50]

In a social world where poverty was viewed as a function of tenancy relations, and debt contracts were legally enforced, Jesus' strategy was articulated in terms of liberation and compassion, in view of debt forgiveness.[51] Indebtedness has been examined as a control mechanism integral to the Roman administration of Palestine and aiming at maintaining the established order.[52] This is the context of the Lord's Prayer intended to liberate people from the burden of perennial debt. The Lord's Prayer (Mt. 6:9–13; Lk. 11:2–4) conceives extreme necessity as release from indebtedness; seeking the reign of God remains the only means to carefree security and genuine well-being (Mk. 10:29–30; Lk. 12:29–31). Luke, in particular, reverses status and prevailing hierarchies in favour of those regarded as dishonoured in an honour-and-shame society.[53]

This distinctively Lukan stance does not necessarily imply repudiation of capital per se. A voluntary restriction of consumption originates in Jesus' belief in the existence of extremes in distribution, which were intolerable in the circle of his followers.[54] Luke's Gospel depicts Jesus as ferociously criticizing Mammon, the personification of dishonest wealth, which is linked to hoarding of possessions. Christopher M. Hays argues that Luke warns against those who hoard their wealth and seem to be preoccupied with financial gain (Lk. 12:16–21, 16:1–13), whereas the book of Acts (4:34–35) endorses the view of a renunciation of property through sharing, divesture and hospitality.[55] The Parable of the Rich Fool in particular reflects the landowner's attempt to increase his level of consumption and pursue pleasure by withdrawing from the community and confining himself to a private sphere of abundance. Unsurprisingly, his hoarding behaviour "can guarantee neither the kind of life he envisioned nor even the continuation of life itself."[56] In contrast to the rich ruler, who was admonished to share all his wealth in the wave of a state of spiritual perfection (Lk. 18:18–30; cf. Mt. 19:16–30; Mk. 10:17–31), Zacchaeus' vow in Luke 19:1–10 was indicative of genuine repentance. His decision to compensate those he had deprived of their possessions was grounded in established Jewish practices of restitution for loss of property.[57]

Hoarding Mitigated Through Circulation of Surplus: Alleviating the Needy in Paul

Paul addresses the value system of a community whose practices entailed a sharp division between the poor and the wealthy. The concept of private administration, situated within a private commercial context in Roman Corinth, is employed to invest his apostolic authority with the social connotations of a divinely appointed administrator.[58] Paul employs a two-fold strategy to alleviate those in extreme necessity.[59] On the one hand, at the micro-level, community meals aim at transcending social boundaries, thus representing a transition from the social code of the Graeco-Roman banquet tradition to another of shared practices coexisting with the Eucharist. On the other hand, Paul's Corinthian correspondence reveals that the collection for Jerusalem, as an expression of a profound Christian solidarity, can be interpreted in a context of balanced reciprocity, an exchange of material support, prayer and grace between Gentile and Jewish converts. Thus, an economic safety network was shaped, centred on the underlying virtue of hope already rooted in, and anticipated by, a long-standing prophetic tradition.[60] This action of raising funds in support of the needy[61] amounts to a circulation of surpluses from prosperous to afflicted areas, a practice that eventuates in a deep thanksgiving to God, the benefactor from whom any beneficence stems (2 Cor. 9:13–15).

Furthermore, a distinctively Pauline work ethic culminates in the ideal of *autarkeia* (self-sufficiency), akin to virtuous living. In Paul's view, a selfish mode of living was reflecting lack of *enkrateia* (self-control), a core value in Hellenistic and Jewish moral literatures.[62] In fact, stewardship of resources entrusted to an extended community of producers and consumers appeared to be not only a practice pertinent to communal integrity, but also an opportunity to exhibit administrative competences and, ultimately, innovative reasoning.[63] It is notable that in subsequent periods, after the emergence of the episcopal organization of churches, efficient management of ecclesiastical property would be a feature of a bishop's successful administration. Paul, in his attempt to address the exigencies of a specific congregational situation in 2 Thessalonians 3:6–13, provides a sound rationale for work engagements consonant to the precept of self-sufficiency that in turn facilitates benevolent action (Eph. 4:28). Accordingly, the emphasis on manual labour (1 Thess. 5:12–15) reflects a work ethic according to which each believer is urged to contribute a fair share to the communal needs.[64]

Middling groups that acquire sufficient resources to channel into such acts of balanced reciprocity are vividly illustrated in Pauline correspondence, in which there is rich textual evidence in support of this claim. In reconsidering Steven J. Friesen's findings on first-century poverty,[65] Bruce W. Longenecker elaborated case-sensitive taxonomies of Graeco-Roman economic stratification that shed new light on the rhetorical conventions of the era.[66] Worth mentioning is the emphasis placed on certain middling groups enjoying excess income—thus claiming a more active engagement in economic affairs—and more specifically, to certain individuals belonging to groups administering resources certainly above subsistence level.[67] Paul addresses the needs of particular groups being around a stable near-subsistence level, although certain individuals fall into higher or lower categories. Fairly wealthy members of the congregations, who accommodated Paul in their homes, included people able to enjoy moderate surplus income and undertake long-distance travel.[68]

Paul's emphasis upon the household-management principles represents the first attempt to accommodate Christian economic practices in the prevailing structures of Graeco-Roman society. Longenecker explains the rise of Christian household affiliations in terms of a shift in reference groups: among the groups represented in this extended household are small business owners enjoying moderate wealth, while landed aristocracy does not seem to be incorporated in Paul's correspondence.[69] Not infrequently, however, divisions within the Christian communities reflected differing degrees of access to monetary resources. Timothy A. Brookins examines divisions within the Corinthian congregations in terms of a comprehensive account of the ancient economy, by underlying the economic connotations of philosophical education and social status within the Corinthian community.[70] In this context, Pauline injunctions reflected a sort of compromise within nascent Christianity, given that idealistic Pauline views of monetary transactions were replete with moral connotations.

Hoarding Abolished: The Ideal of Sharing Possessions

Early Christian responses to economic necessity are illustrated in the book of Acts, in which issues of sharing of resources are considered an integral part of community life (Acts 2:43–47, 4:32–35). Distribution, in particular, is elevated to a key issue of the Luke–Acts theology of possessions, in the context of a communitarian model of ownership[71]: in this context, brotherly love is supportive of a mode of communal living that anticipates Jesus' Parousia (Second Coming). The community's devotional life culminates in bonds of friendship that encompass three kinds of practices: persevering in acts of proclamation, sharing in hospitality and sharing possessions.[72] This community of goods remained a hallmark of sectarian groups, such as the Qumran community.[73] Notable are particular narratives on the requirement for helping needy widows (Acts 6:1–4), engaging in charitable practices and offering hospitality. This has been demonstrated in the case of eminent persons (Acts 12:12, 16:40, 21:8), who retained appreciable financial means, typical of upper-middle social strata.[74] Retaining resources, on the contrary, epitomized in one's unwillingness to share them with fellow believers, was viewed as highly detrimental to these bonds of brotherly communion (Acts 5:1–11).[75]

Hoarding as a Morally Perilous Practice

The Pastoral Epistles appear to be explicitly critical of hoarding wealth in a social context in which Christians were perceived as upwardly mobile as well as culturally accommodative due to an ongoing process of social ascendance of urban Christian groups.[76] Among them, 1 Timothy (and Titus) draws on household-management traditions to delineate and allocate a wide range of pastoral responsibilities within the new congregations.

1 Timothy addresses the needs of hierarchically structured households in a more conventional manner. Strictures placed upon women's economic behaviour, accused of conspicuous display of wealth (1 Tim. 2:9), were perfectly aligned with stereotypical negative perceptions of monetary capital (1 Tim. 6:9–10).[77] Notably, the pursuit of gain is vehemently denounced in the context of the selection of ecclesiastical superintendents (1 Tim. 3:1–8; cf. Tit. 1:7). Profit seeking is spiritually perilous, since egoistic proclivities entrap those who aspire to be wealthy into morally harmful engagements (1 Tim. 6:9).

Profit seeking is a feature of false teachers and is implicitly contrasted with honest stewardship of monetary funds (1 Tim. 6:3–10; 2 Tim. 3:2–9; Tit. 1:10–11).[78] Given the salience of the Pauline metaphor of greed as a form of alienation from God (Eph. 4:18–19),[79] acquisitive behaviour violates God's exclusive rights to primary human allegiances.[80] Virtuous *autarkeia* is reiterated as typical of both Jewish-Christian and Graeco-Roman moral traditions.[81] 1 Timothy differs from other moralists of his day in that he situates his mandates on wealth within a context centred on self-sufficiency and socially responsible use of resources, insofar as believers are urged to entrust not the uncertainty of riches but God the patron and benefactor. In contrast to false teachers unremittingly denounced in the Pastorals, and given the transient nature of wealth,[82] prosperous householders are admonished to engage in generous benefaction as a form of enrichment in charitable acts (1 Tim. 6:18–19).[83]

Moral precepts concerning the administration of community funds are also formulated in the context of 1 Peter, in the form of exhortations to persons of pastoral oversight (1 Pet. 5:1–4).[84] The epistle adopts established household-management ideals: in this context, abstinence from lucrative practices is being alluded to, underlying any primary preoccupation with the administration of monetary capital.[85] An ethic of stewardship opposes the quest for financial gain in return for services offered to the community. In 2 Peter, avaricious behaviour remains a distinctive feature of false teachers who prospered from preaching, extorting a significant amount of resources from their audiences (2 Pet. 2:3, 15).[86]

Hoarding as a Socially Detrimental Practice: Delivering Hoarders to Divine Judgment

The Epistle of James addresses a particular situation in a faith community whereby the wealthy and powerful received honourable treatment, while poor members were frequently demeaned (Jas. 2:1-4), a theme already familiar in Jewish sources (Sir. 13:21-24). The epistle places emphasis on the ephemeral nature of accumulated wealth as a contrast to the excellence of poverty. Scarcity of resources stems from succumbency to the enticement of worldly wealth, particularly from acts that endorse the alleged security of riches. In this respect, the desire to acquire more at the expense of others is disruptive of community integrity and generates disarray and quarrelling, as well as the perspicuous perpetration of sin. Hence, hoarding appears as the social corollary of a corrupted human nature being prone to gluttony and wantonness.[87] The solution to this predicament of the human condition resides in experiencing the favours bestowed by the Father and, more specifically, in participating in Christ's eschatological vindication of the suffering righteous, given that God's care for the poor remains a prominent issue in biblical teaching (Deut. 10:18; Ps. 68:5; Am. 2:6-7; Lk. 1:52-53).[88] It has been argued that both Luke-Acts and the Epistle of James reveal that, despite the lure of enrichment, the sensitivity toward the victims of economic upheavals permeated early Christian practices.[89]

James elaborates on a clear distinction between two distinct groups of the wealthy. On the one hand, traders are criticized because they engage in business planning and place their trust in thoroughly unpredictable outcomes independently of God's will.[90] Given the futility of such long-term planning, business engagements, oriented toward the precariousness of this world, were perceived as propagating injustice, diminishing the opportunity for charity and involving greedy motives (Jas. 4:13-17).[91] On the other hand, wealthy landowners are ferociously attacked for amassing riches, a process that was detrimental to the economically worse off, who felt they were being defrauded of their legitimate goods. Hoarding wealth implied licentious conduct typical of those outsiders who appeared to withhold wages

(Jas. 5:4)[92] and live in luxury at the expense of others (Jas. 5:5).[93] In sum, hoarding is viewed as an irrational and unethical pursuit because of the enhanced social cost of this practice. A rhetoric of divine judgment originates in a reality in which rents were generated by encroachment upon others' resources (Jas. 5:1–6). The agrarian imagery employed by James designates an antithesis to the profit-seeking mentality primarily associated with the urban centres, which is found in the stereotypic representations of the era. James' hostility to capital accumulation resonates with the tendency evident in Graeco-Roman moral literature to employ the topos of a contrast between the rural and the urban as denoting the struggle between the natural and the artificial way of living.[94]

Hoarding as the Corollary of Rapid Economic Growth: Endangering Faithfulness to Christ

In a distinctively apocalyptic worldview, the welfare of merchant classes was primarily related to Rome's capacity to import valuable commodities through maritime trade (enumerated in Rev. 18:12–13). The Roman Empire was successful in securing a decent living standard for social strata other than the upper classes, but also in establishing an effective network of commercial exchanges throughout the Mediterranean Basin. Political networks, institutional stability and, most importantly, the increasing sophistication of contractual law accounted for an unprecedented growth in the volume of monetary transactions. In addition, Rome's efficacy in providing legal enforcement of contracts contributed to an optimal operation of markets by significantly reducing a variety of transaction costs, which resulted in the enhancement of economic efficiency.[95] The *Pax Romana* stimulated Mediterranean trade which in turn promoted regional specialization, comparative advantage and technological change. These factors were critical to the amelioration of living standards, despite the fact that historical conditions were not propitious for those changes that would occur many centuries later during the Industrial Revolution.[96]

The Mediterranean world in the first two centuries AD witnessed such an expansion of economic transactions through long-distance maritime trade, a context portrayed in Revelation 18:11–19. Luxury products referred to in these verses[97] were integral to the Roman trade system that was viewed in Revelation as an efficient means of compromising through indulgence in sinful idolatry.[98] Revelation focuses on the eschatological implications of the impact of wealth on moral behaviours displayed by the pious. In this way Revelation diverges from Jewish wisdom literature, which considers that inequity stems from disparity between rich and poor yet anticipates material wealth for those who seek wisdom. John employs the prophetic tradition with respect to the wealth connotations in Revelation 18.[99] These reflected the injustice perpetrated in pagan cities (Isa. 13:11; Ezek. 27:1–36), whose prosperity made them a source of arrogance (Jer. 50:31–32). This type of abundance is threatened because of the impending affliction vividly portrayed in the violent imagery of the Revelation, in which the implication is that accumulation achieved through reallocation of surplus was securing the interests of the Roman elite. In John's symbolic world, true prosperity and abundant life are experienced as realities pertaining to the future age (Rev. 21:18–21). On the contrary, amassment of material goods, as well as surplus creation, characterize only those who persecute the community of the saints.[100] Christians are viewed as experiencing a persisting social exclusion, not being in a position to conduct their business affairs (Rev. 13:17; also 2:9).[101]

Hoarding as a Form of Alienation from Fellow Believers: The Need for Benevolent Aid

Other New Testament texts elaborate on similar economic concerns from earliest Christianity. The First Epistle of John reiterates the principle of altruistic love as a call to share surplus income, because the ethical implications of faith are reflected in Christians' practical responses to situations of extreme necessity. Distribution of surplus is the economic outcome of the injunction to share wealth with the destitute and the needy (1 Jn. 3:17).[102] In contrast to temporal pursuits (1 Jn. 2:15–17), righteousness is entwined with love through Christ that necessitates acts of sharing wealth. Conversely, accumulation of financial capital for its own sake impedes prospects of salvation. In this respect, sharing surplus is not mandated as a covenantal obligation, but it is viewed as a typical feature of shaping new identities detached from, yet interacting with, prevailing economic practices, an apparent contradiction that we turn to examine in the following chapter.

Notes

1. For an overview of this stance, see G. N. Gotsis and G. Merianos, "Early Christian Representations of the Economy: Evidence from New Testament Texts," *History and Anthropology* 23.4 (2012): 468, 472–474.
2. D. E. Oakman, "The Ancient Economy and St. John's Apocalypse," *Listening: Journal of Religion and Culture* 28 (1993): 200–214.
3. B. J. Malina, "Collectivism in Mediterranean Culture," in *Understanding the Social World of the New Testament*, eds. D. Neufeld and R. E. DeMaris (London: Routledge, 2010), 22–23, argues that in collectivist societies, group-centredness, founded on solidarity, defined the group's identity. J. E. Stambaugh and D. L. Balch, *The New Testament in Its Social Environment*. Library of Early Christianity, 2 (Philadelphia, PA: The Westminster Press, 1986), 63–64, share this view of the ancient economy as a cluster of personified relations.
4. D. A. Fiensy, "Ancient Economy and the New Testament," in *Understanding the Social World of the New Testament*, eds. Neufeld and DeMaris, 199–204.
5. B. J. Malina, *The Social Gospel of Jesus: The Kingdom of God in Mediterranean Perspective* (Minneapolis, MN: Fortress Press, 2001), 103–104.
6. See Malina, *Social Gospel of Jesus*. According to B. J. Malina and J. J. Pilch, *Social-Science Commentary on the Book of Revelation* (Minneapolis, MN: Fortress Press, 2000), 209, taxes were nothing more than a form of extortion, given the inability of a subsistence economy to generate surplus. Elite minorities were oriented to conspicuous consumption intended to serve individual or collective honour.
7. S. Freyne, "Herodian Economics in Galilee: Searching for a Suitable Model," in *Modelling Early Christianity: Social Scientific Studies of the New Testament in Its Context*, ed. P. F. Esler (London: Routledge, 1995), 35.
8. Freyne, "Herodian Economics," 45.
9. Freyne, "Herodian Economics," 43.
10. The prevailing Galilean market structures resorted to value-systems eroding the cultural determinants of an honour-and-shame society (Freyne, "Herodian Economics," 41). These attitudes were opposed to the traditional Judaic beliefs of an inclusive economy; see S. Freyne, "Galilee and Judea: The Social World of Jesus," in *The Face of New Testament Studies: A Survey of Recent Research*, eds. S. McKnight and G. R. Osborne (Grand Rapids, MI and Leicester: Baker Academic and Apollos, 2004), 32–33.
11. Though their positive role in economic welfare is acknowledged, these groups were perceived as being too occupied with their professions,

thus being unable to enjoy leisure and attain wisdom (Sir. 38:24–34). R. Boer, *The Sacred Economy of Ancient Israel*. Library of Ancient Israel (Louisville, KY: Westminster John Knox Press, 2015), provides an investigation of how both aspects of economic life—subsistence and extractive—were embedded in institutionalized forms throughout consecutive periods of ancient Israel's history.
12. On the primitivist–modernist controversy, see indicatively T. Amemiya, *Economy and Economics of Ancient Greece*. Routledge Explorations in Economic History, 33 (London: Routledge, 2007), Chap. 5; A. Bresson, *The Making of the Ancient Greek Economy: Institutions, Markets, and Growth in the City-States*, trans. S. Rendall (Princeton, NJ: Princeton University Press, 2016), Chap. 1.
13. D. Kessler and P. Temin, "Money and Prices in the Early Roman Empire," in *The Monetary Systems of the Greeks and the Romans*, ed. W. V. Harris (Oxford: Oxford University Press, 2008), 137–159.
14. P. F. Bang, "Trade and Empire—In Search of Organizing Concepts for the Roman Economy," *Past & Present* 195.1 (2007): 3–54. P. Erdkamp, "Economic Growth in the Roman Mediterranean World: An Early Good-bye to Malthus?" *Explorations in Economic History* 60 (2016): 1–20, argues that, despite population growth, market-size effects enabled the Roman economy to expand its scope for per capita economic growth, allowing more productive employment of available labour in the Roman world.
15. W. M. Jongman, "Re-Constructing the Roman Economy," in *The Cambridge History of Capitalism*, vol. 1: *The Rise of Capitalism: From Ancient Origins to 1848*, eds. L. Neal and J. G. Williamson (Cambridge: Cambridge University Press, 2014), 75–100.
16. Cf. J.-M. Carrié, "Were Late Roman and Byzantine Economies Market Economies? A Comparative Look at Historiography," in *Trade and Markets in Byzantium*, ed. C. Morrisson. Dumbarton Oaks Byzantine Symposia and Colloquia (Washington, DC: Dumbarton Oaks Research Library and Collection, 2012), 13.
17. See Gotsis and Merianos, "Early Christian Representations," 471, 490.
18. J. Banaji, "Mass Production, Monetary Economy and the Commercial Vitality of the Mediterranean," in idem, *Exploring the Economy of Late Antiquity: Selected Essays* (Cambridge: Cambridge University Press, 2016), 3–4.
19. Cf. P. Sarris, "Integration and Disintegration in the Late Roman Economy: The Role of Markets, Emperors, and Aristocrats," in *Local Economies? Production and Exchange of Inland Regions in Late Antiquity*, ed. L. Lavan. Late Antique Archaeology, 10 (Leiden and Boston, MA: Brill, 2015), 167–188, who underscores the critical role of

markets in late antiquity, in an era of state interventions aiming at stimulating commodified exchange and serving the interests of the elites. For a computational exploration of these market processes behind archaeological evidence, see T. Brughmans and J. Poblome, "Roman Bazaar or Market Economy? Explaining Tableware Distributions through Computational Modelling," *Antiquity* 90.350 (2016): 393–408.
20. Aristotle, *Politica* 1.2 1253b23–27, 1.5 1259b18–21, 3.4 1278b37–39.
21. See Gotsis and Merianos, "Early Christian Representations," 471. The concept of household management was shared by Jewish authors. For instance, Flavius Josephus (*Contra Apionem* 2.181) focuses on the salience of piety (*eusebeia*) as a unifying principle that shapes a diversity of moral duties. See M. Y. MacDonald, "Kinship and Family in the New Testament World," in *Understanding the Social World of the New Testament*, eds. Neufeld and DeMaris, 31–34; eadem, "Beyond Identification of the Topos of Household Management: Reading the Household Codes in Light of Recent Methodologies and Theoretical Perspectives in the Study of the New Testament," *NTS* 57.1 (2011): 68.
22. Aristotle, *Ethica Nicomachea* 1.7 1098a29–33, 2.1 1103a26–34.
23. D. Leshem, "Oikonomia in the Age of Empires," *History of the Human Sciences* 26.1 (2013): 36–37.
24. D. Leshem, "The Ancient Art of Economics," *European Journal of the History of Economic Thought* 21.2 (2014): 205, 207–209.
25. On the contrary, wealth pursued for its own sake was viewed as morally shameful. On the one hand, avarice was considered a root of injustice (Aristotle, *Ars rhetorica* 1.10 1368b14–17); on the other hand, pursuit of wealth, indulgence in insatiable desires and conspicuous consumption entailed moral depravity, detrimental to virtuousness (Aristotle, *Politica* 2.4 1267a10–15; *Ars rhetorica* 1.12 1372b11–13).
26. D. Leshem, "What Did the Ancient Greeks Mean by *Oikonomia*?" *Journal of Economic Perspectives* 30.1 (2016): 230.
27. See D. Leshem, "Oikonomia Redefined," *Journal of the History of Economic Thought* 35.1 (2013): 49–57, for a detailed discussion.
28. The notion of "limited good" has been employed to explore issues of wealth and poverty in first-century Palestine; see, for example, D. H. Reinstorf, "The Rich, the Poor, and the Law," *HTSTS* 60.1–2 (2004): 329–348. On the motives for wealth accumulation in a limited good society, see B. J. Malina, *The New Testament World: Insights from Cultural Anthropology* (3rd edn. Louisville, KY: Westminster John Knox Press, 2001), 97–100; idem, *Social Gospel of Jesus*, 104–105.
29. Gotsis and Merianos, "Early Christian Representations," 474.
30. Old Testament narratives offer a positive account of material possessions; see S. Seiler, "Die theologische Dimension von Armut und Reichtum

2 HISTORICAL BACKGROUND: EARLY CHRISTIAN CONCEPTIONS ...   33

im Horizont alttestamentlicher Prophetie und Weisheit," *Zeitschrift für die Alttestamentliche Wissenschaft* 123.4 (2011): 580–595. P. D. Vrolijk, *Jacob's Wealth: An Examination into the Nature and Role of Material Possessions in the Jacob-Cycle (Gen 25:19–35:29)*. Supplements to Vetus Testamentum, 146 (Leiden and Boston, MA: Brill, 2011), explores riches in the Jacob cycle and the ensuing economic attitudes as integral to a relationship dynamics that entails both conflict and conflict resolution. P. Guillaume, *Land, Credit and Crisis: Agrarian Finance in the Hebrew Bible* (Sheffield: Equinox, 2012), embeds prophetic condemnation of commercial activities in a context of patronage and argues that Palestine was unique in its abundance of land, thus rejecting typical views of peasants as victims of social injustice.

31. C. Perrotta, "The Legacy of the Past: Ancient Economic Thought on Wealth and Development," *European Journal of the History of Economic Thought* 10.2 (2003): 203.

32. For an overview of the state of knowledge on Palestine's economy, see P. A. Harland, "The Economy of First-Century Palestine: State of the Scholarly Discussion," in *Handbook of Early Christianity: Social Science Approaches*, eds. A. J. Blasi, J. Duhaime and P.-A. Turcotte (Walnut Creek, CA: AltaMira Press, 2002), 511–527.

33. J. Pastor, *Land and Economy in Ancient Palestine* (London: Routledge, 1997), 146–150. R. A. Horsley, *Covenant Economics: A Biblical Vision of Justice for All* (Louisville, KY: Westminster John Knox Press, 2009), argues that Jesus envisions a covenant renewal focusing on inalienable rights, not unprecedented in Israel's moral economy. Charity is then construed as an alternative to reciprocal exchange. T. Novic, "Charity and Reciprocity: Structures of Benevolence in Rabbinic Literature," *Harvard Theological Review* 105.1 (2012): 33–52, addresses this relationship between charity and reciprocity in view of identifying reciprocities that suppress the engines of patronage and indebtedness.

34. J. S. Kloppenborg, "The Growth and Impact of Agricultural Tenancy in Jewish Palestine (III BCE–I CE)," *Journal of the Economic and Social History of the Orient* 51.1 (2008): 31–66. For an exploration of the textual and archaeological evidence on tenancy relations in the economy of Roman Palestine, see Z. Safrai, *The Economy of Roman Palestine* (London: Routledge, 1994), 182–191.

35. See K. C. Hanson and D. E. Oakman, *Palestine in the Time of Jesus: Social Structures and Social Conflicts* (Minneapolis, MN: Fortress Press, 1998), 116–125.

36. Estate stewards acted as managers and functioned as intermediaries between households embedded in a cluster of patron–client relationships; see B. Dyck, F. A. Starke and J. B. Weimer, "Toward

Understanding Management in First Century Palestine," *Journal of Management History* 18.2 (2012): 137–165.
37. Slaves engaged in business activities insofar as they managed resources that belonged to their masters or acquired by their own initiatives; see R. Gamauf, "Slaves Doing Business: The Role of Roman Law in the Economy of a Roman Household," *European Review of History* 16.3 (2009): 331–346. A prominent section of freedmen is depicted as economically and socially mobile, engaging in trade and commerce; see H. Mouritsen, *The Freedman in the Roman World* (Cambridge: Cambridge University Press, 2011). From a different lens, D. P. Kehoe, "Law, Agency and Growth in the Roman Economy," in *New Frontiers: Law and Society in the Roman World*, ed. P. J. du Plessis (Edinburgh: Edinburgh University Press, 2013), 177–191, explores the stringent legal requirements imposed on stewards, who protected the financial interests of socially important groups.
38. A body of literature focuses on a social-scientific approach to parable material, which reflects socio-economic structures of Roman Galilee. On the Parable of the Feast, see E. van Eck, "When Patrons are Patrons: A Social-Scientific and Realistic Reading of the Parable of the Feast (Lk 14:16b-23)," *HTSTS* 69.1 (2013). Art. #1375, 14 pp. (10.4102/hts.v69i1.1375). On the Parable of the Sower, see E. van Eck, "The Harvest and the Kingdom: An Interpretation of the Sower (Mk 4:3b–8) as a Parable of Jesus the Galilean," *HTSTS* 70.1 (2014). Art. #2715, 10 pp. (10.4102/hts.v70i1.2715). On the Parable of the Unmerciful Servant, see E. van Eck, "Honour and Debt Release in the Parable of the Unmerciful Servant (Mt 18:23–33): A Social-Scientific and Realistic Reading," *HTSTS* 71.1 (2015). Art. #2838, 11 pp. (10.4102/hts. v71i1.2838). On the Parable of the Pearl, see E. van Eck, "When an Outsider Becomes an Insider: A Social-Scientific and Realistic Reading of the Merchant (Mt 13:45–46)," *HTSTS* 71.1 (2015b). Art. #2859, 8 pp. (10.4102/hts.v71i1.2859). On the Parable of the Vineyard Labourers, see E. van Eck and J. S. Kloppenborg, "An Unexpected Patron: A Social-Scientific and Realistic Reading of the Parable of the Vineyard Labourers (Mt 20:1–15)," *HTSTS* 71.1 (2015). Art. #2883, 11 pp. (10.4102/hts.v71i1.2883); E. K. Vearncombe, "Redistribution and Reciprocity: A Socio-Economic Interpretation of the Parable of the Labourers in the Vineyard (Matthew 20.1–15)," *Journal for the Study of the Historical Jesus* 8.3 (2010): 199–236. On the Parable of the Shrewd Manager, see D. H. Reinstorf, "The Parable of the Shrewd Manager (Lk 16:1–8): A Biography of Jesus and a Lesson on Mercy," *HTSTS* 69.1 (2013). Art. #1943, 7 pp. (10.4102/hts.v69i1.1943).

39. D. A. Fiensy, "Did Large Estates Exist in Lower Galilee in the First Half of the First Century C.E.?" *Journal for the Study of the Historical Jesus* 10.2 (2012): 133–153, contends that, in contrast to the medium-sized estates of the elite in Sepphoris, Lower Galilee, estates were of modest size, exerting a non-significant economic impact.
40. D. A. Fiensy, *Christian Origins and the Ancient Economy* (Eugene, OR: Cascade Books, 2014), 33. The poor were far from comprising a homogeneous group in the Roman Mediterranean Basin. B.-Z. Rosenfeld and H. Perlmutter, "The Poor as a Stratum of Jewish Society in Roman Palestine 70–250 CE: An Analysis," *Historia: Zeitschrift für Alte Geschichte* 60.3 (2011): 273–300, introduce a new approach to the stratification of poverty in Roman Palestine. They employ a typology that differentiates between distinct sub-groups of poor people in accordance with their financial situation, combined with their particular occupation.
41. S. E. Rollens, *Framing Social Criticism in the Jesus Movement: The Ideological Project in the Sayings Gospel Q*. WUNT, 2.374 (Tübingen: Mohr Siebeck, 2014), 200, argues that focusing on middling persons who may experience structural marginality, but are also in a position to interact with their social conditions and participate in social movements, is a more realistic way to conceive of the processes associated with the Jesus movement.
42. The maxim depicting a rich man who enjoys abundance of wealth is reminiscent of similar declarations in Jewish texts that highlight the dissipation of the rich (e.g., Jer. 17:11).
43. Prov. 10:2, 13:21–23, 15:27, 21:6. The sages were suspicious of excess wealth, favouring a moderate amount of resources acquired through careful saving (Prov. 13:11), in contrast to hastily concentrated wealth (Prov. 16:8, 28:20, 22).
44. Prov. 11:28, 20:21, 23:4–5; Eccl. 5:10, 9:11–12; Sir. 11:10–28, 31:5–6.
45. See Eccl. 5:13–17, in the context of which the rich person who accumulates excess wealth runs the risk of losing it completely; in this case, hoarding originates in feelings of insecurity concerning one's financial well-being (Eccl. 5:12), however, stored wealth can be lost through failure in a business venture. See C.-L. Seow, "The Social World of Ecclesiastes," in *Money as God? The Monetization of the Market and Its Impact on Religion, Politics, Law, and Ethics*, eds. J. von Hagen and M. Welker (Cambridge: Cambridge University Press, 2014), 138, 156–157. For an examination of the implications of wealth among rabbinic Judaism, see M. Bar-Ilan, "Wealth in the World of the Sages: Why Were Korach and Moses Rich People?" in *Wealth and Poverty in*

Jewish Tradition, ed. L. J. Greenspoon. Studies in Jewish Civilization, 26 (West Lafayette, IN: Purdue University Press, 2015), 1–12.
46. Philo, *De praemiis et poenis* 104. See T. E. Phillips, "Revisiting Philo: Discussion of Wealth and Poverty in Philo's Ethical Discourse," *JSNT* 83 (2001): 116. On the heavenly treasury, see Chap. 3 in this book.
47. Phillips, "Revisiting Philo," 120.
48. Phillips, "Revisiting Philo," 117.
49. Hanson and Oakman, *Palestine*, 126–127.
50. See Gotsis and Merianos, "Early Christian Representations," 478–479.
51. N. Eubank, *Wages of Cross-Bearing and Debt of Sin: The Economy of Heaven in Matthew's Gospel*. Beihefte zur Zeitschrift für die neutestament-liche Wissenschaft und die Kunde der älteren Kirche, 196 (Berlin and Boston, MA: W. de Gruyter, 2013), employs an economic terminology to describe sin as a debt in Matthew's theology.
52. D. E. Oakman, *Jesus, Debt, and the Lord's Prayer: First-Century Debt and Jesus' Intentions* (Eugene, OR: Cascade Books, 2014), 17–41.
53. A. C. Miller, *Rumors of Resistance: Status Reversals and Hidden Transcripts in the Gospel of Luke* (Minneapolis, MN: Fortress Press, 2014), identifies in Luke's status reversal a call for resistance to, and transformation of, dominant values and an imperially endorsed and maintained status quo. This is evident especially in Mary's Magnificat (Lk. 1:46–55) which, in Miller's view, declares "that God will radically alter the prevailing order and values of this world" amid major social and spiritual transformation (*Rumors*, 253).
54. C. L. Blomberg, *Neither Poverty nor Riches: A Biblical Theology of Material Possessions*. New Studies in Biblical Theology, 7 (Downers Grove, IL and Leicester: InterVarsity Press and Apollos, 1999), 127.
55. C. M. Hays, *Luke's Wealth Ethics: A Study in Their Coherence and Character*. WUNT, 2.275 (Tübingen: Mohr Siebeck, 2010), 210–211. Accordingly, "the Gospel of Luke calls for the development of sustenance economic theory based on a cooperativeness ethic, where actors trust one another to do what is best for the whole"; see B. Dyck, *Management and the Gospel: Luke's Radical Message for the First and Twenty-First Centuries* (New York: Palgrave Macmillan, 2013), 170.
56. J. A. Metzger, *Consumption and Wealth in Luke's Travel Narrative*. Biblical Interpretation Series, 88 (Leiden and Boston, MA: Brill, 2007), 81.
57. Ex. 21:33–22:15; Lev. 6:2–7; Num. 5:6–8. According to C. M. Hays ("Slaughtering Stewards and Incarcerating Debtors: Coercing Charity in Luke 12:35–13:9," *Neotestamentica* 46.1 [2012]: 41–60), Lukan wealth ethics, concerned with stimulating proper use of wealth, is

replete with an eschatological *paraenesis*, underscoring the entwinement of ethics and eschatology in Lukan soteriology.

58. See J. K. Goodrich, *Paul as an Administrator of God in 1 Corinthians*. SNTSMS, 152 (Cambridge: Cambridge University Press, 2012), 189.
59. See Gotsis and Merianos, "Early Christian Representations," 480–484.
60. Paul's efforts to raise relief funds for alleviating poverty in the Church of Jerusalem can be viewed as embedded in a wider cultural context. Pauline churches, like members of Jewish synagogues, or pagan voluntary associations, were bound through their communal economic practices involving sharing of financial resources to fund religious activities, to care for the needy and to establish solidified financial bonds with similar groups in other localities. See D. J. Downs, *The Offering of the Gentiles: Paul's Collection for Jerusalem in Its Chronological, Cultural and Cultic Contexts*. WUNT, 2.248 (Tübingen: Mohr Siebeck, 2008), 118–119. Paul, however, frames his collection in ways inimical to conventional Graeco-Roman values of patronage and euergetism. Drawing on an Old Testament background, his alternate mode of benefaction results in thanksgiving and praise to God rather than to human benefactors (ibid., 158). Paul's view of God as the ultimate source of beneficence was akin to elevating care for the poor to a meaningful public virtue (ibid., 165).
61. J. M. Ogereau, *Paul's Koinonia with the Philippians: A Socio-Historical Investigation of a Pauline Economic Partnership*. WUNT, 2.377 (Tübingen: Mohr Siebeck, 2014), advances the view that Paul's relationship with the Philippian congregations operated within the established pattern of economic partnership (*koinōnia/societas*). Paul provided apostolic labour, and in turn the Philippians supplied the monetary funds. In this view, Paul adopted a more strategic approach toward the organization and funding of his cause, by appropriating this economic model for both its flexible structure and the opportunity it afforded to circumvent bonds of patronage and related social obligations (ibid., 344).
62. Sir. 18:30–19:3; Flavius Josephus, *Bellum judaicum* 4.373; Philo, *De specialibus legibus* 1.149–150. Cf. Acts 24:25; Gal. 5:22–23; 2 Pet. 1:5–7.
63. B. Gordon, *The Economic Problem in Biblical and Patristic Thought*. SupVC, 9 (Leiden: Brill, 1989), 55–56.
64. G. Gotsis and S. Drakopoulou-Dodd, "Economic Ideas in the Pauline Epistles of the New Testament," *History of Economics Review* 35.1 (2002): 13–34.
65. S. J. Friesen, "Poverty in Pauline Studies: Beyond the So-Called New Consensus," *JSNT* 26.3 (2004): 323–361.

66. B. W. Longenecker, "Exposing the Economic Middle: A Revised Economy Scale for the Study of Early Urban Christianity," *JSNT* 31.3 (2009): 262–264.
67. Longenecker, "Exposing the Economic Middle," 263.
68. B. W. Longenecker, *Remember the Poor: Paul, Poverty, and the Greco-Roman World* (Grand Rapids, MI: W. B. Eerdmans, 2010), 257–258. Cf. Gotsis and Merianos, "Early Christian Representations," 481–482.
69. B. W. Longenecker, "Socio-Economic Profiling of the First Urban Christians," in *After the First Urban Christians: The Social-Scientific Study of Pauline Christianity Twenty-Five Years Later*, eds. T. D. Still and D. G. Horrell (London: T & T Clark, 2009), 36–59. D. J. Downs, "Is God Paul's Patron? The Economy of Patronage in Pauline Theology," in *Engaging Economics: New Testament Scenarios and Early Christian Reception*, eds. B. W. Longenecker and K. D. Liebengood (Grand Rapids, MI: W. B. Eerdmans, 2009), 129–156, argues that there was neither a shortage of resources nor the potentially exploitative patronage relationships within the economy of God.
70. T. A. Brookins, *Corinthian Wisdom, Stoic Philosophy, and the Ancient Economy*. SNTSMS, 159 (Cambridge: Cambridge University Press, 2014), 209–211.
71. See D. B. Kraybill and D. M. Sweetland, "Possessions in Luke-Acts: A Sociological Perspective," *Perspectives in Religious Studies* 10.3 (1983): 215–239.
72. D. A. Hume, *The Early Christian Community: A Narrative Analysis of Acts 2:41–247 and 4:32–35*. WUNT 2.298 (Tübingen: Mohr Siebeck, 2011), 117. The ethic advanced in this community opposes the prevailing economic ethos of the Graeco-Roman world, as well as practices detrimental to human identity, i.e. attachment to possessions and egocentric pursuits; see A. J. Kuecker, "The Spirit and the 'Other,' Satan and the 'Self': Economic Ethics as a Consequence of Identity Transformation in Luke-Acts," in *Engaging Economics*, eds. Longenecker and Liebengood, 81–103.
73. For a comparison between Qumran economic organization and Graeco-Roman voluntary associations, see C. M. Murphy, *Wealth in the Dead Sea Scrolls and in the Qumran Community*. Studies on the Texts of the Desert of Judah, 40 (Leiden: Brill, 2002), 13–18.
74. Blomberg, *Neither Poverty*, 171–174.
75. Gotsis and Merianos, "Early Christian Representations," 485–486.
76. Gotsis and Merianos, "Early Christian Representations," 484–485.
77. A. J. Batten, "Neither Gold nor Braided Hair (1 Timothy 2.9; 1 Peter 3.3): Adornment, Gender and Honour in Antiquity," *NTS* 55.4 (2009): 484–501, posits that gendered economic pursuits, evidenced by

enhanced status, were publicly perceived as perilous to the group's social respectability. For an in-depth account of gendered roles in the context of a household economy in Roman Palestine, see A. Sivertsev, "The Household Economy," in *The Oxford Handbook of Jewish Daily Life in Roman Palestine*, ed. C. Hezser (Oxford: Oxford University Press, 2010), 229–245.
78. Attachment to money was perceived as a dimension of deceptive leadership epitomized in those false teachers whose covetousness generated an overall moral crisis.
79. According to B. S. Rosner, *Greed as Idolatry: The Origin and Meaning of a Pauline Metaphor* (Grand Rapids, MI: W. B. Eerdmans, 2007), greed bears a variety of interpretive connotations as the worship of Mammon, as slavery imposed by the economic system, as service to wealth, as inordinate love of and devotion to wealth, as well as confidence in it. Drawing on Old Testament narratives that associate mundane prosperity with oppression of the poor, Rosner identifies in the Pauline texts potential remedies for greed, such as the virtues of compassion, kindness, humility and forgiveness in Col. 3:12–15, and of generosity in 1 Tim. 6.
80. A. J. Malherbe, "Godliness, Self-Sufficiency, Greed, and the Enjoyment of Wealth: 1 Timothy 6:3–19, Part 2," in *idem, Light from the Gentiles: Hellenistic Philosophy and Early Christianity: Collected Essays, 1959–2012*, 2 vols, ed. C. R. Holladay et al. SNT, 150 (Leiden and Boston, MA: Brill, 2014), vol. 1, 555.
81. Sir. 29:21; 2 Cor. 9:8; Diogenes Laertius, *Vitae philosophorum* 6.104.
82. The uncertainty of riches reflects the precarious nature of capital accumulation (1 Tim. 6:17) in alignment with established biblical views. See above, nn. 44–45.
83. Cf. N. Eubank, "Almsgiving is 'The Commandment': A Note on 1 Timothy 6.6–19," *NTS* 58.1 (2012): 144–150.
84. See Gotsis and Merianos, "Early Christian Representations," 489.
85. See G. Gotsis, "Socio-Economic Ideas in the Petrine Epistles of the New Testament," *Storia del Pensiero Economico* 4.2 (2007): 95–96.
86. Cf. Jud. 11. Such excesses of dissipation were consonant to a standard description of unconverted pagans (Eph. 4:19; 1 Pet. 4:3–4; also 2 Pet. 2:13, 18).
87. For a more detailed analysis, see G. N. Gotsis and S. Drakopoulou-Dodd, "Economic Ideas in the Epistle of James," *History of Economic Ideas* 12.1 (2004): 7–35.
88. C. M. Hays, "Provision for the Poor and the Mission of the Church: Ancient Appeals and Contemporary Viability," *HTSTS* 68.1 (2012). Art. #1218, 7 pp. (10.4102/hts.v68i1.1218), investigates the rhetorical

strategies employed by James and other New Testament texts to motivate their readership to charitable action. For a conceptualization of poverty relief, as well as of the attitudes toward wealth and poverty in early rabbinic and tannaitic texts, see G. E. Gardner, "Care for the Poor and the Origins of Charity in Early Rabbinic Literature," in *Wealth and Poverty in Jewish Tradition*, ed. Greenspoon, 13–32.

89. See R. Hoppe, "'Nur sollten wir an die Armen denken...' (Gal. 2:10): Arm und Reich als ekklesiale Herausforderung," *Theologische Quartalschrift* 193.3 (2013): 197–208.

90. See Gotsis and Merianos, "Early Christian Representations," 486–487. The critique of excessive confidence in one's uncertain future was a typical theme not only in Hellenistic (Epictetus, *Diatribae* [*Dissertationes*] 3.21.11–12) but also in Jewish moral literature (Eccl. 11:6).

91. This view resonates a basic tenet of the book of Sirach, which is critical of business engagements and the pursuit of profit, because these activities were thought of as involving deception in the acts of selling and buying (Sir. 26:29-27:3).

92. Cf. Lev. 19:13; Deut. 24:14–15; Sir. 34:27.

93. Cf. Sir. 34:26; Mic. 2:1-2. C. L. Westfall, "Running the Gamut: The Varied Responses to Empire in Jewish Christianity," in *Empire in the New Testament*, eds. S. E. Porter and C. L. Westfall. New Testament Study Series, 10 (Eugene, OR: Pickwick Publications, 2011), 235–237, argues that James challenged the position and power of the wealthy by granting equal, if not higher, honour and status to the poor, by calling believers to operate outside the dominant value system and by encouraging fellowship across social boundaries. Accumulating riches designated a dishonourable line of conduct, given that profit was far from being morally justified in the ancient world. By contrast, the epistle praises those who practice the economics of humility in caring for the needy rather than in storing their wealth, both in a sense of enhancing responsibility and enacting true justice; see M. Kamell, "The Economics of Humility: The Rich and the Humble in James," in *Engaging Economics*, eds. Longenecker and Liebengood, 157–175.

94. See A. J. Batten, "The Urban and the Agrarian in the Letter of James," *Journal of Early Christian History* 3.2 (2013): 4–20.

95. B. Arruñada, "How Rome Enabled Impersonal Markets," *Explorations in Economic History* 61 (2016): 82, argues that, contrary to personal exchanges solely favouring the interests of the elite, institutions of impersonal exchange disseminated the beneficial effects of market transactions within society, therefore expanding trade and specialization opportunities, fostering economic growth and establishing an inclusive social order.

2 HISTORICAL BACKGROUND: EARLY CHRISTIAN CONCEPTIONS ... 41

96. For a detailed analysis of this process, see P. Temin, *The Roman Market Economy*. The Princeton Economic History of the Western World (Princeton, NJ: Princeton University Press, 2013), 220–239.
97. In this narrative, economic arrangements induced a form of religious compromise, stemming from both the consumption of luxuries and active participation in pagan institutions (Rev. 3:17–18). Cf. J. N. Kraybill, *Imperial Cult and Commerce in John's Apocalypse*. JSNTSup, 132 (Sheffield: Sheffield Academic Press, 1996), 135–141; Oakman, "The Ancient Economy and St. John's Apocalypse," 203–205.
98. M. D. Mathews, *Riches, Poverty, and the Faithful: Perspectives on Wealth in the Second Temple Period and the Apocalypse of John*. SNTSMS, 154 (Cambridge: Cambridge University Press, 2013), challenges the view that John's stance was dictated by a mere reaction to the social injustice propagated by the imperial Roman cult. Instead, he ascribes John's appeal to the faith community to resist wealth accumulation to a pervasive influence of later Enochic traditions, according to which the wealthy were perceived as wicked and the poor as righteous. Accordingly, "John is moving his audience to a greater degree of discernment in how they negotiate wealth and whether their commitment is to God or the pursuit of wealth" (ibid., 223).
99. The prophet Nahum depicts merchants as a group integral to a thriving society which is threatened by devastation, as all prominent citizens have to abandon Nineveh in defeat (Nah. 3:16–17).
100. John underscores the fact of overwhelming state control of everyday transactions that promoted new allegiances and therefore posed a substantial threat to faithfulness to Christ (Rev. 13:16–17).
101. Gotsis and Merianos, "Early Christian Representations," 488.
102. Cf. Jas. 2:15–16.

CHAPTER 3

Justifying Savings but not the Pursuit of Wealth: Contradictions, Tensions and Accommodations in Early Patristic Texts

ECONOMIC PURSUITS IN THE GRAECO-ROMAN URBAN CENTRES: THE SOCIAL SETTING

As we highlighted in the previous chapter, a rich diversity of views underpinned early Christian economic perspectives and ensuing practices. This diversity permeates subsequent developments in these issues and helps to explain the underlying reasons for which there is hardly a unified set of views and beliefs on economic matters in early Christianity.[1] Helen Rhee has adequately analysed the multi-level processes through which Christians shaped their socio-economic enclaves in the second and third centuries yet remained integrated into the wider Roman society. The more financially resourceful the new converts were, the greater responsibilities they were assuming in support of the more vulnerable members in their communities. These converts belonged to middling groups (e.g., merchants, artisans and skilled labourers occupying their own private businesses) or to upper social ranks.[2] Honour, inheritance, social influence and wealth were not operating in the same manner in Christian communities, yet they were far from being rejected. They were considered beneficial in serving the nascent communities, provided that they were properly managed through correct intentions and motivation. This new reality posed a considerable problem to those enjoying the greatest financial benefits: that of reconciling their distinctive Christian identity with their elevated socio-economic status, a problem that was significantly accentuated for those aspiring to upward social mobility.[3]

© The Author(s) 2017
G. Merianos and G. Gotsis, *Managing Financial Resources in Late Antiquity*, New Approaches to Byzantine History and Culture, DOI 10.1057/978-1-137-56409-2_3

Extant Christian textual evidence appears almost unanimous in disapproving of the excessive acquisitiveness of persons involved in profitable pursuits, and in designating the substantial threat for those that engage in business affairs, because of their accumulation of earthly fortunes. Business profit was considered to obscure Christian identity and undermine responsibility toward the community. Christian texts were apprehensive about and extremely critical of conducting business, which was thought to result in a perilous compromise of Christian identity with the social exigencies stemming from participation in such activities.[4] These concerns were reflecting what we perceive as "aristocratic"—but was in fact cultural and idealistic—disdain toward trade,[5] as well as the conception that insatiable desire for enrichment governs all business affairs. Furthermore, such a criticism focused on the allegedly idolatrous aspects of commercial enterprises, which were frequently conducted in the pagan temples and sanctuaries as loci of financial capital. Christian leaders, on the one hand, recognized the difficulty of disentangling their faithful from the particular mechanisms through which the Graeco-Roman society operated in a complex economic cluster of civic responsibilities. But, on the other hand, they were constantly seeking to delineate Christian allegiances and to draw theologically unequivocal yet practically ambiguous boundaries for new Christian believers.[6]

Glimpses of Hoarding and Saving in Graeco-Roman Literature of the Imperial Period

Early Christian perceptions of business and entrepreneurial affairs emerged as a response to established practices that were deeply rooted in the socio-cultural background of the era. The Graeco-Roman literature of the imperial period is replete with references to household saving practices.[7] For instance, the first-century Roman Stoic philosopher Musonius Rufus advised despising hoarding and everything superfluous.[8] The second-century rhetorician Maximus of Tyre had an equally strong view, considering wealth buried in the earth as "idle treasure" (*thēsauros argos*).[9] In the same vein of reasoning, Herodes Atticus (ca. 101–177), the extremely wealthy Athenian consul and sophist, exalted the use of riches for the alleviation of the needy, but censured idle ones, characterizing non-circulating wealth as "dead," and the treasure chambers where money was hoarded as "prisons of wealth" (*ploutou desmōtēria*).[10]

The ethical tone of these indicative counsels is obvious, and so is the implicit confirmation of the widespread practices of hoarding and storing wealth. Dio Chrysostom (first–early second century) refers to the *tamieion* (storehouse, strongroom) where goods were safely stored.[11] Apuleius in his second-century *Metamorphoses* depicts citizens (rich and not-so-rich) in cities of central Greece as having accumulated gold and silver coins in the storerooms of their houses.[12] It is notable that hoarding wealth was considered a noticeable aspect of civic life. Philo of Alexandria, for instance, commenting on the customs of the Essenes, wrote that they lived in villages, avoiding all cities, and did not store up treasures of silver and of gold.[13]

Concerning the elite, a reason why it preferred to maintain large monetary reserves was to avoid cash crises, given, for example, its lifestyle and the costly responsibilities it undertook in the context of euergetism. Furthermore, keeping significant cash reserves (especially gold) facilitated bequeathing of assets and their allocation to multiple heirs, as well as providing significant dowries. These were great concerns in a society where social succession was linked with transmission of property.[14] According to Plutarch (first–early second century), money getting was necessary only for kings, for royal stewards and for those that desired pre-eminence and rule over cities.[15] This suggests the need of the elite for cash reserves so as to achieve its political aspirations. It should be noted that members of the elite employed their savings to help family, friends and allies (e.g., for the purchase of land and property), that is, to facilitate other members of the elite. Reserves were also channelled into financing economic activities of the elite or, outside its circles, of others (e.g., entrepreneurs), as well as into lending to dependants in need.[16] It is obvious that in certain cases lending further consolidated personal dependence relations.

Storing wealth in one's household was not a one-way option, since it is well attested that at least a part of private savings was deposited in banks, or even in sanctuaries.[17] Plutarch once again helps us to construe practices and mentalities by stressing that honourable bankers were not expected to bring objections to someone's request for the return of personal deposits.[18] Bankers, as well as elite financiers, offered productive loans (e.g., for business and trade) or non-productive loans (e.g., for conspicuous consumption). In any case, Dio Chrysostom stresses that one of the characteristics that the majority attributed to prosperous men—who were indifferent to the teachings of philosophy—was earning from lending at interest.[19] This implies that the actual impact of moral counsels against practices such as money lending or hoarding should not be overestimated.[20]

Thus, practices of hoarding, maintaining cash reserves, bank depositing, lending at interest and financing entrepreneurial activities were routine in the urban centres of the Roman world, where the majority of early Christians lived.

JUSTIFICATION AND DISTRIBUTION OF SURPLUS

Work Ethic, Business Activities and Trade

Those Christians suspicious of trading activities employed two main arguments. First, they stressed that the desire for enrichment underlies trade, driven by covetousness and the need to acquire superfluous riches beyond a state of virtuous self-sufficiency. Second, accumulated wealth was suspected for the additional reason that it was believed to originate in techniques of deception and fraud inherent to commercial activities, as well as in practices denoting an outright exploitation of the more vulnerable members of the community.

Among early Christian texts outside the New Testament, the *Didache* (ca. late first century) elaborates on a work ethic reminiscent of the ideal of self-sufficiency in the New Testament context.[21] The provenance of the work is unknown, yet there is a scholarly consensus suggesting a Syrian origin, perhaps near Antioch.[22] The author of the *Didache* admonishes believers in Christ not to seek to appropriate others' resources (2.3), not to be motivated by greedy and rapacious intentions (2.6),[23] and not to cultivate a fondness for money, from which derive acts of robbery (3.5). Income that originates in manual labour is invaluable in shaping the base for charity, without favouritism (4.6-7). The *Didache* urges for charity (15.4) but endorses a more radical view on sharing, expanding it to the extent of abhorring one's own right to private property (4.8): "share all things with your brother and do not say that anything is your own. For if you are partners in what is immortal, how much more in what is mortal?"[24] Kurt Niederwimmer observes that "at this point the commandment of compassion and care for the neighbour has attained its sharpest and most consistent development."[25]

The *Didache* develops the doctrine of the Two Ways one could follow in one's lifespan.[26] This tradition, comprising the Way of Life and the Way of Death, introduces a dualistic framework that is profoundly Jewish in origin.[27] The Way of Death, in particular, involves evil and rapacious acts, arrogance, conceit, passions and related vices that make humans insensitive to the needs of others by seeking vanity and mundane rewards. Such persons perpetuate oppressive practices, ignore the needy and strive for pre-eminence while impoverishing the vulnerable (5.1–2). The text (2.4) underscores the internal divide of someone who strives to ineffectively comply with two competing realms, that of the present and that of the future age. This man is called "double-minded" (*dignōmōn*), a theme that other texts repeatedly affirm (for instance, the synonym *dipsychos* is employed in the *Shepherd of Hermas*).[28]

It is notable that the work introduces an ethic of hospitality that draws on earlier traditions: tradesmen are welcome in the community, and persons devoid of an occupation are acceptable on the condition that they will engage in labour activities and avoid idleness (12.3–4). *Didache* distinguishes genuine from false prophets on the grounds of asking (or not) for money (11.3–12); in the same manner, fondness of money was not typical of a church minister (15.1). In conformity to the work ethic elaborated in the *Didache*, the community is not obligated to support those who live at the expense of others, being intolerant of the unemployed who indulge in idleness, as well as of those who misuse Christian faith for personal enrichment.[29] Ignatius of Antioch (early second century) in his *Epistle to the Smyrnaeans* (6.2) also warns of dissidents who are indifferent to the needy, the afflicted and the oppressed.[30] On the contrary, genuine teachers deserve any financial and material support in conformity to the *Didache*'s precise instructions (13). Polycarp of Smyrna (d. ca. 155–160) in his *Epistle to the Philippians* (11.1), referring to an ex-presbyter who abused his office, counsels abstention from the love of money.[31]

Early Christian texts introduce a work ethic that sanctions toil and labour and condemns laziness: this is typical of *1 Clement*, a late-first-century letter concerned with forgiveness and harmony in a community suffering from internal tensions. The letter claims Roman authority over the Church in Corinth and urges believers to engage in well doing and eschew idleness (34.1–2).[32] However, the fruits of labour cannot be reaped in the short run, since one needs to invest in continuous efforts and await the results with patience and endurance.

An implicit distrust toward trading activities and related profitable occupations permeates this view of the economic world. This negative attitude toward lucrative activities remains a distinctive feature of *2 Clement*, a mid-second-century homily on self-control and repentance that claims a different authorship from *1 Clement*.[33] *2 Clement* posits:

> No one who is upright receives the fruit of his labor quickly; he instead waits for it. For if God were to reward the upright immediately, we would straightaway be engaged in commerce rather than devotion to God. For we would appear to be upright not for the sake of piety but for a profit. (20.3–4)[34]

The *Epistle of Barnabas*, a seemingly popular text in early Christianity, was possibly written in the 130s and intended to address the needs of a community probably situated near Alexandria, yet authorship remains inconclusive, suggesting a familiarity with Jewish interpretation.[35] The work denounces the practices of those who benefit from the efforts of others without contributing a fair share to community welfare. Such persons indulge in greed and covet what belongs to others, remaining in idleness and refraining from productive occupations (10.4).

The second-century *Shepherd of Hermas*—another popular work in the early Church,[36] written most probably in Rome or its vicinity—substantiates a similar work ethic. Income from productive occupations is morally legitimate provided that is properly channelled to the needy, that is, by exhibiting impartiality (*Mand.* 2.4 [27]; cf. *Sim.* 9.24.2–3 [101]). Furthermore, the text warns those who fall short of true faith that engagement in business affairs and pursuit of excess wealth subjects them to potential peril, as they are exposed to the influence of outsiders (*Mand.* 10.1.4 [40]). Business dealings, disassociated from virtue, may prove perilous to Christian identity (*Sim.* 8.9.1 [75]). Christians are counselled to restrict the scope of their business pursuits by reducing the volume of their business engagements, because to devote too much time and energy to the sphere of trade does not conform to their spiritual allegiances (*Sim.* 4.7 [53]). Believers are admonished as follows:

> But avoid many business activities and you will not sin at all. For those involved with numerous business dealings are also involved in numerous

sins, since they are distracted by their affairs and do not serve as the Lord's slaves. (*Sim.* 4.5 [53])[37]

There is also another rationale for the reduction of the scope of business activities. Involvement in multiple business projects seems to be quite ineffective because it disorientates the tradesman from his primary business aim, renders the business plan unfeasible due to increasing uncertainty and entails a concomitant loss of control in business pursuits. Such a merchant not only fails to prosper but is also exposed to business failure:

For many people undertake numerous projects but go back and forth in their minds, and nothing at all goes well for them. And they say that they do not prosper in what they do, but it never occurs to them that they have done what is evil; instead, they blame the Lord. (*Sim.* 6.3.5 [63])[38]

The Justification of Moderate Prosperity

The wealth ethics in *2 Clement* draws on established New Testament patterns on the impossibility of serving two irreconcilable realms, the divine and that of Mammon (6.1),[39] expressed in the context of a polarity between this age and the age to come (6.3).[40] One should renounce perishable and ephemeral possessions with a view to acquiring imperishable things in heaven (6.6).

In the *Shepherd of Hermas* there is a rationale for the justification of the prosperous believer, provided that his/her wealth is distributed to those in need. Hermas is the protagonist of the story which is intended to inculcate the need for repentance. The work exhorts Christians to abstain from luxurious living and from ostentatious conduct originating in material abundance, as well as from accumulating excess wealth (*Mand.* 8.3 [38], 12.2.1 [45]). The text also urges them to refrain from fraud, greed, vanity and arrogance (*Mand.* 8.5 [38]). The excesses of dissipation are threatened by the impending judgment,[41] which is inevitable for all those who enjoy luxuries, succumb to ephemeral enticements and deprive others of their goods (*Sim.* 6.4.1–4 [64], 6.5.4–5 [65]). Christians should not concentrate on material possessions, adopting the practices of outsiders, to the detriment of their own distinctive identity (*Sim.* 1.4–6 [50]). On the contrary, they should excel in helping behaviours by offering support toward widows, orphans, the needy or those who suffer from indebtedness (*Mand.* 8.10 [38]).

Hermas provides a justification for wealth that resides in the aforementioned ministry toward the community (*Sim.* 1.9–10 [50]). The text illustrates the position of the rich through a vision of a tower (i.e. the Church) under construction and explains that the round stones that do not properly fit in the building of this tower are those who simultaneously have faith in God and own earthly possessions: just as the round stones have to be trimmed and become square to be integral to the construction process, the rich Christians should learn to manage their wealth in a way that proves its social utility and furthers the common good (cf. *Vis.* 3.6.5–7 [14]).[42]

A model of stewardship of resources underlies these narratives: notably, those who fail in their ministry, since they usurp the livelihood of more vulnerable members of the community, not only betray the expectations of others but also endanger their salvation if they persist in their fallacious behaviour (*Sim.* 9.26.2 [103]). The aforementioned faithful wealthy, who are partially obstructed from the truth by their riches but are able to remain good, will be treated in the following way: the Lord will leave them only a portion of their original wealth in order for these people to become less insensitive to the needs of others and to manage properly the remaining part of their riches (*Sim.* 9.30.4–5 [107]).[43] Eschatological rhetoric is thus intertwined with moral exhortations, with a view to addressing issues of social stratification in the Christian communities and shaping Christian economic and social ethics.[44]

Hermas envisions a socio-economic order in which an adequate self-sufficiency remains the ideal, not the accumulation of wealth through its investment in property, housing or business ventures.[45] The author of *Hermas* articulates a vision of a Christian economic praxis by urging wealthy members to invest otherwise, in acts of benevolence, as well as by distancing themselves from more conventional aspirations typical of the economic attachments of the surrounding environment.[46] In this respect, it would be plausible to argue that *Hermas* construes Christian identity in terms of a primary shift in economic allegiances, from storing economic assets or being involved in complex business arrangements to affirming alternative economic practices focusing on community welfare.[47]

Rhee underscores that, despite the universal denouncement of avaricious behaviours in Christian apocalyptic discourses, there remains an ambiguity with respect to the degree of divestment that generates tension between ideal and practice: the ideal of renunciation of wealth coexists with the fact of relativizing wealth from commercial engagements through the practice of almsgiving.[48]

An Organicist View of Society

The *Shepherd of Hermas* focuses on an ideal of mutuality that is based on the complementarity of socio-economic roles of groups that significantly differ in status, power, wealth and social influence. *Hermas* employs a social metaphor to illustrate the two main groups, the rich and the poor, in terms of a vine and an elm (*Sim.* 2 [51]). By drawing this analogy, the text demonstrates the social utility of both groups: the rich undertake the responsibility to support the needy by liquidating part of their surplus and directing monetary funds to the needy through almsgiving, while the poor offer their prayers for their benefactors in return.[49] Wealthy members assume the responsibility to undertake relief efforts by offering financial aid, but they also engage in patronage relationships with poorer members of the community. According to Carolyn Osiek:

> There is certainly an appeal to the self-interest of the rich here: it is to their advantage to keep the poor happy so that they will continue their effective intercession for the rich. This is a spiritualization of the institution of patronage: the *obsequium* and *operae* owed by the client to a patron takes the form of intercessory prayer.[50]

It seems that the obligation of the wealthy is viewed not so much as a responsibility, but rather as a *diakonia* (ministry) offered by a particular group for the welfare of the community (*SH, Sim.* 2.7 [51]). A new complementarity of social roles transcends the stereotypic antagonism between rich and poor through an entwinement of two distinct biblical traditions, one that focuses on the precedence of the spirituality of the poor over the wickedness of the wealthy, and another that centres on the obligation of the rich to share their surplus with the needy.[51]

Such a social exchange based on balanced reciprocities is probably not addressed to the wealthy members of the upper economic elite, but rather to the middling groups that enjoy sufficient but moderate surplus: for instance, freedmen and related groups involved in trading and business engagements.[52] *Hermas* praises the benevolent wealthy as follows:

Happy are those who have possessions and understand that their riches have come from the Lord: for the one who understands this will also be able to perform a great ministry. (*Sim.* 2.10 [51])[53]

The rhetoric of the text is implicitly depicting the more complicated social stratification of second-century Roman society by providing indirect evidence of the diversity of economic groups situated at the middle of the social hierarchy and enjoying moderate wealth, such as businessmen, traders and merchants, a category of occupations in which freedmen were often involved.[54] *Hermas* implies a view of society that moves beyond the stereotypic binary dichotomy of "rich" and "poor." Yet given that this more complicated picture is not adequately illustrated in such narratives, we have no other choice but to reconstruct the socio-economic reality by speculating about the nature of the groups referred to in patristic texts. *Hermas* adopts an organicist view of society that nurtures the ideal of a harmonious cooperation of distinct groups comprising an orderly society.[55] Harry O. Maier argues that *Hermas* sought to shape ideal communities and effectively reconciled patronage-based economic pursuits with an ensuing curtailment of economic activities that were detrimental to the poor's welfare. The promotion of both care for the poor and widely held civic goals was in fact an unintended consequence of this endeavour.[56]

Undoubtedly, allusions to social stratification are evidenced in this dispute over the proper use of surplus in the *Shepherd of Hermas*, in the narrative world of which we identify issues related to the entrance of higher-status Christians into the community.[57] Women converts played an important role in the formation of this new type of patronage.[58] Interestingly, this ideal coexistence of social groups, which widely differed in their access to and appropriation of material and symbolic resources, was contingent upon balanced reciprocities. Wealth was not accumulated per se, but in order to be channelled to the needy in exchange for prayers promoting the salvation of wealthy members. This is a motif repeatedly affirmed in subsequent patristic rhetoric on wealth and poverty, as we shall argue in the next chapter, although a difference is that the pernicious nature of hoarding is more vividly illustrated in later contributions. In *Hermas*, those who hold riches are now afforded a new opportunity for repentance and participation in the process of community building, that is, to maintain their business but offer their excess wealth to the needy. It is in the self-interest of the rich to give to the poor: the initiative for charity belongs primarily, if not exclusively, to the rich, so the text involves reciprocities, yet within the reciprocal relationship the focus is undoubtedly on the rich.[59]

Nevertheless, the idea of reciprocating the favour permeates all texts, according to which the recipient offers his/her gratitude and prayer to the donor, who may also be rewarded by Christ himself in the impending judgment.

> And so both accomplish their work. The poor person works at his prayer in which he is rich and which he received from the Lord; and he gives it back to the Lord who supplied it to him in the first place. So too the rich person does not hesitate to supply his wealth to the poor person, since he received it from the Lord. And this is a great and acceptable thing to do before God because the rich person has gained understanding by his wealth and has worked for the poor person out of the gifts provided by the Lord, and he has accomplished his ministry well. (*SH, Sim.* 2.7 [51])[60]

Beyond the *Shepherd of Hermas*, organicist views of society pervade *1 Clement*'s narrative structure. *1 Clement* (37.4–5) employs an organic analogy to designate the complementarity of different social groups (the elevated and the lowly) and the significance of each part to the orderly performance of the social body. Accordingly, the wealthy should provide to meet the financial needs of the weaker, while the latter should respond by offering thanksgiving to God for the existence of persons who care for their living (38.1–2).

Welcoming the Rich

Clement of Alexandria (ca. 150–ca. 215) focused on the wealthy and their social responsibilities from an elite standpoint.[61] He was living in the highly urbanized environment of Alexandria, in which participation in business and entrepreneurial activities was totally acceptable, being an integral part of economic life. At the same time, Alexandria was the cultural melting pot of the Mediterranean, where diverse streams of thought crossed each other.[62] This financial and cultural environment had an impact on the way Clement viewed wealth. His most influential work on the subject—*Who Is the Rich Man Who Can Be Saved?*—reveals that Christianity started to be appealing to the well-off social strata.[63] Clement specifies that he is not addressing every rich man in this work but those who have been converted,[64] while he implies that wealthy Christians and Christianity sympathizers were alarmed by both the severe attitude toward wealth in the Gospels and the aloofness with which their not-so-prosperous fellow believers were treating them.[65]

Clement argues that Jesus' command to the young rich man (Mt. 19:21) should not be interpreted in a strictly literal manner,[66] insofar as Jesus' instructions bear a deeper meaning. They imply that one should not renounce riches but rather banish from the soul the excessive desire for and attachment to them and the anxious cares that they cause.[67] Clement was influenced by Stoicism, and in particular by the concept of the Stoic wise man, who stays untouched by the mundane cares of everyday life, regarding them as *adiaphora* (indifferents).[68] In this respect, Clement was addressing the spiritual needs of new converts involved in business engagements, by suggesting that radical divestment was not mandatory for Christians. On the contrary, in managing their financial and material resources Christians had to get rid of the desire for excessive wealth, because it entailed an attachment to secular affairs, aggravated mundane concerns and entrapped them in the lure of ephemeral gratification.

In his *Stromateis* Clement disassociates ownership from the use of wealth, implying that Christians can concentrate capital assets under the constraint that they use them as if their ownership belongs to the community, thus being exhorted to alleviate extreme necessity.[69] This stewardship view of property may be explicated if we consider that, in the urban centre of Alexandria, capital and entrepreneurship could assume a social dimension, a detail that helps to clarify the presuppositions of a rich man's salvation.[70] Clement's position is encapsulated as follows: wealth should not be rejected per se, given that it is nothing more than an instrument (*organon*) granted by God to wealthy men, to be used properly so as to support those in need. Wealth itself, according to Clement, is neither good nor evil, thus he attributes to it the properties of the Stoic concept of *adiaphoron*, as mentioned above, which denotes a morally neutral entity.[71] If the wealthy channel their surplus to alleviate human suffering, then wealth is positively evaluated as a means that serves the ultimate goal of human salvation.

Clement depicts the process of redistribution as an economic exchange, characterizing it as "beautiful trade" and "divine business": the wealthy purchase immortality with money; by giving the perishable possessions of the world, they receive in exchange an eternal abode in heaven.[72] Balanced reciprocities are central to this view, just as in the *Shepherd of Hermas*—with which Clement was acquainted—designating the complementarity of social roles in a Christian community. Both groups, the rich and the poor, are mutually dependent on a system of patronage and benefaction.[73] Sharing proves to be integral to this overarching social system, and wealth becomes an instrument of social benefaction.

In the same cultural environment, that of third-century Alexandria, Origen (ca. 185–ca. 254) adopted a less flexible stance toward the excesses of wealth. Origen does not articulate a comprehensive view on the nature of wealth, yet he occasionally reflects on ethically controversial issues, such as the moral burden of riches and the spiritual benefits of poverty, by highlighting the obligations of all Christians to ensure distribution of surplus, always in accordance with the precepts of justice and charity. It has been argued that the interrelated demands of charity, equity and justice in Origen's thought do not contravene provision for one's necessities in life. What mostly matters is refraining from an avaricious pursuit of excess wealth, accompanied by a process of dispossession of material surplus to sustain the needy.[74]

Origen endorses the ideal of *autarkeia* (self-sufficiency), while he reminds not only wealthy patrons but also those who enjoy even a moderate level of wealth of their obligation to support the economically destitute through almsgiving.[75] In his view, dispossession of riches may move the wealthy in the opposite direction of longing for the lost possessions, thus precluding subtle and sublime disentanglement from earthly things and, ultimately, salvation.[76] Total renunciation of possessions remains a distinctive feature of those who proceed to radical divestment for religious purposes. In common with the involuntarily indigent, such persons can substantially benefit from redistributive initiatives undertaken by more prosperous Christians.[77] It seems that Origen was effective in deconstructing traditional representations of rich and poor. Both groups shared the capacity for moral choice and spiritual freedom, yet they could also succumb to greedy motives that entail attachment to wealth.[78]

Clement of Alexandria's Stoic influences on his treatment of wealth and poverty as indifferent things have been contrasted with Origen's stance on asceticism resulting in a condemnation of riches, which is reminiscent of *Shepherd of Hermas*' more critical attitude toward wealth. Whereas Clement was supportive of an inclusion of the wealthy in the Christian community, Origen considered divestment a prerequisite for resisting avaricious behaviours.[79] In this scholarly view, the Origenian tradition—culminating, for instance, in Evagrius Ponticus' and Rufinus of Aquileia's ascetic ideals—elaborates on a principle of social equality later embraced by other Origenian ascetics.[80]

This tension between Clement and Origen on wealth ethics is contingent on the focal point each one adopts. As already argued, Clement addresses the spiritual needs of his wealthy audience, whereas Origen elaborates on a more comprehensive ethics, addressing prerequisites of salvation for both groups. Commenting on the Gospel of Matthew (19:23), Origen asserts that, though the rich face difficulty in entering the kingdom of God, salvation is far from unattainable for them; the outcome is dependent upon the intervention of God, who alone is in the position to secure their entrance into the heavenly realm.[81] Much like Clement, Origen recognizes the complementarity of social roles between the rich and the poor: the first group controls aggressivity and exhibits love through genuine almsgiving, whereas the second, being in an inferior position, learns humility through poverty. Origen however, broadens his perspective by defining the spiritual obligations of both social groups: the wealthy have to engage in compassionate acts through sharing, while the poor have to learn how to excel in endurance and perseverance.[82]

THE FRAMEWORK OF CHRISTIAN DISCOURSE ON SAVINGS

Universalizing Moral Exhortations for Charity

Early patristic thought offers a set of counsels on the proper lifestyle adopted by new believers. According to *1 Clement*, they should treat one another with kindness and compassion (14.3), refraining from the vices of audacity, insolence and effrontery, and behaving with gentleness, humility and meekness (30.8, 44.3). Greed in particular, in common with arrogance, deceit, slander, vanity and inhospitality, is considered as a form of injustice and lawlessness, entirely inappropriate for genuine Christians (35.5), who would strive for the common good (48.6), even to the detriment of their own welfare (51.2). Therefore, the ideal remains that of social harmony, peace and stability (61.1) based on a virtuous administration of civil and domestic affairs (61.2).

The *Epistle of Barnabas* shares a similar view on the priority of charity in Christian life, interwoven with a strong call for justice and forgiveness. It comments on these issues as follows:

> Loosen every bond of injustice; unravel the strange hold of coercive agreements; send forth in forgiveness those who are downtrodden: tear up every unfair contract. Break your bread to the hungry, and provide clothing for everyone you see naked. Bring the homeless under your roof. And if you see anyone who has been humbled, do not despise him— neither you nor anyone from your children's household. (3.3)[83]

In accordance with the *Didache* (4.8), the *Epistle of Barnabas* exhorts the believers to share all wealth with others by endorsing an ideal of partnership in all things, both perishable and imperishable (19.8). This view supports more radical attitudes toward sharing of surplus, in view of avoiding greed (19.6), and partiality (19.11). The epistle strongly condemns the economic practices of the arrogant wealthy who indulge in vanity and pursue ephemeral success to the detriment of the needy. Individuals who aspire to enrichment tend to disregard the more vulnerable, oppress the afflicted and support the wealthy (20.2).

It is noteworthy that the ideal of sharing resources does not assume the diminution of one's own abundance. On the contrary, it makes the Christian an imitator of God. Happiness cannot be evaluated in material things—a basic patristic view still expressed in the fifth century by Theodoret of Cyrrhus, as we shall see—because the pursuit of wealth and power, the abundance of material goods and the ensuing prosperity do not secure the experience of happiness.

The *Epistle to Diognetus* (ca. second half of the second century) stresses[84]:

> For happiness is not a matter of oppressing your neighbors, or wishing to have more than those who are lowly, or being wealthy and coercing those who are in need. Nor is anyone able to imitate God in these ways, for they form no part of his greatness. (10.5)[85]

The epistle deconstructs the dominant ideals of those who seek happiness in the pursuit of social influence and in the affluence of wealth and possessions, because these mundane goals are inimical to Christians who wish to enter the divine realm. Such selfish motives never cease to pose a threat to others' welfare, often interrelated with coercive and exploitative economic practices. Genuine happiness, on the contrary, may be experienced by those who excel in charity, who make their abundance a means to serve an ulterior goal, that of the alleviation of the needy. The use of possessions to support the destitute is thus elevated to a means of imitating God (10.6). The *Shepherd of Hermas* shares a similar view in affirming that those who refuse to help their brothers who suffer misfortune in their daily lives commit a great sin, in contrast to the supporters of the needy who experience great joy (*Sim.* 10.4.2–3 [114]).

As already argued, Clement of Alexandria's view of wealth as an instrument is invested with providential connotations, since God himself has granted it to the prosperous members of a community for proper stewardship; therefore, none can exert ownership over a God-given good. It is notable that similar views on the divine origin and the temporary possession of wealth by humans are long-standing in Greek and Roman literature.[86] Clement seeks to mitigate the tension experienced by the rich by persuading them that Christians should not accumulate superfluous riches; instead, they should distribute wealth to the poor in a life of discipleship to Christ.[87] If God is the only provider of this affluence of material goods, the rich man is nothing but a steward who should manage these resources justly, being mandated to engage in the redistribution of wealth through almsgiving,[88] a view that resonates well with subsequent patristic thinking on these issues. Concomitantly, in early patristic thought wealth can be morally justified through proper use. On the contrary, amassment of goods in service of purely selfish motives (involving hoarding behaviours) distorts the primary function of wealth as a God-given instrument.[89]

Two Distinct Models of Almsgiving

2 Clement sheds new light on almsgiving by offering a different perspective. Self-restraint, charity and virtuousness are countenanced as being akin to righteousness that precludes any attachment to money and to related worldly affairs (4.3, 5.6). The practice of charity is not only morally laudable but it also lightens the believer of the burden of sin, since love covers a multitude of sins (16.4).[90] It has been argued that *2 Clement* 16.1–4 introduces an alternate view of almsgiving as typical of all believers and not merely of a select segment of the congregation.[91] Sharing of resources within the faith community is thus required of all, and represents the implementation of communal practices of repentance and mercy exhibited by all members as agents of mutual assistance.[92] This is not the mainstream view as it is shown by other second- or third-century Christian texts. Clement of Alexandria, for instance, "clearly advocates a top-down model of redemptive almsgiving where money flows from one group of wealthy believers to another group of impoverished saints."[93] It should be noted that the *Shepherd of Hermas* had already promoted a reciprocal framework of social exchange between two distinct groups, defined as the "rich" and the "poor," in the context of a top-down model of almsgiving.[94]

As it has been pointed out above, this two-fold representation of social stratification evidenced in both the *Shepherd of Hermas* and Clement of Alexandria reflects a binary divide between two opposing groups—the "rich" and the "poor"—that fails to adequately take into account the far more complicated social differentiation in income distribution. Such binary opposition ultimately operates as a mere rhetorical construction deeply entrenched in the social stereotypes of the era. Furthermore, this oversimplification is intended to reinforce the elite social values and worldview and to justify the accumulation of wealth and power by the upper social strata.[95]

David J. Downs plausibly argues for the existence of two distinct models of almsgiving in early Christian texts, one exemplified in Clement of Alexandria, focusing on the philanthropy of the wealthy, and another substantiated in 2 Corinthians 8:13–14 and in the *Didache* 4.5–8, centred on mutualism and reciprocal support.[96] The first model is articulated on a vertical axis ranging from those who enjoy an abundance of financial resources and material prosperity to those who suffer from destitution and lack the necessities of life. We deem that the *Shepherd of Hermas* and Clement of Alexandria refer to Christians in a position to engage in hoarding wealth. The philanthropic exhortation of these early Christian texts may act as a remedy for such behaviours: the top-down transfer of surplus is intended to reduce the scope and mitigate the intensity of hoarding activities.

The second model "involves a more horizontal exchange of resources among those of lesser means."[97] Downs situates *2 Clement* in the second context that prioritizes participation of all believers in a divine economy that is expected to influence distribution of resources within the community of faith. As a consequence, *2 Clement* goes far beyond exhorting prosperous Christians to actively display charitable concern for their passive, impoverished brothers in faith. These believers may have engaged in different occupations, being for instance merchants, artisans and large shop owners or regular wage earners, enjoying moderate surplus or being near subsistence level. They might have also been (skilled and unskilled) labourers, small farm- and shop owners at subsistence level. Regardless of their economic state, all are urged to make their love manifest in almsgiving.[98] In line with Downs' argument, we deem that these groups possessed a moderate level of surplus income that could be directed to practices of mutual support, thus strengthening the bonds of, and substantially affecting patterns of distribution within, the faith community.

Motives for Almsgiving

As already argued, sharing of resources was perceived as a practice designed to cultivate a profound sense of unity and harmony both within and between Christian communities. It was viewed as an obligation associating merciful acts with manifestations of justice. Having common funds and common meals not only reflected a renewed interest in caring for the poor and helpless but also substantiated intra-Christian solidarity.[99]

Christopher M. Hays enumerates a set of stimuli that facilitated believers to display such active concern for others.[100] Appeals to charitable giving that are not grounded in self-interest but highlight the spiritual benefits accrued by the donors are typical of early Christian literature. The wealthier members of the community, who enjoyed sufficient financial means and were willing to share them with the weakest, may have served as patrons of the community, expecting to receive the compensation valued in a patronage system, that is, honour. Yet this might not have been an easy task to perform, given the role ambiguities arising from their dual responsibility, both as patrons and true members of the community.[101] As a result, early Christian teaching and practice sought to overcome these tensions, envisioning in almsgiving a fundamental expression of altruistic and disinterested love.[102] Furthermore, almsgiving can be integral to the invocation of a *koinōnia* (Christian fellowship) language in texts that exhort their readers to proceed with a generous sharing of their possessions, like the *Didache* and the *Epistle of Barnabas*. As argued earlier, these texts favour a more radical view of divestment that makes hoarding entirely unfeasible.

Almsgiving can also help prosperous Christians to effectively resist their internal passions, as evidenced in Clement of Alexandria's affirmation that an ongoing voluntary deprivation of excess wealth can contribute to subduing one's vicious impulses that might otherwise lead to apostasy.[103] In this respect, the rhetoric of almsgiving helps to deconstruct hoarding as a dominant economic practice. Furthermore, almsgiving can be deemed as a means to restore one's spiritual health by cancelling the sinful infection incurred by post-baptismal sins. Almsgiving embodies a redemptive potential originating in texts, such as Tobit (4:10, 12:8–9) and Proverbs (10:2, 11:4, 14:21, 28:8), that elaborate on a theology of charity.[104] Gary A. Anderson discusses the view that such a theology of charity was prevalent in the Old Testament, rabbinic midrash and Second Temple literature, and the New Testament, as well as in the sermons of the Church Fathers; he also considers a set of related topics, such as the nature and purpose of ephemeral riches or the concepts of atonement and reparation. Anderson deems that Tobit 4:7, Proverbs 19:17 and Sirach 29:8–12 elaborate on the idea of a heavenly treasury of merit, created through human acts of genuine charity, the main function of which is the formation of a deposit in heaven that benefits the donor in the afterlife.[105] The concept of the heavenly treasury had a great impact on patristic thought.

Early Christian charitable *paraenesis* also draws on the rhetoric of the impending judgment as a real menace that threatens the false security riches offer to their holders. 2 *Clement* 16.1–4 and the *Shepherd of Hermas* elaborate on such a motive, yet the frequency with which Christians appealed to this eschatological judgment was reduced as the expectation of Christ's Second Coming began to gradually diminish.[106] Other noteworthy stimuli for charity either reveal purely disinterested motives—ranging from hospitality to self-sacrifice itself—or reflect a deeper conviction that true wealth resides in virtue or wisdom alone, or even refuse temporal riches in this very age.[107]

This rich diversity of motives for engaging in charitable practices in the second- and third-century patristic literature shares the view of excess wealth as rather intolerable within the faith community, let alone the accumulation of riches for self-interested pursuits. The model of redemptive almsgiving adopted by the Church was entwined with underlying ideological changes that significantly affected the status of poverty. Devoting more scant resources to almsgiving and devaluing efforts for affluence probably resulted in a reduction of labour force participation in productive engagements.[108] Although these contentions are in need of further elaboration, it remains an undeniable reality that the fourth-century Christian Fathers warned the faithful of the perils that are endemic in hoarding behaviours in a more vivid manner, highlighting the need for a conscious disengagement from the burden of excess wealth. This would have been a first step toward a more just and equitable Christian society, as that of the increasingly Christianized fourth-century Roman Empire was envisioned to be.

NOTES

1. These issues become more complicated if we consider the diversity of apocryphal sources beyond the accepted New Testament canon. In the apocryphal *Acts of Peter and the Twelve Apostles* (11–12), for instance, the apostles are urged not to address the needs of the rich, since the latter enjoy partiality due to their influence and excel in revelling in their wealth. In a similar vein of reasoning, the *Acts of Thomas* (20, 62) depicts a more ascetic lifestyle and endorses ideals that were not undisputed in the nascent communities. The *Acts of Thomas* reflects a dualistic tension between transient and corruptible earthly possessions on the one hand, and everlasting heavenly riches on the other. See H. Rhee, *Loving the Poor, Saving the Rich: Wealth, Poverty, and Early Christianity* (Grand Rapids, MI: Baker Academic, 2012), 67–68. It is equally important that the *Hymn of the Pearl* highlights the allegorical tension between the lure of illusory wealth and the promise of true wealth. See E. Moore, "Wealth, Poverty, and the Value of the Person: Some Notes on the *Hymn of the Pearl* and Its Early Christian Context," in *Wealth and Poverty in Early Church and Society*, ed. S. R. Holman. Holy Cross Studies in Patristic Theology and History (Grand Rapids, MI: Baker Academic, 2008), 56–63.
2. Rhee, *Loving the Poor*, 166–167.
3. Rhee, *Loving the Poor*, 159–160; also *eadem*, "Wealth, Business Activities, and Blurring of Christian Identity," *SP* 62 (2013): 245–257.
4. For a detailed discussion of these views on wealth creation and maintenance, see H. Rhee, "A Patristic View of Wealth and Possessions," *Ex Auditu: An International Journal of the Theological Interpretation of Scripture* 27 (2011): 51–77.
5. J. Banaji, "Economic Trajectories," in *The Oxford Handbook of Late Antiquity*, ed. S. F. Johnson (Oxford: Oxford University Press, 2012), 602–603 (= *idem*, "The Economic Trajectories of Late Antiquity," in *idem*, *Exploring the Economy of Late Antiquity: Selected Essays* [Cambridge: Cambridge University Press, 2016], 68–69).

6. Rhee, *Loving the Poor*, 187–188; *eadem*, "Wealth, Business Activities, and Blurring of Christian Identity."
7. For an assessment of the relevant sources, see N. Giannakopoulos, "Μορφές αποταμίευσης, διαχείρισης και αξιοποίησης του χρήματος στην Ελλάδα κατά τους αυτοκρατορικούς χρόνους (27 π.Χ.–περ. 280 μ.Χ.). Μια αποτίμηση των πηγών," in *Αποταμίευση και διαχείριση χρήματος στην ελληνική ιστορία*, eds. K. Bouraselis and K. Meidani (Athens: Tachydromiko Tamieutērio Hellados, 2011), 105–150.
8. Gaius Musonius Rufus, *Ep.* 1.6.
9. Maximus of Tyre, *Or.* 15.5; cf. 35.3.
10. Philostratus, *Vitae sophistarum* 2.547.
11. Dio Chrysostom, *Or.* 65.10–11.
12. Apuleius, *Metamorphoses* 3.28, 4.9, 4.13–18.
13. Philo of Alexandria, *Quod omnis probus liber sit* 76.
14. W. Jongman, "A Golden Age: Death, Money Supply and Social Succession in the Roman Empire," in *Credito e moneta nel mondo romano*, ed. E. Lo Cascio. Pragmateiai, 8 (Bari: Edipuglia, 2003), 189–196; also Giannakopoulos, "Μορφές αποταμίευσης," 143–144.
15. Plutarch, *De cupiditate divitiarum* 5 (*Moralia* 525d).
16. J. Andreau, *Banking and Business in the Roman World*, trans. J. Lloyd. Key Themes in Ancient History (Cambridge: Cambridge University Press, 1999), 27–28. Especially on the elite lending to the elite, see Jongman, "A Golden Age," 196.
17. On the latter, see R. Bogaert, *Banques et banquiers dans les cités grecques* (Leiden: A. W. Sijthoff, 1968), 281–288. For banks and bankers in the Roman world, see Andreau, *Banking and Business*, 32–49. See also S. Cosentino, "Banking in Early Byzantine Ravenna," *Cahiers de Recherches Médiévales et Humanistes* 28.2 (2014): 245 n. 1, for a bibliography on banking in the late antique and early Byzantine periods.
18. Plutarch, *Consolatio ad Apollonium* 28 (*Moralia* 116a).
19. Dio Chrysostom, *Or.* 27.7.
20. See Giannakopoulos, "Μορφές αποταμίευσης," 129.
21. For a review of the extant scholarly discussion on the possible relationship of the *Didache* with the Gospel of Matthew, see J. Verheyden, "Matthew and the *Didache*: Some Comments on the Comments," in *The Didache: A Missing Piece of the Puzzle in Early Christianity*, eds. J. A. Draper and C. N. Jefford. Early Christianity and Its Literature, 14 (Atlanta, GA: SBL Press, 2015), 409–426. J. A. Draper ("The Moral Economy of the *Didache*," *HTSS* 67.1 [2011]. Art. #907, 10 pp. [10.4102/hts.v67i1.907]) applies Polanyi's notion of moral economy to the economic relations referred to in the *Didache*. Draper partly supports A. Milavec's (*The Didache: Faith, Hope and Life of the Earliest*

Christian Communities, 50–70 C.E. [New York: Newman Press, 2003]) contention that the *Didache*'s injunctions were intended to shape an economic safety network for community members through systems of generalized reciprocity and mechanisms of redistribution of surplus. The community was conceived in terms of an economic system that resisted its assimilation into the Roman imperial system. In Draper's view, the text reflects some ambiguities in its adoption of a Christian house table ethic and, primarily, in the adoption of a patron–client conception of the relationship between prophets and teachers on the one hand, and bishops and deacons on the other. For an introduction in the *Didache*, see J. A. Draper, "The *Didache*," in *Writings of the Apostolic Fathers*, ed. P. Foster (London: T&T Clark, 2007), 13–20.

22. For a discussion of issues of date and provenance, see H. van de Sandt and D. Flusser, *The Didache: Its Jewish Sources and Its Place in Early Judaism and Christianity.* Compendia Rerum Iudaicarum ad Novum Testamentum, Sect. 3, Jewish Traditions in Early Christian Literature, 5 (Assen and Minneapolis, MN: Royal Van Gorcum and Fortress Press, 2002), 48–52. On Antioch as the home of the *Didache*, see C. N. Jefford, "The Milieu of Matthew, the *Didache*, and Ignatius of Antioch: Agreements and Differences," in *Matthew and the Didache: Two Documents from the Same Jewish-Christian Milieu?* ed. H. van de Sandt (Assen and Minneapolis, MN: Royal Van Gorcum and Fortress Press, 2005), 37–38.

23. Warning against greed and covetousness is well documented in the early Christian literature (e.g., Eph. 5:3; Col. 3:5; *1 Clem.* 35.5; *SH, Mand.* 8.5 [38]; Polycarp of Smyrna, *Ep. to the Philippians* 2.2).

24. Eng. trans. Ehrman 1, 425.

25. K. Niederwimmer, *The Didache: A Commentary*, trans. L. M. Maloney, ed. H. W. Attridge. Hermeneia (Minneapolis, MN: Fortress Press, 1998), 108. A. Giambrone, "'According to the Commandment' (*Did.* 1.5): Lexical Reflections on Almsgiving as 'The Commandment'," *NTS* 60.4 (2014): 448–465, investigates the semantic use of the term "commandment" as an injunction for charity and argues that the *Didache* draws on Tobit's and Sirach's use of charity as a paradigmatic precept, but through a more systematically developed expression. Tobit, in particular, with its emphasis on almsgiving and care for the poor, became a fundamental source of later Christian discourse on poverty relief; see S. R. Holman, *The Hungry Are Dying: Beggars and Bishops in Roman Cappadocia.* Oxford Studies in Historical Theology (Oxford: Oxford University Press, 2001), 43.

26. This doctrine is also elaborated on in the context of the *Epistle of Barnabas* in which it functions as a means of strengthening the

communal identity of the audience by nurturing a strong sense of in-group awareness, in conformity to the author's teaching authority; see J. C. H. Smith, "The *Epistle of Barnabas* and the Two Ways of Teaching Authority," *VC* 68.5 (2014): 465–497. For an overview of the Two Ways instruction, see Draper, "The *Didache*," 16–17.

27. On the question of the *Sitz im Leben* of the Two Ways doctrine, see W. Rordorf, "An Aspect of the Judeo-Christian Ethic: The Two Ways," in *The* Didache *in Modern Research*, ed. J. A. Draper (Leiden: Brill, 1996), 153–159.
28. E.g., *1 Clem.* 11.2, 23.2–3; *2 Clem.* 11.5, 19.2; *SH*, *Vis.* 2.2.7 [6], 3.2.2 [10], 3.4.3 [12], 3.7.1 [15], 3.10.9 [18], 3.11.2 [19], 4.1.4 [22], 5.2.4, 6 [23]; *Mand.* 9.7–12 [39], 10.1.1–2 [40], 10.2.4 [41], 11.2, 13 [43], 12.4.2 [47]; *Sim.* 1.3 [50], 6.1.2 [61], 8.7.2 [73], 8.10.2 [76], 9.21.1–3 [98]; *Ep. of Barnabas* 19.7. On "double-mindedness," see, e.g., Rhee, *Loving the Poor*, 61–62.
29. Cf. *2 Clem.* 20.4; also Chap. 2, pp. 26–27, in this book. See Niederwimmer, *The Didache*, 187.
30. For an overview of Ignatius' epistles, see P. Foster, "The Epistles of Ignatius of Antioch," in *Writings of the Apostolic Fathers*, ed. Foster, 81–107.
31. On Polycarp's epistle to the Philippians, see indicatively M. Holmes, "Polycarp of Smyrna, *Epistle to the Philippians*," in *Writings of the Apostolic Fathers*, ed. Foster, 108–125. During the late second century, Irenaeus of Lyons differentiated between heretical and orthodox teaching on the grounds of similar economic considerations. In contrast to false teaching that was entwined with a love of money and imposed a price on those adhering to it, the apostolic teaching incurred no monetary cost. In Irenaeus' view, the Church is conceived in terms of a rich man whose invaluable treasure, the water of life, is not available at a price but shared by, and accessible to, all. See D. J. Bingham, "Heresy and Catholicity in Economic Perspective: Irenaeus on Wealth," *Ephemerides Theologicae Lovanienses* 92.3 (2016): 381–405.
32. For an introduction in *1 Clem.*, see A. Gregory, "*1 Clement*: An Introduction," in *Writings of the Apostolic Fathers*, ed. Foster, 21–31.
33. On *2 Clem.*, see, e.g., P. Parvis, "*2 Clement* and the Meaning of the Christian Homily," in *Writings of the Apostolic Fathers*, ed. Foster, 32–41.
34. Eng. trans. Ehrman 1, 199.
35. For an introduction in the *Ep. of Barnabas*, see J. C. Paget, "The *Epistle of Barnabas*," in *Writings of the Apostolic Fathers*, ed. Foster, 72–80.
36. On the reception of the *Shepherd of Hermas*, see C. Osiek, *Shepherd of Hermas: A Commentary*. Hermeneia (Minneapolis, MN: Fortress Press, 1999), 4. For an overview of the writing, see J. Verheyden, "The

Shepherd of Hermas," in *Writings of the Apostolic Fathers*, ed. Foster, 63–71.
37. Eng. trans. Ehrman 2, 319.
38. Eng. trans. Ehrman 2, 345.
39. Cf. Mt. 6:24; Lk. 16:13.
40. Tensions between temporal and eternal realities are pertinent to Christian spirituality. C. L. de Wet ("'No Small Counsel about Self-Control': *Enkrateia* and the Virtuous Body as Missional Performance in 2 *Clement*," HTSTS 69.1 [2013]. Art. #1340, 10 pp. [10.4102/hts. v69i1.1340]) convincingly links the process of virtuousness and virtue formation in 2 *Clem.* with discourses of suffering (14.1–5), martyrdom (5.1–7) and apocalyptic anticipation (17.1–7) as akin to early Christian missional performance.
41. The imminence of the Parousia is a theme with which early Christian texts are familiar, see *1 Clem.* 23.5; *2 Clem.* 16.3; *Ep. of Barnabas* 21.3; Ignatius of Antioch, *Ep. to the Ephesians* 11.1.
42. See also *SH*, *Vis.* 3.2.4–9 [10], 3.3.3 [11], 3.5 [13], 3.8.9 [16]; *Sim.* 9.5.1–2 [82], 9.7.6 [84], 9.20 [97], 9.31.2 [108].
43. The peril of wealth is perceived in terms of the entanglement of the wealthy with this world through their business affairs; yet their wealth is not denounced per se nor completely cut away, insofar as it represents an opportunity for repentance through charity before the completion of the tower and the return of its master, the latter implying the *eschaton*. See Rhee, *Loving the Poor*, 60–61.
44. For a discussion of these issues, see H. Rhee, "Wealth, Poverty, and Eschatology: Pre-Constantine Christian Social Thought and the Hope for the World to Come," in *Reading Patristic Texts on Social Ethics: Issues and Challenges for the Twenty-First Century*, eds. J. Leemans, B. J. Matz and J. Verstraeten. CUA Studies in Early Christianity (Washington, DC: The Catholic University of America Press, 2011), 64–84.
45. B. H. Dunning, *Aliens and Sojourners: Self as Other in Early Christianity*. Divinations: Rereading Ancient Religion (Philadelphia, PA: University of Pennsylvania Press, 2009), 86.
46. Dunning, *Aliens and Sojourners*, 88.
47. Dunning, *Aliens and Sojourners*, 89–90.
48. Rhee, *Loving the Poor*, 71.
49. Osiek, *Shepherd of Hermas*, 162–163.
50. Osiek, *Shepherd of Hermas*, 163–164.
51. Osiek, *Shepherd of Hermas*, 164.
52. Osiek, *Shepherd of Hermas*, 20–22; cf. R. Newhauser, *The Early History of Greed: The Sin of Avarice in Early Medieval Thought and Literature*.

Cambridge Studies in Medieval Literature, 41 (Cambridge: Cambridge University Press, 2000), 5.
53. Eng. trans. Ehrman 2, 315.
54. Beyond *Hermas*, there is further textual evidence of prosperous freedmen, who benefitted from easier access to capital and to the business networks of their former masters, and, as a result, were in a position to enter into a prolonged collaboration with the latter in significantly reducing transaction costs and enhancing opportunities of entrepreneurial success. Relying on freedmen to manage business interests was also a rational option for owners, because they addressed problems of informational asymmetry in finding trustworthy agents. See W. Broekaert, "Freedmen and Agency in Roman Business," in *Urban Craftsmen and Traders in the Roman World*, eds. A. Wilson and M. Flohr (Oxford: Oxford University Press, 2016), 222–253.
55. Osiek, *Shepherd of Hermas*, 162–164; Newhauser, *Early History of Greed*, 5; S. J. Friesen, "Injustice or God's Will? Early Christian Explanations of Poverty," in *Wealth and Poverty*, ed. Holman, 33–34.
56. H. O. Maier, "From Material Place to Imagined Space: Emergent Christian Community as Thirdspace in the *Shepherd of Hermas*," in *Early Christian Communities between Ideal and Reality*, eds. M. Grundeken and J. Verheyden. WUNT, 1.342 (Tübingen: Mohr Siebeck, 2015), 159.
57. Entrance of new members was associated with efforts to redefine Christian identities. Dunning, *Aliens and Sojourners*, demonstrates—especially in his fourth chapter on the *Shepherd of Hermas*—the mechanisms through which Christians occupying a conflicted social space capitalized on the tension of being marginal and simultaneously potent to render Christian identities more attractive amid a wide range of emerging social identities.
58. P. Lampe, *From Paul to Valentinus: Christians at Rome in the First Two Centuries*, trans. M. Steinhauser, ed. M. D. Johnson (London: Continuum, 2003), 67–159.
59. M. Grundeken, *Community Building in the Shepherd of Hermas: A Critical Study of Some Key Aspects*. SupVC, 131 (Leiden and Boston, MA: Brill, 2015), 125; also 136 n. 32.
60. Eng. trans. Ehrman 2, 313.
61. A. van den Hoek, "Widening the Eye of the Needle: Wealth and Poverty in the Works of Clement of Alexandria," in *Wealth and Poverty*, ed. Holman, 74–75.
62. On late antique Alexandria, see C. Haas, *Alexandria in Late Antiquity: Topography and Social Conflict* (Baltimore, MD: Johns Hopkins University Press, 1997).

63. H. F. Hägg, *Clement of Alexandria and the Beginnings of Christian Apophaticism*. OECS (Oxford: Oxford University Press, 2006), 66; P. Garnsey, *Thinking about Property: From Antiquity to the Age of Revolution*. Ideas in Context, 90 (Cambridge: Cambridge University Press, 2007), 88.

64. Clem. Alex., *Quis div.* 2.4 (ed. O. Stählin and L. Früchtel, *Clemens Alexandrinus*, vol. 3. GCS, 17 [2nd edn. Akademie-Verlag: Berlin, 1970], 161).

65. Clem. Alex., *Quis div.* 3.1 (ed. Stählin and Früchtel, *Clemens Alexandrinus*, vol. 3, 161). Cf. Garnsey, *Thinking about Property*, 88; van den Hoek, "Widening the Eye of the Needle," 70.

66. A. Lindemann, "Eigentum und Reich Gottes: Die Erzählung 'Jesus und der Reiche' im Neuen Testament und bei Clemens Alexandrinus," *Zeitschrift für Evangelische Ethik* 50.2 (2006): 89–109, reframes the ethical dimension of the wealth and property debate by considering the exegetical contribution of Clement's "economic" interpretation of the Rich Young Man's story in the Synoptic Gospels, thus demonstrating the lack of a uniform and coherent treatment of the problem of possessing wealth in early Christian literature.

67. Clem. Alex., *Quis div.* 11.2 (ed. Stählin and Früchtel, *Clemens Alexandrinus*, vol. 3, 166). Cf. van den Hoek, "Widening the Eye of the Needle," 75; H. Stander, "Economics in the Church Fathers," in *The Oxford Handbook of Christianity and Economics*, ed. P. Oslington (Oxford: Oxford University Press, 2014), 28. Drawing on Clement's suggestion not to make any speculations with regard to the rich man's subsequent response to Jesus' challenge, Andrew Clark underscores that the young man's reaction conceals his deeper realization of the cost of discipleship, rather than a rejection of Jesus' call, given that God achieves the impossible for anyone who approaches him with genuine intentions, even for those burdened by excess wealth; see A. D. Clark, "'Do Not Judge Who Is Worthy and Unworthy': Clement's Warning Not to Speculate about the Rich Young Man's Response (Mark 10.17-31)," *JSNT* 31.4 (2009): 447–468.

68. Garnsey, *Thinking about Property*, 89. Cf., for instance, the view of the Emperor (161–180) and Stoic philosopher Marcus Aurelius that the indispensable condition leading to the noblest of lives is for a man to be indifferent toward indifferent things (*Ad se ipsum* 11.16). For Clement's relation to classical philosophy, see H. Chadwick, *Early Christian Thought and the Classical Tradition: Studies in Justin, Clement, and Origen* (Oxford: Clarendon Press, 1966), 31–65.

69. Clem. Alex., *Stromateis* 4.13.94.3 (ed. O. Stählin, L. Früchtel and U. Treu, *Clemens Alexandrinus*, vol. 2. GCS, 52 [4th edn. Berlin:

Akademie-Verlag, 1985], 289–290). See B. Gordon, *The Economic Problem in Biblical and Patristic Thought*. SupVC, 9 (Leiden: Brill, 1989), 85.
70. Gordon, *Economic Problem*, 85, 87.
71. Clem. Alex., *Quis div.* 14 (ed. Stählin and Früchtel, *Clemens Alexandrinus*, vol. 3, 168–169). Cf. van den Hoek, "Widening the Eye of the Needle," 73.
72. Clem. Alex. *Quis div.* 32.1 (ed. Stählin and Früchtel, *Clemens Alexandrinus*, vol. 3, 181). Cf. van den Hoek, "Widening the Eye of the Needle," 74.
73. van den Hoek, "Widening the Eye of the Needle," 74.
74. B. Blosser, "Love and Equity: The Social Doctrine of Origen of Alexandria," *Studies in Christian Ethics* 27.4 (2014): 391–394.
75. Blosser, "Love and Equity," 399–401.
76. E.g., Origen, *Commentarii in Matthaeum* 15.16 (ed. E. Klostermann and E. Benz, *Origenes Werke* 10: *Origenes Matthäuserklärung*, 1: *Die griechisch erhaltenen Tomoi*. GCS, 40 = Origenes, 10 [Leipzig: J. C. Hinrichs'sche Buchhandlung, 1935], 395–397). See Rhee, *Loving the Poor*, 84.
77. Blosser, "Love and Equity," 402–403.
78. Rhee, *Loving the Poor*, 102.
79. Newhauser, *Early History of Greed*, 13–14.
80. I. L. E. Ramelli, *Social Justice and the Legitimacy of Slavery: The Role of Philosophical Asceticism from Ancient Judaism to Late Antiquity*. OECS (Oxford: Oxford University Press, 2016), 239.
81. Origen, *Commentarii in Matthaeum* 15.20 (ed. Klostermann and Benz, *Origenes Werke* 10: *Origenes Matthäuserklärung*, 1, 405–409).
82. Origen, *Expositio in Proverbia* 22 (PG 17, 217).
83. Eng. trans. Ehrman 2, 19.
84. For an overview of the text, see P. Foster, "The *Epistle to Diognetus*," in *Writings of the Apostolic Fathers*, ed. Foster, 147–156.
85. Eng. trans. Ehrman 2, 153.
86. See, for instance, Euripides, *Phoenissae* 555–557; Plutarch, *Consolatio ad Apollonium* 28 (*Moralia* 116a).
87. E. Osborn, *Clement of Alexandria* (Cambridge: Cambridge University Press, 2005), 251–253.
88. C. M. Hays, "Resumptions of Radicalism: Christian Wealth Ethics in the Second and Third Centuries," *Zeitschrift für die Neutestamentliche Wissenschaft* 102.2 (2011): 261–282, reviews contributions to the formation of second- and third-century Christian wealth ethics. He suggests that sharing and divesture, albeit strongly recommended by Clement, Cyprian of Carthage and other streams of patristic thought, were always

meant to be voluntary, a matter of personal choice in the service of community welfare.

89. See G. Merianos, "Αντιλήψεις περί αποταμιεύσεως στο Βυζάντιο: Πατερικές διδαχές, ψυχωφελείς διηγήσεις και κοσμικές θεωρήσεις," in *Αποταμίευση και διαχείριση χρήματος*, eds. Bouraselis and Meidani, 184–185.
90. Cf. Prov. 10:12; 1 Pet. 4:8. D. J. Downs, "'Love Covers a Multitude of Sins': Redemptive Almsgiving in 1 Peter 4:8 and Its Early Christian Reception," *Journal of Theological Studies* 65.2 (2014): 512, argues that early Christian texts and authors like *1 Clement*, *2 Clement*, the *Didascalia Apostolorum*, Clement of Alexandria and Origen are aligned with 1 Pet. 4:8 "in using the phrase 'love covers a multitude of sins' to promote the social, ecclesiological and material embodiment of ἀγάπη among the people of God." In this respect, *2 Clement*'s and Clement of Alexandria's affirmation that concern for others reduces the burden of sin for donors cannot be deemed incompatible with the atonement offered through Jesus' sacrifice for humankind (ibid., 513–514).
91. D. J. Downs, "Redemptive Almsgiving and Economic Stratification in *2 Clement*," *JECS* 19.4 (2011): 493–517.
92. It is noteworthy that this conception of almsgiving, as involving all believers in alleviating the needy through sharing of surplus, is also adopted, at least in part, by Cyprian of Carthage in the third century. His promotion of almsgiving was not linked to patronage. Cyprian resorted to Paul in view of promoting a counter-cultural attitude based on care and concern for all, rather than cultivating particular clients through the construction of vertical relationships. See E. Murphy, "Cyprian, Paul, and Care for the Poor and Captive: Offering Sacrifices and Ransoming Temples," *ZAC* 20.3 (2016): 418–436.
93. Downs, "Redemptive Almsgiving," 496.
94. Downs, "Redemptive Almsgiving," 497.
95. Downs, "Redemptive Almsgiving," 500–501.
96. Downs, "Redemptive Almsgiving," 504.
97. Downs, "Redemptive Almsgiving," 504.
98. Downs, "Redemptive Almsgiving." D. K. Buell ("'Be Not One Who Stretches Out Hands to Receive but Shuts Them when It Comes to Giving': Envisioning Christian Charity when Both Donors and Recipients Are Poor," in *Wealth and Poverty*, ed. Holman, 42) argues that early Christian texts such as the *Didache*, *1 Clement* and the *Shepherd of Hermas* "offer strategies, at least implicitly, for generating funds for donations under near subsistence conditions." On the contrary, a top-down almsgiving model has been frequently employed to justify and maintain economic divisions within the community rather

than providing the foundations for challenging economic differences as unjust.
99. Rhee, *Loving the Poor*, 137.
100. C. M. Hays, "By Almsgiving and Faith Sins Are Purged? The Theological Underpinnings of Early Christian Care for the Poor," in *Engaging Economics: New Testament Scenarios and Early Christian Reception*, eds. B. W. Longenecker and K. D. Liebengood (Grand Rapids, MI: W. B. Eerdmans, 2009), 260–280.
101. J. A. Draper, "Social Ambiguity and the Production of Text: Prophets, Teachers, Bishops, and Deacons and the Development of the Jesus Traditions in the Community of the *Didache*," in *The Didache in Context: Essays on Its Text, History, and Transmission*, ed. C. N. Jefford. SNT, 77 (Leiden: Brill, 1995), 292–293. J. A. Draper ("Children and Slaves in the Community of the Didache and the Two Ways Tradition," in *The Didache: A Missing Piece*, eds. Draper and Jefford, 91–92, 98, 100) argues that the community of goods in texts such as the *Didache* and the *Epistle of Barnabas* is subject to specific limitations that undermine a full scale implementation of egalitarian practices.
102. Hays, "By Almsgiving," 263.
103. Hays, "By Almsgiving," 266.
104. See D. J. Downs, *Alms: Charity, Reward, and Atonement in Early Christianity* (Waco, TX: Baylor University Press, 2016), especially the analysis of Tobit (pp. 58–70) and Sirach (pp. 71–81), in which merciful acts are deemed as a means of expiating and purifying those who perpetrated sin. For a thorough account of the origins of communal and institutional almsgiving in rabbinic Judaism, see G. E. Gardner, *The Origins of Organized Charity in Rabbinic Judaism* (Cambridge: Cambridge University Press, 2015), who argues that these practices enabled collective support for the poor that benefitted the entire community of faith.
105. G. A. Anderson, *Charity: The Place of the Poor in the Biblical Tradition* (New Haven, CT: Yale University Press, 2013), 54 and 197 (n. 1), focuses on this redemptive dimension of almsgiving as comparable to a treasury that is in a position to deliver from death (Prov. 10:2, 11:4). Anderson argues that, in Jewish and Christian thought, charity was construed as a privileged means of serving God (*Charity*, 18), and more specifically as a loan that believers made to God (ibid., 50). The sacrificial function of almsgiving resides in directly helping Jesus himself through alleviating the needy (ibid., 160). For the heavenly treasury in the Gospels, see Mt. 6:19–21; Lk. 12:33–34; also Mt. 19:21; Mk. 10:21; Lk. 18:22.
106. Hays, "By Almsgiving," 276.
107. Hospitality: *1 Clem.* 1.2, 35.5; self-sacrifice: *1 Clem.* 55.2; true wealth residing in virtue or wisdom: e.g., Clem. Alex., *Quis div.* 19.1 (ed.

Stählin and Früchtel, *Clemens Alexandrinus*, vol. 3, 171); refusal of temporal riches: *SH*, *Sim.* 1.8–11 [50].
108. M. Silver, "The Business Model of the Early Christian Church and Its Implications for Labor Force Participation in the Roman Empire," *Marburger Beiträge zur Antiken Handels-, Wirtschafts- und Sozialgeschichte* 32 (2014): 99, 106.

CHAPTER 4

Savings for Redistributive Purposes: Stewardship of Wealth in the Teachings of Basil of Caesarea and John Chrysostom

Sketching Out the Setting: New Responsibilities and Challenges

The formation of fourth-century patristic economic thought was mainly affected by three factors: the progressive identification between Christianity and the Empire, the economic crisis of the previous period and the emergence of monasticism.[1] The Christian bishops attempted to transform the social responsibility that their role entailed into action for the reformation of late Roman society according to Christian standards. Most influential among them were the Cappadocian Fathers—Basil of Caesarea (d. ca. 379), Gregory of Nyssa (d. after 394) and Gregory of Nazianzus (d. ca. 390)—and their younger contemporary John Chrysostom (d. 407), all of them highly educated prelates of elevated socio-economic background.[2] These Fathers devoted much of their work to the formation and promotion of a Christian ethics that sought to eliminate social dysfunctions and inequalities. In this chapter we focus on the social teachings of Basil of Caesarea and John Chrysostom, although we occasionally refer to the two Gregories too.

As their earlier counterparts, the Cappadocians and Chrysostom continued to condemn the accumulation of wealth as manifest evidence of greed, and at the same time they praised its proper use for self-sufficiency and poverty relief. But they no longer addressed small congregations mainly comprised of members from lower and middle social strata. Their audiences now gradually represented the entire social scale in the Graeco-Roman urban centres. This meant that they had to make the rich and the not-so-rich believers face their social responsibilities in an increasingly Christian society. This development theoretically opened new possibilities for the realization of the ideal of a more equitable society through models of a more or less radical redistribution of wealth, but at the same time it brought the Fathers face to face with the mentalities and economic practices of the elites which contradicted this very ideal.

Being members of the civic elite themselves, the Cappadocians and Chrysostom knew first-hand these mentalities and practices. Although oversimplified as a categorization, practices such as hoarding, usury and luxury consumption posed great obstacles to the alleviation of the "needy." The latter seem to have grown in number in the fourth century in the urban centres of the East, since, for instance, immigration from the countryside and lesser provincial centres to the cities was increased.[3] At the same time, the Church Fathers had to show the advantages of being Christian, in terms of social care and cohesion, to civic audiences that remained pagan to different degrees. They also had to compete with similar Jewish and in particular pagan attempts, such as the effort of Emperor Julian (361–363), to awaken pagan practitioners to their social responsibilities.

By the time of the death of Theodosius I (395), Christianity had become the official religion of the Empire. Despite the anti-pagan legislation—which, however, was difficult to impose—pagan temples and celebrations did not immediately decline. What led to their gradual decline was rather the support and patronage offered to Christianity from the reign of Constantine I (306–337) onwards and the respective withdrawal of imperial favour and funding from pagan cults.[4] Constantine confiscated the treasures of the pagan temples, a measure that the contemporary anonymous author of the *De rebus bellicis* (*On Military Affairs*) implies partly funded the introduction of Constantine's gold coinage, the *solidus*,[5] which we shall further discuss in the sixth chapter. Furthermore, lands that had once been confiscated and returned by Julian to the pagan temples were reconfiscated by Valentinian I (364–375).[6] The social status of Christians was fundamentally altered by the open favour, wealth and privilege bestowed upon their Church. Besides the lack of public funding for and financial impoverishment of the pagan cults,[7] further reasons made Christianity appealing, especially to elites. For example, Christians were preferred for the highest administrative posts under the

Constantinian and Theodosian dynasties, a stance which will have culminated in the decision of Theodosius II (408–450) to make imperial posts accessible to Christians only.[8]

Julian attempted to stem the advance of Christianity in the fourth century and reform traditional priesthoods. The spearhead of Christian social rhetoric and ethics, philanthropy, was also a traditional concept in Hellenic ethics.[9] *Philanthrōpia* was identified with the love of the gods for humanity, but it was also considered the crowning virtue of a ruler. Julian tried to show the connection of Hellenism with the active concern for social welfare; nonetheless, it has been argued that his assertion that the Greeks historically practiced poverty relief is not affirmed by any evidence of structured aid to the poor as such.[10]

Certain epistles of Julian, such as the one addressed to Arsacius, High Priest of Galatia, are often employed as evidence of the rivalry between contemporary pagan and Christian clergies on philanthropic efforts. Julian urges Arsacius to observe Christian benevolence to strangers, care for the graves and the holiness of their lives, and to practice these virtues; not just he, but every priest in Galatia.[11] Peter Van Nuffelen, however, has disputed the authenticity of the epistle, considering it a fifth-century forgery that reflects Christian institutional charity of that time and aims to present Julian as an imitator of Christians.[12] Jean Bouffartigue, on the other hand, has defended the letter's authenticity.[13] Interestingly, Susanna Elm has shifted the focus from the oft-discussed Christian influence on Julian's measures and his attempt to compete with the Christian Church[14] to a different aim of philanthropy as conceived by this emperor:

> Julian's notions of philanthropy had a different aim: true worship of the real gods with sacrifices initiating and enabling *oikeiōsis* with them. That aim does not minimize the ethical components of such affiliation, especially imperial benevolence, clemency, and juridical mildness, none of which required, however, a pagan church or a Christian precedent.[15]

Be all that as it may, in one other epistle of his, Julian stresses:

> You must above all exercise philanthropy, for from it result many other blessings, and moreover that choicest and greatest blessing of all, the good will of the gods. […] we must suppose that God, who naturally loves human beings, has more kindness for those men who love their fellows.[16]

Concerning poverty, Julian employs in the same epistle an argument echoing Stoics[17]: people should not blame the gods for poverty but the insatiable greed of men of property instead. To denote the appropriation of public goods by the rich, he employs a vivid image: if God was to rain gold, the rich would send their slaves to place buckets everywhere and drive off the rest, so that they "alone might seize upon the gifts of the gods meant for all in common."[18] Thus, it is the greed of the rich that generates poverty. It is interesting that he then presents sharing possessions with one's fellow human beings as economically advantageous: he himself had often given lavishly to the needy, and the gods had returned his gifts many times over.[19] Benefaction is not only divinely reciprocated but also recovered multiplied, an argument also used by Paul (2 Cor. 9:5–12), who stresses: "the one who sows sparingly will also reap sparingly, and the one who sows bountifully will also reap bountifully."[20]

Julian completes his argument in the aforesaid epistle with the claim: "We ought then to share our money with all men, but more generously with the good, and with the helpless and poor so as to suffice for their need."[21] This exhortation sounds so "Christian," and it was the direct connection of philanthropy with Christian—and to a lesser extent with Jewish—religion that must have frustrated him. Christians manifestly engaged in charitable activities, "such as the so-called love-feast, or hospitality, or service of tables," attracting new members to their communities.[22] Julian was not willing to let the Christian clergy monopolize the notion of philanthropy.

Years after Julian's death, John Chrysostom, as a presbyter in Antioch, employed the image of the pagans as a counter-force to Christians in his city, reversing at the same time the mythological aspect of pagan religions that was emphasized by Christian authors: "Let's become the laughing-stock of the pagans: our beliefs seem to be myths."[23] Libanius (d. ca. 393) attests that pagan temples in Antioch served as the shelter of poverty-stricken groups, such as aged people, orphans, *et cetera*,[24] in the way Julian seems to have envisioned the assumption of social duties by his priests.

Yet we should not construe this religious "rivalry" in terms of a bipolar opposition between Christians and pagans. In a city such as Chrysostom's Antioch, where an active Jewish community also existed, it is most probable that the latter followed traditional Jewish precepts concerning care of orphans, widows and other needy categories.[25] Late antique rabbinic texts pointed to poverty relief as a moral obligation inside a Jewish community, an activity which should be performed showing respect to the recipient's dignity, and which was identified as a good deed, pleasing to God.[26] The Christian clergy had to prompt Christian believers to excel in terms of social cooperation in the religiously pluralistic cities of the late antique Eastern Mediterranean.

ASPECTS OF BASIL OF CAESAREA'S VIEWS ON PROPERTY AND WEALTH

Famine in Cappadocia, 368/9

In the late 360s a severe drought afflicted Cappadocia, causing a famine that struck the poorest population.[27] This oft-discussed famine cannot be fully perceived without sketching some of the particularities of the region. Cappadocia was a vast rural area with relatively few cities, creating a picture that was in sharp contrast with that of the Eastern Mediterranean city ports. It was famous for its horses, their breeding being important for the imperial cavalry, and as a result imperial horse ranches dominated the area. In the middle of this region stood Caesarea, whose particularity as a consumption centre was that it was not supported by a nexus of minor towns. The Cappadocian cities were not poor, as they were placed along the main routes of communication, and the products of local animal husbandry, agriculture and industry enjoyed strong demand from other markets. Yet in a time of crisis and famine, "armies" of the destitute would reach the few major urban centres of the region as the main consumption centres, and especially Caesarea, which was not supported by lesser towns as intermediate points of distribution.[28]

This happened in 368/9. In his funeral oration for Basil of Caesarea (*Or.* 43), Gregory of Nazianzus depicts the dire situation, as well as the attempts that Basil, as a priest, made to relieve the poor. Gregory depicts the geographical particularity of Caesarea, but besides this he holds in great part liable for the famine those with access to grain:

> There was a famine, the most severe one ever recorded. The city was in distress, and there was no source of assistance, or relief for the calamity. [...] an inland city like ours can neither turn its superfluity to profit, nor supply its need, by either disposing of what we have, or importing what

we have not: but the hardest part of all such distress is the insensibility and insatiability of those who possess supplies. For they watch their opportunities, and turn the distress to profit, and thrive upon misfortune [...].[29]

It is obvious that the great landowners of the region accumulated grain that generated considerable profits.

The economic history of the Roman world provides significant examples of the regulation of stocks and bans on hoarding, the latter also being a part of imperial instructions to provincial governors.[30] Concerning hoarding of products, three types dominated economic behaviour in the Roman world: private hoarding by consumers, commercial hoarding by traders and farmers, and public hoarding by imperial, provincial or local authorities. Among them, private and public hoarding were intended to ensure the availability of basic goods in times of necessity, the first through a decrease in demand, the second through an increase in supply when the stock of goods was returned to the market. Commercial hoarding was supposed to ensure a firm supply of goods in as many areas as possible, though through artificial price regulation.[31]

Not infrequently, wealthy landowners in many eras and areas of the Empire were thought to be hoarding grain, insofar as these surpluses yielded higher levels of profit in times of food shortages. During such periods, the reactions of the lower strata were directed against members of the elites who failed to address expectations of public generosity and civic virtue. For instance, during a riot in the city of Prusa in the late first century AD, the prosperous landowner Dio Chrysostom was accused by the populace of hoarding grain instead of channelling the surplus to the local markets and selling at cheaper prices. Dio appeared also to frustrate peoples' expectations, according to which prominent citizens had to contribute capital to the common fund.[32] It is probable that leaders in provincial communities often acted like Dio, who had to pacify the rioters by reminding them of his past benefactions, as well as by incurring the fear of imperial retribution.[33]

Things were not different in major urban centres. In a late-fourth-century letter addressed to Nicomachus Flavianus, Symmachus turns against Pinianus, his successor as the prefect of Rome, for his incompetence in managing food supply; this resulted in shortages of commodities and speculative selling that benefitted those who enjoyed an abundance of stored goods.[34] In such times of crisis, scarcity and famine offered new opportunities for the hoarders to intervene in the black market and turn necessity into a source of indecent wealth.[35] It is noteworthy that not only elite members but also the populace were engaging in hoarding behaviours.[36] Undoubtedly, such individual consumers were far from being in the position to manipulate market prices typical of speculative hoarding, as their wealthier counterparts could. Traders and prosperous landowners, on the contrary, were afforded the opportunity to transform extreme necessity into a possibility of extracting considerable gain, an attitude detrimental to social welfare and therefore deemed as inappropriate to Christians.[37]

Both Basil and Gregory of Nazianzus deplored the greedy behaviours of great landowners who resorted to hoarding as a principal lucrative strategy that increased shortages in supply.[38] It has thus been argued that Basil was facing not a complete lack of grain in Caesarea but rather its hoarding by those who intended to secure vast profits during a period of crisis. Since hoarding was responsible for food shortage, Basil's goal was to convince the hoarders to sell their surplus in the market or offer it freely to the needy.[39] He did so in an oration explicitly linked with the famine (*Hom.* 8).[40]

In this sermon Basil strongly urges the wealthy who withheld surplus in grain to share it with the afflicted population.[41] The consequences of deprivation were felt at all levels of the social structure: the community was facing an utter lack of food, households were inflicted by famine because of market speculation, usury and insufficient reserves, while individuals were being cut off from the household as well as from the community.[42] Basil, echoing Stoic arguments,[43] states that men, who are equipped with reason, should not appear crueller than the irrational beasts that use what nature provides as common possession. But men, he stresses, make private that which is common. He then reverses Julian's exhortations to his priests by saying: "we should be put to shame by what is said for the philanthropy of the Greeks."[44] Basil attempts to persuade those holding grain in their silos to share it, by presenting them as patrons to the poor, the latter being the dependents of the former according to the Graeco-Roman ideal of civic order. He promises the *tropheus* (nourisher) the honour that a Greek benefactor would traditionally have enjoyed, although this honour is placed eschatologically in the Last Judgement.[45]

As Peter Brown has observed, Basil "challenged the rich to act as *euergetai* to the poor [...]. Basil's sermons were intended to be the swansong of the ancient city."[46] It is important for our theme that the aforementioned sermon and its context help us realize that hoarding not only concerns valuables and money but often foodstuffs and everything that could be used for profiteering by those withholding it. Basil does not deal with the typical hoarding of wealth but, even worse, with a kind that threatens the sustenance of life itself. Storing goods, especially in times of crisis, resulted in the failure of market mechanisms to meet the excess demand for food. The Church Fathers were not alone in reproaching local elites for this practice. In 362–363, famine inflicted Antioch. According to Emperor Julian, its causes were a drought and the wealthy, who stored the grain produced on their land so as to maximize their profits.[47] Of course, the practice of grain hoarding was not an exclusive late antique phenomenon; in late Medieval Italy, for instance, it was considered a crime against community.[48]

Basil did not just preach in order to prompt the rich to assume their social obligations. He was a man of action and did not hesitate to employ his patrimony so as to purchase grain and relieve the famine-stricken with food and medical care.[49] In the same period, the foundation of his *ptōchotropheion* (poor hospice) also commenced, which we shall discuss shortly.

Private Vs. Common Property, Hoarding Vs. Sharing

Channelling surplus to the needy through almsgiving was germane to a Christian community viewed as a social organism based on the interdependence of its members. This mutual interdependence, though, was disrupted by the greedy behaviour of the rich. Basil touches upon the issue of property in *Hom.* 6,[50] employing two main arguments: (a) the rich are not owners but managers of common resources received by God for proper stewardship[51]; (b) as a consequence, what is withheld by the rich from this common property is actually stolen from the poor.[52] To the seemingly logical and much-used argument, "whom do I harm by keeping what is mine," Basil responds using an image of Stoic origin: the public theatre.[53] A rich person resembles someone who, after occupying a seat in the theatre, shuts out those who come after him, believing that what is intended for common use is his own property.[54] Basil here twists Cicero's image of the theatre, which the latter used to defend the right of private property: the theatre is a shared amenity, yet a seat in it belongs rightfully to whomever occupies it first.[55] Basil attacks the principle of first occupancy, juxtaposing that he who takes first a seat does not claim occupancy only on it but on the whole theatre.[56] His arguments recall the ones employed by Julian (through the image of the rain of gold), on which we commented earlier.

Basil concludes in *Hom.* 6 that a greedy person is one who does not adhere to *autarkeia* (self-sufficiency),[57] while a robber is one who deprives everyone else of his property. And thus we have finally arrived at our main subject, as we read his words: "the silver you buried belongs to the needy person."[58] Such positions seem quite radical and imply the sharp inequalities of the Cappadocians' era. Gregory of Nazianzus shares Basil's view, and in his oration *On the Love of the Poor* (*Or.* 14) he stresses in a likely manner that some people toil to hoard, while others suffer from poverty: "Let us not labour to gather up treasure and protect it, while others labour in poverty," implying that the former worsen the condition of the latter.[59]

Barry Gordon argues that scarcity is a man-made phenomenon, entwined with behaviours relating to consumption and distribution. Hence, he underscores that:

> In any society, the rich create the problem of scarcity for themselves by continually expanding their consumption horizons, and by anxiously hoarding wealth against the threat of future need. The poor, by contrast, have the problem thrust upon them by institutionalised economic inequality.[60]

The fourth-century patristic view of the economic problem seems to coincide with this assessment. In *Hom.* 7 Basil comments on the story of the Rich Young Man in Mt. 19:16–26.[61] The sermon's theme rotates around the vanity of pursuing and accumulating wealth. Basil challenges the argument that hoarding may prove effective in addressing the uncertainty of the future and other unpredictable events, as well as the necessity of bequeathing a part of this wealth to one's children.[62] Here Basil rejects a significant aspect of the mentality of the property-conscious elites that linked social succession with transmission of property. For Basil, holding wealth on account of the children's future is a mere excuse for greed.[63] On the whole, reducing uncertainty through hoarding remains highly ambivalent. The only tangible outcome of it is the punishment for cruelty, since the hoarder along with his wealth buries also his heart (cf. Mt. 6:21). Basil makes a notable observation in the same sermon: after having described indicative cases of luxury and conspicuous consumption he states that, no matter how much the wealth is scattered, it continues to abound and, as a result, it is buried underground or stored in secret places. We may conclude that, for Basil, hoarding follows consumption as a practice, as he states that when someone fails to fully spend his wealth, he then conceals it in the earth.[64]

Susan R. Holman, commenting on *Homilies* 6 and 7, argues that Basil may seem to claim a radical reform, yet he does not wish to undermine the social order. He rather seeks to "apply a social control that reflects his own view of biblical justice." This justice necessitates an authoritative structure that, on the one hand, can channel the donations of the rich to their communities, and, on the other hand, can recognize the motives of suppliants asking for help.[65] The Church could guarantee the proper functioning of such a redistributive mechanism.

The wealthy occupied a prominent position in Basil's teaching, since they should assume an enhanced social responsibility toward the community. In a Christian society wealthy members had to undertake the social function of redistribution of wealth through proper management of their surplus income. The rationale for such a social practice was multi-level: it was perceived as a precondition for the giver's salvation and as a means of imitating Christ's benignity and realizing godlikeness,[66] while transforming the wealthy into supporters of the less privileged. As a result, a more complicated system of reciprocities emerged, in which generalized reciprocity, the unconditional concern for others as constitutive of Christian identities, coexisted with balanced reciprocities akin to an orderly society. Those consistently engaging in charitable activities were benefitted by accumulating reputation and honour.

Equally important is the fact that an undisrupted flow of resources to the least privileged members was thus secured. In the absence of organized social welfare state policies in late antique societies, the redistributive nature of alms ensured that both the salvation and need for reputation of one group was perfectly compatible with the need for survival of the other. The societal ideal that Basil seems to endorse recalls the organicist view of society evidenced in earlier Christians texts, such as the *Shepherd of Hermas*,[67] adapted to the conditions of the fourth century.

Institutionalizing Poverty Relief: Basil's Ptōchotropheion *and the Bequest of Gregory of Nazianzus*

The foundation of Basil's *ptōchotropheion*, also known as "Basileias" or "new city," was closely linked with the experience he gained through the Cappadocian famine of 368/9. This crisis, far from being unprecedented, contributed to the shaping of a model of institutionalized poverty relief, which was not novel in ecclesiastical practice, but its most emblematic realization was Basil's *ptōchotropheion*. It was completed in ca. 372, after the famine and his election as bishop. Built outside the walls of Caesarea, on his family's estates, it was a complex of apartments for needy travellers, the poor and the sick, but also the bishop and his guests. Thus, this compound combined a hostel, a poorhouse and a hospital where the sick were medically treated and the able poor were trained or employed in trades.[68]

Basil must have realized that appeals to the rich in times of crisis were hardly enough. The bishop could organize his own safety net through his initiatives, not having to exclusively rely on the untrustworthy wealthy for immediate aid. As a bishop, he had to meet his responsibilities and be prepared not only for the everyday care for the poor but also for the next crisis. As an ecclesiastical patron he also had to prove to the emperor and his officials that the wealth and privileges enjoyed by his Church were used for the benefit of local society.[69] He did so by founding both a conspicuous edifice and a welfare institution. As Peter Brown puts it: "The incident is a striking outcome of the Constantinian settlement, by which the church was granted its privileges in return for a fully public commitment to the care of the poor."[70]

The foundation of the Basileias also pointed to the patristic awareness that, even if the wealthy were convinced to share a part of their riches with the poor, this had to be realized in an effective way. One-off donations, no matter how significant, were a drop in the ocean. Sustainable care for the poor required projects, such as the Basileias, which could be undertaken by the Church but required the steadfast support of the state and/or the wealthy in order to be viable. The concept of the rich man as a proper administrator of his wealth coincides with this model of benefaction, which called for the wholehearted response of the well off to fundraising attempts, or, even better, for the endowment of assets that could produce recurring revenue. It is in this context—as we shall see in the sixth chapter, discussing Melania the Younger—that total dispossession on behalf of the rich was considered an heroic act, but hardly economically efficient.

Gregory of Nazianzus must also have financed some kind of institution for the poor in Nazianzus—not as ambitious as Basil's attempt, but he must have provided a "soup kitchen" at least.[71] It is notable that, in his famous testament (dated 381),[72] Gregory states that he has consecrated all his possessions, with certain exceptions, "to the Catholic Church which is in Nazianzus, for the service of the poor who are under the care of the aforesaid Church."[73] The management of the bequest was to be undertaken by three *ptōchotrophoi* (nourishers of the poor): Marcellus the deacon and monk, Gregory the deacon and monk, and Eustathius the monk. Gregory the deacon and monk, a freedman, was named the heir of all the property, both moveable and immoveable, having the task to deliver everything to the Church of Nazianzus, with the exception of what was to be left to some individuals by way of legacy or *fideicommissum* (roughly interpreted as "trust").[74] The term used for the three administrators, *ptōchotrophoi*, brings into mind Basil's *ptōchotropheion*, and probably implies its influence.[75]

Gregory of Nazianzus' testament is very telling in the fact that some of the most eminent Church Fathers did not die in voluntary poverty. The possessions of Gregory as described in the text give the impression of an average provincial property.[76] References are made to land, flocks, precious garments, slaves and unspecified sums of money, but also specific sums of *solidi*. The latter show that even a Church Father had savings.

Concerning especially sums of money in his testament, Gregory bequeathed his namesake heir 50 *solidi*, the largest amount he left to anyone. To him, along with the monk Eustathius, Gregory also left the estate at Arianzus with the breeding mares and sheep in it.[77] Among the arrangements he made in favour of the virgin Roussiane, a relative of his and seemingly a woman of status who had embraced the ascetic lifestyle, he ordered that an unspecified annual allowance be given to her, in order that she might live decently.[78] Gregory mentions his servant Theophilus, a freedman, but also Theophilus' brother, Eupraxius, and his notary, Theodosius, who would be manumitted after his death. Gregory left a legacy of five *solidi* to each of them.[79] Lastly, three close friends and associates were also to receive, besides his garments, a sum of *solidi*: Evagrius the deacon, 30; Theodoulus the deacon, 20; and Elaphius the notary, 20.[80]

A modern reader may find the combination of references to money and slaves disturbing, and it seems that a Father of the calibre of Gregory did not exactly live up to his ideals; but did these ideals include total dispossession? Of course, we should not overlook the fact that he was willing to make his property an endowment to the Church of Nazianzus for the benefit of the poor. This was not a one-off donation but an endowment of the kind that a bishopric needed in order to keep taking care of the poor effectively. Yet it is notable that he appointed the three *ptōchotrophoi*, men of his trust, to manage his bequest. Perhaps the fact that the bishopric of Nazianzus was vacant at the time he was composing his will played a role in his decision.[81] Anyhow, Gregory remained a property-conscious aristocratic benefactor who wanted to have the last word on his patrimony, which could not just be assimilated into the Church's property. It was his legacy. In the fifth century, Melania the Younger, as we shall see in the sixth chapter, had a similar stance toward the fate of her monastic institutions after her death. Gregory as an aristocratic patron was also responsible for those who would lose his protection after his death. It comes as no surprise, then, that he left significant sums to his close friends and associates, some of whom were freedmen or slaves to be manumitted after his death.[82]

We think that the notion of proper stewardship of one's wealth concerning Cappadocian patristic ideals should be viewed under the lens of the foundation of Basil's *ptōchotropheion* and Gregory's bequest to the Church of Nazianzus. From dispossession to sporadic donations, many options existed to alleviate those in need, all being better than leaving one's wealth hoarded. Yet founding an institution or actively supporting the Church's work through endowed assets generating income made the real difference. In this way, social benefaction could be tangible in the long run. Even so, the question of who controlled the endowments of the elite would be a thorny issue, as we shall see in the sixth chapter.

Delineating John Chrysostom's Views on Hoarding

The Ideals of Self-sufficiency and Stewardship of Wealth

John Chrysostom is one of the most suitable cases for studying fourth-century patristic trends in social issues in an urban context. He lived in two prominent cities of his time, Antioch and the relatively recent imperial capital Constantinople.[83] He was born (ca. 350), studied and served as a priest in the former, and in 397 he was elected bishop of the latter. John met in these two cities some of the wealthiest aristocrats in the Eastern Mediterranean, as well as well-off representatives of the upper strata of middling groups which prospered through the flourishing industry and trade.[84] Concerning Antioch, for instance, Chrysostom himself informs us that its marketplace had an abundance of goods, and that it was frequented until very late in the evening, while Libanius in his encomium on the city proudly refers to the constant building activity there[85]; both attest to the fact that the city was prospering. On the other hand, Chrysostom witnessed in both Antioch and Constantinople poverty in different forms and degrees: from beggars to ascetics; from those near or at subsistence level to those below it; from women of status choosing to live an ascetic life to destitute women having no other choice but to sell their bodies for food. Chrysostom's work refers to all kinds of poverty: socio-economic (analysed into endemic, episodic and epidemic), spiritual and voluntary. These categories in Chrysostomic texts have been comprehensively studied by Wendy Mayer.[86]

It should be noted, however, that Chrysostom was concerned in his preaching with both the poor and the rich, caring for the salvation of every member of the Christian community. His call for almsgiving denotes a form of redistribution of wealth that is beneficial to both the donor and the recipient. Mayer, in her analysis of Chrysostom's discourse on poverty, underlines that:

> [...] John's repositioning of the poor within a transformed Christian society in which traditional social values concerning wealth and poverty are turned upside down is secondary to his main purpose. This is not to argue that John does not personally feel for the plight of the economic poor or that he is disinterested in their care. [...] his spotlight is not confined to them, but shines equally on the rich [...]. If we are obliged to label him at all, it is more accurate to call him not a champion of the poor, but of poverty—not economic poverty, but voluntary poverty.[87]

Chrysostom wanted the rich to be saved as much as he wished the poor to be fed.

In this respect, John, following the long-standing views on the issue, did not consider wealth to be evil and neither did he contest its possession, provided that it was properly administered, but he rather opposed greediness and wealth's gluttonous accumulation.[88] Gold embodied the notion of wealth in the post-Constantinian era, as we shall discuss in the sixth chapter, and Chrysostom encapsulates in a homily its licit and illicit uses:

> Is gold good? It is good for almsgiving, for the aid of the poor; it is not good for unprofitable use, to be hoarded up, to be buried in the earth, to be worn on the hands and the feet and the head. It was discovered for this

purpose, not that we should bind the image of God with it, but that we should release those who are bound.[89]

Almsgiving, poverty relief and release of captives are opposed to unprofitable use, hoarding, luxury and conspicuous consumption. Release of captives, in particular, points to a basic episcopal duty, the ransoming of captives who had fallen into the hands of foreign military raiders, brigands and pirates, but also slave and prostitute dealers, and it required the collection of large sums in a very short time.[90]

Elsewhere, Chrysostom offers a functional definition of wealth that seems to fit the particularities of a typically mercantile economic system: wealth comprises a set of precious metals, in particular gold and silver, ornaments and jewellery, luxuries and so on.[91] The generation of surplus can be justified in this economic framework, subject to moral and spiritual constraints. In Chrysostom's view, God bestowed goods on the wealthy to alleviate the needy through sharing, thus abstaining from immediate gratification. Enjoyment of both material and symbolic goods (e.g., reputation and honour) should be grounded in mindfulness and prudence, given that amassing perishable goods is considered a shameful behaviour. Behind hoarding practices that violate the premises of self-sufficiency, Chrysostom identifies greed, a grave moral transgression that renders someone prosperous through unremittingly perpetrating injustice.[92]

On the contrary, self-sufficiency is valued in the sense that one should be content with what he/she already has. It is notable that an abundance of goods does not denote genuine prosperity—a view already discernible in certain Apostolic Fathers, as we have seen—while he who is not content with what he has is considered to covet other people's property.[93] For Chrysostom, maintenance of wealth presupposes the concomitant relativization of its intrinsic worthiness and, primarily, its evaluation through the lenses of eternity.[94] Christian believers, like true philosophers, should have no need of possessions and other worldly pursuits,[95] a view replete with Stoic ethical connotations.[96]

The Parable of the Rich Man and Lazarus in Luke 16:19–31 offers fruitful material from which Chrysostom draws in view of not only of a theology of salvation, but also of pastoral concerns about wealth, poverty and care for others.[97] Greedy wealthy persons indulge in their insatiable desires that urge them to appropriate others' resources[98] and exploit the needy.[99] Concomitantly, accumulation of wealth denotes an economic process inimical to the precept of social justice. Chrysostom views excess wealth as eroding the ideal of justice; hoarding riches and seeking justice are two inconsistent human pursuits, a fact that is emphatically declared, often through the use of social metaphors.[100]

Overall, Chrysostom, like Basil of Caesarea, argues that the concentration of excess wealth is nothing but theft originating in some kind of injustice.[101] A latent injustice lurks even in the case of inherited wealth, for which one cannot employ the argument that we cannot be held responsible for the inequities of our ancestors. Wealth is morally justified if it is dissociated from the vice of greed, since amassing riches is detrimental to community welfare, thus making it an irrational pursuit. This superfluity of riches contravenes the principle of self-sufficiency by triggering ostentatious lifestyles that reflect moral depravity and corruption.[102]

According to Chrysostom, self-sufficiency was a typical case of Old Testament patriarchs in whom material possessions were thought of as stemming from just acquisition—they were not products of fraud, deprivation of others' legitimate resources or iniquity.[103] In such a case, wealth originated in personal toil and comprised a primitive form of productive capital in an early agrarian economy. On the contrary, accumulation of gold and silver objects for their own sake was thought of as an unnatural process akin to the lifestyles of the arrogant wealthy, which transgressed the premises of self-sufficiency. In his *Homily 7 on Colossians*, delivered in Antioch, Chrysostom censures in this context especially the vanity and coquetry of the wealthy female members of his audience:

> How do the women differ (I am embarrassed, but have to say it) who make silver chamber-pots? [...] Christ is starving and you're indulging like that? [...] Possessing silver plates is not even in accord with a philosophical spirit, but is total wantonness. Making unclean vessels from silver too, is that wantonness?[104]

And later on he adds: "I think that they will desire much more to have golden hair and lips and eyebrows and thus to anoint themselves all over with liquid gold."[105] His conclusion is striking and encapsulates the manifest inequality in Antioch, but also the indifference of the Christian rich to assuming their social responsibilities:

There are so many beggars standing around the church, and the church has so many children so rich, it can't come to the aid of a single beggar. One is hungry, the other is drunk; one relieves herself in silver, the other doesn't even have bread. What's this madness?[106]

The Monastic Stewardship Paradigm

John Chrysostom envisions a Christian *conditio humana* in which all social conflict, which arises from sharp socio-economic divisions and concomitant inequality, would be mitigated. This ideal might be realized through abstinence from conspicuous consumption and luxurious living and, more specifically, through the pursuit of a monastic paradigm of stewardship of resources even in more secular spheres of life.[107]

At the extreme, the monastic stewardship paradigm necessitates common ownership of possessions, a state that was once akin to the human condition. Chrysostom stresses that God did not create the rich and the poor; on the contrary, the Earth belonged to all.[108] As is the case with Basil, in Chrysostom's view, individual property rights induce situations which could be described through the modern premise of a "zero-sum game," in which any individual advancement with respect to finite resources is feasible at the expense of others. Accordingly, those who succumb to an individual appropriation of goods of which they do not hold possession *stricto sensu* (as everything belongs to God only) are motivated by greedy dispositions, seeking to usurp resources which otherwise should be held in common. According to Chrysostom, private property is nothing more than a linguistic invention, a pure social convention that is by no means typical of the primordial state of humanity, in particular of that before the Fall.[109]

Underlying his ideal are the principles of social cooperation, unanimity and mutuality that attenuate acquisitive behaviour and facilitate sharing, as in the case of the early Jerusalem Church, depicted in Acts (2:42–47, 4:32–37), that held everything in common.[110] Chrysostom stresses that the words "mine" (*emon*) and "yours" (*son*), often employed in his orations to denote acquisitiveness, were not used in the early Christian community.[111] This social endeavour was in fact effective in transcending the boundaries between wealthy and needy members.[112] Chrysostom implies that the inherent goodness of this mode of economic organization would have ultimately eradicated all social evils, yet this social experiment was discontinued.[113] Common ownership survived through coenobitic monasticism, and found its historical culmination in the respective practices that perpetuated the communal nature of the Jerusalem Church. According to Chrysostom, the words "mine" and "yours" were still not heard in monasteries.[114]

Private property is a social institution that violates the premises upon which such an ideal *conditio humana* is grounded. Furthermore, individual ownership not only distorts the initial abundance of goods intended to serve primary human needs, but also deviates from the principle of self-sufficiency. In this view, holding goods in common is entwined with a virtuous standard of living that precludes hoarding of possessions. This stewardship ideal is intended to suppress all proclivities associated with greedy conduct, the intention to acquire more at the expense of others. Hoarding as a process appears to be harmful to social cohesion, incurring attitudes conducive to inequity and the exploitation of the economically worse off.[115] Chrysostom is seemingly aware of the impediments to the process of realizing such an egalitarian ideal. For him, the most serious obstacle to the endeavour of implementing a communal organization remains the cruel and uncompassionate personality of the rich, who strongly oppose an obligation of sharing.[116] In this view, the acquisitiveness (the "mine" and "yours") of the wealthy pervades all manifestations of economic life, distorting the primordial harmony and generating tensions and societal conflict.[117]

Despite the obstacles, the monastic stewardship paradigm retains its social attractiveness. In its proponents' view, communal ownership was expected to improve social welfare and to foster a better allocation of resources through redistribution rather than individual acquisition, since the origins of poverty lie within the division of the common property. This model presupposes an enhanced level of trust in divine providence so as to meet the problems unleashed by an eventual lack of capital assets.[118] Such negative prospects necessitate a strategy to motivate believers accordingly, by providing proper rationales centred on Christian experience. It was, however, through persuasion rather than sound rational arguments that this paradigm might be implemented in the secular sphere.[119]

It has been argued that Chrysostom envisioned a much deeper societal transformation, based on a transition from the institutional sphere of the Graeco-Roman city, entrenched in patronage and benefaction, to a communal mode of organization founded on the new institution of ascetic households.[120] It seems that, according to Chrysostom, the gap between worldly life in the urban centres and ascetic life in the countryside could be bridged. Jan R. Stenger stresses that for Chrysostom:

> [...] the monastic community, shaped after biblical models, represents a perfectly equal society, an excellent antidote to the elitist vision of a society based on class and education. He therefore suggests ways in which the monastic life, or rather philosophy, can greatly influence and finally transform life in the city so that the classical *polis* is virtually turned into a monastery.[121]

Accordingly, wealth, reputation, status and philosophy are subservient to a life of virtue and devotion underlying Christianity's strong preference for an equal society.[122]

Hoarding as a Socially and Individually Inefficient Practice

Commenting on 1 Timothy 6:9, Chrysostom treats those who succumb to the enticements of worldly pursuits as following individual but irrational goal setting: what underlies the pursuit of riches is greed, the love of wealth that contravenes right reason. Chrysostom seeks to designate the profound irrationality of hoarding goods by employing the metaphor of human life as a journey, in which possessions amount to a burden devoid of practical utility,[123] a view that resonates with a Stoic philosophical framework.[124] Furthermore, hoarding is deemed to be socially shameful, as we have already seen, because those impoverished are deprived of the necessities of life, whereas the prosperous spend their excess income on luxuries devoid of immediate utility.[125] This critique is full of ethical overtones, reminiscent of the Hellenistic moral literature, which regards conspicuous consumption as originating in human vanity.[126]

Storing wealth is often intertwined with a disposition for conspicuous consumption that reinforces power and status recognition pertinent to the elite. In Chrysostom's rhetoric, the dissipation of the wealthy is at odds with the vulnerability of the needy who suffer from hunger, lack of necessities and, ultimately, homelessness.[127] The wealthy are strongly admonished to proceed to generous almsgiving, yet they are reassured that such an activity will not render the donors themselves impoverished and devoid of their economic benefits.

Hoarding, however, is a sub-optimal activity, according to Chrysostom, and he employs a set of arguments to support his view. First of all, hiding wealth is a highly uncertain and risky process, given its ephemeral character and constant mobility.[128] Second, the human relationship with material goods should not be one of ownership (*despoteia*), since nothing really belongs to human beings, but one of proper administration planned to serve the common good. Thus, one can only claim ownership of the achievements of the soul, charity and benevolence.[129]

Chrysostom advances a third argument in favour of diminishing the intrinsic value of accumulated wealth. He argues that the act of admiring certain goods makes them worthy: we subjectively render precious metals valuable even if they are devoid of such a quality. In other words, precious metals (frequently objects of hoarding) are valued as a result of human assumptions and societal beliefs. Hoarding as such is rather a matter of anticipation, incorporating socially constructed criteria of worthiness that can be easily relativized and, ultimately, challenged. Only higher ideals, such as piety and righteousness, are not prone to such fluctuations of value because they are good by nature.[130]

It seems that Chrysostom proposes what in modern terminology is considered a "subjective theory of value," according to which the value of a commodity or good depends upon our subjective evaluation of its worthiness due to the satisfaction we derive from its consumption. In this respect, the value of goods is contingent upon a set of interdependent opinions and beliefs concerning their ability to satisfy human needs. This set shapes what the Romans would call the *communis aestimatio* (common estimation) of a particular community of producers and consumers interacting in free market exchanges that preclude compulsion and coercion (the latter is typical of monopolistic market conditions).

A Call for Almsgiving

According to Chrysostom, those who prosper have to properly use their surplus and refrain from storing it. Just as the artisans have cultivated their particular art by developing skills and competences pertinent to their specific occupation, in a similar way the rich should learn how to properly use their wealth by giving alms to the needy. Thus, the rich would excel in this very art of the beneficial stewardship of wealth.[131]

Almsgiving, instead of hoarding riches, is viewed not only as a moral precept facilitating the redistribution of wealth, but also as an economic practice constitutive of an orderly and equitable society. In fact, almsgiving is conceived of in terms of a reciprocal exchange in which the donor obtains much more utility than the recipient: without the existence of the needy, remittance of innumerable sins perpetrated by the wealthy would hardly occur.[132] Almsgiving tends to assume a form of micro-economic management of financial resources oriented toward the eschatological fate of humankind, yet its short-term benefits are also visible, because it protects the Christian household against danger.[133]

Church Fathers had to address the indifference toward the indigent and poor, since the rich engaged in conspicuous consumption, yet believed that church institutions should undertake the obligation of relieving the poor. Chrysostom comments in his *Homily 21 on 1 Corinthians*, delivered in Antioch:

> Indeed I'm acutely ashamed when I see many of the rich riding horses with golden bridles, with a train of servants clad in gold. They have silver couches and an excessive amount of other ostentation, and when they're asked to give an offering to a poor person, they become poorer than the extremely poor. But what's their constant talk? "He's got the common church allowance," they say.[134]

The "destitute" were situated at the fringes of society, suffering humiliation and unequal treatment,[135] and experiencing strong feelings of social inferiority. These marginalized groups, frequently viewed as exhibiting certain forms of deviant behaviour, were perceived as being prone to laziness, devoid of social responsibility and unable to contribute to the welfare of the city. They were considered to display blatant anti-social behaviour, violating their legal obligations and seeking to attract compassion through deception and related strategies.[136]

Chrysostom, being aware of the socio-economic conditions of his time, employs the language of market transactions to describe almsgiving as a form of balanced reciprocity between donors and recipients, based on an exchange of money for grace. Almsgiving comprises a heavenly deposit, a kind of savings in heaven, that has to be repaid during the final judgment, and as such it cancels debts originating in sinful activities perpetrated by the donor.[137] Almsgiving as a form of circulation of wealth through generalized reciprocities seems to be more preferable than practices of devoting objects of value to local churches.[138]

Chrysostom strives to transform the mindsets of his audience by focusing not so much on addressing issues of structural poverty as on the attitudes of the poor, who fail to meet social exigencies.[139] He discourages socially sanctioned types of benevolence—for instance, those addressing the needs of wandering ascetics—since such giving is contingent upon institutionalized forms of reputation and recognition, rewarding status rather than the genuine need of the recipient.[140]

As already mentioned, a redistribution on behalf of the wealthy would by no means endanger the self-sufficiency enjoyed by powerful households. Consequently, it could not pose a threat to the stability of social structures by subverting prevailing patronage relationships promoted by wealthy members of the congregations.[141] Chrysostom is willing to accept established social arrangements.[142] Being prosperous does not necessarily imply a sinful human condition, a thesis reminiscent of Clement of Alexandria's attempt to accommodate rich Christians.[143] Evidently, Chrysostom advocates the existence of a righteous wealthy, not demanding a total renunciation of possessions.

Commenting on Chrysostom's interpretation of the declaration of Zacchaeus in Luke 19:8b, Ronald H. van der Bergh considers almsgiving as embedded in Zacchaeus' personal decision for the manifold restitution of stolen property. Chrysostom evokes an adequate compensation for those who had been wronged, thus viewing almsgiving as integral to the restitution of specific unjust acts.[144] Persistent inequalities and, ultimately, inequity are grounded in human sin entrenched in all social formations. Economically speaking, sinful behaviours emerge in a social space privileging the hoarding of wealth, involving two core connotations: the primacy of individual gratification and the very negation of sharing excess wealth with those in extreme necessity.[145]

Chrysostom seeks to specify a socially desirable and morally binding level of almsgiving that is contingent upon the level of income enjoyed by a particular believer. Prosperous believers are urged to offer to the needy no less than a tenth of all income and returns.[146] This very act of charitable giving renders the wealthy just stewards of resources entrusted to them by divine providence in view of supporting the economically worse off.[147]

Chrysostom's "statistics" concerning the socio-economic stratification of Antioch have been discussed often. According to him, 10 percent of the population of Antioch were rich, 10 percent were poor and the remaining 80 percent were in a middling economic position.[148]

Obviously, rich and poor represent in this picture the far ends of the social scale—the extremely rich and the extremely poor—while the 80 percent is roughly identified with those in between. Chrysostom's aim was to show that if the rich and the not-so-rich assumed their social roles, it would have been very easy for the 90 percent of the population to feed and clothe the remaining 10 percent, and thus to eradicate poverty. He intentionally reduces the level of poverty and at the same time exaggerates the level of relative wealth so as to show that the solution to poverty in an urban context is a matter of choice and determination on behalf of the wealthy and the less wealthy.[149] Thus, Chrysostom stresses the responsibilities not only of the super-rich toward the "needy," but of whoever was above the level of extreme poverty. In the third chapter we discussed the two models of almsgiving in early Christianity proposed by David J. Downs,[150] one based on the philanthropy of the wealthy and the other on mutualism and reciprocal support. Chrysostom's exhortations imply that adapted versions of both models were still being proposed in the fourth century.

In a similar way, Gregory of Nyssa admonishes even the poor to be charitable, since there is always someone poorer. "Give what you have," he says, and he considers the level of offering as being dependent upon the economic capacity of the donor. According to Gregory, joint contribution and mutual dependence could deliver someone from misfortune.[151] The often unreliable wealthy had to be to convinced to engage in charitable activities, but the middle and low social strata could shape the real safety network for the sustenance of the destitute; the great numbers of small-scale donors compensated for their small donations for the needy. Gregory, commenting on the offerings for the construction of the tabernacle (Ex. 35:5–9), sketches a rough social stratification of the Israelites based on wealth: the rich offered gold, others silver, the poor offered skins and the poorer-than-poor hair.[152] This stratification probably reflects an outline of the social hierarchy with which he was acquainted, beyond the stereotypic polarity between the "rich" and the "poor."

Stewardship of wealth on behalf of everyone above extreme poverty could make the difference, and both Fathers stress that offerings should be proportionate to one's economic condition. Yet, Chrysostom's constant appeals to the determination of the rich and the not-so-rich to eradicate poverty imply that his arguments did not succeed in adequately motivating them to act accordingly. Wealth was used more for luxury and conspicuous consumption, money lending and the funding of political aspirations than for the care of the poor. Poverty relief was more often than not considered the task of the Church alone.[153]

USURY IN BASIL OF CAESAREA AND JOHN CHRYSOSTOM

If hoarding is an anti-social practice because it withdraws resources that could otherwise be used for the benefit of others, usury is considered a moral and social evil, an utter misuse of one's surplus to profiteer to the detriment of others. Usury is depicted as expanding unconstrainedly, consuming even life itself; as Susan R. Holman observes, it has been described in terms of "metastatic cancer."[154] It is strongly condemned in Old Testament, early Christian and subsequent patristic literature, while Basil of Caesarea, Gregory of Nyssa and John Chrysostom also dealt with this problem in their attempt to warn both lenders and debtors of the grave implications of such a practice.[155]

Much like the hoarder, the usurer has concentrated a great amount of financial resources but with a view to engaging in the activity of lending financial capital. He employs a justificatory basis, that of the presumed alleviation of those in search of financial resources, but his primary aspiration remains the pursuit of profit from money lending. Such a justification is devoid of a genuine moral basis, since the usurer employs fraud and deception to entrap the needy in an exploitative relationship from which he is intended to benefit. Gregory of Nyssa, in conformity with Aristotelian reasoning, considers interest as unnatural both because the lender expects *tokos*—meaning both "offspring" and "interest on money"—from inanimate things, but also because the lender does not labour for the generation of profit.[156] Interestingly, both Gregory and Basil of Caesarea compare creditors to homicidal physicians.[157]

Instead of alleviating economic necessity, usurers propagate injustice by extorting significant amounts of resources from borrowers by charging extremely high interest rates on the pretext of scarcity of monetary capital.[158] Basil even mentions some of the usurers' eloquent nicknames: "exactors of a hundred percent" (*ekatostologoi*) and "tithe exactors" (*dekatēlogoi*).[159] Basil's advice is quite simple: "Are you rich? Do not borrow. Are you poor? Do not borrow." In the first case one does not need a loan, while in the second case one cannot repay it.[160] Basil observes that those who take out a loan are not the destitute, since the creditors would have no confidence in their ability to repay; it seems that the borrowers are usually members of the middling groups, who engage in unconstrained luxury and conspicuous consumption, seeking to achieve higher status and to imitate the elite's way of life. The debtor has a house and servants, lives lavishly, and desperately needs the loan to continue funding his conspicuous way of living: expensive garments, gold plate, an abundance of food and so on.[161] This is unproductive borrowing, not used, for example, to finance a commercial enterprise.[162] Basil's alternatives to getting a loan, namely using one's hands or craft to work for wages or even to beg, serve to show that there are many ways of getting a living, all of them preferable to and less burdensome than borrowing. As Basil admits, his intention is not to lay down the law but rather to advise,[163] and indeed canonical legislation of the early period did not forbid laymen to lend at interest.[164]

Basil's solutions must not have sounded very appealing to individuals who were accustomed to patronage.[165] They would have preferred to further enter into the vicious circle of borrowing, paying off the prior loans with subsequent ones; Basil observes that these persons only appear to possess resources.[166] Holman argues that: "interest-bearing loans had an accepted place in gift patronage and the social promotion of intangible obligations."[167] The act of lending, thus creating an obligation, was perceived in terms of beneficence, and being in debt was not considered socially shameful, provided that the debtor could pay in time. A prudent citizen had to protect his patrimony in a society that valued his status with respect to his property, and borrowing seemed less appalling than selling a part of his property in order to meet his needs.[168] Basil, however, attempted to warn that sooner or later this would happen, with severe individual and social consequences. As Holman notes:

> [...] the creditor reduces a citizen to a beggar and deprives the community of a contributing member. To lose one's patrimony was a form of social death: the end of family land, the end of a stable civic identity, the end of all political rights that may be tied to land ownership. The creditors are thus robbing their victims of intrinsic civic rights [...].[169]

Basil's solution in order for one to avoid the risks of borrowing is to upkeep the ideal of self-sufficiency, to cover needs step by step based on personal resources and abilities, rather than to be raised up suddenly using external means, only to be ultimately stripped of everything.[170] Interestingly, socio-economic advancement accomplished through borrowing is considered as irrational, futile and dangerous, reflecting Basil's life experience but also his concern for societal order. The debtor, as depicted in Basil, is mainly the victim of his own aspirations and his persistence for social status and power. His management of resources is irrational: not only is he not content with what he has, he enters into indebtedness so as to succumb to extravagance. He is not rich, but he wants others to think that he is. As the hoarder withdraws resources from circulation, in the same manner Basil's debtor becomes the accomplice of the usurer in directing the finite surplus to anti-social practices, for the benefit of the latter. All three—hoarder, usurer and (Basil's type of) debtor—are insatiable and mismanage financial resources.

Chrysostom presents the debtor in somewhat different terms. He argues, for instance, that tradespeople, specifically bronze-, gold- and silversmiths, prefer to borrow in order to face a need, rather than sell their tools, which are a significant asset. They know that if they keep hold of their tools, it is possible to surpass the state of indebtedness through their work.[171] In this case, Chrysostom's debtor takes out a loan not to indulge in luxury consumption but to overcome financial difficulties. He is in true need but still he is not a destitute. Most probably, his tools are the reason why a creditor agreed to give him a loan in the first place, while as a specialized artisan, who may additionally own a shop, he is a member of the middling groups. Once again the rhetoric on poverty could be misleading.

In any case, the interest charges on loans are considered to aggravate the situation of the poor.[172] It seems that, for most, Christian ethics and financial dealings were not compatible.[173] Chrysostom presents poor people as being physically abused by their creditors when they delay repaying their loan,[174] and also as victims of lawsuits.[175] In the latter case, he makes a distinction between the "poor" and the beggars. The former are characterized as the poor who wish to prosper, and it is they who are dragged to courts as they obviously possess assets coveted by the litigant.[176]

For Basil and Gregory of Nyssa, the only praiseworthy kind of usury is the heavenly one, the practice of lending to Christ himself.[177] Basil states that a gift to a poor person is at the same time a loan to Christ, who undertakes to repay it on behalf of the poor. He should be the most coveted guarantor.[178] In a similar manner, a major theme in Chrysostom's discourse on almsgiving is that this practice renders God one's debtor through forging bonds of mutual friendship.[179] His attempt, much like Basil's, was not to prohibit lending at interest but to convince believers to assume their responsibilities toward their less fortunate fellow citizens by distributing their surplus and receiving interest in heaven in return.[180]

The imagery of lending to Christ through the poor, like the one of hoarding in the heavenly treasury, reveals the Fathers' acquaintance with contemporary economic practices.[181] At the same time, the Fathers' economic vocabulary implies that they realized they had to meet their audiences on their own terms and address them in a manner that they could understand. Thus, they attempted to give new content to an economic vocabulary with which their congregations were familiar, and to shift the focus from economic to spiritual profit.[182] In doing so, they indirectly attested the prevailing position of the mentality of financial practices in late antique urban centres. Ultimately, it seems that their preaching had a greater impact in the intellectual field—since their ideas decisively influenced contemporary and subsequent authors—than in the practical.

Notes

1. B. Gordon, *The Economic Problem in Biblical and Patristic Thought*. SupVC, 9 (Leiden: Brill, 1989), 89–101.
2. B. E. Daley, "1998 NAPS Presidential Address. Building a New City: The Cappadocian Fathers and the Rhetoric of Philanthropy," *JECS* 7.3 (1999): 433; C. Rapp, *Holy Bishops in Late Antiquity: The Nature of Christian Leadership in an Age of Transition*. TCH, 37 (Berkeley, CA: University of California Press, 2005), 181, 185. On John Chrysostom in particular, see J. N. D. Kelly, *Golden Mouth: The Story of John Chrysostom—Ascetic, Preacher, Bishop* (Ithaca, NY: Cornell University Press, 1995), 4–5; W. Mayer and P. Allen, *John Chrysostom*. ECF (London: Routledge, 2000), 5.
3. P. Brown, *Power and Persuasion in Late Antiquity: Towards a Christian Empire* (Madison, WI: University of Wisconsin Press, 1992), 93; E. Patlagean, *Pauvreté économique et pauvreté sociale à Byzance, 4ᵉ–7ᵉ siècles*. Civilisations et Sociétés, 48 (Paris: Mouton, 1977), 231–235.
4. D. M. Gwynn, "The 'End' of Roman Senatorial Paganism," in *The Archaeology of Late Antique 'Paganism'*, eds. L. Lavan and M. Mulryan. Late Antique Archaeology, 7 (Leiden and Boston, MA: Brill, 2011), 135, 156.
5. *De rebus bellicis* 2.2 (ed. A. Giardina, *Anonimo, Le cose della guerra*. Scrittori Greci e Latini [Milan: Mondadori, 1989], 12).
6. *CTh* 5.13.3 (364); also 10.1.8 (364). See B. Caseau, "Late Antique Paganism: Adaptation under Duress," in *Archaeology of Late Antique 'Paganism'*, eds. Lavan and Mulryan, 123.
7. Caseau, "Late Antique Paganism," 120–127.
8. *CTh* 16.10.21 (415); see Rapp, *Holy Bishops*, 188–189.

9. On the Greek concept of philanthropy, see D. J. Constantelos, *Byzantine Philanthropy and Social Welfare*. Rutgers Byzantine Series (New Brunswick, NJ: Rutgers University Press, 1968), 3–11. On the importance of *philanthrōpia* for Julian, see R. Smith, *Julian's Gods: Religion and Philosophy in the Thought and Action of Julian the Apostate* (London: Routledge, 1995), 42–44, 211–213; Daley, "Building a New City," 434–437. However, S. R. Holman, *The Hungry Are Dying: Beggars and Bishops in Roman Cappadocia*. Oxford Studies in Historical Theology (Oxford: Oxford University Press, 2001), 57, observes that "the fact remains that even in the fourth century, the Graeco-Roman concept of philanthropy as such did not readily consider poverty as a special category."
10. Holman, *The Hungry Are Dying*, 42.
11. Julian, *Ep.* 84.429d–430a (ed. J. Bidez, *L'empereur Julien, œuvres complètes*, vol. 1.2. Collection des Universités de France [2nd edn. Paris: Les Belles Lettres, 1960], 144).
12. P. Van Nuffelen, "Deux fausses lettres de Julien l'Apostat (la lettre aux Juifs, *Ep.* 51 [Wright], et la lettre à Arsacius, *Ep.* 84 [Bidez])," *VC* 56.2 (2002): 136–150.
13. J. Bouffartigue, "L'authenticité de la Lettre 84 de l'empereur Julien," *Revue de Philologie, de Littérature et d'Histoire Anciennes* 79.2 (2005): 231–242.
14. On Julian's competitive effort to outshine the Christian philanthropic practices, see, e.g., R. Finn, *Almsgiving in the Later Roman Empire: Christian Promotion and Practice (313–450)*. Oxford Classical Monographs (Oxford: Oxford University Press, 2006), 87–88. Finn argues that Julian's claim that pagan philosophy had long incorporated similar principles to Christian scriptures is untrustworthy (ibid., 172). Finn also stresses that pagans did not usually consider almsgiving as an expression of generosity (ibid., 214–218).
15. S. Elm, *Sons of Hellenism, Fathers of the Church: Emperor Julian, Gregory of Nazianzus, and the Vision of Rome*. TCH, 49 (Berkeley, CA: University of California Press, 2012), 327.
16. Julian, *Ep.* 89b.289a–b (ed. Bidez, *L'empereur Julien, œuvres complètes*, vol. 1.2, 156); Eng. trans. W. C. Wright, *The Works of Emperor Julian*, 3 vols. LCL, 13, 29, 157 (London: W. Heinemann, 1913–1923), vol. 2, 299.
17. Daley, "Building a New City," 436 and n. 20.
18. Julian, *Ep.* 89b.290a–b (ed. Bidez, *L'empereur Julien, œuvres complètes*, vol. 1.2, 157); Eng. trans. Wright, *The Works of Emperor Julian*, vol. 2, 301.
19. Julian, *Ep.* 89b.290c (ed. Bidez, *L'empereur Julien, œuvres complètes*, vol. 1.2, 158).

20. Eng. trans. NRSV. For a thorough examination of 2 Cor. 9:5–12, the term "blessing" and Paul's impact on the formation of the notion of "miraculous economy," see D. Caner, "Towards a Miraculous Economy: Christian Gifts and Material 'Blessings' in Late Antiquity," *JECS* 14.3 (2006): 329–377; *idem*, "Wealth, Stewardship, and Charitable 'Blessings' in Early Byzantine Monasticism," in *Wealth and Poverty in Early Church and Society*, ed. S. R. Holman. Holy Cross Studies in Patristic Theology and History (Grand Rapids, MI: Baker Academic, 2008), 230–231.
21. Julian, *Ep.* 89b.290d (ed. Bidez, *L'empereur Julien, œuvres complètes*, vol. 1.2, 158); Eng. trans. Wright, *The Works of Emperor Julian*, vol. 2, 303.
22. Julian, *Ep.* 89b.305c–d (ed. Bidez, *L'empereur Julien, œuvres complètes*, vol. 1.2, 173–174); Eng. trans. Wright, *The Works of Emperor Julian*, vol. 2, 337–339.
23. Chrysostom, *In Col. hom.* 7.5 (PG 62, 350); Eng. trans. Mayer and Allen, *John Chrysostom*, 83.
24. Libanius, *Or.* 2.30 (ed. R. Foerster, *Libanii opera*, 12 vols. in 13. BSGRT [Leipzig: B. G. Teubner, 1903–1923], vol. 1.1, 248); *Or.* 30.20 (ibid., vol. 3, 97–98).
25. Mayer and Allen, *John Chrysostom*, 50.
26. Holman, *The Hungry Are Dying*, 42–48.
27. On the famine, its implications and Basil's attempts to overcome them, see Holman, *The Hungry Are Dying*, 64–98. See also P. Brown, *Poverty and Leadership in the Later Roman Empire*. The Menahem Stern Jerusalem Lectures (Hanover, NH: University Press of New England, 2002), 35–36, 39–41; D. C. Stathakopoulos, *Famine and Pestilence in the Late Roman and Early Byzantine Empire: A Systematic Survey of Subsistence Crises and Epidemics*. Birmingham Byzantine and Ottoman Monographs, 9 (Aldershot: Ashgate, 2004), no. 21, pp. 200–201; I. G. Telelis, Μετεωρολογικά φαινόμενα και κλίμα στο Βυζάντιο, 2 vols. Ποιήματα, 5.1–2 (Athens: Akadēmia Athēnōn, Kentron Ereunēs tēs Hellēnikēs kai Latinikēs Grammateias, 2004), vol. 1, no. 43, pp. 117–119.
28. On Cappadocian geography, landscape, farming, industry, pastoralism and stocking, see J. E. Cooper and M. J. Decker, *Life and Society in Byzantine Cappadocia* (Houndmills, Basingstoke: Palgrave Macmillan, 2012), 11–103. For a quick but informative glance at Caesarea's position, see Brown, *Poverty and Leadership*, 39.
29. Greg. Naz., *Funebris oratio in laudem Basilii Magni* 34 (ed. J. Bernardi, *Grégoire de Nazianze, Discours 42–43*. SC, 384 [Paris: Les Éditions du Cerf, 1992], 200–202); Eng. trans. NPNF 2, vol. 7, 407. Cf. Patlagean, *Pauvreté*, 83–84. For another occasion on which Gregory censured

grain hoarders, see R. Van Dam, *Families and Friends in Late Roman Cappadocia* (Philadelphia, PA: University of Pennsylvania Press, 2003), 51.
30. B. E. Hawk, *Law and Commerce in Pre-Industrial Societies* (Leiden: Brill, 2016), 277.
31. B.-Z. Rosenfeld and J. Menirav, *Markets and Marketing in Roman Palestine*, trans. C. Cassel. Supplements to the Journal for the Study of Judaism, 99 (Leiden: Brill, 2005), 164.
32. Dio Chrysostom, *Or.* 46; cf. P. Erdkamp, *The Grain Market in the Roman Empire: A Social, Political and Economic Study* (Cambridge: Cambridge University Press, 2005), 278; also A. Zuiderhoek, *The Politics of Munificence in the Roman Empire: Citizens, Elites, and Benefactors in Asia Minor.* Greek Culture in the Roman World (Cambridge: Cambridge University Press, 2009), 138. Dio Chrysostom, defending himself against charges of unjust profiteering in a period of dearth, tried to convince his audience that he was a buyer not a seller of grain; his harvest of grain could hardly meet the requirements of his estates (Dio Chrysostom, *Or.* 46.8; Erdkamp, *The Grain Market*, 53).
33. C. J. Fuhrmann, *Policing the Roman Empire: Soldiers, Administration, and Public Order* (Oxford: Oxford University Press, 2012), 83.
34. J. J. Ferrer-Maestro, "Speculation and Crisis: Some Examples in the Eastern Provinces of the Later Roman Empire," in *New Perspectives on Late Antiquity in the Eastern Roman Empire*, eds. A. de Francisco Heredero, D. Hernández de la Fuente and S. Torres Prieto (Newcastle upon Tyne: Cambridge Scholars Publishing, 2014), 250. See also *PLRE* 1, 345–347 (Nicomachus Flavianus 14), 702 (Pinianus 1), 865–870 (Q. Aurelius Symmachus *signo* Eusebius 4).
35. Ferrer-Maestro, "Speculation," 257.
36. M. Silver ("The Plague under Commodus as an Unintended Consequence of Roman Grain Market Regulation," *Classical World* 105.2 [2012]: 224) argues that forced sales and maximum price edicts, by undermining profit expectations and disrupting grain markets, incurred feelings of anxiety among the urban populace, a fact that urged urban consumers to hoard grain in their homes. Yet the primary motivation of these consumers was self-sufficiency in times of distress, rather than the expectation of profiteering from others' needs.
37. In the early fourth century the holy man Severinus of Noricum, a small town on the Danube River, engaged in grain provisioning during a period of severe distress. Severinus "was able to rebuke a wealthy woman for hoarding grain during a famine, presumably to speculate for a higher price," and his initiative alleviated a serious shortage; see Rapp, *Holy Bishops*, 233.

38. Cooper and Decker, *Byzantine Cappadocia*, 182.
39. P. Garnsey (*Famine and Food Supply in the Graeco-Roman World: Responses to Risk and Crisis* [Cambridge: Cambridge University Press, 1988], 22–23) arrives at the conclusion that "Caesarea suffered a serious food shortage but not a famine." See also R. Van Dam, *Kingdom of Snow: Roman Rule and Greek Culture in Cappadocia* (Philadelphia, PA: University of Pennsylvania Press, 2002), 45.
40. Basil, *Hom. temp. fam.* (PG 31, 303–328).
41. E.g., Basil, *Hom. temp. fam.* 4 (PG 31, 313).
42. S. R. Holman, "The Hungry Body: Famine, Poverty, and Identity in Basil's *Hom.* 8," *JECS* 7.3 (1999): 357.
43. Daley, "Building a New City," 446–447.
44. Basil, *Hom. temp. fam.* 8 (PG 31, 325). Cf. Daley, "Building a New City," 447; Holman, "Hungry Body," 349.
45. Basil, *Hom. temp. fam.* 7 (PG 31, 324). Cf. Holman, "Hungry Body," 348–350, 362. On Basil and the concept of *tropheus*, see Holman, *The Hungry Are Dying, passim.*
46. Brown, *Poverty and Leadership*, 39–40.
47. Julian, *Misopogon* 368c–d (ed. C. Lacombrade, *L'empereur Julien, œuvres complètes*, vol. 2.2. Collection des Universités de France [Paris: Les Belles Lettres, 1964], 195–196). The problem Julian encountered in Antioch was one of rising prices due to food shortage, accompanied by the ensuing hoarding. Julian first urged the Antiochene elite to supply the market, but without result. He then issued an edict of maximum prices and ordered the importation of additional grain from less afflicted areas outside the city territory; he also transported 22,000 *modioi* from his imperial estates in Egypt to be sold at lower-than-market prices. The Emperor justified his measure of imposing a fair price for all basic goods by the avaricious behaviour of those who supplied the market, yet the imposition of maximum prices dried up the market supply. Julian reacted by accusing the landed aristocracy of Antioch of speculation through withdrawing their supplies from the market just to profiteer on the misery of the common population. The Antiochene elite was far from willing to see its allegedly "just" profits significantly curtailed by being deprived of the opportunity to control the agricultural produce in the region: wealthy speculators bought cheap imperial grain and sold it at elevated prices in the countryside, thus subverting the imperial intervention. Merchants of a more modest status fell short of undertaking initiatives to alleviate the crisis, as they were hesitant to challenge the local monopoly position enjoyed by the landed aristocracy. This fact demonstrates the limited ability of the Antiochene middle tradesmen to effectively compete with those who forced the purchase of goods at

exorbitant prices in a way that impeded the efficient operation of market mechanisms. See Garnsey, *Famine and Food Supply*, 22–23; Holman, *The Hungry Are Dying*, 58; Stathakopoulos, *Famine*, no. 16, pp. 193–197; Erdkamp, *The Grain Market*, 291; P. F. Bang, "Imperial Bazaar: Towards a Comparative Understanding of Markets in the Roman Empire," in *Ancient Economies, Modern Methodologies: Archaeology, Comparative History, Models and Institutions*, eds. P. F. Bang, M. Ikeguchi and H. G. Ziche. Pragmateiai, 12 (Bari: Edipuglia, 2006), 71–72; Elm, *Sons of Hellenism*, 273–275; J. Harries, *Imperial Rome AD 284 to 363: The New Empire*. The Edinburgh History of Ancient Rome (Edinburgh: Edinburgh University Press, 2012), 70.
48. Cf. T. Dean, *Crime and Justice in Late Medieval Italy* (Cambridge: Cambridge University Press, 2007), 59.
49. Holman, *The Hungry Are Dying*, 73, 128; eadem, "Constructed and Consumed: The Everyday Life of the Poor in 4th c. Cappadocia," in *Social and Political Life in Late Antiquity*, eds. W. Bowden, A. Gutteridge and C. Machado. Late Antique Archaeology, 3.1 (Leiden and Boston, MA: Brill, 2006), 444.
50. Basil, *Hom. Destr. horr.* (PG 31, 261–277). See Holman, *The Hungry Are Dying*, 102–104, 107–109; eadem, "Constructed and Consumed," 450. In this oration Basil elaborates his view of detachment from excess wealth and property, because they impede salvation; see B. Matz, "The Principle of Detachment from Private Property in Basil of Caesarea's *Homily* 6 and Its Context," in *Reading Patristic Texts on Social Ethics: Issues and Challenges for Twenty-First-Century Christian Social Thought*, eds. J. Leemans, B. J. Matz and J. Verstraeten. CUA Studies in Early Christianity (Washington, DC: The Catholic University of America Press, 2011), 161–184. *Hom.* 6, as well as *Hom.* 7, which we will discuss shortly, is probably included in the works triggered by the famine in Cappadocia; see Holman, "Hungry Body," 338; eadem, *The Hungry Are Dying*, 73; eadem, "Constructed and Consumed," 443.
51. Basil, *Hom. Destr. horr.* 2 (PG 31, 264–265).
52. P. Garnsey, *Thinking about Property: From Antiquity to the Age of Revolution*. Ideas in Context, 90 (Cambridge: Cambridge University Press, 2007), 216.
53. R. Newhauser, *The Early History of Greed: The Sin of Avarice in Early Medieval Thought and Literature*. Cambridge Studies in Medieval Literature, 41 (Cambridge: Cambridge University Press, 2000), 29 and 158 (n. 21).
54. Basil, *Hom. Destr. horr.* 7 (PG 31, 276).
55. Cicero, *De finibus bonorum et malorum* 3.20.67.
56. Garnsey, *Thinking about Property*, 116–117, 216.

57. On *autarkeia* as an unrealizable literary construct with respect to Byzantium, see A. E. Laiou, "Economic Thought and Ideology," in *The Economic History of Byzantium: From the Seventh through the Fifteenth Century*, 3 vols., ed. A. E. Laiou. Dumbarton Oaks Studies, 39 (Washington, DC: Dumbarton Oaks Research Library and Collection, 2002), vol. 2, 1125–1130.
58. Basil, *Hom. Destr. horr.* 7 (PG 31, 276–277).
59. Greg. Naz., *De pauperum amore* 24 (PG 35, 889); Eng. trans. B. E. Daley, *Gregory of Nazianzus*. ECF (London: Routledge, 2006), 89. On this oration, see J. A. McGuckin, *Saint Gregory of Nazianzus: An Intellectual Biography* (Crestwood, NY: St. Vladimir's Seminary Press, 2001), 145–155; C. A. Beeley, *Gregory of Nazianzus on the Trinity and the Knowledge of God: In Your Light We Shall See Light*. Oxford Studies in Historical Theology (Oxford: Oxford University Press, 2008), 254–258; B. J. Matz, "Deciphering a Recipe for Biblical Preaching in *Oration* 14," in *Re-Reading Gregory of Nazianzus: Essays on History, Theology, and Culture*, ed. C. A. Beeley. CUA Studies in Early Christianity (Washington, DC: The Catholic University of America Press, 2012), 49–66. For Gregory of Nazianzus' views on wealth, see B. Coulie, *Les richesses dans l'œuvre de saint Grégoire de Nazianze. Étude littéraire et historique*. Publications de l'Institut Orientaliste de Louvain, 32 (Louvain-la-Neuve: Institut Orientaliste, 1985); also C. Moreschini, "Gregory Nazianzen and Philosophy, with Remarks on Gregory's Cynicism," in *Re-Reading Gregory of Nazianzus*, ed. Beeley, 117; A. Hofer, *Christ in the Life and Teaching of Gregory of Nazianzus*. OECS (Oxford: Oxford University Press, 2013), 220–223. McGuckin stresses that Gregory elaborated on the moral dimensions of holding wealth in view of the evangelic dimensions of dispossession, yet in a way differing from the stringent ascetic ethos of Basil of Caesarea. For Gregory, the quest for wisdom and sobriety took precedence over a formal discipline of the body; see J. A. McGuckin, "St. Gregory of Nazianzus on the Love of the Poor (Oration 14)," in *The Ecumenical Legacy of the Cappadocians*, ed. N. Dumitraşcu. Pathways for Ecumenical and Interreligious Dialogue (Houndmills, Basingstoke: Palgrave Macmillan, 2016), 139–157.
60. Gordon, *Economic Problem*, 104–105.
61. Basil, *Hom. div.* (PG 31, 277–304). See Holman, *The Hungry Are Dying*, 104–106, 107–109.
62. Basil, *Hom. div.* 2 (PG 31, 284).
63. Basil, *Hom. div.* 7 (PG 31, 297).

64. Basil, *Hom. div.* 2–3 (PG 31, 285). Overspending as being indicative of conspicuous consumption is not countenanced in the biblical literature. The book of Proverbs among Jewish wisdom literature incorporates warnings against indulgence in overspending (Prov. 21:20). Indictment of conspicuous consumption is not infrequent in prophetic judgment discourse. The prophet Amos, for instance, targets the elite groups of the eighth-century Kingdoms of Israel and Judah, as accustomed to luxurious spending and leading a life of dissipation (Am. 6:4–6). Faithfulness to the Lord appears inimical to Israelite tokens of conspicuous consumption (Am. 3:15), and primarily to the luxurious excesses of the greedy (Am. 4:1–3). Luxurious spending is subject to the impending judgment in several prophetic narratives (e.g., Isa. 3:18–24) because such practices were detrimental to the welfare of the needy (Am. 2:6–8, 6:7).
65. Holman, *The Hungry Are Dying*, 109.
66. See G. A. Nigro, "L'esegesi di 2 Cor 8,9 nei Padri Cappadoci," *Vetera Christianorum* 51 (2014): 197–212.
67. See Chap. 3 in this book.
68. On Basileias, see Constantelos, *Byzantine Philanthropy*, 154–155; T. S. Miller, *The Birth of the Hospital in the Byzantine Empire*. The Henry E. Sigerist Supplements to the Bulletin of the History of Medicine, new ser., 10 (2nd edn. Baltimore, MD: Johns Hopkins University Press, 1997), 85–88; Holman, *The Hungry Are Dying*, 74–76, 145–148; Brown, *Poverty and Leadership*, 35–36, 40, 125 n. 150; A. T. Crislip, *From Monastery to Hospital: Christian Monasticism & the Transformation of Health Care in Late Antiquity* (Ann Arbor, MI: The University of Michigan Press, 2005), 103–120, 141; A. Müller, "'All das ist Zierde für den Ort...'. Das diakonisch-karitative Großprojekt des Basileios von Kaisareia," *ZAC* 13.3 (2010): 452–474; M. Girardi,"Basilio di Cesarea: le coordinate scritturistiche della 'Basiliade' in favore di poveri e indigenti," *Classica et Christiana* 9.2 (2014): 459–483. Training in trades, besides offering a means to relieve poverty, must have also been entwined with a particular ethos of work that is strongly countenanced in Basil's thought. Work could serve as a training ground for the virtues; see J. Ballan, "Basil of Caesarea on the Ascetic Craft: The Invention of Ascetic Community and the Spiritualization of Work in the *Asketikon*," *Heythrop Journal* 52.4 (2011): 559–568; A. Dinan, "Manual Labor in the Life and Thought of St. Basil the Great," *Logos: A Journal of Catholic Thought and Culture* 12.4 (2009): 133–157.
69. Brown, *Poverty and Leadership*, 39.
70. Brown, *Poverty and Leadership*, 42.

71. F. Vasileiou, "For the Poor, the Family, the Friends: Gregory of Nazianzus' Testament in the Context of Early Christian Literature," in *Inheritance, Law and Religions in the Ancient and Mediaeval Worlds*, eds. B. Caseau and S. R. Huebner. Centre de Recherche d'Histoire et Civilisation de Byzance, Monographies, 45 (Paris: ACHCByz, 2014), 145. On distribution of food to the hungry by the Church, see B. Caseau, "Autour de l'autel: le contrôle des donateurs et des donations alimentaires," in *Donation et donateurs dans le monde byzantin*, eds. J.-M. Spieser and É. Yota. Réalités Byzantines, 14 (Paris: Desclée de Brouwer, 2012), 47–73.
72. On the testament, see R. Van Dam, "Self-Representation in the Will of Gregory of Nazianzus," *Journal of Theological Studies* 46.1 (1995): 118–148; Vasileiou, "For the Poor."
73. Greg. Naz., *Test.*, ll. 10–12 (ed. J. Beaucamp, "Le testament de Grégoire de Nazianze," *Fontes Minores* 10 [1998]: 30); Eng. trans. Daley, *Gregory of Nazianzus*, 186.
74. Greg. Naz., *Test.*, ll. 12–31 (ed. Beaucamp, "Le testament," 30–32). On the legacy and *fideicommissum*, see Beaucamp, "Le testament," 86; Daley, *Gregory of Nazianzus*, 255–256 (n. 11). Especially on the latter, see D. Johnston, *The Roman Law of Trusts* (Oxford: Clarendon Press, 1988).
75. Vasileiou, "For the Poor," 145.
76. Cf. Patlagean, *Pauvreté*, 347, 382.
77. Greg. Naz., *Test.*, ll. 36–43 (ed. Beaucamp, "Le testament," 32).
78. Greg. Naz., *Test.*, ll. 44–47 (ed. Beaucamp, "Le testament," 32). On Roussiane, see Holman, "Constructed and Consumed," 457–458.
79. Greg. Naz., *Test.*, ll. 58–62 (ed. Beaucamp, "Le testament," 34).
80. Greg. Naz., *Test.*, ll. 82–92 (ed. Beaucamp, "Le testament," 36).
81. Vasileiou, "For the Poor," 149–150.
82. Vasileiou, "For the Poor," 157.
83. On Antioch, see, e.g., G. Downey, *A History of Antioch in Syria: From Seleucus to the Arab Conquest*. (Princeton, NJ: Princeton University Press, 1961); J. H. W. G. Liebeschuetz, *Antioch: City and Imperial Administration in the Later Roman Empire* (Oxford: Clarendon Press, 1972); A. U. De Giorgi, *Ancient Antioch: From the Seleucid Era to the Islamic Conquest* (Cambridge: Cambridge University Press, 2016). On Constantinople, see G. Dagron, *Naissance d'une capitale. Constantinople et ses institutions de 330 à 451*. Bibliothèque Byzantine, Études, 7 (Paris: Presses Universitaires de France, 1974); R. Krautheimer, *Three Christian Capitals: Topography and Politics*. Una's Lectures, 4 (Berkeley, CA: University of California Press, 1983), 41–67; C. Mango, *Le développement urbain de Constantinople, IVe–VIIe siècles*. Travaux et Mémoires, Monographies,

2 (2nd edn. Paris: De Boccard, 1990); S. Bassett, *The Urban Image of Late Antique Constantinople* (Cambridge: Cambridge University Press, 2004). For a quick glance at Antioch and Constantinople in Chrysostom's time, see Mayer and Allen, *John Chrysostom*, 11–16; W. Mayer, "John Chrysostom on Poverty," in *Preaching Poverty in Late Antiquity: Perceptions and Realities*, eds. P. Allen, B. Neil and W. Mayer. Arbeiten zur Kirchen- und Theologiegeschichte, 28 (Leipzig: Evangelische Verlagsanstalt, 2009), 71–76. On the topography of Antioch in Chrysostomic texts, see W. Mayer, "The Topography of Antioch Described in the Writings of John Chrysostom," in *Les sources de l'histoire du paysage urbain d'Antioche sur l'Oronte*, ed. C. Saliou (Paris: Université Paris 8, Vincennes-Saint-Denis, 2012), 81–100. On Chrysostom's Antiochene and Constantinopolitan congregations, see W. Mayer, "John Chrysostom and His Audiences: Distinguishing Different Congregations at Antioch and Constantinople," *SP* 31 (1997): 70–75; Mayer and Allen, *John Chrysostom*, 34–40; especially on his Antiochene congregation, see J. L. Maxwell, *Christianization and Communication in Late Antiquity: John Chrysostom and His Congregation in Antioch* (Cambridge: Cambridge University Press, 2006).

84. On socio-economic and archaeological aspects of the early Byzantine "middle class," see E. Zanini, "Artisans and Traders in the Early Byzantine City: Exploring the Limits of Archaeological Evidence," in *Social and Political Life in Late Antiquity*, eds. Bowden, Gutteridge and Machado, 373–411; S. Ellis, "Middle Class Houses in Late Antiquity," in *Social and Political Life in Late Antiquity*, eds. Bowden, Gutteridge and Machado, 413–437.

85. Chrysostom, *De stat. hom.* 17.2 (PG 49, 179); Libanius, *Or.* 11.227 (ed. Foerster, *Libanii opera*, vol. 1.2, 516).

86. W. Mayer, "Poverty and Society in the World of John Chrysostom," in *Social and Political Life in Late Antiquity*, eds. Bowden, Gutteridge and Machado, 465–484; eadem, "Poverty and Generosity toward the Poor in the Time of John Chrysostom," in *Wealth and Poverty*, ed. Holman, 149–154; eadem, "John Chrysostom on Poverty," 82–111.

87. Mayer, "John Chrysostom on Poverty," 110. She concludes (ibid., 111) by underscoring that: "It is also clear from John's constant attempts to reframe the beggar as someone who does not merely take but also gives back to society that, due to an underlying cultural belief in the concept of limited good, hostility towards and suspicion of members of the lowest socio-economic level were endemic at both Antioch and Constantinople and stubbornly resistant to any attempt to combat them. In such a climate direct and indiscriminate giving toward the

'needy' poor is unlikely to have been widely practiced, despite John's constant attempts to persuade people to do so."
88. Chrysostom, *In Ioh. hom.* 64.4 (PG 59, 360). Cf. A. D. Karayiannis and S. Drakopoulou-Dodd, "The Greek Christian Fathers," in *Ancient and Medieval Economic Ideas and Concepts of Social Justice*, eds. S. Todd Lowry and B. Gordon (Leiden: Brill, 1998), 198. On Chrysostom's view of wealth and poverty as "indifferents," see Mayer, "John Chrysostom on Poverty," 85.
89. Chrysostom, *In 1 Tim. hom.* 7.3 (PG 62, 538–539).
90. Rapp, *Holy Bishops*, 228–232.
91. Chrysostom, *In 1 Cor. hom.* 34.5 (PG 61, 292). See M. M. Mitchell, "Silver Chamber Pots and Other Goods Which Are Not Good: John Chrysostom's Discourse against Wealth and Possessions," in *Having: Property and Possession in Religious and Social Life*, eds. W. Schweiker and C. Mathewes (Grand Rapids, MI: W. B. Eerdmans, 2004), 91–99, for a detailed discussion.
92. Cf. Chrysostom, *De Laz. conc.* 7.5 (PG 48, 1052).
93. Chrysostom, *De Laz. conc.* 2.1 (PG 48, 982).
94. Chrysostom, *In 1 Tim. hom.* 11.2 (PG 62, 556).
95. Chrysostom, *In Eph. hom.* 21.4 (PG 62, 153–154).
96. Cf. Seneca, *Ep. morales* 110.
97. See W. Mayer, "John Chrysostom's Use of Luke 16:19–31," *Scrinium* 4 (2008): 45–59. F. Cardman, "Poverty and Wealth as Theater: John Chrysostom's Homilies on Lazarus and the Rich Man," in *Wealth and Poverty*, ed. Holman, 159–175, argues that Chrysostom, commenting on this parable, employs a metaphor of wealth as an extended theatrical performance, in which preacher and audience negotiate their roles: the preacher seeks to move his audience from the deception of the appearance of ephemeral riches to the reality of salvation.
98. Chrysostom, *De Laz. conc.* 2.1 (PG 48, 982).
99. Chrysostom, *De Laz. conc.* 1.12 (PG 48, 980); 4.4 (PG 48, 1011); 6.3 (PG 48, 1030).
100. Chrysostom, *In Eph. hom.* 13.3 (PG 62, 97).
101. Chrysostom, *In 1 Tim. hom.* 12.4 (PG 62, 562–564). See Mitchell, "Silver Chamber Pots," 92.
102. H. Stander, "Economics in the Church Fathers," in *The Oxford Handbook of Christianity and Economics*, ed. P. Oslington (Oxford: Oxford University Press, 2014), 29.
103. Chrysostom, *In 1 Cor. hom.* 34.6 (PG 61, 294–295). See Mitchell, "Silver Chamber Pots," 93. In this context, diligence and prudence in managing scant resources entailed material prosperity (Prov. 10:4–5). Prosperity was thus viewed as a reward of the righteous in accordance

with the doctrine of retribution (Prov. 14:21-23), whereas the riches of the wicked would eventually pass to the righteous (Job 27:13-17).
104. Chrysostom, *In Col. hom.* 7.4 (PG 62, 349); Eng. trans. Mayer and Allen, *John Chrysostom*, 81. It is indicative that, despite the fact that hoarding was vehemently denounced in Christian preaching and teaching, precious objects of silver or gold were retained not only by the aristocracy and bishops, but also by the wider public, as demonstrated by late antique textual and archaeological evidence. See F. Baratte, "Les objets précieux dans la vie économique et sociale du monde romain à la fin de l'Antiquité," *Revue Numismatique* 159 (2003): 205-216.
105. Chrysostom, *In Col. hom.* 7.5 (PG 62, 350); Eng. trans. Mayer and Allen, *John Chrysostom*, 82. Cf. J. H. W. G. Liebeschuetz, *Ambrose and John Chrysostom: Clerics between Desert and Empire* (Oxford: Oxford University Press, 2011), 231-232.
106. Chrysostom, *In Col. hom.* 7.5 (PG 62, 351-352); Eng. trans. Mayer and Allen, *John Chrysostom*, 83. P. M. Blowers explores the emotional culture of pity and compassion in late antique Christianity, a context in which Chrysostom sought to convince his audience that "wealthier Christians deserved pity, not envy in view of the unique miseries associated with wealth, and that envious, covetous, or greedy persons themselves, whether rich or poor, should be supreme objects of compassion because of their self-inflicted emotional pain" ("2009 NAPS Presidential Address. Pity, Empathy, and the Tragic Spectacle of Human Suffering: Exploring the Emotional Culture of Compassion in Late Ancient Christianity," *JECS* 18.1 [2010]: 13).
107. Underlying this archetypical mode of economic organization remain the familial institutions, the Christian households, the primary house churches (Chrysostom, *In Act. apost. hom.* 26.4 [PG 60, 203]) that seem to draw on the ancient household traditions (Xenophon, *Oeconomicus* 1.5-47, 6.4-5; Plato, *Leges* 809c; Aristotle, *Politica* 1.3 1258a25-30). In the patristic conception of household, economic practices are invested with new connotations pertinent to Christian spirituality. Economic goods are viewed as a kind of particular favour bestowed by God's providence (Chrysostom, *In Mt. hom.* 55.5 [PG 58, 545]). Therefore, generous almsgiving is a manifestation of proper stewardship of goods given by God. For a detailed approach to medieval and early modern developments of the ideal of stewardship of riches, see P. G. Schervish and K. Whitaker, *Wealth and the Will of God: Discerning the Use of Riches in the Service of Ultimate Purpose* (Bloomington, IN: Indiana University Press, 2010).
108. Chrysostom, *In 1 Tim. hom.* 12.4 (PG 62, 563).

109. Chrysostom, *De virginitate* 68.3–4 (ed. H. Musurillo, trans. B. Grillet, *Jean Chrysostome, La virginité*. SC, 125 [Paris: Les Éditions du Cerf, 1966], 340–342).
110. Chrysostom, *In 1 Thess. hom.* 2.4 (PG 62, 404).
111. On the words "mine" and "yours" as viewed by Chrysostom, see Mitchell, "Silver Chamber Pots," 96–97, 119–120.
112. Chrysostom, *In Act. apost. hom.* 7.2 (PG 60, 66).
113. Cf. Chrysostom, *In Act. apost. hom.* 7.3 (PG 60, 67).
114. Chrysostom, *In 1 Tim. hom.* 14.3 (PG 62, 575). See Mitchell, "Silver Chamber Pots," 96–97.
115. For an Old Testament background of these views that focus on the prophetic condemnation of hoarding, see P. K. Tull, "Consumerism, Idolatry, and Environmental Limits in Isaiah," in *The Book of Isaiah: Enduring Questions Answered anew: Essays Honoring Joseph Blenkinsopp and His Contribution to the Study of Isaiah*, eds. R. J. Bautch and J. T. Hibbard (Grand Rapids, MI: W. B. Eerdmans, 2014), 205.
116. E.g., Chrysostom, *In Mt. hom.* 66.3 (PG 58, 630).
117. Chrysostom, *In 1 Tim. hom.* 12.4 (PG 62, 564).
118. Chrysostom, *In Act. apost. hom.* 11.3 (PG 60, 97–98).
119. See Mitchell, "Silver Chamber Pots," 116–119, for further discussion; cf. Mayer, "Poverty and Generosity," 142.
120. Mitchell, "Silver Chamber Pots," 120, argues that Chrysostom's vision of a communistic, concordant and just economic order is entrenched in his overall endeavour of societal transformation.
121. J. R. Stenger, "Where to Find Christian Philosophy? Spatiality in John Chrysostom's Counter to Greek *Paideia*," *JECS* 24.2 (2016): 197.
122. Stenger, "Where to Find Christian Philosophy?" 191.
123. Chrysostom, *In Eph. hom.* 13.4 (PG 62, 98–99).
124. Seneca, *Ep. morales* 17.3. Cf. Mitchell, "Silver Chamber Pots," 105–106.
125. Chrysostom, *In Col. hom.* 7.5 (PG 62, 351–352).
126. Cf. Plutarch, *De Stoicorum repugnantiis* 30 (*Moralia* 1048b–c).
127. For an interpretation of the social construction of poverty and hunger in Chrysostom's world, see H. Stander, "Chrysostom on Hunger and Famine," *HTSTS* 67.1 (2011). Art. #880, 7 pp. (10.4102/hts.v67i1.880).
128. Chrysostom, *In 1 Cor. hom.* 35.6 (PG 61, 305). Chrysostom, highlighting the transience and precariousness of wealth, draws an analogy between the nature of wealth and human nature. Possession of wealth is brief as is life expectancy: enjoying riches is an ephemeral experience, and one may be deprived of his wealth before his biological end; see *In illud: Ne timueritis hom. 1* (PG 55, 502).

129. Chrysostom, *In 1 Tim. hom.* 11.2–3 (PG 62, 556).
130. Chrysostom, *In 1 Tim. hom.* 17.3 (PG 62, 596). Cf. Mitchell, "Silver Chamber Pots," 107–108.
131. Chrysostom, *In Mt. hom.* 49.3 (PG 58, 500).
132. For an assessment of Chrysostom's stance toward the indigent and poor, see S. Sitzler, "Identity: The Indigent and the Wealthy in the Homilies of John Chrysostom," *VC* 63.5 (2009): 468–479, who advances the view that through his discourse on almsgiving, Chrysostom was seeking to negotiate Christian identities for the wealthy within a Christian community in a way that supplemented rather than opposed those identities operating in a secular, Graeco-Roman environment.
133. Chrysostom, *In 2 Tim. hom.* 7.4 (PG 62, 642).
134. Chrysostom, *In 1 Cor. hom.* 21.6 (PG 61, 179); Eng. trans. Mayer and Allen, *John Chrysostom*, 173.
135. Beyond the ethical and symbolic dimensions of suffering, the more pragmatic ones could hardly be underestimated. Church Fathers like Chrysostom, Gregory of Nazianzus and Gregory of Nyssa helped a renewed sensitivity to the pain incurred by the isolation and marginalization of the needy to emerge, forging an emotional community of cosufferers. See A. Samellas, "Public Aspects of Pain in Late Antiquity: The Testimony of Chrysostom and the Cappadocians in their Graeco-Roman Context," *ZAC* 19.2 (2015): 260–296.
136. See Mayer, "Poverty and Generosity," 149–151.
137. Chrysostom, *De stat. hom.* 2.5–7 (PG 49, 39–43).
138. Chrysostom, *In Mt. hom.* 50.3 (PG 58, 508–509).
139. Chrysostom, *In Heb. hom.* 11.4 (PG 63, 96). Cf. Mayer, "Poverty and Generosity," 151.
140. Chrysostom, *In Phil. hom.* 1.5 (PG 62, 188). Cf. Mayer, "Poverty and Generosity," 151, 156.
141. Mayer, "Poverty and Generosity," 156.
142. C. L. de Wet, *Preaching Bondage: John Chrysostom and the Discourse of Slavery in Early Christianity* (Oakland, CA: University of California Press, 2015), argues that the seeming mitigation of certain of the most pernicious aspects of slavery in Chrysostom's discourses actually functions as a justification of this institution and, ultimately, contributes to maintaining it. Exhortations for a reduction of the number of slaves retained by Christian masters were a corollary of Chrysostom's renunciation of excess wealth, rather than a particular project aiming at the abolition of slavery.
143. See Chap. 3 in this book.
144. R. H. van der Bergh, "Chrysostom's Reception of Luke 19:8b (the Declaration of Zacchaeus)," *HTSTS* 70.1 (2014). Art. #2730, 6 pp. (10.4102/hts.v70i1.2730).

145. Chrysostom, *In 1 Cor. hom.* 13.5 (PG 61, 113).
146. Chrysostom, *In 1 Cor. hom.* 43.4 (PG 61, 374). Cf. R. Brändle, "This Sweetest Passage: Matthew 25:31–46 and Assistance to the Poor in the Homilies of John Chrysostom," in *Wealth and Poverty*, ed. Holman, 129.
147. Chrysostom, *In 1 Cor. hom.* 43.1 (PG 61, 368–369). Cf. Brändle, "This Sweetest Passage," 130.
148. Chrysostom, *In Mt. hom.* 66.3 (PG 58, 630).
149. Brown, *Poverty and Leadership*, 14; Mayer, "Poverty and Society," 467–468.
150. D. J. Downs, "Redemptive Almsgiving and Economic Stratification in *2 Clement*," *JECS* 19.4 (2011): 493–517.
151. Greg. Nyss., *Paup.* 1 (ed. A. van Heck, GNO 9.1 [Leiden: Brill, 1967], 98). Gregory of Nyssa elaborates on the ideal of ascetic domestic households that might anticipate later institutional developments; see P. Rousseau, "The Pious Household and the Virgin Chorus: Reflections on Gregory of Nyssa's *Life of Macrina*," *JECS* 13.2 (2005): 165–186.
152. Greg. Nyss., *Paup.* 1 (ed. van Heck, GNO 9.1, 98). On Gregory of Nyssa's tabernacle imagery, see A. Conway-Jones, *Gregory of Nyssa's Tabernacle Imagery in Its Jewish and Christian Contexts*. OECS (Oxford: Oxford University Press, 2014).
153. Mayer, "Poverty and Generosity," 156; *eadem*, "John Chrysostom on Poverty," 105, 111.
154. Holman, "Constructed and Consumed," 458.
155. See J. L. González, *Faith and Wealth: A History of Early Christian Ideas on the Origin, Significance, and Use of Money* (Eugene, OR: Wipf and Stock Publishers, 1990), 175–176; M. La Matina, "Basilio di Cesarea, Gregorio di Nissa e le passioni dell'usura," *Pan* 15–16 (1998): 131–168; M. E. Biddle, "The Biblical Prohibition against Usury," *Interpretation: A Journal of Bible and Theology* 65.2 (2011): 117–127; Holman, *The Hungry Are Dying*, 114–134; B. L. Ihssen, "Basil and Gregory's Sermons on Usury: Credit where Credit Is Due," *JECS* 16.3 (2008): 403–430; *eadem*, "'That Which Has Been Wrung from Tears': Usury, the Greek Fathers, and Catholic Social Teaching," in *Reading Patristic Texts on Social Ethics*, eds. Leemans, Matz and Verstraeten, 124–160; *eadem*, *They Who Give from Evil: The Response of the Eastern Church to Moneylending in the Early Christian Era* (Eugene, OR: Pickwick Publications, 2012); M. D. Meeks, "The Peril of Usury in the Christian Tradition," *Interpretation: A Journal of Bible and Theology* 65.2 (2011): 128–140; H. Boersma, *Embodiment and Virtue in Gregory of Nyssa: An Anagogical Approach*. OECS (Oxford: Oxford University Press, 2013), 163–165, 171–174, 176–177.

156. Greg. Nyss., *Usur.* (ed. E. Gebhardt, GNO 9.1, 197, 200). Cf. Aristotle, *Politica* 1.10 1258b2–8; Basil, *HPs.*14b.3 (PG 29, 273–276). See A. E. Laiou, "The Church, Economic Thought and Economic Practice," in *The Christian East, Its Institutions and Its Thought: A Critical Reflection*, ed. R. F. Taft. Orientalia Christiana Analecta, 251 (Rome: Pontificio Istituto Orientale, 1996), 441 (repr. in *eadem, Economic Thought and Economic Life in Byzantium*. CS, 1033 [Farnham: Ashgate, 2013], no. II); Holman, *The Hungry Are Dying*, 115–116.
157. Basil, *HPs.*14b.1 (PG 29, 268); Greg. Nyss., *Usur.* (ed. Gebhardt, GNO 9.1, 197). For the similarities and dissimilarities of Basil's and Gregory's sermons on usury, see Ihssen, "Basil and Gregory's Sermons."
158. Basil, *HPs.*14b.1 (PG 29, 265–268).
159. Basil, *HPs.*14b.5 (PG 29, 280). See Lampe: svv. ἑκατοστολόγος and δεκατηλόγος.
160. Basil, *HPs.*14b.3 (PG 29, 272–273).
161. Basil, *HPs.*14b.4 (PG 29, 276). See A. Samellas, "The Anti-Usury Arguments of the Church Fathers of the East in Their Historical Context and the Accommodation of the Church to the Prevailing 'Credit Economy' in Late Antiquity," *Journal of Ancient History* 5.1 (2017): 141–142.
162. Laiou, "Church," 441 (repr. in *eadem, Economic Thought*, no. II).
163. Basil, *HPs.*14b.4 (PG 29, 276).
164. Laiou, "Church," 441 (repr. in *eadem, Economic Thought*, no. II).
165. Holman, "Constructed and Consumed," 459.
166. Basil, *HPs.*14b.4 (PG 29, 276–277).
167. Holman, *The Hungry Are Dying*, 116.
168. Holman, *The Hungry Are Dying*, 117.
169. Holman, *The Hungry Are Dying*, 121–122.
170. Basil, *HPs.*14b.2 (PG 29, 269).
171. Chrysostom, *De Laz. conc.* 3.2 (PG 48, 993). Cf. Mayer, "Poverty and Society," 470.
172. Chrysostom, *Princ. Act. hom.* 4.1 (PG 51, 97).
173. Mayer, "Poverty and Society," 470.
174. Chrysostom, *De dec. mill.* 5 (PG 51, 24).
175. Chrysostom, *In Act. apost. hom.* 13.4 (PG 60, 110–111).
176. Mayer, "Poverty and Society," 471.
177. See Ihssen, "Basil and Gregory's Sermons," 420–425. On Gregory of Nyssa in particular, see Greg. Nyss., *Usur.* (ed. Gebhardt, GNO 9.1, 198–199).
178. Basil, *HPs.*14b.5 (PG 29, 277).

179. Brändle, "This Sweetest Passage," 130. M. Verhoeff, "A Genuine Friend Wishes to be a Debtor: John Chrysostom's Discourse on Almsgiving Reinterpreted," *Sacris Erudiri* 52 (2013): 47–66, argues that, despite the abundance of expressions reflecting lending practices in Chrysostom, the economic dimension remains subordinate to the spiritual one. Drawing on Graeco-Roman euergetism and Christian gift-giving traditions, Chrysostom envisions in almsgiving the cultivation of proximity to Christ, rather than a redemptive activity in itself.
180. E.g., Chrysostom, *In Mt. hom.* 66.4–5 (PG 58, 630–632). Cf. A. E. Laiou, "Trade, Profit, and Salvation in the Late Patristic and the Byzantine Period," in *Wealth and Poverty*, ed. Holman, 247.
181. C. Rapp, "Spiritual Guarantors at Penance, Baptism, and Ordination in the Late Antique East," in *A New History of Penance*, ed. A. Firey. Brill's Companions to the Christian Tradition, 14 (Leiden and Boston, MA: Brill, 2008), 132 and n. 36.
182. Laiou, "Church," 441–442 (repr. in *eadem, Economic Thought*, no. II). Cf. Cardman, "Poverty and Wealth," 171 n. 51.

CHAPTER 5

Fifth-Century Patristic Conceptions of Savings and Capital: Isidore of Pelusium and Theodoret of Cyrrhus

Isidore of Pelusium

The main phases in Isidore of Pelusium's life (360–449/50?) could be roughly sketched out as follows: he acquired a classical education, he exercised the profession of teacher of rhetoric, he was then ordained priest in Pelusium and he finally became a monk and withdrew nearby.[1] The nature of his known work is notable: a huge epistolary corpus comprising approximately 2000 letters, in which he addresses a large number of recipients, from the highest echelons of secular and ecclesiastical hierarchy—Emperor Theodosius II and Cyril, bishop of Alexandria (412–444)—to simple professionals and monks, from members of the classically cultured civic elite to uneducated clerics. The maintenance of a social network with several groups with which Isidore interacted, and through which he stayed informed and exercised influence on various matters, was no meagre achievement, since the multitude, status and interconnection of the recipients ensured better chances of promoting any cause. This was not exceptional as a practice—it was employed by prelates such as Theodoret of Cyrrhus as a tool for mediating patronage[2]—but it was highly effective. His voice could be heard through his "pen" in Egypt and beyond on a wide variety of matters, from doctrine and social responsibility to more mundane aspects of everyday life, such as the public spectacles.[3]

The range of his interests affirms Peter Brown's assessment: "Isidore lived with one foot in the desert and the other firmly planted in his

© The Author(s) 2017
G. Merianos and G. Gotsis, *Managing Financial Resources in Late Antiquity*, New Approaches to Byzantine History and Culture,
DOI 10.1057/978-1-137-56409-2_5

city."[4] Isidore's particularity derives also from the fact that after his withdrawal as a monk he was beyond the hierarchy of the secular Church, being free to act willingly in a way that a bishop could rarely have been. He did not overlook the significance of ecclesiastical and secular hierarchy or the social status of a recipient, but as an ascetic monk who acted as the spokesman of Pelusium, he appeared to be more dependent on such aspects for the promotion of his city's benefit. One of the key characteristics of Isidore's reputation was his celebrated *parrhēsia* (outspokenness).[5] He intervened in both secular and ecclesiastical affairs with the courage of an Old Testament prophet and with a relevant stance: living outside but nearby Pelusium. The welfare—spiritual and material—of Pelusium was one of his main concerns, in a particular way that was not typical of other contemporary ascetics.[6]

Pelusium

In Isidore's times, Pelusium, an ancient Egyptian coastal city at the north-eastern corner of the Nile Delta, was the capital of the province of Augustamnica Prima and a diocesan town. It was the major economic centre of that area and the second most important port after Alexandria. For instance, in the *Chronicle* of Theophanes the Confessor, an incident dated 452/3 confirms the significance of Pelusium as a port:

> After Dioscorus' banishment and Proterius' promotion, the supporters of Dioscorus and Eutyches created an enormous amount of trouble and even threatened to stop the transport of corn. When Marcian learned of this, he ordered that the Egyptian corn be brought down the Nile to Pelusium instead of Alexandria, and so be shipped to the capital. As a result the Alexandrians, who were starving, asked Proterius to supplicate the emperor on their behalf and so they stopped making trouble.[7]

The favourable geostrategic position of Pelusium permitted it to be connected with Constantinople and the provinces of the Empire through the seaways, and with the rest of Egypt through the River Nile. Furthermore, it was an obligatory point of passage on the route connecting Palestine with Egypt, and it is indicative that all invasions of Egypt from the East passed through it.[8]

In his work, Isidore addresses or refers to *nauklēroi* (ship owners and merchants). For instance, he sends a letter to *eparchos* Isidorus, the *praefectus praetorio per Orientem* (praetorian prefect of the East) in 435–436, and one other to Sozomenus, the *domesticus* of the aforementioned prefect, requesting their mediation in favour of *nauklēros* Bonus, who lost state grain due to a storm at sea.[9] In one other epistle to *nauklēros* Theophilus, Isidore argues pragmatically against administering an oath to somebody (one will speak the truth or lie regardless of an oath),[10] a practice which perhaps was of interest to Theophilus when making a business deal. Epistles such as these offer glimpses into the everyday and administrative life of a significant and wealthy city port, but also into practices and mentalities.

Isidore's Attitude Toward Wealth: Benefaction vs. Accumulation and Luxury Consumption

Proper personal economic conduct and care of the poor were core issues in Isidore's correspondence, related to his stance toward wealth. Isidore employs the traditional argument, which was based on Stoic concepts and used by Clement of Alexandria, that both wealth and poverty are nothing but mere *organa* (instruments) in view of their proper use. In this respect, one should not blame wealth or poverty, for it is innate human disposition that renders all things the means for perpetrating virtuous or vicious deeds.[11] Although he recognizes that a rich man can be virtuous, he deems that in an alleged comparison between a virtuous wealthy person and a virtuous poor person, the latter deserves more praise.[12] Here he follows the mainstream patristic view—also adopted by Theodoret of Cyrrhus, as we shall see—that the poor have the precedence in virtue. Isidore was not against material prosperity, provided that it was channelled properly into retaining self-sufficiency and offering the surplus resources to the less fortunate. In this context, Isidore defines prosperity as self-sufficiency,[13] this being the ideal economic state. Again, he underlines that bliss does not consist in abundant tables, languorous songs or flowing wealth but in self-sufficiency and in not lacking anything necessary.[14]

For him, taking care of the needy is inseparable from circulating stored wealth, as is obvious in his following words:

> You possess wealth justly but you cling to it unjustly; make it common to make it yours, to be your ransom and atonement in time of need.[15]

It should be noticed that this is not a generic exhortation but is addressed to *hēgemōn* Cyrenius, the *corrector* (governor) of Augustamnica, one of the high civil officials with whom Isidore did not hesitate to be at loggerheads.[16] In another epistle to the same Cyrenius, Isidore accentuates that to keep property from being shared is to disobey Jesus' command: "If you wish to be perfect, go, sell your possessions, and give the money to the poor, and you will have treasure in heaven; then come, follow me"[17] (Mt. 19:21).[18]

In one of several epistles to *politeuomenos* (*curialis*) Hypatius—who, as it seems, was enamoured of money—Isidore argues that almsgiving and beneficence to the needy quench avarice, these being the best remedies for someone who wishes to extinguish the furnace of the love of money.[19] No matter how licit one's possession of riches is, it is nonetheless illicit if it is not being dispersed so as to become common. Isidore displays a seemingly paradoxical feature of ownership: only when wealth is dispersed can one claim to be its rightful owner, because only then can one redeem it as a means for personal salvation. Wealth is a ticket to Paradise, but the owner's name is on this ticket only if he has previously distributed this wealth. Of course, nothing less than active engagement in almsgiving is expected; as he stresses to the presbyter Hermesandros, it is not enough to sympathize with (*synalgein*) the misfortunes of others, especially as long as someone is capable of amending the situation of his poor fellow citizens. Otherwise, the expressed sympathy is nothing more than hypocrisy.[20]

In most cases, Isidore censures mismanagement of wealth in the form of barren accumulation or luxury consumption. Concerning the former, he considers that amassing riches is not just a manifestation of avarice but is also worthless as a factor to enhance satisfaction in one's life: he who desires more and more, even if he possesses countless treasures, is never satisfied, since he does not know satiation.[21] In the same sense, mad desire for money is purposeless and unreasonable: it constantly acquires but it is never sated. It resembles a hydra with numberless heads: as it eats, so its appetite grows.[22] Concerning luxury consumption, he emphatically stresses that anything superfluous (e.g., in food, clothing, housing and furniture) must be cut away.[23] Isidore also shares the common line of reasoning that wealth—like beauty, strength, glory and power—is impermanent.[24] Furthermore, he employs a rationalistic argument to display the vainness of possessions due to constant threats: moths, the great length of time, slanderers, thieves, household servants, the uncertainty of the future and, finally, death. Isidore then resignifies the censured practice of hoarding through a traditional counsel: one should "stow" wealth on Earth through almsgiving and benefactions in order to find a refuge where none of the evils cited can enter; this place is heaven.[25]

Theodosius II Exhorted to Disperse Wealth

Isidore did not hesitate to counsel even Emperor Theodosius II[26] with his usual *parrhēsia* on matters of the beneficial administration of wealth:

> If you are trying to gain the kingdom of Christ—may persistence unworn away crown this—and the prize of immortality that God gives to those who administer it honestly, blend authority with mildness and lighten yourself of the weight of wealth by the necessary dispersion of it, for a king is not saved through ample power, nor does he escape the impiety of idolatry by keeping for himself abundant wealth.[27]

Generosity was considered to be one of the most important features of an emperor,[28] and, as we shall see in the sixth chapter, it was often expressed through the distribution of largesse to his subjects. Yet the aforementioned exhortation reveals that Isidore conceived the solution to the problem of stored wealth as unidirectional, applying even to imperial policy: no wealth is good when stored; it is imperative to disperse it. The Emperor should lighten himself of the weight of wealth, implying thus its immense size but also the moral burden it imposed on the Emperor's shoulders. Isidore employs the known biblical topos of identifying excessive wealth—and therefore greed—with idolatry, since it resulted in worshipping money and not God.[29] Apart from this, the Pelousiote's counsel had a basis in reality: wealth in the imperial treasury was primarily associated with tax revenues, while its remarkable "weight" could be interpreted as the result of heavy taxation. Themistius in the fourth century wrote in a similar context: "the less the king exacts, the more he bestows,"[30] associating imperial generosity with alleviation of taxation.

Peter Brown has written a memorable sentence in a different context; however, his words also fit here:

> The [...] prodigy of administrative effort that brought the imperial tax collectors and the collectors of rents to shops and villages all over the Roman world raised the issue of the legitimacy of wealth itself and of the empire that extracted it.[31]

We are not in the position to know if Isidore's letter refers to heavy taxation; after all, this is but speculation. Yet certain fiscal measures of Theodosius II aimed at increasing revenue through taxation.[32] Furthermore, the barbarian migrations impelled emperors to accumulate substantial reserves in order for them to be ready to respond to the increasing military and diplomatic demands (tributes).[33] Concerning the latter, from 422 Theodosius was obliged to pay annual tributes to the Huns imposed by humiliating treaties (especially in the reign of Attila). According to an estimate, the total tribute payments must have reached at least 1,335,600 *solidi*, not including ransom payments for captives, ranging from 8 to 12 gold coins per head.[34] It comes as no surprise that, after the defeat of 447 in particular, taxation was increased to meet the monetary demands of Attila. According to the rhetorician and writer Priscus of Panium (d. after 472), neither those previously exempted from land taxes nor members of the Senate were excluded.[35] However, it is noteworthy that, despite these payments—and other causes of heavy expenditure—Theodosius and his successor Marcian (450–457) managed to accumulate a reserve of over 100,000 pounds (lb) of gold (or 7.2 million *solidi*), according to the bureaucrat John Lydus (490–ca. 565?).[36] This could not have happened without an effective fiscal policy, which nonetheless was burdensome to the population.

We do not know if Theodosius ever read this epistle, but this is not what really matters. More important for our theme is that Isidore urged the Emperor to comply with the only model of licit use of wealth that he had in mind and which applied to everyone: distribution, although its exact nature is not specified. Even in the case that this was actually an implicit exhortation to persuade Theodosius to alleviate taxation, and to show his generosity in an apophatic way, a particular conception of the appropriate management of wealth by the Emperor is discernible. He should not amass vast wealth because he has the power and the means to do so, this being an act of avarice, but he should let it be diffused; otherwise, he risks not entering the kingdom of heaven.

Mismanagement of Church Property: "Who Watches the Watchers?"

One of Isidore's main concerns through his epistolary work is to censure unbecoming practices, which seem to have occurred more often than not in the Church of Pelusium, and to ameliorate the behaviour of certain members of the clergy. Although not a novel situation in ecclesiastical affairs, the deplorable state of the administration of church property,[37] as illustrated by Isidore, touches upon a delicate issue in the Fathers' conception of the moral use of wealth. Patristic views appear to presuppose roughly two levels in the redistribution of riches. The first was personal, concerning every Christian individually, and required an active engagement in almsgiving and other charitable activities.[38] This kind of activity could be conducted on one's own. Nevertheless, the ecclesiastical network guaranteed an even, reasonable, regular and anonymous distribution of the offerings to the needy.[39] Individual attempts were praiseworthy but they lacked coordination which only the ecclesiastical mechanism could offer, as well as the element of anonymity. The latter should not be regarded lightly, and Isidore, commenting on the related evangelical precept (Mt. 6:1), emphasizes the need for secrecy when practicing almsgiving, since otherwise the beneficiaries are publicly exposed.[40]

Therefore, the "transformation" of wealth from private to common, from stored to flowing, required not only extensive, frequent charitable activity but also an effective redistribution of the offerings, made possible by an efficient episcopal administration. This gradually resulted in an institutionalized conception of philanthropy,[41] which was the second level. The requirement for the haves and the have-nots to be wholehearted givers presupposed that the clergy would administer their donations appropriately. But the whole attempt seemed to be negated if the church officials responsible for the administration of ecclesiastical property appropriated these offerings or used them for purposes other than feeding the poor. And with this concern in mind Isidore touched upon a delicate matter, ever-present in his correspondence. Persuading, even obliging, the well off to share their riches was one issue, but having a virtuous ecclesiastical personnel to properly manage the shared wealth was another.

John Chrysostom in his *Homily* 21 *on 1 Corinthians* explicitly mentions that people used suspicions of improper conduct on the part of clerics as an excuse for not engaging in almsgiving.[42] The bishop was to be kept ultimately accountable for the proper or improper management of the ecclesiastical wealth. He had, of course, officials under his authority who were responsible for specific aspects of administration, most notably the *oikonomos*, the steward of ecclesiastical property. This office was known since the beginning of the fourth century, but the Council of Chalcedon (451) rendered the appointment of an *oikonomos*, chosen from the local clergy, obligatory for every see.[43] Apart from the obvious benefits that the retention of a specialized and dedicated administrator offered to a bishopric, it also helped to keep the bishop himself clear of suspicions of financial abuse. It is noteworthy that such rumours of financial impropriety, which sometimes had a basis in reality, were now directed toward the *oikonomos*.[44]

Eusebius, Bishop of Pelusium
By the time of Isidore, it was usual for local Churches to possess substantial wealth, especially if they were situated in an economically advantageous position, like Pelusium.[45] This prosperity could attract the greediness of the wrong persons in the right positions, which appears to have been the case during the episcopate of Eusebius of Pelusium. Not only the bishop himself, but also members of the clergy, including certain *oikonomoi*, were involved in unbecoming practices and the plundering of the ecclesiastical finances.[46] In one of his epistles, Isidore eloquently describes the state of the Church, presumably in Pelusium. Church, he says, resembles a woman deprived of her former prosperity, now only left with insignia. She still has the jewellery boxes and chests, but riches have been taken away from her. This happened to the Church not because of the negligence of the one who adorned it for the first time, but because of the dishonesty of those who mismanaged its fortunes.[47] Bishop Eusebius and his minions shared the love for power, money and lavish living, but the tone was set by Eusebius' ill conduct, he being the guiltiest of all, since he was solely responsible for maintaining the good order of his Church.[48] Isidore never misses an opportunity to censure him in a harsh and blunt way, covering a multitude of issues. Although his overall criticism seems liable to some suspicion of exaggeration, Pierre Évieux deems that Isidore's censure most likely reflects reality.[49] In what follows we will deal with economic aspects of Eusebius and his minions' misconduct, as portrayed by Isidore.

Eusebius sold the priesthood to anyone, especially to rich yet unworthy people, and this is after all how he became acquainted with some of his accomplices.[50] As his primary goal was the fulfilment of his personal ambitions, he did not hesitate to appropriate money that ought to have benefitted the poor.[51] Isidore warns him that "judgment will be without mercy to anyone who has shown no mercy" (Jas. 2:13).[52] The bishop was so uncharitable and greedy that he deprived the poor not only of the offerings of others but also of the goods that he administered as a bishop, although he was obliged to distribute them voluntarily.[53] A noteworthy charge that Isidore levels against him is that he was preoccupied with the building of a magnificent church that was nonetheless founded on actions of corruption and unlawfulness, such as simoniac sales.[54] Eusebius focused his activities on this goal, selling ordinations, squeezing out the poor, devouring what was intended for them, and so on.[55] Isidore stresses that the bishop did not discern the difference between the *Ekklēsia* (Church) and an *ekklēsiastērion* (church). As Isidore points out, *Ekklēsia* is the gathering of saints, assembled together by means of the right faith and an excellent way of life, while *ekklēsiastērion* is just the church building. The former is composed of unblemished souls, the latter is built of stone and wood; Eusebius should stop destroying the former and excessively adorning the latter. Isidore states that if he was presented with the choice, he would have chosen to have been born in the past—when there were no such embellished churches and the Church was crowned with divine and heavenly gifts of grace—rather than in his days—when churches are adorned with all kinds of marble but the Church is deprived of all those spiritual gifts of grace.[56] In a nutshell, Eusebius took care of walls and columns to the detriment of his flock, devoted himself to a life of luxury and strove after money.[57] After this, it is no surprise that Isidore bitterly characterizes Eusebius, his *bête noire*, as "devourer of the people" (*dēmoboros*).[58]

Of course, Eusebius of Pelusium was not the only prelate preoccupied with making impressive churches in Egypt. Isidore, on one other occasion, refers to Theophilus, bishop of Alexandria (385–412), for his excessive building activity, calling him "mad on stones" (*lithomanēs*) and also "worshipper of gold" (*chrysolatrēs*).[59] Both Palladius and Sozomen lay emphasis on the willingness of Theophilus to misappropriate money for poverty relief to finance the erection of churches. Palladius, in particular, says that Theophilus was occupied by a "mania for stones [i.e. building] proper to pharaohs" ("*lithomania* [...] *pharaōnios*").[60] The project of the "Christianization of space" mainly with the conversion of pagan temples to churches, and also with the construction of *martyria* (shrines to martyrs) and urban monasteries, seemed inevitable for a powerful bishop of the Church such as Theophilus, whose city's character remained nonetheless pagan.[61] It is true that some bishops exaggerated with ambitious building projects with a view to demonstrating their power to their flocks and also to civic rivals and pagan adherents. Even so, the accusation of excessive church-building activity was often used by ecclesiastical opponents to bring discredit upon bishops (cf. the case of Hiba of Edessa in the section on Theodoret of Cyrrhus).[62] Isidore's aversion to *lithomania* derives from the reallocation of financial resources destined for the poor in order for a bishop to serve personal projects reflecting mere self-centred ambition, as well as from the shift of the focus from the spiritual Church to the church as a building. He seems to suggest that a scarcity dilemma consisting in a trade-off (i.e. a relationship of substitution) between two options—"sustenance of the needy" and "building patronage"—is simply a pseudo-dilemma, since, ultimately, only the poor matter.

Two of Eusebius' Accomplices

Presbyter Zosimus

The vices of Eusebius' minions are portrayed by Isidore as vividly as those of their bishop. These clergymen either had a fair share in Eusebius' unscrupulous activities or managed to organize their own. Their shortcomings were one of the issues that preoccupied Isidore in his epistolary work, and it is indicative that the most notorious among them, Zosimus, is associated with 178 of Isidore's epistles (as direct recipient, corecipient, or being explicitly mentioned). In a total of approximately 2000 letters, this is quite a high figure.[63] Zosimus' origins were very low: his father was a slave, he experienced extreme poverty in his youth and his education was negligible. As a result he was uncultured and ignorant, not being acquainted with the philosophers, not to mention his limited familiarity with the Scriptures.[64] He received the priesthood at an advanced age through purchase, seeing it as an opportunity to acquire power and make an investment that would return profit.[65] To fulfil the latter goal, he used his function to amass money.

Isidore, addressing him, stresses that he was intoxicated with avarice, and exhorts him to follow the example of those living in self-sufficiency, those living by just labour, those satisfied with the fruits of their own toil. He should stop getting his unclean and greedy hands on the property and money of others.[66] An aspect of his cruelty was evidenced by the fact that he did not practice almsgiving and, as if this were not enough, he robbed the needy of their possessions.[67] Isidore reserves for him, too, a harsh characterization: "heart of stone."[68] In brief, Zosimus lived a life of laziness and luxury, making money, exploiting the misfortunes of others, appropriating the commons and what belonged to the poor.[69] These were not his only shortcomings, as there were more tiles in the mosaic of charges levelled against him by Isidore, such as succumbing to the vices of the flesh, having inappropriate theological views or exercising tyranny over other clerics.[70] It is most interesting that Isidore explicitly states that Zosimus' ill conduct offered an excuse to pagans and Jews to attack and reproach the Church using his bad example.[71]

Martinianus the *Oikonomos*

Another unworthy presbyter attached to Eusebius was Martinianus, whose case presents the additional interest of having a direct relationship with the administration of the property of Pelusium's see.[72] The majority of details concerning him are drawn from a letter that Isidore addressed to Cyril of Alexandria.[73] We do not know who Martinianus' parents were, or from where he originated. Yet it is known that he was a runaway slave who arrived at Pelusium in extreme poverty, and there he received aid from many people. He took the monastic habit, but this was not enough for him, since his was seeking to become a cleric as a way of acquiring power, according to Isidore. Bishop Ammonius, the predecessor of Eusebius (and quite his opposite in every way), realized Martinianus' hypocrisy and refused flatly to ordain him. The latter tried in vain to achieve his goal elsewhere. However, the news of Ammonius' death and Eusebius' ordination made him return to Pelusium.

This time he succeeded in becoming a priest, but he did not stop there. The next step in his plan was to be appointed as the *oikonomos* of the Church of Pelusium, a goal which he achieved by persuading Eusebius that he was going to leave everything he would acquire to the Church. The way he administered the Church's finances was worse than a "barbaric war," since he knew that the appointment to this key position was his only chance to make a lot of money fast. Thus, he appropriated church property, sold ordinations, cast out the virtuous and applauded those who acted like him. He brought under his control Eusebius the bishop, who even recorded in the ecclesiastical accounts that the Church was indebted to Martinianus: this was the only way for the latter to keep safe what he improperly acquired, because the Church, being in debt to him, would not demand back everything he had stolen. Isidore continues his account to Cyril of Alexandria of Martinianus' impropriety, informing him, among other things, that when charges and accusations were brought against Martinianus, he claimed that it was Eusebius who was selling ordinations and appropriating church riches, not him.

Eventually, with the riches he had appropriated and—according to his own testimony—shared with Eusebius, Martinianus was ready to carry out his final plan: to acquire an episcopal see. He first sent money to Alexandria, probably with a view to bribing the electorate or certain ecclesiastical officials who were in the position to propose his name to Cyril for a particular see. Cyril found out about his machinations and threatened him with severe punishment so that he would quit his plan. Despite Cyril's pressure, Martinianus did not give up and went in person to Alexandria to achieve his ambition.[74] Isidore closes his letter to Cyril by urging him to take measures that would safeguard the see of Pelusium, including: to send Martinianus back to Pelusium escorted by pious and unbribable bishops, to whom he would account for the ecclesiastical revenues; to return everything he owed; and also to prove his accusations against Eusebius for complicity in theft. As for Bishop Eusebius, who was either Martinianus' fellow thief or had thoughtlessly signed everything the former had given him, Cyril should make "the episcopate inaccessible"; otherwise, should he decide to forgive him, he should appoint an *epitropos* (administrator) so as to prevent Eusebius from committing unforgivable mistakes in the future.

We do not know the actual impact of Isidore's exhortations to Cyril,[75] yet his letter is very instructive: not only does it attest the supremacy and authority of the Church of Alexandria all over Egypt,[76] it also highlights two notable points. The first is Isidore's request for control over the finances of Pelusium by administrators sent from Alexandria. This would aim not only at the consolidation of Pelusium's ecclesiastical finances but also at the protection of Alexandria's economic interests. Since every see in Egypt had to pay a percentage of its revenue to the bishopric of Alexandria,[77] the appropriation of income belonging to the Church of Pelusium eventually meant financial loss for the Church of Alexandria as well. The second point concerns the bishop of Alexandria himself: Isidore states with his *parrhēsia* that Martinianus' attempt injured Cyril's reputation, since it implied that he actually ordained for money. In order for Cyril to shake off suspicion, he should realize the threatened punishment against Martinianus.[78] Of course, Isidore refers to Cyril's stained reputation in his attempt to rouse him to action against the corrupt *oikonomos*. However, one cannot help but speculate that, had Isidore not taken action, Martinianus might well have been ordained bishop. Selling a bishopric to the highest bidder was neither novel nor rare.[79]

An Assessment of Isidore's Accusations of Ecclesiastical Mismanagement

Cases such as that of Martinianus help us conceive of simoniac sales also as economic actions, as an investment from the perspective of the buyer, who after acquiring the desired office would have seen it as capital ready to return profit. Priesthood, and primarily the episcopal office, despite the undeniable importance of the financial opportunities it presented, was attractive to wealthy members of the municipal elite primarily due to the social prestige it entailed.[80] On the other hand, for men of low origins and high ambitions, the priesthood promised both economic and social advancement within their lifetime and for a lifetime. But it also required an investment of money and resources proportionate to the sought-after office or episcopate, which these people usually did not possess. To recall Martinianus' case, he first achieved being ordained presbyter and then he persuaded Bishop Eusebius to appoint him as the *oikonomos* of Pelusium's see. From this post, he started selling ordinations and appropriating ecclesiastical property until he gathered enough money to bid for an episcopal seat. Martinianus was not the only corrupt *oikonomos* in Pelusium. His successor, Maron, is accused by Isidore of secretly buying the priesthood[81] and, among his numerous vices and misdeeds, of collecting the goods of the Church and the poor in his house.[82] He was an accomplice of Eusebius, and like his bishop he appeared to enjoy luxury and comfort, living an "Epicurean life."[83] Thus, persons who became priests, let alone bishops, by simoniac sale, would have been eager to recoup their initial investment and make profit too, with a view to living luxuriously, even engaging in conspicuous consumption, but also further financing their aspirations.

Bribery, like simony, was also not rare in ecclesiastical affairs. Although not connected with Isidore, a certain epistle concerns one of the most striking examples of bribing because of the immense sums and luxury items it involved, but also due to its context and purpose. It was written by Epiphanius, Cyril of Alexandria's archdeacon and *syncellus* (adviser and fellow boarder),[84] to Maximianus, the bishop of Constantinople (431–434) and successor of Nestorius (428–431). The epistle, preserved in Latin, lists the rich gifts (called euphemistically *benedictiones*, blessings)[85] that Cyril had ordered to be sent to Constantinople to be used as a means of influencing officials in the court—and consequently imperial policy—on doctrinal matters during the Nestorian controversy. Besides valuable and luxurious carpets, tapestries, ivory furniture,[86] peacocks, *et cetera*, the epistle refers to the massive amount of 1080 lb of gold,[87] which, according to an estimate, was "the equivalent of the annual stipends of 38 bishops or of a year's food and clothing for 19,000 poor persons."[88] The immense sum and luxury gifts imply the prosperity of the Church of Alexandria, and at the same time the volume of the stored wealth in the church treasury.[89]

The Church of Alexandria was involved, with its ships, in the Mediterranean grain shipment and trade (cf. the threats of Dioscorus' supporters to stop the grain transport after his banishment, at the beginning of this chapter), administrated landed property, owned artisan workshops and received state funds for the relief of the poor (cf. Isidore's accusations for the appropriation of money for the poor).[90] If we add to all these the less licit methods for the acquisition of money, such as simoniac sales and bribes, it comes as no surprise that Cyril was able to offer such sums and gifts to the capital's courtiers. On the other hand, it suggests that Cyril was administrating the Church's property like it was his own. Even though it was used in this case to achieve theological and ecclesiastical supremacy and not personal financial gain, it was used arbitrarily.[91] The purpose of the gifts was to buy influence and perhaps, at a second level, to tacitly proclaim prosperity and power, and thus to express status and hierarchy; these are diachronic features of gift giving.[92] After all, the epistle in which all these sums and gifts are listed was sent to the bishop of Constantinople, aiming both at informing and impressing him.[93] Bribery in the form of gifts was a method of political intervention and investment, typical of the way in which late Roman society, and especially the elite, used to influence the administration; yet Cyril's gifts were beyond customary. Years later, Nestorius remembered in his exile how Cyril's methods, such as the channelling of an abundance of wealth, led to his fall.[94]

Appropriation of church property and of funds destined for the poor, simony, excessive building activity and bribery are closely related to the management of ecclesiastical financial resources. Isidore's references to the mismanagement of alms and church property by members of the clergy, in accordance with other contemporary testimonies, reveal a real situation. If a clergyman sought to appropriate money, he had great chances to succeed, at least for a short time and given his proximity to financial resources. This did not escape the notice of flocks, not to mention of authorities, both lay and ecclesiastical.[95]

Isidore's testimony expresses, of course, a certain mindset. It is notable, for instance, that Bishop Eusebius and his accomplices were men of no or very little education and of foreign, low or servile origin (here Isidore seems to build on the stereotypic contrast between a free citizen and a slave).[96] Eusebius' speech was "barbaric" and he had an unsubstantial education.[97] Presbyter Zosimus seemed to be worse: uneducated, ignorant of the philosophers but also of basic Christian precepts.[98] Interestingly, their lack of knowledge is directly associated by Isidore with their wrongdoing and their inability to engage in virtuous activities. Isidore deems that one's life should be arranged according to reason.[99] Hence, the exploitation of ecclesiastical property was connected with lack of knowledge and education on behalf of these clergymen, as they were incapable of in-depth examination of the spiritual, ethical and practical aspects of an action. In a sense, they were victims of their unrestrained vices, such as avarice. This is not to say that Isidore believed that every humble person was susceptible to ill conduct; he rather suggested that ill conduct was consistent with ignorance in positions of responsibility. Even so, Isidore appears somewhat elitist toward the uneducated and greedy clerics. He implicitly depicts a contemporary reality: people of low social origin (even runaway slaves) who managed to enter the clergy, or even climbed the ladder of ecclesiastical hierarchy, made up a special case of vertical social mobility in the late antique Roman society. The opportunities that ecclesiastical service presented to persons of modest origin were significant, as was the opportunity for fast enrichment. In the latter case, the wealth of the Church was at the mercy of untrustworthy servants.

No matter how harshly Isidore censures individual clerics for their shortcomings, he is not simplistic. The way he expresses his exhortation to Cyril to take action against Martinianus the *oikonomos* reveals his awareness of the fact that the existence of deplorable practices in the Church was mostly due to the tolerance or even the involvement of higher ecclesiastical officials. How did all this affect the management of Church savings and financial resources? If, according to patristic exhortations, a wealthy man should be a proper administrator of his riches with a view to redistributing part of his wealth through his benefactions, then the request for proper administration of the finances of the Church, as the institution which managed donations and offerings, was equally pressing. This was not just an idealistic approach, as it concerned aspects such as the bishop's role in overseeing the proper administration of ecclesiastical property, as well as the requirement for him to act more as its trustee than its owner. After all, nobody was more entitled to this property than the needy.

THEODORET OF CYRRHUS

Theodoret (393–ca. 466), a younger contemporary of Isidore, spent most of his life in Antioch, his native city, and Cyrrhus, his diocese.[100] He was born to a well-off Antiochene family whose social status can be inferred from the classical education Theodoret received, as well as from his social associations which are revealed in his epistolary work.[101] Theodoret himself offers meagre information or hints about his past, but these are not devoid of exaggeration. In a celebrated epistle to Pope Leo I (440–461) dated to 449, Theodoret implies his well-heeled past by declaring that he had distributed his inherited property on the death of his parents, a fact he claims that all the inhabitants of the East knew. This is said in the context of poverty, which Theodoret wanted to show he voluntarily embraced, and it follows his assertion that during the 26 years of his service as bishop he never obtained a residence, a plot of land, an *obol* or a tomb.[102] Thus, he implies that the episcopate had never been for him a means for personal financial gain. Abandonment of private property for an aspiring bishop was explicitly required from the fourth century, in theory at least,[103] and Theodoret wished to show that he complied with this obligation. But why did he feel urged to do so?

Theodoret as a Civic Patron

In 423, Theodoret was ordained bishop of Cyrrhus, a city in the province of Euphratensis in Syria. This happened against his own will and while living in a monastery, as he declares in an epistle to *hypatos* (consul) Nomus,[104] a statement which most probably is a topos. In the same letter, he offers information on his activity as a bishop: he financed from the revenues of his Church the building of public porticoes and two large bridges, the maintenance of the public baths and also the construction of an aqueduct in Cyrrhus, supplying the once dry town with water.[105] More or less the same tangible results of his building patronage, financed by significant amounts of ecclesiastical revenue, are also demonstrated in one other epistle of his to the patrician Anatolius.[106] Both letters are dated to 448, a year earlier than the one sent to Pope Leo. Interestingly, the description of Theodoret's building patronage in these letters is preceded by a statement, which is different in each epistle. In the epistle to Nomus, Theodoret stresses: "in so many years I never took an *obol* nor a garment from any one (cf. his similar assertion to Pope Leo, mentioned earlier). Not one of my domestics ever received a loaf or an egg. I could not endure the thought of possessing anything save the rags I wore."[107] In the epistle to Anatolius, he asks rhetorically: "when did I ever make myself offensive about anything to his serene majesty [the emperor] or his chief officers? Or when was I ever obnoxious to the many and illustrious owners here?"[108] After each of these remarks, Theodoret refers to his aforementioned building activity.

These letters (and several others to different recipients) were sent to the imperial court to seek support and mediation from high-ranking officials, because by 448 Theodoret and his clerical allies had been accused first of misconduct and later of heresy (Nestorianism).[109] It is notable that a major part of the accusations involved church mismanagement in various forms, an indication that the administration of a see's property was considered a primary concern for any bishop, but also a pretence used by his opponents to discredit him. Irenaeus of Tyre (bishop ca. 445–448), formerly *comes Orientis* (count of the East), was the first to be accused in late 447. The indictment against him included charges of mismanagement, immoral conduct and defiance of the emperor's authority. Hiba (Ibas) of Edessa (bishop ca. 436–449, 451–457) was accused of nepotism as well as of misallocation of money to building activity, to the detriment of the poor.[110] Theodoret, for his part, in order to refute the initial, non-doctrinal accusations—codified by Adam M. Schor as "neglecting his flock while conspiring to tyrannize other dioceses"[111]— attempted to highlight in epistles to courtiers his good record in the fields of asceticism, patronage and the eradication of heresies.[112]

Nevertheless, no matter how much Theodoret's role as a civic patron is projected—in parallel with his denunciation of possessions—his role as patron of the poor, and the weak in general, is absent in the epistles in question. One could contradict that the nature of the charges did not render references to his patronage of the poor necessary. But is not this activity considered one of the key features of a bishop?[113] Furthermore, his building activity, as described in the aforesaid epistles, on the one hand aimed at serving the whole city with infrastructure, but on the other hand did not have the character of a charitable project. The way Theodoret refers to the benefactions he bestowed upon Cyrrhus lays emphasis on the significance of building activity for a bishop, as it combines the civic aspect of his office with his capacity as a prominent citizen.[114] Such a citizen would have been interested in useful but also noticeable works to proclaim his patronage to his city. One cannot assess Theodoret's stance toward the poor by a handful of letters, yet we deem that such indications lend support to the argument of Pauline Allen, Bronwen Neil and Wendy Mayer that the view of the bishop as a lover and promoter of the poor, especially in the fourth and fifth centuries, needs to be put in certain contexts.[115]

Theodoret's "aristocratic" approach is discernible, insofar as he attempts to show to his peers his efficiency as a local leader and as a manager of resources, while at the same time aims at impressing them too. The public euergetism that he as a patron had undertaken was even more impressive because it was conducted through the finances of his Church, without him becoming annoying to the local elite or to the capital with fundraising attempts. Thus, he was able to boast that in so many years he never took money from anyone—shaking off at the same time suspicions of bribery, if any. His confidence suggests that he was so efficient as an administrator that he was able to finance his benefactions to Cyrrhus through his capacity as bishop only. This feature of effective property management must have been appealing to high-ranking officials who, as members of the elite, always sought to make their own property more productive and economically efficient.[116] Theodoret, as in many other instances, seems to comply with aspects related to the social role and experiences of the early Byzantine elite.[117]

One is rightfully prepared to allow for exaggeration in relevant statements. Even so, the aforementioned tacitly point to a crucial feature of the patristic discourse on hoarding, saving and the proper management of wealth. Often, and besides individual views, beliefs and inclinations, the formulation and expression of such concepts in patristic works are also related to the literary genre, the occasion and the audience. In this case, proper management of resources is exemplified by building patronage in the letters that Theodoret addresses to high-ranking officials and members of the elite, as he faces accusations of neglecting his flock.

Theodoret did care for the poor and regarded generosity toward them as an utmost virtue. In a letter to Irenaeus of Tyre, for instance, he praises the prelate for his contempt of money and his generosity to the needy.[118] But, as we shall see, care of the poor was not exactly the spearhead in his call for social harmony, in the way the Cappadocians and Chrysostom employed it; rather it was social cooperation due to mutual interdependence between the rich and the poor. His role concerning this social dipole was a mediating one. In his epistles, but also in other works, he displays himself—through carefully employed performative techniques—as an indispensable and trustworthy broker, ready to bridge any gap between the powerful and the weak, and to foster further links between his clients and potential patrons by motivating them to reach one another. His office guaranteed impartiality and at the same time pastoral concern for the benefit of both sides; his ascetic lifestyle certified his imperviousness to misconduct.[119] Theodoret seemed to be an asset for Cyrrhus.

Theodoret as a Mediator

What was the situation in his see? Theresa Urbainczyk points out that not much is known of Theodoret's diocese before he wrote about it.[120] About 60 miles north-east of Antioch, in northern Syria, the city of Cyrrhus was a suffragan see of Hierapolis.[121] According to Theodoret, his diocese included 800 churches,[122] a rather high number. In an epistle addressed to Constantinus, *praefectus praetorio per Orientem*,[123] he provides some information about his region, noting that it is forty miles long and forty miles broad, with numerous high mountains, some entirely barren and others shaded by fruitless trees.[124] Given that in this epistle and several others Theodoret requests the reduction of taxation upon the farmers of Cyrrhus, it is evident that he attempts to lay emphasis on the infertility of a mountainous land. As a result, he probably exaggerates to an extent the bareness of his region and draws a rather gloomy depiction of Cyrrhus' territory.[125]

Theodoret sympathized with the citizens and peasants of his diocese, as his correspondence shows. For instance, in 445 and 446 he addresses prominent persons and officials, attempting to achieve a settlement of taxation that would relieve the taxpayers of Cyrrhus.[126] In another case, he addresses two of his epistles to Areobindus, *magister utriusque militiae* (master of both services, i.e. infantry and cavalry), who owned land within the territory of Cyrrhus; his tenant farmers were unable to pay Areobindus the dues of olive oil owed to him, because of poor harvests, and Theodoret requested him to abate their dues.[127]

Wealth, Poverty and Divine Providence[128]

Theodoret was undoubtedly eager to mediate as a patron between ordinary people and members of the elite, between the "poor" and the "rich," but what was his conception of economic inequalities and therefore of the licit use of wealth? Answers can be found in a particular work of his entitled *On Providence*.[129] Modern scholars deem that it was composed subsequent to the Council of Ephesus (431) and more precisely after 435, probably in 437.[130] It is believed that Theodoret delivered the 10 discourses the work is made up of (provided that they were not just written exercises) in his native city, Antioch, as their style and arguments imply an audience acquainted with philosophy, which was not likely to be found in Cyrrhus.[131] *On Providence* is Theodoret's attempt at a high-level popularization of a subject scrutinized in the sixth chapter of his *The Cure of Pagan Maladies*,[132] although there it is analysed under a more philosophically oriented approach, resorting to numerous quotations from profane authors. In contrast, *On Providence* abounds with biblical quotations, being the backbone of Theodoret's primary sources.[133]

Everyday life in Antioch, as well as in the other major cities of the Empire, provided a wellspring of arguments in support of a wider scepticism toward the existence of providence. Slavery, scarcity, the huge discrepancy between rich and poor, the excessive wealth and provoking wickedness of some of the prosperous, and the grinding poverty of a great part of the population made the Christians sceptical about God's providence, since he allowed such anomalies to continue.[134] The problem was not new: John Chrysostom, for instance, wrote on the subject.[135] Theodoret was so familiar with the criticism of some pagans and the complaints of the Christian flock as to write a treatise on providence himself. According to him, nobody should object to the notion of providence, especially if one recognizes a Creator, since every visible object, phenomenon and part of creation embodies design, beauty, harmony and utility.[136]

One of his objectives was to demonstrate that wealth and poverty alike are providential, as they are essential for the preservation of human society. He meets this goal mostly in the sixth discourse of *On Providence* under the title *That Wealth and Poverty Both Have Their Uses in Life*.[137] Those who reject the existence of divine providence, according to Theodoret, "while enjoying these manifold blessings, rebel and rave, calling all this care a want of care, throwing aside riches and poverty and complaining about the inequalities of life."[138] It would not be difficult to assume from Theodoret's polemical overtones that inequality of wealth turned into a major argument against providence.

As we have seen in previous chapters, the Church Fathers knew that poverty was a heavy burden to carry, but they did not consider it to be an anomaly, something unnatural and incompatible with divine providence. On the contrary, inequality of wealth was considered providential. On the one hand, the condition of necessitous poverty that stemmed from such inequality was primarily a means for the salvation of the rich. The prosperous should engage in charitable acts to the needy, thus obtaining an opportunity to save their souls. On the other hand, poverty was beneficial even to the poor because their penury forced them to work: accordingly, they entered into a compulsory state, a form of coercion, which secured them from the evils of idleness.[139] This system combined reciprocities and division of labour.

Wealth demanded different treatment. Theodoret follows the mainstream patristic tendency that does not denounce wealth; after all, being rich was one of the major features of the elite. Thus, he (like Isidore of Pelusium) employs the solution that Clement of Alexandria gave to the issue of wealth, who considered it as an *organon* (instrument), building on the Stoic concept of *adiaphoron* (indifferent)[140]:

> [...] if riches were evil, the fault would rebound to their Giver. What we maintain is that wealth and poverty, like raw materials or instruments, are given to men by the Creator and that with these, men, like sculptors, either fashion the statue of virtue or strike the figure of evil. With riches, however, only a few can fashion even a few parts of virtue while with poverty it is possible for many to make them all. Let us not scoff, then, at poverty, the mother of virtue; and let us not slander wealth, but let us blame those who do not use them for the proper end.[141]

Evidently, Theodoret gives poverty the precedence in virtue. In the ninth discourse he describes the licit use of wealth:

> The Guardian of the universe has not given men wealth to squander on luxury, or to use for immoral purposes, but rather to administer it wisely and well so as to provide the necessities of life for themselves and to give what is over and above to those in need.[142]

Theodoret considers wealth as a kind of grave impediment to an upright life, insofar as the rich man succumbs to his passions, living without measure; in this respect, wealth "turns the master of the passions into a slave."[143] Following the patristic worldview, he deems it quite difficult (but not impossible) for a rich man to live in virtue. On the contrary, the state of a poor man guarantees the only certain road leading to virtue.[144]

In any case, Theodoret affirms in other works too that God does not disallow possessions but rather being enamoured of money, portraying the latter as the source of greed. Hence, he opposes the ideal of self-sufficiency—in which one is content with what is at hand—to the increase of one's possessions.[145] In this context, Theodoret states that possessions are allowed, provided that they are administered properly. For this reason, he highlights the difference between being a master and a slave of economic resources.[146] We should stress at this point that Theodoret accentuates two essential and interconnected aspects of riches, reinforcing his point that wealth is an instrument provided by God, belonging to no one but him. The first characteristic is mobility of wealth that leads many people to fall from riches to poverty or to rise from poverty to riches.[147] Consequently, the other feature of wealth is precariousness, given that no one can claim possession over it, due to the constant passing of riches from one man to another.[148] Thus, people do not really possess riches; they are rather provided with the opportunity to administer them properly. Up until now, Theodoret's justification of property and wealth draws heavily on the earlier patristic tradition.

Having proved in *On Providence* that wealth is not reprehensible per se, only its misuse, Theodoret feels compelled to answer another plausible question: "Why has the Creator not given the gift of wealth to all men instead of allotting wealth to some and poverty to others, leaving life full of anomalies?"[149] His answer is once again embedded in Christian tradition. He employs an organic analogy, invoking the celebrated image of the diversity of functions characterizing the parts of the human body: the eyes, the ears, the nose, the tongue, *et cetera* have different faculties, granted to them wisely by the Creator with one purpose, their collaboration and contribution to the perfection of the body as a whole. To strengthen his point Theodoret resorts to Paul (1 Cor. 12:21–23).[150] In proportion, God confers different functions to men ("the bodily parts") commensurate to their natures and abilities, and by this providential planning each person proves to be an integral part of the community ("the body").[151]

Theodoret seems to exalt the social character of the division of labour—due to necessity—that is beneficial to the whole community. If wealth was equally distributed, nobody would be eager to serve others and to perform the various professions essential for human survival. As a result, "one of two things would happen. Either everybody would eagerly take to every kind of work through necessity, or we would all perish simultaneously through lack of the necessities of life."[152] The first case is unachievable, because (as Plato has also shown in *Republic* 370b–c) it is impossible for a single man to master every craft.[153] Inevitably, "if there were equal provision of wealth, the result would be that all would face annihilation."[154] It is noteworthy that John Chrysostom also shared this view.[155] It is safe then to infer that Theodoret strongly supports division and specialization of labour, which prevent lack of skill and promote the production of every necessity.

Economic Exchange Viewed as Social Cooperation

In Theodoret's view, divine providence ensures, through inequality in wealth, the proper foundations of human coexistence. He stresses that, apart from this disparity, the rich and the poor are equal in terms of natural law.[156] Therefore, all humans were created equal and inequality is nothing but a form of social organization sustaining life, since it compels the rich and the poor to provide each other with what they are short of, satisfying their complementary needs.[157] It would not be difficult to describe the kind of services the poor offer to the rich: the products of their crafts. But what service would the rich offer to the poor in return? Theodoret replies: "money," which probably denotes the creation of a market for their products.[158] According to his words:

> Those who live in poverty derive their equal share of enjoyment from the wealth of the rich. For God who created both classes equipped the poor with all kinds of crafts which cause the rich to come to their doors and give them money to get what they want from them. And since their wants are proportioned to their wealth, they are in need of every necessity of life.[159]

Therefore, it would not be implausible to assume that Theodoret regards inequality as the foundation of the socio-economic edifice of his era, which he strongly defends. Every aspect of this institutional structure demonstrates the care of God and his providence to humanity: "by giving money to some and crafts to others, unites them by their needs in harmonious friendship."[160] Economic inequalities are constituent parts of the social system and guarantee social harmony.

In this view, the wealthy and the poor are conceptualized as the two functional parts of an overarching social entity: in modern phraseology, these two groups seem to represent the two poles of an informal dyadic contract that does not necessarily acquire institutional shape (as in patron–client relationships), but rather serves as an analytical category appropriate to Theodoret's rhetorical framework. This concept appears consonant to the social rhetoric employed in his text, being reflective of an attempt to eliminate social disruption by reminding the respective groups of the mutual obligations imposed upon them by God. Ultimately, Theodoret's rhetoric was not at all lacking in normative implications. Issues of normativity that arise as ethical dilemmas, originating in the relevant social choices enacted by the two groups, could hardly be dismissed.

Theodoret was aware of this moral dimension, and this is reflected in his attempt to seek a convincing answer to another objection: the fact that the majority of the rich live unjustly. He responds by placing an emphasis on human freedom of will, once again employing the argument that poverty and riches are like raw materials provided by God, yet neither of them implies lack of human responsibility, being eventually an excuse for evil living.[161] At this point he draws a distinction between the unjust and the just, either rich or poor. The actions of the unjust are discredited by the actions of the just:

> Those who husband their riches properly, and do not increase them at the expense of other people's misfortunes, but rather share all they have with those in need, are a sufficient reproach to those who spend their wealth on wickedness and in a spirit of selfishness. Those, too, who accept their poverty philosophically and endure its attacks with courage and patience, are standing reproaches to those who have learned evil doing while living in poverty.[162]

The case of the rich appears to be far more interesting, since it allows for reading between the lines and interpreting Theodoret's words in a context of social roles and responsibilities: wealth is morally justified insofar as current inequities emerge as a by-product of personal rather than institutional weaknesses.[163] As people are gifted with free will, and poverty and wealth are nothing more than mere instruments, man has no sufficient reason to blame providence or the social organization, but exclusively human faults and shortcomings.

In the fifth discourse, Theodoret lays emphasis on another celebrated image that nature provides, life in a beehive, which proposes a model of social harmony.[164] Bees do not own private property, since riches are common and possession is undivided. They do not harm one another, they do not desire more than their share and they persistently work. Consequently, they expel the drones, which avoid toil and prefer to live on that of others. Finally, they detest rule by many and democratic rule, instead obeying one leader.[165] Theodoret continues after a few lines:

> You, a rational creature, learn from the irrational creatures to abhor an idle life as dangerous, pursue works of virtue with zeal, and collect this treasure from every source; not to seek for power that does not become you, but administer what you have with integrity and justice, bear in mind that what exists is common property, and extend its enjoyment to those who stand in need of it.[166]

Due attention should be paid to certain points of Theodoret's depiction of life in a beehive: the absence of private property, a view in agreement with fourth-century patristic ideals; the appreciation of productive toil; the aversion to "democratic" rule; and the subsequent predilection for submission to one leader. Furthermore, Theodoret's last words condense his views on the indispensable conditions for harmonious social organization: the aspiration to beneficial labour,[167] the preservation of the social structure and hierarchy (given that no one wishes to surpass his rank, yearning for status that he is not entitled to have) and the endorsement of the view that everything should be held in common. Theodoret's concern with justifying and above all proving that the extant socio-economic organization should remain unaltered is evident. Elsewhere, he asserts that he who desires to acquire riches falls into sin, but he who is already wealthy by status does not. For Theodoret, inherited wealth, if it is administered according to the divine laws, is completely justified and free of accusations, in sharp contrast to the pursuit of enrichment (especially in the case of a former "poor" person), which leads to sin.[168] To cut a long story short, what seems to be at stake here is social mobility or at least an aspiration to socio-economic advancement.

According to Theodoret, a virtuous way of life must incorporate the aforementioned precepts. Nevertheless, objections to providence do not cease to emerge, especially with regard to the unrewarded efforts of the virtuous. In the ninth discourse of his treatise, he recapitulates the main arguments for the dubious usefulness of a righteous living, since it does not guarantee an apparent advancement in one's status in return.[169] Theodoret replies to such criticism in the following way. He disagrees with the current view of well-being, and he uses the long-standing patristic argument that the standard by which someone is characterized as blissful should not be his material possessions ("your idea of well-being is a lofty carriage, a string of slaves, an elaborate wardrobe"). According to Theodoret, luxury and comfort should not be considered as happiness but as the greatest unhappiness.[170]

Theodoret's Conception of Social Dynamics: An Appraisal[171]

On Providence exemplifies Theodoret's stance on the licit management of wealth. Defending divine providence with respect to economic issues, he draws on earlier patristic approaches to the problems of wealth creation, retention and accumulation, as well as of the impoverishment of the economically worse off. In doing so, he elaborates a coherent system of thought in which both poverty and riches are considered as mere instruments that should be properly evaluated depending on human inward dispositions. His justification of wealth does not substantially differ from that of Clement of Alexandria's, while his organicist view of the social structure is reminiscent of that in the *Shepherd of Hermas*. Though not innovative, Theodoret's perception of the complex relations between the rich and the poor seems to be somewhat differentiated from the mainstream patristic literature since it appears not to be invested with a strong call to almsgiving. There are constant allusions to the allocation of productive resources and division of labour, but specific issues of the distribution of economic surplus, generated by the respective economic activities, are hardly taken into consideration.

The absence of references to the salvific necessity of charity in certain of Theodoret's epistles, as well as in *On Providence*, should not be puzzling. In the first case, Theodoret addresses his peers facing accusations of mismanagement. He probably preferred to show tangible results by resorting to his building activity in comparison to a vague reference to the care of the poor. In the second case, his stance is far from addressing issues of a structural or enduring poverty that might be conducive to deprivation and ultimately to destitution. Theodoret's "poor" seem not to be those at the margin of subsistence or those lacking regular employment, who are constantly exposed to the risk of starvation. It seems that he does not have in mind those without profession but the majority of those who engage in productive labour. Undoubtedly, the language of poverty employed by Theodoret in *On Providence* offers little specification of beggars, widows and orphans: the "poor" in question appear to be mainly craftsmen at the risk of indebtedness, rather than the irredeemably impoverished. The existing divide between the destitute and the self-sufficient is properly relocated and reshaped, as one between two distinct groups with different degrees of access to scant resources. Arguably, Theodoret's poverty emerges as a by-product of an economic rather than a social problem: it is a matter of inadequate resources, not one of inequity or misdistribution of the economic surplus.

In this respect, Theodoret appears not to be primarily concerned with almsgiving as a moral justification of property and wealth. He seems to imply that the solution to poverty is labour: if a person works then someone will purchase the products of his/her toil. Presumably, there is a partial shift of emphasis from distributive to productive economic mechanisms. Great cities such as Antioch were full of professionals and craftsmen who earned enough not to face impoverishment, roughly ranging from individuals with moderate surplus resources (especially artisans who employed others) to those at subsistence level. We should bear in mind that, according to John Chrysostom, self-employed artisans were in a far better position than wage-employed ones, since employers tended to withhold a sizeable part of the wages of the latter on the pretext that they were feeding them.[172] Furthermore, a large number of wage earners in the cities were employed casually.[173] Thus, people of industry at all levels would not have been in need of charity but rather of frequent commissions and the employment possibilities they enabled.

It is probable that those who earned more also aspired to social advancement. Theodoret employs his mediating experience to promote social cooperation between the so-called "rich" and "poor," while at the same time elevating order to a societal ideal, which an overall antagonism between competing social groups with unequal access to economic resources might eventually threaten. Wealth is considered the cohesive agent between the two groups, even though it cannot be distributed equally to all.

An interesting aspect of the crafts–money circuit of Theodoret is that it presupposes full engagement on behalf of the rich in the consumption of a diversity of goods, including luxury products.[174] Here Theodoret seems to distance himself from the traditional patristic requirement for abstinence from luxury and conspicuous consumption. It seems that in fifth-century major urban centres such as Antioch, the luxury goods market was so vigorous that it permitted Theodoret (at least) to include this kind of consumption in a larger conception of socio-economic collaboration, regulated by what could be roughly characterized as the "laws of supply and demand."

We can thus plausibly infer that his model of cooperation fitted in an urban environment involving several industrial sectors and respective markets, the efficient functioning of which necessitated relative socio-economic and political stability. Stability probably derived from the restriction of social mobility. This probably explains why luxurious spending, a traditional feature of the elite and part of his solution, is puzzlingly censured in the ninth discourse, in Theodoret's effort to persuade those who are not rich that the "trappings of a life of softness, license, and luxury" do not constitute genuine well-being. It is in this context that he mentions that "the Guardian of the universe has not given men wealth to squander on luxury."[175] This double standard is indicative of the integration of Christian ethics with economic pragmatism and prevailing social norms in Theodoret's thinking, at least in the way it is depicted in *On Providence*.

To sum up, according to Theodoret, consumption and the channelling of surplus into the market rather than more conventional patristic views on stewardship of savings were required to achieve the redistribution of wealth and social harmony.

Notes

1. On Isidore's life and work, see P. Évieux, *Isidore de Péluse*. Théologie Historique, 99 (Paris: Beauchesne, 1995); *idem*, "Isidore de Péluse, moine égyptien du Ve siècle," *SP* 29 (1997): 451–454; C. M. Fouskas, *Saint Isidore of Pelusium: His Life and His Works* (Athens: n.p., 1970). On the secondary bibliography concerning Isidore, see M. Toca, "Isidore of Pelusium's Letters to Didymus the Blind," *SP* 96 (2017) (forthcoming): n. 3.

2. A. M. Schor, *Theodoret's People: Social Networks and Religious Conflict in Late Roman Syria*. TCH, 48 (Berkeley, CA: University of California Press, 2011).
3. On the latter, see R. Lim, "Isidore of Pelusium on Roman Spectacles," *SP* 29 (1997): 66–74.
4. P. Brown, *Power and Persuasion in Late Antiquity: Towards a Christian Empire* (Madison, WI: University of Wisconsin Press, 1992), 140.
5. See Brown, *Power and Persuasion*, 61–69 (on the concept of *parrhēsia*), 140 (on Isidore's *parrhēsia*). On the classical roots of Christian outspokenness, see J. H. W. G. Liebeschuetz, *Ambrose and John Chrysostom: Clerics between Desert and Empire* (Oxford: Oxford University Press, 2011), 43–54. On the term and its conception by Isidore's contemporary Shenoute of Atripe, see A. G. López, *Shenoute of Atripe and the Uses of Poverty: Rural Patronage, Religious Conflict, and Monasticism in Late Antique Egypt*. TCH, 50 (Berkeley, CA: University of California Press, 2013), 34–41, 157 (nn. 91, 97).
6. López, *Shenoute of Atripe*, 23, compares the relation of Isidore to Pelusium with that of Shenoute to Panopolis.
7. Theophanes the Confessor, *Chronographia* (ed. C. de Boor, *Theophanis Chronographia*, vol. 1 [Leipzig: B. G. Teubner, 1883], 106–107); Eng. trans. (adapted from) C. Mango and R. Scott, *The Chronicle of Theophanes the Confessor. Byzantine and Near Eastern History, AD 284–813* (Oxford: Clarendon Press, 1997), 164. Cf. Fouskas, *Isidore of Pelusium*, 74; Évieux, *Isidore de Péluse*, 32–33 and n. 14.
8. On Pelusium, see Fouskas, *Isidore of Pelusium*, 71–76; A. H. M. Jones, *The Cities of the Eastern Roman Provinces* (2nd edn. Oxford: Clarendon Press, 1971), 312, 314, 342–343; S. Timm, *Das christlich-koptische Ägypten in arabischer Zeit*, vol. 2 (Wiesbaden: Reichert, 1984), 926–935, s.v. al-Faramā; Évieux, *Isidore de Péluse*, 30–46.
9. Isidore, *Ep.* 299 [1.299] (PG 78, 356–357); *Ep.* 300 [1.300] (PG 78, 357). See *PLRE* 2, 631–633 (Fl. Anthemius Isidorus 9), 1023 (Sozomenus 1); Évieux, *Isidore de Péluse*, 101–104. On the same Isidorus as *praefectus urbi Constantinopolis* (410–412), see G. Dagron, *Naissance d'une capitale. Constantinople et ses institutions de 330 à 451*. Bibliothèque Byzantine, Études, 7 (Paris: Presses Universitaires de France, 1974), 265.
10. Isidore, *Ep.* 155 [1.155] (PG 78, 285–287).
11. Isidore, *Ep.* 972 [3.172] (PG 78, 864).
12. Isidore, *Ep.* 1511 [5.222] (Évieux 2, 184–186).
13. Isidore, *Ep.* 1470 [5.186] (Évieux 2, 120).
14. Isidore, *Ep.* 1434 [5.158] (Évieux 2, 42).
15. Isidore, *Ep.* 411 [1.411] (PG 78, 412).

16. *PLRE* 2, 333-334 (Cyrenius); Évieux, *Isidore de Péluse*, 56-61, 131 (on Isidore's troubled relation with Cyrenius), 104 (on the terminology Isidore uses to designate the governor of a province).
17. Eng. trans. NRSV.
18. Isidore, *Ep.* 420 [1.420] (PG 78, 416).
19. Isidore, *Ep.* 1465 [5.181] (Évieux 2, 104-106). Cf. *Ep.* 1387 [5.120] (Évieux 1, 454); *Ep.* 1513 [5.224] (Évieux 2, 188).
20. Isidore, *Ep.* 1645 [5.312] (Évieux 2, 388-390).
21. Isidore, *Ep.* 1315 [5.67] (Évieux 1, 352-354).
22. Isidore, *Ep.* 1297 [5.55] (Évieux 1, 320).
23. Isidore, *Ep.* 1664 [5.328] (Évieux 2, 412).
24. Isidore, *Ep.* 1216 [5.3] (Évieux 1, 184).
25. Isidore, *Ep.* 1381 [5.112] (Évieux 1, 446-448).
26. On various aspects of the reign of Theodosius II, see J. Harries, "'Pius princeps': Theodosius II and Fifth-Century Constantinople," in *New Constantines: The Rhythm of Imperial Renewal in Byzantium, 4th-13th Centuries*, ed. P. Magdalino. Society for the Promotion of Byzantine Studies, Publications, 2 (Aldershot: Variorum, 1994), 35-44; A. D. Lee, "The Eastern Empire: Theodosius to Anastasius," in *The Cambridge Ancient History*, vol. 14: *Late Antiquity: Empire and Successors, A.D. 425-600*, eds. A. Cameron, B. Ward-Perkins and M. Whitby (Cambridge: Cambridge University Press, 2000), 34-42; F. Millar, *A Greek Roman Empire: Power and Belief under Theodosius II, 408-450*. Sather Classical Lectures, 64 (Berkeley, CA: University of California Press, 2006); C. Kelly, ed., *Theodosius II: Rethinking the Roman Empire in Late Antiquity*. CCS (Cambridge: Cambridge University Press, 2013).
27. Isidore, *Ep.* 35 [1.35] (PG 78, 204); Eng. trans. from "Roger Pearse: Thoughts on Antiquity, Patristics, putting things online, information access, and more" (http://www.roger-pearse.com/weblog/2009/01/22/isidore-of-pelusium-some-newly-translated-letters/).
28. Cf. Themistius, *Or.* 8.112a-d (ed. H. Schenkl and G. Downey, *Themistii orationes quae supersunt*, vol. 1. BSGRT [Leipzig: B. G. Teubner, 1965], 169-170). See J. Vanderspoel, *Themistius and the Imperial Court: Oratory, Civic Duty, and Paideia from Constantius to Theodosius* (Ann Arbor, MI: The University of Michigan Press, 1995), 169.
29. See B. S. Rosner, *Greed as Idolatry: The Origin and Meaning of a Pauline Metaphor* (Grand Rapids, MI: W. B. Eerdmans, 2007).
30. Themistius, *Or.* 8.112d-113a (ed. Schenkl and Downey, *Themistii orationes*, vol. 1, 170); Eng. trans. D. Moncur, annotated in P. Heather and J. Matthews, *The Goths in the Fourth Century*. Translated Texts for

Historians, 11 (Liverpool: Liverpool University Press, 1991), 24. On the context, see Vanderspoel, *Themistius*, 169–170. Cf. N. Lenski, *Failure of Empire: Valens and the Roman State in the Fourth Century A.D.* TCH, 34 (Berkeley, CA: University of California Press, 2002), 303.

31. P. Brown, *Through the Eye of a Needle: Wealth, the Fall of Rome, and the Making of Christianity in the West, 350–550 AD* (Princeton, NJ: Princeton University Press, 2012), xxiv.
32. *CTh* 11.20.5 (424), 11.20.6 (430).
33. K. W. Harl, *Coinage in the Roman Economy, 300 B.C. to A.D. 700*. Ancient Society and History (Baltimore, MD: Johns Hopkins University Press, 1996), 176.
34. Harl, *Coinage*, 310; also S. Moorhead, "The Coinage of the Later Roman Empire, 364–498," in *The Oxford Handbook of Greek and Roman Coinage*, ed. W. E. Metcalf (Oxford: Oxford University Press, 2012), 608. On the Huns, Attila, the treaties and the tributes, see B. Croke, "Anatolius and Nomus: Envoys to Attila," *Byzantinoslavica* 42.2 (1981): 159–170 (repr. in *idem*, *Christian Chronicles and Byzantine History, 5th–6th Centuries*. CS, 386 [Aldershot: Variorum, 1992], no. XIII); C. Zuckerman, "L'Empire d'Orient et les Huns. Notes sur Priscus," *Travaux et Mémoires* 12 (1994): 159–182; M. Whitby, "The Balkans and Greece, 420–602," in *Cambridge Ancient History*, vol. 14: *Late Antiquity*, eds. Cameron, Ward-Perkins and Whitby, 704–712; P. Guest, "Roman Gold and Hun Kings: The Use and Hoarding of Solidi in the Late Fourth and Fifth Centuries," in *Roman Coins outside the Empire: Ways and Phases, Contexts and Functions*, eds. A. Bursche, R. Ciołek and R. Wolters. Collection Moneta, 82 (Wetteren: Moneta, 2008), 295–307; C. Kelly, *Attila the Hun: Barbarian Terror and the Fall of the Roman Empire* (London: The Bodley Head, 2008); M. Maas, ed., *The Cambridge Companion to the Age of Attila*. Cambridge Companions to the Ancient World (New York: Cambridge University Press, 2015).
35. Priscus, *Excerpta* 5.6–7 (ed. P. Carolla, *Priscus Panita, Excerpta et fragmenta*. BSGRT [Berlin: W. de Gruyter, 2008], 10); Eng. trans. J. Given, *The Fragmentary History of Priscus: Attila, the Huns and the Roman Empire, AD 430–476*. Christian Roman Empire Series, 11 (Merchantville, NJ: Evolution Publishing, 2014), 38: "As for the agreements and the money owed to the Huns, the Romans compelled everyone to contribute who paid taxes towards tribute payments as well as those who at any time had been relieved of the burdensome property taxes, whether through judges' decision or emperors' generosity. Men registered in the Senate on account of their net worth also

contributed promised gold." Cf. Lee, "The Eastern Empire: Theodosius to Anastasius," 41; Kelly, *Attila the Hun*, 109.

36. John Lydus, *De magistratibus populi romani libri tres* 3.43 (ed. A. C. Bandy, *Ioannes Lydus, On Powers, or, The Magistracies of the Roman State*. Memoirs of the American Philosophical Society, 149 [Philadelphia, PA: The American Philosophical Society, 1983], 200); Cf. M. F. Hendy, *Studies in the Byzantine Monetary Economy, c. 300–1450* (Cambridge: Cambridge University Press, 1985), 224; Harl, *Coinage*, 176, 310; Moorhead, "Coinage," 607.

37. See, for example, the information deriving from episcopal correspondence, concerning corruption within the Church during the fifth and sixth centuries; P. Allen and B. Neil, *Crisis Management in Late Antiquity (410–590 CE): A Survey of the Evidence from Episcopal Letters*. SupVC, 121 (Leiden and Boston, MA: Brill, 2013), 153–157.

38. As we have seen, almsgiving was not considered an obligation for the wealthy only. The view that almsgiving can also be construed as a method of mutual support between the poor is already discernible in certain contexts in some apostolic patristic writings; see D. K. Buell, "'Be Not One Who Stretches Out Hands to Receive but Shuts Them when It Comes to Giving': Envisioning Christian Charity when Both Donors and Recipients Are Poor," in *Wealth and Poverty in Early Church and Society*, ed. S. R. Holman. Holy Cross Studies in Patristic Theology and History (Grand Rapids, MI: Baker Academic, 2008), 37–47.

39. Cf. C. Rapp, *Holy Bishops in Late Antiquity: The Nature of Christian Leadership in an Age of Transition*. TCH, 37 (Berkeley, CA: University of California Press, 2005), 224–225.

40. Isidore, *Ep.* 1909 [4.41] (PG 78, 1092–1093); *Ep.* 1946 [4.227] (PG 78, 1321). Certain rabbinic texts stress the need for respect of the dignity of those who receive alms; see S. R. Holman, *The Hungry Are Dying: Beggars and Bishops in Roman Cappadocia*. Oxford Studies in Historical Theology (Oxford: Oxford University Press, 2001), 47.

41. Christian almsgiving underwent a major transformation, as the process of institutionalization resulted in the concentration of charitable ministry around the clergy. H. Rhee, "'Every Good and Perfect Gift Comes from Above': The Episcopal Control of Charity and Christian(-ized) Patronage," *Scrinium* 9.1 (2013): 165–181, examines rationales for such a centralized control of almsgiving through church patronage that began to take precedence over the individualized initiatives favoured by earlier texts.

42. Chrysostom, *In 1 Cor. hom.* 21.6–7 (PG 61, 179–180).

43. *Concilium universale Chalcedonense*, can. 26 (ACO 2.1.2, 163 [359]). On the office of *oikonomos*, see V. A. Leontaritou, Εκκλησιαστικά αξιώματα και υπηρεσίες στην πρώιμη και μέση βυζαντινή περίοδο. Forschungen zur byzantinischen Rechtsgeschichte, Athener Reihe, 8 (Athens and Komotini: Ekdoseis Ant. N. Sakkoula, 1996), 352–435.
44. Rapp, *Holy Bishops*, 218–219.
45. On the Church's economic activities in Egypt (fourth–eighth c.), see E. Wipszycka, *Les ressources et les activités économiques des églises en Égypte du IVe au VIIIe siècle*. Papyrologica Bruxellensia, 10. (Brussels: Fondation Égyptologique Reine Élisabeth, 1972).
46. On Eusebius of Pelusium, see Évieux, *Isidore de Péluse*, 206–212; Fouskas, *Isidore of Pelusium*, 66–67. On his accomplices, see Évieux, *Isidore de Péluse*, 212–223; Fouskas, *Isidore of Pelusium*, 67–69.
47. Isidore, *Ep.* 1208 [3.408] (PG 78, 1041).
48. Évieux, *Isidore de Péluse*, 208, 210–211; cf. Fouskas, *Isidore of Pelusium*, 67.
49. Évieux, *Isidore de Péluse*, 206–207.
50. E.g., Isidore, *Ep.* 1945 [5.532] (PG 78, 1628). See Évieux, *Isidore de Péluse*, 209–210.
51. Isidore, *Ep.* 250 [1.250] (PG 78, 333); also *Ep.* 521 [2.21] (PG 78, 472).
52. Eng. trans. NRSV.
53. Isidore, *Ep.* 492 [1.492] (PG 78, 449).
54. Isidore, *Ep.* 113 [1.113] (PG 78, 257).
55. Isidore, *Ep.* 37 [1.37] (PG 78, 205).
56. Isidore, *Ep.* 746 [2.246] (PG 78, 684–685). On the term *ekklēsiastērion*, see Lampe, s.v. ἐκκλησιαστήριον. On Isidore's references to the primitive Church, see Évieux, *Isidore de Péluse*, 199–202. Cf. Chrysostom's similar differentiation between the church as a building and the Church as the sum of the souls in it, which constitute its true adornment (*In Eph. hom.* 10.2–3 [PG 62, 78]; A. E. Siecienski, "Gilding the Lily: A Patristic Defense of Liturgical Splendor," in *Wealth and Poverty*, ed. Holman, 219–220).
57. Isidore, *Ep.* 700 [2.200] (PG 78, 645).
58. Isidore, *Ep.* 1630 [5.301] (Évieux 2, 366). In the *Iliad* 1.231, Achilles calls Agamemnon *dēmoboros*.
59. Isidore, *Ep.* 152 [1.152] (PG 78, 285). Cf. Évieux, *Isidore de Péluse*, 202–203; Fouskas, *Isidore of Pelusium*, 61. On the term λιθομανής (*lithomanēs*), see Lampe; Sophocles.
60. Palladius, *Dialogus de vita S. Ioannis Chrysostomi* 6.62 (ed. A.-M. Malingrey, with P. Leclercq, *Palladios, Dialogue sur la vie de Jean Chrysostome*, 2 vols. SC, 341–342 [Paris: Les Éditions du Cerf, 1988],

vol. 1, 134); also Sozomen, *Historia ecclesiastica* 8.12.6 (ed. J. Bidez and G. C. Hansen, *Sozomenus, Kirchengeschichte*. GCS NF, 4 [2nd edn. Berlin: Akademie-Verlag, 1995], 365). See Brown, *Power and Persuasion*, 120; López, *Shenoute of Atripe*, 164 (n. 36); cf. C. Haas, Alexandria *in Late Antiquity: Topography and Social Conflict* (Baltimore, MD: Johns Hopkins University Press, 1997), 207; N. Russell, *Theophilus of Alexandria*. ECF (London: Routledge, 2007), 10. On the term λιθομανία (*lithomania*), see Lampe; Sophocles.

61. Russell, *Theophilus of Alexandria*, 6–7, 10–11.
62. Rapp, *Holy Bishops*, 221. On this accusation against Hiba of Edessa, see Schor, *Theodoret's People*, 175.
63. Évieux, *Isidore de Péluse*, 213; cf. Fouskas, *Isidore of Pelusium*, 67.
64. On Zosimus, see Évieux, *Isidore de Péluse*, 213–217; Fouskas, *Isidore of Pelusium*, 67.
65. Isidore, *Ep.* 1945 [5.532] (PG 78, 1628); *Ep.* 1762 [5.393] (PG 78, 1561).
66. Isidore, *Ep.* 613 [2.113] (PG 78, 553).
67. Isidore, *Ep.* 544 [2.44] (PG 78, 485).
68. Isidore, *Ep.* 1229 [5.13] (Évieux 2, 206).
69. Isidore, *Ep.* 685 [2.185] (PG 78, 636).
70. For a much more complete list of Zosimus' vices and misdeeds, see Évieux, *Isidore de Péluse*, 214–216; also Fouskas, *Isidore of Pelusium*, 67.
71. Isidore, *Ep.* 890 [3.90] (PG 78, 796).
72. On Martinianus, see Évieux, *Isidore de Péluse*, 217–218; Fouskas, *Isidore of Pelusium*, 68.
73. Isidore, *Ep.* 627 [2.127] (PG 78, 565–572).
74. On Martinianus' attempt to buy a bishopric, see Évieux, *Isidore de Péluse*, 82, 156–158, 218; P. Van Nuffelen and J. Leemans, "Episcopal Elections in Late Antiquity: Structures and Perspectives," in *Episcopal Elections in Late Antiquity*, eds. J. Leemans et al. Arbeiten zur Kirchengeschichte, 119 (Berlin and Boston, MA: W. de Gruyter, 2011), 18; E. Wipszycka, "Les élections épiscopales en Égypte aux VIe-VIIe siècles," in *Episcopal Elections*, eds. Leemans et al., 266.
75. See also Isidore, *Ep.* 1328 [5.79] (Évieux 1, 370). Cf. Évieux, *Isidore de Péluse*, 81–82.
76. On the personal dependence of the Egyptian bishops on the bishop of Alexandria, see indicatively Russell, *Theophilus of Alexandria*, 5–6; E. Wipszycka, "The Institutional Church," in *Egypt in the Byzantine World, 300–700*, ed. R. S. Bagnall (Cambridge: Cambridge University Press, 2007), 331–332.
77. Évieux, *Isidore de Péluse*, 158; Wipszycka, "Institutional Church," 335.
78. Isidore, *Ep.* 627 [2.127] (PG 78, 572).

79. Cf. P. Évieux et al., *Cyrille d'Alexandrie, Lettres festales*, vol. 1: *I–VI*. SC, 372 (Paris: Les Éditions du Cerf, 1991), 38.
80. E. Wipszycka, "Le istituzioni ecclesiastiche in Egitto dalla fine del III all'inizio dell'VIII secolo," in *L'Egitto cristiano. Aspetti e problemi in età tardo-antica*, ed. A. Camplani. Studia Ephemeridis Augustinianum, 56 (Rome: Institutum Patristicum Augustinianum, 1997), 250; Rapp, *Holy Bishops*, 212.
81. Isidore, *Ep.* 145 [1.145] (PG 78, 280). On Maron, see Évieux, *Isidore de Péluse*, 218–219; Fouskas, *Isidore of Pelusium*, 67–68.
82. Isidore, *Ep.* 269 [1.269] (PG 78, 341).
83. Isidore, *Ep.* 522 [2.22] (PG 78, 472).
84. On the term *syncellus/synkellos*, see A. Papadakis, "Synkellos," in *ODB*, vol. 3, 1993–1994.
85. D. Caner, based on his thorough examination of *eulogiai*, stresses that the term "blessing," used to characterize Cyril's gifts, should not be regarded in general as a euphemism for "bribe" ("Towards a Miraculous Economy: Christian Gifts and Material 'Blessings' in Late Antiquity," *JECS* 14.3 [2006]: 353).
86. On ivory production in Alexandria in the fifth and later centuries, see E. Rodziewicz, "Ivory, Bone, Glass and Other Production at Alexandria, 5th–9th Centuries," in *Byzantine Trade, 4th–12th Centuries: The Archaeology of Local, Regional and International Exchange*, ed. M. Mundell Mango. Society for the Promotion of Byzantine Studies, Publications, 14 (Farnham: Ashgate, 2009), 83–91.
87. *Collectio Casinensis* 293 (ACO 1.4.2, 222–224). Cf. P. Batiffol, "Les présents de Saint Cyrille à la cour de Constantinople," in *idem*, *Études de liturgie et d'archéologie chrétienne* (Paris: J. Gabalda, 1919), 159–173; A. H. M. Jones, *The Later Roman Empire, 284–602: A Social, Economic and Administrative Survey*, 3 vols. (Oxford: Blackwell, 1964), vol. 1, 346; K. G. Holum, *Theodosian Empresses: Women and Imperial Dominion in Late Antiquity* (Berkeley, CA: University of California Press, 1982), 179–181; Brown, *Power and Persuasion*, 16–17; N. Russell, *Cyril of Alexandria*. ECF (London: Routledge, 2000), 52, 131; C. Kelly, *Ruling the Later Roman Empire*. Revealing Antiquity, 15 (Cambridge, MA: The Belknap Press of Harvard University Press, 2004), 171–172; S. Wessel, *Cyril of Alexandria and the Nestorian Controversy: The Making of a Saint and of a Heretic*. OECS (Oxford: Oxford University Press, 2004), 262 and n. 25; Rodziewicz, "Ivory, Bone, Glass," 87; Allen and Neil, *Crisis Management*, 99, 155. See now W. F. Beers, "Furnish Whatever is Lacking to Their Avarice': The Payment Programme of Cyril of Alexandria," in *From Constantinople to the Frontier: The City and the Cities*, eds. N. S. M. Matheou, T.

Kampianaki and L. M. Bondioli. The Medieval Mediterranean, 106 (Leiden and Boston, MA: Brill, 2016), 67-83.
88. Brown, *Power and Persuasion*, 16.
89. Batiffol ("Les présents de Saint Cyrille," 168), and Kelly (*Ruling the Later Roman Empire*, 172) argue that this extravagant offering depleted the church treasury of Alexandria, but this may be an exaggeration; cf. Beers, "Furnish," 80.
90. M. J. Hollerich, "The Alexandrian Bishops and the Grain Trade: Ecclesiastical Commerce in Late Roman Egypt," *Journal of the Economic and Social History of the Orient* 25.2 (1982): 187-207; Wipszycka, *Les ressources*, 57-63; Évieux et al., *Cyrille d'Alexandrie, Lettres festales*, vol. 1, 34.
91. L. R. Wickham (*Cyril of Alexandria: Select Letters*. OECS [Oxford: Clarendon Press, 1983], xxv) states, concerning Cyril's intentions behind this immense bribery: "The bankrupting size is the sincerest testimony to Cyril's wish for a united Church and should, in fairness, bring him credit."
92. On gift giving viewed through the lens of economic anthropology, see indicatively S. Gudeman, *The Anthropology of Economy: Community, Market, and Culture* (Oxford: Blackwell, 2001), 80-89; Y. Yan, "The Gift and Gift Economy," in *A Handbook of Economic Anthropology, Second Edition*, ed. J. G. Carrier (Cheltenham: E. Elgar, 2012), 275-290.
93. Holum, *Theodosian Empresses*, 180.
94. D. Caner, *Wandering, Begging Monks: Spiritual Authority and the Promotion of Monasticism in Late Antiquity*. TCH, 33 (Berkeley, CA: University of California Press, 2002), 222.
95. Rapp, *Holy Bishops*, 211.
96. Cf. the use of this stereotype by Theodoret of Cyrrhus; Schor, *Theodoret's People*, 162.
97. Isidore, *Ep.* 1409 [5.140] (Évieux 1, 494). Cf. Évieux, *Isidore de Péluse*, 208. On good education as a desirable qualification for a bishop, linked nonetheless with his social status, see Rapp, *Holy Bishops*, 178-183.
98. Isidore, *Ep.* 128 [1.128] (PG 78, 268); *Ep.* 881 [3.81] (PG 78, 788-789); *Ep.* 1035 [3.235] (PG 78, 916). Cf. Évieux, *Isidore de Péluse*, 214.
99. Isidore, *Ep.* 1249 [5.28] (PG 78, 1345).
100. T. Urbainczyk, *Theodoret of Cyrrhus: The Bishop and the Holy Man* (Ann Arbor, MI: The University of Michigan Press, 2002), 11.
101. Urbainczyk, *Theodoret of Cyrrhus*, 18, 21; also P. Canivet, *Le monachisme syrien selon Théodoret de Cyr*. Théologie Historique, 42 (Paris: Beauchesne, 1977), 37-38. On the year of his birth, see I.

Pásztori-Kupán, *Theodoret of Cyrus*. ECF (London: Routledge, 2006), 3; Schor, *Theodoret's People*, 6. Urbainczyk (*Theodoret of Cyrrhus*, 10) believes that the date of his birth is uncertain and, even though it is often stated that he was born in 393, we have no precise evidence for this year.
102. Theodoret, *Ep.* 113 (Azéma 3, 62, 66). Cf. Urbainczyk, *Theodoret of Cyrrhus*, 22. On this letter to Pope Leo, see Schor, *Theodoret's People*, 176–178.
103. Rapp, *Holy Bishops*, 212–213.
104. Theodoret, *Ep.* 81 (Azéma 2, 196). On Nomus, see *PLRE* 2, 785–786 (Nomus 1).
105. Theodoret, *Ep.* 81 (Azéma 2, 196).
106. Theodoret, *Ep.* 79 (Azéma 2, 186). On Anatolius, see *PLRE* 2, 84–86 (Fl. Anatolius 10).
107. Theodoret, *Ep.* 81 (Azéma 2, 196); Eng. trans. *NPNF 2*, vol. 3, 277.
108. Theodoret, *Ep.* 79 (Azéma 2, 186); Eng. trans. *NPNF 2*, vol. 3, 275.
109. On the letters in question and their context, see Schor, *Theodoret's People*, 4–5, 124–125, 174–176, 196–197; also Pásztori-Kupán, *Theodoret of Cyrus*, 5–6, 20. On the letter to Anatolius, in particular, see also Rapp, *Holy Bishops*, 222.
110. For an overview of the charges, see Schor, *Theodoret's People*, 175. On charges against Irenaeus, see Theodoret, *Ep.* 110 (Azéma 3, 38–42). On charges against Hiba, see ACO 2.1.3, 24–26. On Irenaeus, see *PLRE* 2, 624–625 (Irenaeus 2). On Hiba, see R. Doran, *Stewards of the Poor: The Man of God, Rabbula, and Hiba in Fifth-Century Edessa*. Cistercian Studies Series, 208 (Kalamazoo, MI: Cistercian Publications, 2006). On bishops of senatorial background, like Irenaeus, see Rapp, *Holy Bishops*, 188–195.
111. Schor, *Theodoret's People*, 175.
112. Besides the letters to Anatolius and Nomus, mentioned above, see also one to *hyparchos* (*praefectus urbi Constantinopolis*) Eutrechius: Theodoret, *Ep.* 80 (Azéma 2, 188–190). On this official, see *PLRE* 2, 440 (Eutrechius).
113. As the seminal studies of Évelyne Patlagean and Peter Brown have shown; Patlagean, *Pauvreté économique et pauvreté sociale à Byzance, 4e–7e siècles*. Civilisations et Sociétés, 48 (Paris: Mouton, 1977); also *eadem*, "The Poor," in *The Byzantines*, ed. G. Cavallo, trans. T. Dunlap, T. L. Fagan and C. Lambert (Chicago, IL: The University of Chicago Press, 1997), 15–42; Brown, *Power and Persuasion*, 89–103; *idem*, *Poverty and Leadership in the Later Roman Empire*. The Menahem Stern Jerusalem Lectures (Hanover, NH: University Press of New England, 2002).

114. On the building activity of late antique bishops and its significance, see Rapp, *Holy Bishops*, 220–223.
115. P. Allen, B. Neil and W. Mayer, eds., *Preaching Poverty in Late Antiquity: Perceptions and Realities*. Arbeiten zur Kirchen- und Theologiegeschichte, 28 (Leipzig: Evangelische Verlagsanstalt, 2009).
116. Cf. P. Sarris, "The Early Byzantine Economy in Context: Aristocratic Property and Economic Growth Reconsidered," *Early Medieval Europe* 19.3 (2011): 255–284.
117. Cf. Schor, *Theodoret's People*, 160.
118. Theodoret, *Ep.* 35 (Azéma 2, 96).
119. Schor, *Theodoret's People*, 163–166.
120. Urbainczyk, *Theodoret of Cyrrhus*, 21.
121. On Cyrrhus and its surrounding area, see Jones, *Cities of the Eastern Roman Provinces*, 244, 252, 262–263, 267–268. For a brief overview of the city, see M. Mundell Mango, "Cyrrhus," in *ODB*, vol. 1, 574. Evidence of the ruins of Cyrrhus and its environs today is found in W. Dalrymple, *From the Holy Mountain: A Journey in the Shadow of Byzantium* (London: Harper Collins, 1997), 159–171.
122. Theodoret, *Ep.* 113 (Azéma 3, 62).
123. On Constantinus, see *PLRE* 2, 317–318 (Fl. Constantinus 22).
124. Theodoret, *Ep.* 42 (Azéma 2, 110).
125. See I. G. Tompkins, "Problems of Dating and Pertinence in Some Letters of Theodoret of Cyrrhus," *Byzantion* 65.1 (1995): 182 n. 27; Urbainczyk, *Theodoret of Cyrrhus*, 22. In the sixth century, Cyrrhus revived to an extent, as Procopius of Caesarea records that Justinian I provided the city with a wall, a garrison, many public buildings and a roofed aqueduct. See Procopius, *De aedificiis libri VI* 2.11.2-7 (ed. J. Haury and G. Wirth, *Procopii Caesariensis opera omnia*, 4 vols. BSGRT [Leipzig: B. G. Teubner, 1962–1964], vol. 4, 80–81).
126. Tompkins, "Problems of Dating," 176–195; Schor, *Theodoret's People*, 167–168. Among the recipients was Pulcheria Augusta, the sister of Theodosius II; see J. Harries, "Men without Women: Theodosius' Consistory and the Business of Government," in *Theodosius II: Rethinking the Roman Empire*, ed. Kelly, 67–68. On Pulcheria, see *PLRE* 2, 929–930 (Aelia Pulcheria); Holum, *Theodosian Empresses*, 79–111.
127. For an overview of these epistles, see Tompkins, "Problems of Dating," 178–183; Schor, *Theodoret's People*, 168–170; Allen and Neil, *Crisis Management*, 94–96; D. Lee, "Theodosius and His Generals," in *Theodosius II: Rethinking the Roman Empire*, ed. Kelly, 97–98. On Areobindus, see *PLRE* 2, 145–146 (Fl. Ariobindus 2).

128. What follows is in great part based on G. N. Gotsis and G. A. Merianos, "Wealth and Poverty in Theodoret of Cyrrhus' *On Providence,*" *Journal of Eastern Christian Studies* 59.1-2 (2007): 11-48.
129. For an insightful discussion of *On Providence* from a theological and cultural point of view, see P. Wood, "Social Heresy in Theodoret of Cyrrhus: The Sermon *On Divine Providence*," in *Hérésies: une construction d'identités religieuses*, eds. C. Brouwer, G. Dye and A. van Rompaey. Problèmes d'Histoire des Religions, 22 (Brussels: Éditions de l'Université de Bruxelles, 2015), 43-54. See also the introduction of the French translation of the text: Y. Azéma, *Théodoret de Cyr, Discours sur la Providence* (Paris: Les Belles Lettres, 1954).
130. T. Halton, *Theodoret of Cyrus, On Divine Providence.* Ancient Christian Writers, 49 (New York: Newman Press, 1988), 3. Cf. B. Croke, "Dating Theodoret's *Church History* and *Commentary on the Psalms*," *Byzantion* 54.1 (1984): 74 (repr. in idem, *Christian Chronicles and Byzantine History*, no. VII).
131. Halton, *Theodoret of Cyrus*, 3.
132. Theodoret, *Graecarum affectionum curatio* 6 (ed. P. Canivet, *Théodoret de Cyr, Thérapeutique des maladies helléniques*, 2 vols. SC, 57 [Paris: Les Éditions du Cerf, 1958], vol. 1, 254-287).
133. Halton, *Theodoret of Cyrus*, 3-4. Nemesius of Emesa, *De natura hominis* 42-43 (ed. M. Morani, *Nemesii Emeseni, De natura hominis.* BSGRT [Leipzig: B. G. Teubner, 1987], 120-136), could have provided a useful source for *On Providence*, even though this has been persuasively questioned by R. W. Sharples, "Nemesius of Emesa and Some Theories of Divine Providence," *VC* 37 (1983): 141-156. For modern discussions on providence, see indicatively P. Helm, *The Providence of God. Contours of Christian Theology* (Downers Grove, IL: InterVarsity Press, 1994); J. Sanders, *The God Who Risks: A Theology of Providence* (2nd edn. Downers Grove, IL: IVP Academic, 2007); M. W. Elliott, *Providence Perceived: Divine Action from a Human Point of View.* Arbeiten zur Kirchengeschichte, 124 (Berlin and Boston, MA: W. de Gruyter, 2015).
134. Halton, *Theodoret of Cyrus*, 6.
135. Chrysostom, *Ad eos qui scandalizati sunt* (ed. A.-M. Malingrey, *Jean Chrysostome, Sur la providence de Dieu.* SC, 79 [Paris: Les Éditions du Cerf, 1961]).
136. Theodoret, *De prov.* 1 (PG 83, 561).
137. Theodoret, *De prov.* 6 (PG 83, 644); Eng. trans. Halton, *Theodoret of Cyrus*, 73.
138. Theodoret, *De prov.* 6 (PG 83, 644); Eng. trans. Halton, *Theodoret of Cyrus*, 73-74. On this common objection to divine providence, see also

Titus of Bostra, *Adversus Manichaeos* 2.8 (PG 18, 1148); Chrysostom, *De Anna serm.* 5.3–4 (PG 54, 672–674).
139. B. Gordon, *The Economic Problem in Biblical and Patristic Thought.* SupVC, 9 (Leiden: Brill, 1989), 110.
140. Clem. Alex., *Quis div.* 14.1 (ed. O. Stählin and L. Früchtel, *Clemens Alexandrinus*, vol. 3. GCS, 17 [2nd edn. Berlin: Akademie-Verlag, 1970], 168).
141. Theodoret, *De prov.* 6 (PG 83, 652); Eng. trans. Halton, *Theodoret of Cyrus*, 77–78.
142. Theodoret, *De prov.* 9 (PG 83, 720); Eng. trans. Halton, *Theodoret of Cyrus*, 121. Cf. Theodoret, *Interpr. 2 Cor.* 8.13–15 (PG 82, 425); *Interpr. 1 Tim.* 6.18 (PG 82, 829).
143. Theodoret, *De prov.* 6 (PG 83, 648); Eng. trans. Halton, *Theodoret of Cyrus*, 76. The rich usually succumb to the sin of avarice, which Theodoret strongly condemns: see, e.g., *In Michaeae* 6.11–12 (PG 81, 1777); *In Habacuc* 2.9 (PG 81, 1821).
144. Theodoret, *De prov.* 6 (PG 83, 648–649). Theodoret, *In Isaiae* 14.6 (PG 81, 360), presents poverty as a means of curing the excesses of prosperity, given that a state of affluence generates dissipation and leisure. On the divine retribution against the wealthy, see Theodoret, *In Sophoniae* 1.18 (PG 81, 1845).
145. Theodoret, *Interpr. Heb.* 13.5 (PG 82, 780).
146. Theodoret, *Interpr. 1 Tim.* 3.3 (PG 82, 805–808).
147. See, e.g., Theodoret, *Or. de div. et s. char.* (PG 82, 1512).
148. See, e.g., Theodoret, *Interpr. 1 Tim.* 6.17 (PG 82, 828).
149. Theodoret, *De prov.* 6 (PG 83, 652); Eng. trans. Halton, *Theodoret of Cyrus*, 78.
150. Theodoret, *De prov.* 6 (PG 83, 652–653).
151. Chrysostom also uses this organic analogy to emphasize that each person depends on the others; *In Act. apost. hom.* 37.3 (PG 60, 266). In the same context, Theodoret in his fourth discourse on providence presents the beneficial interdependence of the crafts: "Behold, then, all the crafts borrowing something useful from one another: the contractor gets his tools from the smith; the smith gets his house from the contractor; both get food from the farmer; the farmer gets the equipment for his house from them and also what can help him in his agricultural pursuits"; *De prov.* 4 (PG 83, 616–617); Eng. trans. Halton, *Theodoret of Cyrus*, 54. Cf. Chrysostom, *In Mt. hom.* 52.4 (PG 58, 523).
152. Theodoret, *De prov.* 6 (PG 83, 656); Eng. trans. Halton, *Theodoret of Cyrus*, 81.
153. Theodoret, *De prov.* 6 (PG 83, 656). Cf. Chrysostom, *In Mt. hom.* 77.6 (PG 58, 710). On the patristic argument that the variety of natural

inclinations leads to the division of labour, thus generating social life, see A. D. Karayiannis and S. Drakopoulou-Dodd, "The Greek Christian Fathers," in *Ancient and Medieval Economic Ideas and Concepts of Social Justice*, eds. S. Todd Lowry and B. Gordon (Leiden: Brill, 1998), 174. On Theodoret and Plato, see N. Siniossoglou, *Plato and Theodoret: The Christian Appropriation of Platonic Philosophy and the Hellenic Intellectual Resistance*. CCS (Cambridge: Cambridge University Press, 2008).

154. Theodoret, *De prov.* 6 (PG 83, 656); Eng. trans. Halton, *Theodoret of Cyrus*, 81.
155. Chrysostom, *De Anna serm.* 5.3 (PG 54, 673).
156. Theodoret, *De prov.* 6 (PG 83, 657).
157. J. Viner, "The Economic Doctrines of the Christian Fathers," *History of Political Economy* 10 (1978): 19.
158. Ibid.
159. Theodoret, *De prov.* 6 (PG 83, 660); Eng. trans. Halton, *Theodoret of Cyrus*, 83.
160. Theodoret, *De prov.* 6 (PG 83, 661); Eng. trans. Halton, *Theodoret of Cyrus*, 84.
161. Theodoret, *De prov.* 6 (PG 83, 664).
162. Theodoret, *De prov.* 6 (PG 83, 664); Eng. trans. Halton, *Theodoret of Cyrus*, 85.
163. Viner, "Economic Doctrines," 19.
164. Cf. Basil, *In Hexaemeron hom.* 8.4 (PG 29, 172–173); Chrysostom, *De stat. hom.* 12.2 (PG 49, 129).
165. Theodoret, *De prov.* 5 (PG 83, 625).
166. Theodoret, *De prov.* 5 (PG 83, 628); Eng. trans. Halton, *Theodoret of Cyrus*, 62.
167. Employing a comparative perspective, P. Brown (*Treasure in Heaven: The Holy Poor in Early Christianity*. Page-Barbour and Richard Lectures Series, Richard Lectures, 2012 [Charlottesville, VA: University of Virginia Press, 2016]) convincingly argues that typical Christian responses to the need for supporting the holy poor as an effective means of accumulating treasure in heaven were not identical in a Syrian and an Egyptian context. Monks in Egypt, unlike their Syrian counterparts, adopted more positive attitudes with respect to manual labour, becoming less dependent on almsgiving, thus affecting subsequent Western developments on hoarding heavenly treasure through charity and labour. In sum, Brown identifies inner contradictions within Eastern Christianity by exploring such issues as the meaning of labour, the impact of wealth and the social connotations of the angelic life of ascetics.

168. Theodoret, *Interpr. 1 Tim.* 6.9 (PG 82, 825).
169. Theodoret, *De prov.* 9 (PG 83, 717–720).
170. Theodoret, *De prov.* 9 (PG 83, 720); Eng. trans. Halton, *Theodoret of Cyrus*, 121. Cf. Theodoret, *Or. de div. et s. char.* (PG 82, 1512). Theodoret's response to this issue is partly reminiscent of an earlier Christian ethical tradition. Consider, for instance, *2 Clem.* 20.4; Eng. trans. Ehrman 1, 199: "For if God were to reward the upright immediately, we would straightaway be engaged in commerce rather than devotion to God. For we would appear to be upright not for the sake of piety but for a profit."
171. See also the conclusions in Gotsis and Merianos, "Wealth and Poverty in Theodoret," 46–48.
172. Chrysostom, *In 1 Cor. hom.* 43.3 (PG 61, 372). Cf. J. Banaji, "Economic Trajectories," in *The Oxford Handbook of Late Antiquity*, ed. S. F. Johnson (Oxford: Oxford University Press, 2012), 607 (= *idem*, "The Economic Trajectories of Late Antiquity," in *idem*, *Exploring the Economy of Late Antiquity: Selected Essays* [Cambridge: Cambridge University Press, 2016], 76).
173. Banaji, "Economic Trajectories," 608 (= *idem*, "Economic Trajectories of Late Antiquity," 76).
174. Theodoret, *De prov.* 6 (PG 83, 660–661).
175. Theodoret, *De prov.* 9 (PG 83, 720); Eng. trans. Halton, *Theodoret of Cyrus*, 121.

CHAPTER 6

Contextualizing Patristic Concepts of Hoarding and Saving

Economic, Monetary and Social Transformations

Debasements, Inflation and Reforms in an Age of Crisis

Debasement, inflation and attempts to reform the monetary system and reverse the vicious circle characterize the period during which "classical" patristic views on wealth accumulation and its proper management were expressed. What follows does not intend to give an extensive picture of the economic and monetary situation from the late second to the late fifth century, but rather to highlight certain developments with serious repercussions.

The pivot of the Roman monetary system was the silver *denarius*, which suffered from a steady decline in its precious metal content after the death of Marcus Aurelius (180).[1] Diminished state funds in relation to increased expenditure (wars, largesse, building projects, *et cetera*) culminated in protracted debasement, which permitted more coins to be produced and to be spent by imperial governments.[2] Caracalla (198–217) introduced in 215 a new denomination, the *antoninianus*, which circulated as the double of the *denarius*, although the former had 1½ times the latter's weight and just 80% of the silver content of two *denarii*. This inevitably led to extensive hoarding of the coins with finer silver alloy, the *denarii*,[3] a phenomenon which is traditionally ascribed to Gresham's Law (expressed as "bad money drives out good under legal tender laws").[4] We should stress at this point that it is probable that the

© The Author(s) 2017
G. Merianos and G. Gotsis, *Managing Financial Resources in Late Antiquity*, New Approaches to Byzantine History and Culture,
DOI 10.1057/978-1-137-56409-2_6

159

Fathers' criticism of hoarding sometimes corresponds to contemporary monetary developments and situations, such as the aforementioned.

The fate of the *antoninianus* embodied the troubles and shortcomings of the late Roman monetary system. A tendency to debase the silver coinage was discernible from the Severan period; it was accelerated from 253 and resulted in the silver content of the *antoninianus* hitting its nadir in the reign of Claudius II Gothicus (268–270), with a fineness of ca. 2%.[5] At this point, the *antoninianus* had been transformed into a complex copper alloy (Cu–Sn–Pb–Ag) coin with a silver-clad surface.[6] The population was aware of these developments and lost its faith in the monetary system, one of the pillars of a stable currency. Furthermore, people became experts in extracting the silver coating, which was then sold as bullion.[7]

The situation concerning gold coinage was not better: every debasement of the billon *antoninianus* led to the decrease of the *aureus*' weight standard, so as to preserve official rates of exchange. Yet this did not result in a decrease in the fineness of the gold currency before 253, since the emperors needed proper gold coins for their largesse. After 253, the purity of the *aureus* was reduced, while the need for proper *aurei* destined for donatives (*donativa*) to the army resulted in issuing two or more parallel series of different standards (in weight and fineness). It comes as no surprise that gold coins of different standards "could not provide an anchor in monetary chaos."[8]

Andrew Burnett has observed:

> The result of these changes to the gold and silver coinage was that the currency of the empire became almost completely a token coinage. The departure of precious metal left the coinage without any real or intrinsic value, and thus the link between the rising level of prices and the rising purchasing power of coinage metal was broken, leaving the currency at the mercy of the market. The purchasing power of the coins would not increase, so while they remained tariffed in denarii, the fact that prices rose in terms of denarii led to the need for more and more coins, and hence rampant inflation.[9]

Needless to say that the hoarding of "good" coins (e.g., *denarii* or *antoniniani* issued before the sole reign of Gallienus, 260–268) contributed to their disappearing from circulation.[10] Vital in everyday transactions and taxation, token bronze coins were also devaluated. It is interesting that bronze coins were not considered small change anymore, but were hoarded as a rampart against inflation.[11]

Aurelian (270–275) and Diocletian (284–305) tried to reverse the dreadful situation and to reform the currency. Aurelian's reform took place in 274, after he had reunited the Empire by defeating the Gallo-Roman Empire in the West and the Palmyrene Empire in the East, and managed to restore some degree of monetary stability.[12] The great reform of Diocletian took place in ca. 293/4; it systematized Aurelian's measures and set the tone for the monetary developments in the fourth century.[13] Diocletian stabilized the standard of the gold coin, the *denarius aureus*, at 1/60 of the *libra/litra* (pound)[14]; he restored silver coinage, the *argenteus* (1/96 lb, 80% silver); and he introduced a silvered billon coin, the *nummus* (1/32 lb, 4% silver).[15] The *aureus* and the silver-clad *nummus* were considered the principal coins. However, the *nummus* encountered the public's distrust from the beginning, as the latter declined to accept the former at its stated value, and this resulted in prices rising. In order for billon currency to be successful, it presupposed acute regulation of quantity and exchange rates. On the contrary, the *nummus* was struck in great numbers that inevitably instigated a rise in prices while it circulated along with gold and silver denominations, not to mention older billon coins. The population gradually became aware of the gap between the official and intrinsic value of the circulating coins. This resulted once again in phenomena in the context of Gresham's Law[16]: for instance, the *aurelianiani*—the silvered billon coins introduced by and named after Aurelian, with a fineness of silver from 4.5 to 5%—were considered worthy of being hoarded in great numbers, or melted down or sweated for their precious metal (especially after the revaluations in 300–301).[17]

Diocletian's successive legislative attempts to restrain rampant inflation only prompted the aforementioned tendency. In 301 he issued the Price Edict. "Diocletian's attempt to end inflation consisted of trying to make it illegal, by establishing a maximum legal price for virtually all commodities,"[18] and for wages as well. In a moralizing tone in the preface of the Price Edict, the Tetrarchs attributed inflation to avarice (that of vendors, money-changers, profiteers and so on). Concern was expressed for the protection of the buying power of the soldiers, who experienced their donatives and salary being evaporated through the purchase of a single item.[19] It is noteworthy that the maximum price for a pound of refined gold, whether in the form of ingots, coins or spun gold, was 72,000 *denarii communes* (common *denarii*, employed as a unit of account),[20] while the highest price for a pound of refined silver (not defined in terms of gold) was set to 6000 *denarii communes*, resulting in a gold–silver ratio of 1:12. Therefore, gold was treated as a commodity in whatever form, while silver was treated as such only in its bullion form.[21] Death was reserved for those who breached the provisions of the Edict, such as those who withdrew commodities from the market to acquire a better price.[22] Yet, according to Lactantius (d. ca. 325), this is exactly what happened. He considers Diocletian as the main culprit of the bad financial situation, due to his unjust measures (presumably his currency reform) and especially the ineffectiveness of his Edict, which led to both the withdrawal of products from the market and even higher inflation. As a result, the Edict was abandoned.[23]

After the withdrawal of the Price Edict, Diocletian issued in 301 (September 1) the Monetary Edict, doubling the value of every denomination above one *denarius communis*. Thus, Diocletian reduced in half all prices, salaries and taxes which were calculated in *denarii communes*, but preserved the rates of exchange among the higher denominations. The Monetary Edict did not improve the coinage, neither did it reverse inflation: "coins were worth whatever they could fetch in the marketplace on any given day and not what edicts pronounced."[24] By doubling the salaries of many officials after 301, the government itself contributed to weakening its own currency.[25] Transactions made in cash, as well as official salaries (mainly those of soldiers and civil servants), were subject to the effects of inflation.[26]

Shifting Gradually into the "Byzantine" World

Debasement of coinage was not abandoned as a method after Diocletian. The Roman world faced civil wars from 306 to 324—until the final prevalence of Constantine I—and the rival emperors were in need of troops and money. The introduction of a stable gold currency, known as the *solidus*, by Constantine was a great achievement (which we shall discuss in the next section), yet the situation concerning silver, billon and base-metal denominations remained precarious. In 307 Constantine debased the silver-clad *nummus* and his opponents followed.[27] In the next years, prices rose again, with the public reacting as usual: older *nummi* with more silver content were preferred, being subject to Gresham's Law.[28] In the

East, probably in 321, Licinius (308–324) reduced the silver content and halved the face value of the *nummus* (from 25 to 12.5 *denarii communes*), recognizing that it was overvalued. This development has been recorded in papyri, the most informative of which is P. Ryl. 4 607.[29] This is actually a letter written by one Dionysius to one Apion. The former, obviously having inside knowledge of the imminent retariffing ("the Italian coinage be reduced to the half of a *nummus*"), urges the latter to spend, on the sender's behalf, all the "Italian silver" that he has in purchases of goods of every description at whatever prices he finds them.[30] This letter has been interpreted in the wider context of the panic to which the retariffing led, rushing people to convert their *nummi* into other commodities.[31] However, it is probable in this particular case that the sender of the letter intended to hold and resell the goods after the measure would have been made public.[32] The Fathers' criticism of speculative hoarding and profiteering in times of crisis must have also addressed cases like this.

In 324 the *nummus* of Licinius was demonetized. By 336–337, the Constantinian *nummus* had been transformed into a tiny coin with 15% of the weight and less than 2% of the silver content of the Diocletianic *nummus*. As the government did not revalue this miniscule currency from the rate of 25 *denarii communes*, the market responded by marking prices in *denarii communes*, which resulted in further inflation. By the mid-fourth century inconceivable prices occurred even for the humblest of purchases. From the 330s *nummi* sealed up in leather purses (*folles*) with their value (in *denarii communes*) inscribed on them were the only way to conduct everyday transactions. The value of the *nummus* continued to fall through the fourth and the fifth century. Hypothetical rates of exchange for the *solidus* and the *nummus* have been proposed: in 323 a *solidus* was equivalent to 240 *nummi* or 6000 *denarii communes*; in 338–341 it was equivalent to 11,000 *nummi* or 275,000 *denarii communes*; around 360 it was equivalent to 4004 *nummi* or 20,020,000 *denarii communes*; and in 395–410 a *solidus* was equivalent to 8000 *nummi* or 40,000,000 *denarii communes*.[33] It is obvious that the purchasing power and the status of someone with regular access to gold coinage were beyond comparison.

Despite intermediate attempts, it was not until the reign of Anastasius I (491–518) that a stable and flexible coinage in base metal was provided, the large copper *follis*, filling the alleged gap in the circulating currency between the gold *tremissis* (the third of a *solidus*)[34] and the *nummus*. A *follis* was equivalent to 40 small *nummi*, which nonetheless did not cease to circulate immediately.[35] Anastasius preferred to reform the base coinage instead of debasing and revaluating the *nummi* once again.[36]

The Constantinian Solidus: *A Lever for Change*

The reign of Constantine I signified a new era not only for the Christian Church but also for the late Roman economy. A major change, with repercussions that transformed even social hierarchies, took place from his reign onwards: money surpassed land as the general form (and indication) of wealth.[37] It is a consensus now that Constantine and his successors "flooded" the market with gold[38] in the form of *solidi*.[39] The *solidus* (also known as *nomisma*) was introduced in 309 and weighed approximately 4.50 g, corresponding to 1/72 of the Roman pound, in place of Diocletian's gold coin (*aureus*), corresponding to 1/60. Simply put, a Roman pound of gold theoretically produced 72 *solidi*.[40] Constantine managed to introduce a stable gold coinage and to circulate it as a mass currency, in contrast to the previous monetary practice.[41] Anyhow, perhaps we should not overemphasize the foresight behind this achievement. Constantine's gold coin was actually a debasement in comparison to that of Diocletian, while his victories and the reminting of the heavier *aurei* of his rivals probably led to the imposition of the *solidus* in the Roman world.[42]

Jairus Banaji has adequately traced the monetary, economic and social reverberations caused by the successful introduction of the *solidus*. A major consequence was that gold became the absolute representative of value; this is not to say that values could not be expressed in other lower monies or units of account, but rather that the expression of value in lower currencies implied their own underlying expression of value in terms of gold. Silver and bronze became symbols for gold, representing various quantities of it.[43] If it is accurate that during the last years of Constantius II's reign (337–361) the gold–silver ratio shifted dramatically in favour of the latter, and with the presupposition that this ratio reflected demand factors, Banaji suggests that this development implies not the elevated demand for silver but rather the sudden flooding of the economy with gold in relation to the strong demand for it.[44]

A key text to help us construe this turning point in economy is the anonymous fourth-century treatise *De rebus bellicis* (*On Military Affairs*). The text reproaches Constantine I for his economic policy, which triggered ruinous social repercussions, especially for the lower social strata.⁴⁵ Banaji has proposed an interpretation of the anonymous criticism of the Constantinian monetary policy, describing the interdependent consequences of the novel measures. Constantine imposed a new monetary standard, a development mainly characterized by: (a.i) flooding the market with gold (thus, many transactions were made in gold instead of bronze, even in retail trade),⁴⁶ and subsequently (a.ii) "eliminating any possible duplication of the measure of value by displacing the function of that measure to gold, with the general expression of commodity prices as gold prices (prices expressed in gold)"; (b) accumulation of capital, incited by this general transformation, in the form of gold, which proved to be an indispensable factor in the formation of a new aristocracy, based economically on gold at the expense of the "poor"; and (c) notable violence against the masses triggered by these socio-economic changes. However, Banaji notes that there is no direct attestation of the latter in the extant contemporary sources.⁴⁷

Santo Mazzarino drew attention to the significant association made in the *De rebus bellicis* between the expansion in the circulation of gold and the emergence of a new aristocracy under Constantine and his heirs. What is more, he noticed that the new salaries being paid in gold and their high purchasing power were fundamental constituents of the transformed hierarchical social order.⁴⁸ The anonymous author of the *De rebus bellicis* perhaps was a provincial aristocrat who witnessed his status and interests being threatened by the new situation, evidently not belonging to the new elite that emerged and was benefitted by the expanding flow of gold, partly made possible by the pillaging of pagan temples, according to his own testimony.⁴⁹ This "massive dishoarding of gold [...] led to the (renewed) accumulation of monetary wealth in private hands and sparked a veritable 'passion for spending gold'."⁵⁰

The commutation of the late Roman tax system, as Banaji has pointed out, furnished provincial governors with substantial profits.⁵¹ Ammianus Marcellinus (ca. 330–after 392) states that "the first of all to open the jaws of those nearest to him was Constantine, but it was Constantius who fattened them with the marrow of the provinces."⁵² The anonymous author of the *De rebus bellicis* likewise stresses that provincial governors thought they had been sent into the provinces as merchants (*velut mercatores*).⁵³ Late Roman bureaucracy took shape especially in the reign of Constantius, but the *militares* (military officials) gradually became the dominant group within it.⁵⁴ Valentinian I was the first emperor who set the conditions for the social dominance of the *militares*, according to

Ammianus.[55] Commutation of taxes was further prompted by the pressure of the *militares* to extract considerable monetary payments.[56] As a result, the bureaucracy in general exploited the opportunities for fiscal speculation and profiteering that its involvement in tax collection presented.[57] The stage was gradually being set for the emergence of a new East Roman (Byzantine) elite.

The Emperor as the "Lord of the Gold"

Reforms introduced by Valentinian I and Valens (364–378) consolidated the close association of gold with the emperor. In 366–367 they issued two laws reforming the tax collection and management of *solidi* taken in tax.[58] The laws imply that a series of officials often had the chance to replace proper coins with forgeries sometime in the process between tax collection and delivery to the treasury.[59] The emperors decreed that the collected *solidi* should be weighed and melted into *obryza* (ingots of refined gold). After being delivered without delay directly to the *comitatus* (imperial residence) to be stored in the *sacrae largitiones* (sacred largesses), these certified ingots were used as new *solidi* to be struck by the comitatensian mint. This was operating wherever the emperor's current residence was, and nearly all gold was to be struck by this mint. New *solidi* bore, along with additional letters denoting the mint, the abbreviation COMOB: the COM probably stands for *comitatus*, while the OB denotes *obryzum* (certified pure gold). Parallel, not surviving, measures regulated silver coinage, since *miliarensia* and *argentei* bore the abbreviation PS for *pusulatum* (certified pure silver). In this case, new coins, medallions and ceremonial plate were produced. These measures resulted in the restoration of the *solidus* to 99.5% fineness and to the improvement of the *argenteus* to 97.5–98% fineness, granting the former international standing.[60] It was inevitable that severe laws were reserved against the adulteration of the gold coinage, which had to circulate and return to the imperial treasury impeccable.[61] Other measures stipulated, for example, the proper measuring of gold weight in tax payments, or imposed the use of all *solidi* regardless of the emperor that was depicted on the obverse (meaning that occasionally only the coinage of a reigning emperor was considered as standard).[62]

The gold coin's functions roughly included usage in imperial propaganda (it bore the emperor's image), in imperial largesse and in the expenditure–taxation cycle. Precious metals, especially gold, being so closely associated with the emperor, inevitably formed indispensable constituents of his generosity. The *comes sacrarum largitionum* (count of the sacred largesses) was in charge of the production, supply and distribution of imperial wealth, while his supervision of the exploitation of mines, quarries, mint(s) and imperial workshops for textiles is indicative of the variety of the largesse. Coins, but also silver plates, buckles, collars, armlets, phalerae, *et cetera*, were given to beneficiaries on various occasions, and especially to the aristocracy and the military. This variety also attests to the fact that hoarding concerned not only coins but some of the aforementioned items as well. Largesse was also directed to the citizens of Rome and Constantinople; coins were distributed, for instance, on the occasions of accessions and their anniversaries, triumphs, New Year's celebrations, as well as nominations of the consuls in the capital. As we have already seen, beneficiaries of imperial generosity could also have been foreigners and especially the Barbarian leaders.[63]

Silver was the main instrument for imperial largesse, used, for instance, for the donatives of lower military ranks. Small silver ceremonial issues along with copper coins were distributed to people on several occasions. It is noteworthy that a law of 384 forbade anyone else except ordinary consuls from giving a gift in gold, while it decreed that silver coins, the size of which should not exceed 1/60 of a pound, should be used for scattering in public ceremonies.[64] A law of Marcian in 452 prohibited every distribution of largesse,[65] although it was later permitted again. In the same manner that the consulship was gradually identified with the emperor, the privilege of scattering largesse in gold was narrowed down to the ordinary consuls, until it was finally confined to the Byzantine emperor.[66] Distribution of gold was the prerogative of the emperor, being at the top of a gift-exchange pyramid in the early Byzantine society.[67]

Imperial Reserves

As we have already mentioned in the fifth chapter, commenting on Isidore of Pelusium's letter to Theodosius II, it was usual for Byzantine emperors to create a reserve, which was handy in times of need. Literary sources affirm this tendency and sometimes even offer figures on the size of reserves created during individual reigns. Concerning the fifth century in particular, accumulation of large amounts of gold is attested for certain emperors. Theodosius II and Marcian managed to amass over

100,000 lb of gold—or 7,200,000 *solidi*—according to John Lydus.[68] It is notable that they were able to gather this sum despite heavy expenditure, for example in the form of tributes. From 422, Theodosius paid to the Huns gradually increasing annual subsidies estimated to total at least 1,335,600 *solidi*, without including in this sum ransom payments for the release of captives. Marcian ceased to pay Attila, but on the other hand he settled the Ostrogoths in Pannonia, who are calculated to have received, until their departure to Italy in 489, no less than 2,304,000 *solidi*.[69] These were enormous sums, especially if we take into consideration the suggestion that the annual expenditure of the state during the fifth century was perhaps 5,000,000 *solidi*.[70] The last figure is based on speculation, of course; however, it offers a plausible indication.

A reserve such as the one that Theodosius and Marcian managed to accumulate was not difficult to squander. Marcian's successor Leo I (457–474) undertook, along with the Western Emperor Anthemius (467–472), a naval expedition against the Vandals of North Africa in 468, which turned into a disaster. The tremendous cost of the expedition, partly paid for by Anthemius, ranged between 7,500,000 and 9,500,000 *solidi* and consumed the reserve that had been created by Theodosius and Marcian.[71] This oscillation between "accumulation" and "squandering" as imperial practices is typical throughout Byzantine history.[72] The most famous example of an emperor who depleted a reserve which had been meticulously built up by his predecessors is Justinian I (527–565). He squandered in military expeditions and building programs the mythical reserve of Anastasius I—3200 *centenaria* or at least 23,040,000 *solidi*—which had been further increased by Justin I (518–527) and reached the amount of 4000 *centenaria* or 28,800,000 *solidi*.[73]

It has been suggested that Anastasius was able to accumulate this great reserve partly because reforms in taxation prompted extensive commutation of taxes in his reign. The amount of revenue in widespread commutation depends on the state of the market, and by the sixth century the volume of commercial exchanges was an expanding one.[74] It has also been suggested that the state was employing various means in its attempt to retrieve in the treasury as much gold as possible, for instance, through the *collectarii* (money-changers). In this context, a novel of the Western Emperor Valentinian III (425–455), issued in 445, shows that money-changers could buy a *solidus* from the public for 7000 *nummi* at least, and sell it to the treasury for 7200; the Eastern tariff would not have been substantially different.[75] As we shall argue shortly, the imperial treasury with its accumulated wealth from all over the Empire probably contributed a vivid model to the rhetoric of the heavenly treasury.

The Formation of a "Golden" Elite

Although Constantine's monetary revolution and its consequences affected both East and West and resulted in the formation of new upper social strata, the nature of the new elites was far from being identical in East and West. The Constantinian elite in the West consisted of potent aristocratic families originating in the second- and third-century Western Mediterranean provinces that prospered, most notably Africa; some of these families had managed to survive the protracted civil war prior to the prevalence of Septimius Severus (193–211). On the other hand, the early Byzantine world witnessed the gradual rise of an aristocracy of service, which was not of "traditional" origin like its Western counterpart.[76]

From the fourth (but most evidently from the mid-fifth) to the sixth century, a new elite—to be distinguished from local (municipal) aristocracy in terms of resources and bureaucratic character—was gradually formed concentrating landownership in its hands.[77] This new imperial aristocracy of service in great part originated in the *curiae* (city councils) of the Eastern Mediterranean and dominated the state's offices, the land and the social relations in what was becoming "Byzantium." The formation of an expanding bureaucratic state in the late antique East created numerous civil and military posts, which were occupied by members of the prominent families of the local city councils.[78] Given that these were official governmental posts, wealth, prestige and a closer relationship with imperial authorities in the capital were the unquestionable benefits for their holders, who took care to fully exploit them in their interest. At a provincial level, these advantages were used by members of the new elite to expand their land at the expense of other *curiales* who were less favourably positioned for the pursuit of their own interests, as well as to the detriment of other members of local society.[79]

Imperial governments were preoccupied with the stability of the *solidus*, since both an important part of the state's revenues and the payment of the bureaucratic mechanism was based on it. On the other hand, from the fourth century onwards, there occurred a notable economic expansion, with money flowing into agriculture as well as trade. Therefore, if stability of the gold currency was a prerequisite for fiscal policy, liquidity was vital to the level of monetary activity in the economy.[80]

The members of the new elite contributed to the progressive monetization of the economy by adopting economically efficient methods of organizing and exploiting their production, especially discernible from the fifth century onwards. The papyrological evidence of the estates of the Apion family near the Egyptian city of Oxyrhynchus provides an atypically amply documented testimony of the way elite landholding was structured from the fifth to the seventh century. The bipartite character of the Apion estates was based on a division between land directly managed by the household and its employees (*autourgia*), and allotments (*ktēmata*) rented to farmers of small villages belonging to the estate (*epoikia* or *chōria*). The family also owned land in larger villages (*kōmai*) and urban property in Oxyrhynchus. It seems that the backbone of the Apions' income came from highly commodified production on the *autourgia* (and not from rents) that depended on wage labour.[81] Peter Sarris has observed concerning "bipartitism" that it:

> [...] offered landowners two great advantages: it maximised both the labour at their disposal and the dependence of the estate's labourers on the estate itself. It thus minimised opportunities for peasant autonomy whilst curtailing incentives to peasant resistance."[82]

The elite would have exploited the opportunities for profit making that the favourable conditions of growing monetization and increased liquidity presented in the urban centres of the Eastern Mediterranean. Banaji comments that "relations between business and the state, and between the aristocracy and business, were altogether more involved here, completely at odds with conventional dichotomies between 'public' and 'private' or between 'aristocrats' and 'entrepreneurs'."[83] In this context, Alexandra Čekalova, for instance, has argued that the senatorial aristocracy of Constantinople was "more urban than landed," having its assets mainly in liquid form.[84] The favourable conditions were also exploited by the large urban "middle class" of the Eastern Mediterranean. The commercial flourishing of the fifth century could be interpreted to a degree by the suggestion that merchants had unimpeded access to capital resources that permitted them to establish trade networks both in the Eastern and the Western Mediterranean. Entrepreneurs, silversmiths, jewel traders, silk merchants and, of course, money-changers and bankers were some of the most prosperous groups which interacted with the elite in the conduct of business.[85]

Contemporary economic reality was depicted in the writings of the Fathers. For instance, Gregory of Nazianzus employs the term *megalemporos* (lit. "great merchant," usually translated as "wholesale merchant")[86] in context with the Parable of the Pearl in Matthew 13:45–46.[87] Alternatively, he uses the term *megas emporos*, which denotes the same thing.[88] Nevertheless, the parable originally refers to an *emporos* (merchant), which probably means that Gregory must have adapted the term to better reflect the economic conditions of his time, when *megalemporoi* conducted their large-scale entrepreneurial activities and were easily discerned from simple *emporoi*. A *megalemporos* who sells all that he has so as to buy the priceless pearl would have made a greater impression, since audiences would have easily recalled his alleged socio-economic status. It is hardly a coincidence that the anonymous contemporary author of the *De rebus bellicis* includes the *negotiatores* (large-scale merchants and bankers) in his sketchy depiction of late Roman society.[89]

Concerning bankers, increasing references to them occur in written sources from the second half of the fourth century, a phenomenon to be linked with the revival of banking activity due to the widespread dissemination of the *solidus*.[90] Basil of Caesarea informs us that it was usual for people in Alexandria to give money to the *trapezitai* (private bankers) so as to gain profit from their deposit (*eis porismon*), which means that they were making an investment deposit.[91] John Chrysostom illustrates banking activities too, and it has been proposed that his use of financial terminology is perhaps due to his knowledge of banking.[92] These Fathers were aware both of the language of finance and commerce and the conduct of business, as members of the elite. Given that the formation of early patristic economic reasoning is often entrenched in concrete socio-economic realities, fourth-century Fathers were elaborating their views on the economy as a potential response to certain types of economic activities, and in particular to those arising from the major monetary reforms described earlier. In this respect, we can plausibly infer that they were relating the large-scale business affairs of their era, as well as banking activities, to monetary accumulation and investment processes.

The elite was eager to show its association with gold and consequently with the emperor who offered it to his officials and officers. Gold was a symbol but also evidence of authority and wealth; its appearance instantly conveyed connotations of beauty, purity, largesse, incorruptibility (as it does not rust) and, inevitably, scarcity.[93] But possessors of wealth had to demonstrate it so as to convince others that they truly held it,[94] and luxury and conspicuous expenditure must have reached great heights of excess. Asterius, bishop of Amasea in Pontus (380/90–420/5), reproaches in his homily *Against Avarice* those who "dwell under roofs overlaid with gold,"[95] showing that the use of gilding was not exceptional for architectural details. Theodoret of Cyrrhus' testimony on luxury consumption at the end of the previous chapter is also associated with the conspicuous practices of the elite.

The Church itself could not avoid being associated with gold. This phenomenon has a multi-layered interpretation, but two of its defining aspects have been encapsulated by Dominic Janes. He underlines that, on the one hand, for churchmen "in fighting to denigrate gold":

> It was much easier and more persuasive to say, "indeed everyone knows that gold is very precious, but I know something better." This, however, legitimated gold as something of excellence, albeit lesser excellence, which was then related to Christian divinity as it was already related to pagan divinity.[96]

On the other hand, there was also a necessity from the state's perspective to invest religious imagery with gold and grandeur:

> [...] Church splendour was associated with the patronage of emperors. They wished to associate themselves with divinity and associate the Church with their government. For that to work, the two institutions needed to adopt the same styles, otherwise a bare religious style of the church would seem an explicit criticism of the golden style of the Empire. In tandem, each could do honour to the other.[97]

The Christian Church triumphed, and although born from poverty, at the time of its triumph it had already been an institution associated with wealth and the rich.[98] Yet, in the fourth and the fifth century it gradually encompassed the truly wealthy, in a process that made necessary adaptations and transformations of ideals and norms, not only from the side of the elite but also from the side of the Church. The latter had to compromise both with the fact that it possessed significant wealth itself and that not all the wealthy were actually expected to denounce their riches. A new reasoning had to accommodate the lay members of the elite, as well as the well off of the middle social strata, now that the Church was identified with the Empire and its higher clergy more often than not derived from these social groups. Charity, church building, the foundation and patronage of monastic institutions, and donations made on one's deathbed were virtuous activities through which wealth was spiritually legitimized and stored in the "heavenly treasury."

Earlier Jewish and Christian traditions, discussed in the second and the third chapters, and probably the coffers, chests and depositories of the contemporary elite, contributed to the formation of the imagery of the heavenly treasury as the place and refuge of "spiritual wealth," accumulated there by "transmuting" earthly riches into benefactions. The imperial treasury might have also contributed to the development of this imagery with a compelling analogy. In the same manner that taxation gathered gold throughout the Empire and accumulated it in the imperial treasury, benefaction could be perceived as voluntary subjection to a "blessed kind of taxation" that collected earthly gold (through a beneficiary) and accumulated it as "spiritual gold" in the divine treasury.

In this and related imagery, the gold *solidus* seems to have become the embodiment of wealth. It hardly comes as a surprise that the texts of the fourth- and fifth-century Church Fathers are replete with references to the *chrysion*, a term which means gold in general and gold coin in particular (depending on the context). Indeed, laws such as one issued by Constantine I in 325 assert the common identification of *solidi* with bullion.[99] Just to make a rough comparison, in the second-century *Shepherd of Hermas* we only come across four references to gold, and these are found in an allegorical context, not related to counsels for the proper management of one's property.[100] This is not unexpected, since the socio-economic and monetary realities were much different then; however, the difference is still suggestive.

Christian texts sometimes visualized the seductive radiance of a great amount of gold, as in the *Life* of Saint Melania the Younger (d. 439), a Roman-born ascetic of senatorial status, who along with her equally noble and rich husband, Pinianus, renounced their enormous wealth and liquidated their vast properties in order to follow their ascetic ideals[101]:

[...] "one day we had collected a massive, extraordinary amount of gold to send for the service of the poor and the saints: 45,000 pieces of gold. When I went into the *triclinium*, it seemed, by the operation of the Devil, as if I were lighting up the house with fire from the multitude of gold pieces. In my thoughts, the Enemy said to me, 'What sort of place is this Kingdom of Heaven, that it can be bought with so much money?'"[102]

The depiction of shimmering gold was probably used to emphasize the intensity of the inner struggle the saint faced in bridling the attraction of gold. The Devil clearly associated gold with power, implying that money could buy a kingdom, even that of heaven. The symbolism of gold is recurring in the *Life of Melania the Younger*. During an audience of the ascetic couple with the "Empress" Serena, the latter "was greatly moved when she saw the blessed woman in that humble garment, and having welcomed her, she had her sit on her golden throne."[103] Melania's ascetic prowess is associated with gold, either as the object of a powerful but eventually bridled temptation (the shiny gold coins) or as a symbolic acknowledgement of her spiritual status (the golden throne). Indeed, gold could be perceived either as a symbol of sin or, in different contexts, a symbol of majesty and spiritual radiance. But Melania's relation to gold was not just a symbolic one: her *Life* abounds with references to gold and wealth, since it is the narration of the virtuous deeds of a super-rich person.

MELANIA THE YOUNGER: A CASE STUDY OF A SUPER-RICH PERSON'S DIVESTMENT

The First Steps of Divestment: Italy

The *Life* of Saint Melania the Younger, granddaughter of Melania the Elder, hardly needs an introduction to those who study late antique Roman elites and especially themes such as gender, patronage and spiritual authority. This work is preserved in two anonymous versions, a Greek one (*BHG* 1241) and a Latin one (*BHL* 5885)—which are similar but not identical[104]—and its authorship is attributed to Gerontius.[105] There we read about Melania's and Pinianus' ascetic endeavour—triggered after the death of their children[106]—their slow journey from Rome to Jerusalem, with an intermediate seven-year stay in North Africa, and their deeds (especially Melania's) in the Holy Land. Melania's case is very instructive on the complexities a member of the elite had to face in his/her wish to renounce wealth, but also on the implications the realization of this decision had for Christian societies. Melania was Roman, yet her decision to divest herself of her wealth and the plan to carry out this decision affected East as much as West. In what follows, we will attempt to focus on certain aspects of Melania's and her husband's efforts to denounce the world.

To begin with, Melania herself shows that one of the hardest tasks she undertook on her way to ascetic perfection was to detach herself from the wealth linked with her status. In order to achieve renunciation of wealth,[107] she and her husband had to engage in a three-fold divestment: (a) dispersion of their annual income (notably, Pinianus claimed that his annual revenue in gold reached 120,000 [presumably] *solidi*, without including that of his wife's)[108]; (b) liquidation of their estates or the endowment of them for religious use; and (c) sale or manumission of their slaves.[109] Divestment at such a great scale was an easy thing to say but not an easy thing to achieve, not only due to the enormous size of the property in question but also due to dominant familial, societal and gender norms against which the ascetic couple had to struggle.[110] Bad timing was a further complexity, since in 408 the Visigothic army of Alaric (395–410) arrived outside Rome, a move which culminated in the city's sack in 410.

Melania and Pinianus' decision to follow the evangelical precept in Matthew 19:21[111] and divest themselves of their wealth was taken when they were not yet of age (20 and 24 respectively).[112] Thus, they depended on their peers' tolerance and the authorities' protection to achieve their goal. Their first move was not wisely chosen: in ca. 408 they enthusiastically commenced their renouncing endeavour by selling their estates in the *suburbium* of Rome, first-rate land cultivated by slaves, the production of which was highly commodified. The couple freed 8000 slaves, an act which led those remaining to revolt, as they did not wish to be freed or sold to new, dubious masters and probably be subjected to different conditions to which they had been accustomed. It seems that Pinianus failed to meet his obligations as *dominus* toward his inherited slaves. Freedom, on the other hand, especially with Alaric outside Rome, meant for slaves that they would lose their sustenance and protection in a time of crisis. Severus, Pinianus' brother, intervened to restrict this "folly" and to restore order to the family property and control over the workforce; he proposed to buy the slaves that remained at a low price. The slaves preferred Severus' solution, which the *Life* attributes to the Devil's influence, to their manumission.[113]

The Role of Imperial Intervention
in the Sale of the Couple's Property

It was in this context that, in early 408, the couple sought for the intervention of the "Empress" Serena—the niece and adopted daughter of Theodosius I (379–395), wife of the *magister militum* (master of the soldiers, i.e. commander-in-chief) Stilicho (d. 408), the most powerful man in the Western Empire, and mother-in-law of the Western Emperor Honorius (393–423).[114] They sought for her to facilitate the sale of their assets (including their slaves) throughout the Empire and to gain protection against those relatives who objected to the sale of family property (or wished) to appropriate the couple's property, according to the *Life*).[115] Serena persuaded Emperor Honorius to issue "a decree in every province that their possessions should be sold by the agency of the governors and ministers, and that [...] the money [...] should be remitted to Melania and Pinianus."[116] Peter Brown has plausibly interpreted this excerpt as follows:

> [...] an imperial edict [...] placed the couple's estates under a state of "positive proscription." The edict ruled that the estates [...] were considered, technically, to have been confiscated by the emperor. They became imperial property that could be sold off in public auctions. The governors, official staffs, and town councils of every province were made responsible for this sale. But the money thus raised would go to Pinianus and Melania, not to the imperial fisc.[117]

The story implies two further conjectures. The first is that the emperor could function as the ultimate arbiter in familial disputes within the elite concerning sensitive issues of ethos, status and property. The second is that this is yet another testimony attesting to the fact that the emperor was the regulator of the flow of gold. A hardly imaginable property, such as the one belonging to Melania and Pinianus, was probably difficult to liquidate without the emperor's consent and intervention. A vast amount of gold was required for such a sale, as well as a safe and relatively fast transfer of it from the provinces to Rome. Only the state was in a position to transform a large-scale sale into an immense amount of gold,[118] to validate its accumulation and to safeguard its transfer. Without the emperor's aid the couple would have never been able to liquidate their assets fast enough to avoid the sack of Rome by Alaric.

An unexpected turn of events occurred in August 408, when the once mighty Stilicho was executed, followed by Serena, after being accused by the Senate of complicity with Alaric. The Senate, feeling Alaric's breath on its neck and with the population on the brink of starvation, started to covet Melania and Pinianus' wealth so as to fill the public treasury. In February 409, Pompeianus, the prefect of Rome,[119] proposed to the Senate the confiscation of the couple's property, the pretext for this measure probably being their past association with Serena and Stilicho. But before Pompeianus had the chance to carry out this plan, he was killed by an angry crowd that rioted because of the shortage of bread; the riot was attributed to divine providence by the *Life of Melania*.[120]

Melania's "Poverty"

The couple, accompanied by Melania's mother, Albina, fled from Rome shortly before Alaric's entrance, to their estates first in Sicily and then in North Africa. Evidently they had not yet sold their estates in these regions, although they had already sold their property around Rome, Italy, Spain and Campania, according to the *Life*.[121] This remark offers an opportunity to comment on the couple's divesting strategy. Even though they did live ascetically and started dispersing their wealth before fleeing from Rome, they never reached such a level of renunciation as to be considered stripped of riches. In fact, they continued to hold substantial wealth. This is attested by recurring references throughout the *Life* concerning donations and the foundation or benefaction of monasteries by them.[122] Despite the massive generosity of Melania and Pinianus, portrayed as total renunciation of their wealth, a more careful examination shows that their income-generating capital investment in fixed assets was not disrupted. This permitted them to pursue benefaction for a long period of time, the only exception to this strategy being their initial attempts for property divestment, mentioned above.[123] It is notable that, despite her largesse, Melania's wealth appeared to be inexhaustible, and it is indicative that her *Life* mentions that she was left with only 50 gold coins before her death.[124] Fifty gold coins seem unimportant compared to other amounts of money mentioned in the *Life*, but this was not a pitiable sum for an ascetic. To make a rough comparison, when John Lydus in the early sixth century was appointed first *chartoularios* (a subaltern official) under Zoticus (*praefectus praetorio per Orientem* [praetorian prefect of the East], 511–512),[125] he earned an annual salary of 24 gold coins.[126] In any case, total disposal of wealth was never expected from women with the status of Melania.

A similar example is that of Saint Olympias (d. 408 [*BHG* 1374]) from Constantinople, who was also of elite status and enormously wealthy.[127] After being widowed, she embraced an ascetic way of life and was ordained deaconess. Apart from endowing the Constantinopolitan Church with estates and money, she supported John Chrysostom in his ministry and later in his exile. She became the patron of several other bishops, and supported priests and ascetics. She even founded a female monastery adjacent to the Great Church in Constantinople, which she populated with her relatives and chambermaids but also with women of senatorial status. It seems that for the elite, asceticism was not associated with absolute personal poverty but rather with a conceptual shift in the proper use of wealth, from civic to ecclesiastical benefaction.[128] It is worth mentioning that Palladius in the *Lausiac History* likens the offering of Melania's silk dresses to the altars to a similar donation by Olympias.[129]

Melania's *Life* makes interesting allusions to her aristocratic relation to money: she was still using it as a means to impose her will. For instance, her hagiographer readily admits that "Melania yearned so exceedingly for chastity that by *money* [emphasis ours] and admonitions she persuaded many young men and women to stay clear of licentiousness and an impure manner of life."[130] During a pilgrimage to the cells of anchorites in Egypt, she literally tried to stuff them with gold as she witnessed their poverty. However, a hermit, *abbas* Hephaestion, implicitly pointed to her stubborn naivety. After she unsuccessfully attempted to hide gold in his salt, he asked her of what use was gold in the desert. When she advised him to give it to those in need, the hermit reasonably replied that the poor were not able to come to the desert. After a long conversation the hermit remained adamant, and he finally threw the gold into a nearby river. But Melania did not give up, as she was not used to not having things go her way; although many other anchorites and virgins declined her offer, she nonetheless, "through a spiritual ruse" (*dia panourgias pneumatikēs*), left the gold in their cells.[131]

Coveted Patrons in Africa

Melania and Pinianus chose as the place of their residence in Africa a familial estate in the vicinity of the town of Thagaste, whose bishop was Alypius (since 394). Melania endowed the church of Alypius with revenue, offerings of gold and silver, and precious silk veils,[132] and thus she, the wealthy ascetic, made Alypius the bishop a client and dependent of her patronage.[133] This was not unprecedented, and bishops themselves often sought the active engagement of members of the elite in patronage practices which would benefit their sees and also offer the bishops credit as successful mediators between the "rich" and the "poor." Furthermore, Alypius was of a curial background himself and cognizant of the patronage system of relationships.[134]

According to the *Life of Melania*, other bishops in the province envied Alypius and the formerly poor church of Thagaste for their good fortune.[135] However, the *Life* does not mention that the flock of Augustine (bishop 396–430), in particular, was not restricted to envy but sought to actively promote its own prosperity. We only know from two epistles by Augustine (*Epp.* 125–126) that when Melania and Pinianus, escorted by Alypius, visited him at Hippo in 411, the local congregation forcefully demanded during a church service that Pinianus be made a priest there. Augustine's flock thought that this was a golden opportunity to bind to their city this idiosyncratic rich couple who freely scattered money. Yet the attempt failed, this incident remaining as a reminder that it was truly rare for the African congregations to encounter wealth such as that of Pinianus and Melania. The provinces were desperately looking for such patrons, and cities such as Hippo could not tolerate that others such as Thagaste were solely benefitted by their presence. Apparently, intercity rivalry and envy which used to stimulate philanthropy in the ancient world still appeared between—once pagan, now largely Christianized—communities.[136]

The African Bishops' Advice: A Turning Point in the Couple's Benefaction

It seems that the wealthy couple, and especially Melania, had a strong view on how to spend their riches. They could not be forced to live where others wanted, nor to use their wealth the way others desired. Freedom of choice was after all a privilege of their class. The *Life* implicitly points to the assumption that Melania and Pinianus' largesse in its "mature phase" was dispersed neither randomly nor indiscriminately, but that there was a rationale behind their generosity. Yet this rationale evolved gradually, from the first "amateurish" attempt to liquidate and simply scatter their wealth to organized patronage practices.[137] In a similar and related way, both versions of Melania's *Life*, the Greek and the Latin, reveal that in her "slow way" from Rome to Jerusalem she experimented with various forms of ascetic community: the villa-monastery in Rome, the traditional monastery in Africa and the private foundation in Palestine.[138] The holy couple tried different forms of beneficence and ascetic life on their "way to perfection." In this context, the counsel that was given to them by prominent bishops during the first period of their stay in Africa seems to have signalled a turning point in their dispersing strategy.

> When they arrived there, they immediately sold their property in Numidia, Mauretania, and in Africa itself. Some of the money they sent for the service of the poor and some for ransoming captives. Thus they distributed the money freely [...]. When the blessed ones decided to sell all their property, the most saintly and important bishops of Africa (I mean the blessed Augustine, his brother Alypius, and Aurelius of Carthage) advised them, saying, "The money that you now furnish to monasteries will be used up in a short time. If you wish to have memorial forever in heaven and on earth, give both a house and an income to each monastery."[139]

The African prelates' responsibilities involved the efficient management of ecclesiastical property (including what they had donated to their Churches),[140] and they knew first-hand the limitations of one-off donations. The deeper meaning behind their counsel was that the ever-present need for sustainable benefaction both to the religious and the lay poor required "efficient investment projects," rather than praiseworthy yet occasional acts of beneficence. Steadfastness was the key, and this was not the first time that Church Fathers offered lessons on economic efficiency. Late Roman bishops were preoccupied not only with prompting the elite's philanthropic activity but also with attempting to channel the elite's patronage practices into regular recurring donations, as we have discussed in the fourth chapter. As the manager of his Church, a bishop had to develop a plan for long-term staffing, church maintenance and poor relief; the more recurrent the revenues, the more feasible the bishop's planning. However, the patronage class more often than not preferred one-off donations (e.g., the foundation of a building), which engaged visibility and caused envy among their peers, unlike endowments, which produced recurring revenue (e.g., an estate) but were less visible.[141]

The African bishops' advice signifies the top level of benefaction in patristic exhortations, that is, steadfast benefaction which could be undertaken by elite members. Liquidating an estate and donating the money was less preferable than endowing the estate upon a monastic institution. Following this line of reasoning, the liquidation and random dispersal of one's wealth, besides being a spectacular act, could hardly be considered economically efficient in the long run.

The *Life* stresses that Melania and Pinianus eagerly conformed to this advice. They founded in Thagaste two great monasteries, a male and a female, providing them with a sufficient income, as the bishops had advised.[142] Yet these African foundations were the starting point which led Melania to the establishment of new ascetic communities in private foundations in Jerusalem (the couple and Albina arrived there probably in 417). The establishment of institutions like these raised various ecclesiastical, economic and legal issues, among which was the thorny question of the level of episcopal control.[143] Until the mid-fifth century, private founders/owners were almost uncontrolled in the construction, endowment and management of their foundations. The Council of Chalcedon (451) strengthened the bishop's authority, stipulating, for example, that no foundation was to be constructed without episcopal approval (can. 4) or that all clergy was to be subordinated to the local bishop (can. 8).[144]

It seems that the African bishops' advice was finally adapted to the new aristocratic euergetism that Melania and Pinianus represented. Instead of endowing established monasteries under a bishop's control, they preferred to found and support their own. Melania created monumental buildings and monastic communities in Jerusalem that constituted her legacy, which she was determined to maintain, unlike the temporal property she and Pinianus once had in Rome. It appears that she never really lost her property consciousness, which was peculiar to the elite (as we have already discussed in the fourth chapter, commenting on the bequest of Gregory of Nazianzus); it was just transformed by her ascetic ideals.[145] Moreover, the fact that she had prematurely lost her children perhaps promoted her preference for spiritual over familial bonds, which was a Christian attitude.[146] She was now the mother of a new, extended family comprising her monastic institutions, and her transformed elite mentality dictated the bequest and allocation of her assets to her spiritual children. This was the family line that she wanted to preserve. Was it a coincidence that, on her deathbed, she asked Gerontius to assume the care of the monasteries, exhorting him "to be even more solicitous to submit to toil for their sakes"?[147]

Transferring Monetary Capital in the Mediterranean

From the third century onwards, wealthy Christians in the West employed new strategies in the pursuit of salvation, by channelling their financial surplus to devotional activities that served the need for protecting their souls in the afterlife. This fact resulted in a deeper change in the perceptions of the proper use of money that resonated with the new socio-economic transformations and initiated further reflection on the spiritual implications of monetary resources.[148] In this context, pious donations were in no way unprecedented for the aristocracy in the western part of the Empire, but the Barbarian intrusions in the early fifth century gave an impetus to this trend.[149] The precariousness of landed wealth could be counter-balanced by its liquidation (partial at least) into gold, and the ascetic ideals that were appealing to some members of the senatorial aristocracy guaranteed that a considerable part of this gold would be channelled toward monastic communities.

Melania's status, wealth and network of monastic institutions which received her benefactions made her a formidable ecclesiastical patron. Palladius makes an appraisal of Melania's munificence in the *Lausiac History*, and refers to the transfer of significant sums to the East, which Melania sent by sea as soon as she and Pinianus had partially liquidated their properties: 10,000 *solidi* to Egypt and the Thebaid; 10,000 to Antioch and its district; 15,000 to Palestine; and 10,000 to the churches in the islands and the places of exile.[150] These sums were part of the wealth that rich refugees brought to the East due to the Barbarian incursions.[151] They are also indicative of the fact that the couple's benefactions were channelled primarily toward monks, not the poor.[152] This is not to say that Melania and Pinianus were indifferent to the needs of the lay poor; indeed, references to their benefaction toward them are found throughout the *Life*. Yet emphasis was given to supporting the needs of the religious poor: entire islands were bought for ascetics, and monasteries were purchased to be given to the monks and virgins living there, and were also endowed with sufficient income.[153]

Melania and Pinianus' strategy of wealth dispersion also included an active involvement in church politics.[154] This seems unavoidable for senatorial aristocrats who dispersed huge sums of money; sooner or later they would have to choose sides and affect with their wealth the outcome of ecclesiastical controversies. Melania and Pinianus financially supported the "Johannites," John Chrysostom's adherents, who, after their leader's deposition and exile from Constantinople (404), had been scattered all over the East. The ascetic couple's active support of the Johannites sustained this ecclesiastical faction until its return to Constantinople.[155] The wealth from the West supported the cause of an ecclesiastical party in the East.

The *Life* of Melania reveals in many ways how complex and unpredictable were the consequences of the call for wealth divestment and redistribution. The surplus of the thoughtful rich was not necessarily channelled into almsgiving. Often it was carefully "invested" in establishing and supporting private institutions or shaping church politics.

Notes

1. K. W. Harl, *Coinage in the Roman Economy, 300 B.C. to A.D. 700*. Ancient Society and History. (Baltimore, MD: Johns Hopkins University Press, 1996), 126.
2. C. Howgego, *Ancient History from Coins*. Approaching the Ancient World (London: Routledge, 1995), 125.
3. Harl, *Coinage*, 128. See also Howgego, *Ancient History*, 131.
4. On Gresham's Law, especially in connection with coin finds, see M. Asolati and G. Gorini, eds., *I ritrovamenti monetali e la legge di Gresham*. Numismatica Patavina, 8 (Padua: Esedra, 2006). R. Mundell ("Uses and Abuses of Gresham's Law in the History of Money," *Zagreb Journal of Economics* 2.2 [1998]: 3–38 [repr. in *I ritrovamenti monetali*, eds. Asolati and Gorini, 195–222]) corrects the common expression that summarizes Gresham's Law, "bad money drives out good," to "cheap money drives out dear, if they exchange for the same price." On the relationship of this economic law to debasement processes, see, e.g., T. J. Sargent and B. D. Smith, "Coinage, Debasements, and Gresham's Laws," *Economic Theory* 10.2 (1997): 197–226.
5. Harl, *Coinage*, 128–131.
6. C. Vlachou-Mogire, B. Stern and J. G. McDonnell, "The Application of LA-ICP-MS in the Examination of the Thin Plating Layers Found in Late Roman Coins," *Nuclear Instruments and Methods in Physics Research* B 265 (2007): 558.
7. Harl, *Coinage*, 132.
8. Harl, *Coinage*, 132–134.
9. A. Burnett, *Coinage in the Roman World* (London: Seaby, 1987), 113–114.

10. S. Estiot, "The Later Third Century," in *The Oxford Handbook of Greek and Roman Coinage*, ed. W. E. Metcalf (Oxford: Oxford University Press, 2012), 544. These years also witnessed the gradual demise of the Roman Provincial coinages, most of which did not survive the 270s; a major exception is the coinage of Alexandria, which was ended under Diocletian. See Harl, *Coinage*, 136–143, 150.
11. Harl, *Coinage*, 134–135.
12. On Aurelian's reform, see Burnett, *Coinage*, 124–126; Harl, *Coinage*, 143–148; Estiot, "Later Third Century," 545–548.
13. Burnett, *Coinage*, 128–129.
14. It should be stressed that the *aureus* was henceforth known as *solidus*, but by convention scholars prefer to reserve this name for the Constantinian gold coin; Harl, *Coinage*, 149; R. Abdy, "Tetrarchy and the House of Constantine," in *Oxford Handbook of Greek and Roman Coinage*, ed. Metcalf, 589.
15. M. F. Hendy, *Studies in the Byzantine Monetary Economy, c. 300–1450* (Cambridge: Cambridge University Press, 1985), 449; Harl, *Coinage*, 149; Estiot, "Later Third Century," 548.
16. For an excellent overview of the phenomena of saving from late Roman to early Byzantine times (ca. 301–650), see Y. Stoyas, "Φαινόμενα αποταμίευσης από τους υστερορωμαϊκούς στους βυζαντινούς χρόνους, περ. 301–650," in *Αποταμίευση και διαχείριση χρήματος στην ελληνική ιστορία*, eds. K. Bouraselis and K. Meidani (Athens: Tachydromiko Tamieutērio Hellados, 2011), 219–246. For the practices of saving and coin hoards in the fourth to fifth centuries, see Y. Stoyas, "Πρακτικές αποταμίευσης και νομισματικοί «θησαυροί», 4ος–15ος αι.," in *Αποταμίευση και διαχείριση χρήματος*, eds. Bouraselis and Meidani, 364–369.
17. Harl, *Coinage* 149, 152–156. On the *aurelianianus*, see ibid., 146.
18. Burnett, *Coinage*, 117. The Price Edict contains invaluable evidence of the prosperity Romans enjoyed and, more importantly, of the living standards of labourers who were in a position to earn just enough to have access to a minimal subsistence consumption basket. For a comparative perspective on different historical periods and geographical areas regarding these issues, see R. C. Allen, "How Prosperous Were the Romans? Evidence from Diocletian's Price Edict (AD 301)," in *Quantifying the Roman Economy: Methods and Problems*, eds. A. Bowman and A. Wilson. Oxford Studies on the Roman Economy (Oxford: Oxford University Press, 2009), 327–345.
19. Hendy, *Studies*, 458–459.
20. Harl, *Coinage*, 477 (glossary); Abdy, "Tetrarchy," 586.
21. Hendy, *Studies*, 450–451; Harl, *Coinage*, 153; Abdy, "Tetrarchy," 588–589.

22. A. H. M. Jones, *The Later Roman Empire, 284–602: A Social, Economic and Administrative Survey*, 3 vols. (Oxford: Blackwell, 1964), vol. 1, 61; Burnett, *Coinage*, 117.
23. Lactantius, *De mortibus persecutorum* 7.6–7 (ed. A. Städele, *Laktanz, De mortibus persecutorum / Die Todesarten der Verfolger*. Fontes Christiani, 43 [Turnhout: Brepols, 2003], 106).
24. Harl, *Coinage*, 154.
25. Harl, *Coinage*, 153–154.
26. Burnett, *Coinage*, 119.
27. Harl, *Coinage*, 158–159.
28. Harl, *Coinage*, 164.
29. Cf. P. Oslo 3 83. See Trismegistos nos. 17308 [P. Ryl. 4 607] and 21530 [P. Oslo 3 83] in: www.trismegistos.org.
30. See R. S. Bagnall, *Currency and Inflation in Fourth Century Egypt*. Bulletin of the American Society of Papyrologists, Supplements, 5 ([Chico, CA]: Scholars Press, 1985), 12–15; Hendy, *Studies*, 463–464; Burnett, *Coinage*, 116; Harl, *Coinage*, 165; Abdy, "Tetrarchy," 591–592.
31. Harl, *Coinage*, 165.
32. Hendy, *Studies*, 464.
33. Harl, *Coinage*, 167–168, Table 7.3.
34. On the *tremissis*, see Harl, *Coinage*, 175, 177–178; S. Moorhead, "The Coinage of the Later Roman Empire, 364–498," in *Oxford Handbook of Greek and Roman Coinage*, ed. Metcalf, 604–605.
35. Hendy, *Studies*, 475–492; Burnett, *Coinage*, 154–155; Harl, *Coinage*, 192–193.
36. Harl, *Coinage*, 178–179.
37. J. Banaji, "Economic Trajectories," in *The Oxford Handbook of Late Antiquity*, ed. S. F. Johnson (Oxford: Oxford University Press, 2012), 597 (= *idem*, "The Economic Trajectories of Late Antiquity," in *idem*, *Exploring the Economy of Late Antiquity: Selected Essays* [Cambridge: Cambridge University Press, 2016], 61).
38. For the discussion of the policy of gold coining in the Constantinian Empire, see P. Bruun, *Studies in Constantinian Chronology*. Numismatic Notes and Monographs, 146 (New York: American Numismatic Society, 1961), 76–77, and also L. Ramskold, "Constantine's Vicennalia and the Death of Crispus," *Niš & Byzantium* 11 (2013): 412, 415–418.
39. J. Banaji, *Agrarian Change in Late Antiquity: Gold, Labour, and Aristocratic Dominance*. Oxford Classical Monographs (2nd edn. Oxford: Oxford University Press, 2007), 41, 47; P. Brown, *Through the Eye of a Needle: Wealth, the Fall of Rome, and the Making of Christianity in the West, 350–550 AD*. (Princeton, NJ: Princeton University Press, 2012), 14.

40. Harl, *Coinage*, 159; Abdy, "Tetrarchy," 591.
41. Banaji, *Agrarian Change*, 45.
42. Harl, *Coinage*, 159.
43. Banaji, *Agrarian Change*, 40.
44. Banaji, *Agrarian Change*, 41.
45. *De rebus bellicis* 2.1–4 (ed. A. Giardina, *Anonimo, Le cose della guerra*. Scrittori Greci e Latini [Milan: A. Mondadori, 1989], 12); Eng. trans. E. A. Thompson, *A Roman Reformer and Inventor, Being a New Text of the Treatise* De Rebus Bellicis (Oxford: Clarendon Press, 1952), 110: "It was in the age of Constantine that extravagant grants assigned gold instead of bronze (which earlier was considered of great value) to petty commercial transactions; but the greed I speak of is thought to have arisen from the following causes. When the gold and silver and the huge quantity of precious stones which had been stored away in the temples long ago reached the public, they enkindled all men's possessive and spendthrift instincts. And while the expenditure of bronze itself [...] had seemed already vast and burdensome enough, yet from some kind of blind folly there ensued an even more extravagant passion for spending gold, which is considered more precious. This store of gold meant that the houses of the powerful were crammed full and their splendour enhanced to the destruction of the poor, the poorer classes of course being held down by force." See the comments of S. Mazzarino, *Aspetti sociali del quarto secolo. Ricerche di storia tardo-romana*. Problemi e Ricerche di Storia Antica, 1 (Rome: "L'Erma" di Bretschneider, 1951), 110; Jones, *The Later Roman Empire*, vol. 1, 108–109.
46. Banaji, *Agrarian Change*, 88.
47. Banaji, *Agrarian Change*, 47–48. See also Banaji, "Economic Trajectories," 597 (= *idem*, "Economic Trajectories of Late Antiquity," 61).
48. Mazzarino, *Aspetti sociali*.
49. For an interesting discussion on the anonymous author's identity and rationale behind the writing of this treatise, see C. Grubaugh, "The Anonymous *De rebus bellicis* and the Ethics of Empire in Late Antiquity: A Problem in Intellectual History," *Clio's Scroll* 17.1 (2015): 3–25 (where earlier bibliography is cited).
50. J. Banaji, "Precious Metal Coinages and Monetary Expansion in Late Antiquity," in *idem, Exploring the Economy of Late Antiquity*, 112.
51. Banaji, *Agrarian Change*, 48.
52. Ammianus Marcellinus, *Rerum gestarum libri* 16.8.12 (ed. W. Seyfarth, *Ammianus Marcellinus, Römische Geschichte. Lateinisch und Deutsch und mit einem Kommentar*, 4 vols. Schriften und Quellen der Alten Welt, 21.1–4 [Berlin: Akademie-Verlag, 1968–1971], vol. 1, 172); Eng.

trans. J. C. Rolfe, *Ammianus Marcellinus*, 3 vols. LCL 300, 315, 331 (Cambridge, MA: Harvard University Press, 1935–1939), vol. 1, 239.
53. *De rebus bellicis* 4.1–2 (ed. Giardina, *Anonimo, Le cose della guerra*, 14).
54. Banaji, *Agrarian Change*, 49–51.
55. Ammianus Marcellinus, *Rerum gestarum libri* 27.9.4 (Seyfarth, *Ammianus Marcellinus, Römische Geschichte*, vol. 4, 78–79).
56. Banaji, "Economic Trajectories," 600 (= *idem*, "Economic Trajectories of Late Antiquity," 65).
57. Banaji, *Agrarian Change*, 116.
58. *CTh* 12.6.12 (366), 12.6.13 (367). Cf. two later but relevant laws *CTh* 10.24.3 (381), 1.10.7 (401); see Hendy, *Studies*, 388.
59. Moorhead, "Coinage," 602.
60. Hendy, *Studies*, 386–394, 399; Harl, *Coinage*, 159–160; Moorhead, "Coinage," 602–603.
61. On forging and clipping the coinage and the legislation against these practices, see P. Grierson, "The Roman Law of Counterfeiting," in *Essays in Roman Coinage Presented to Harold Mattingly*, eds. R. A. G. Carson and C. H. V. Sutherland (London: Oxford University Press, 1956), 240–261; Hendy, *Studies*, 316–328, 363–364; V. Penna, "Βυζαντινό νόμισμα και παραχαράκτες," in *Έγκλημα και τιμωρία στο Βυζάντιο*, ed. S. N. Troianos (Athens: Idryma Goulandri-Horn, 1997), 273–294; Moorhead, "Coinage," 612–614. On the definition of counterfeit, forgery and imitation, see the relevant entries in R. G. Doty, *The Macmillan Encyclopedic Dictionary of Numismatics* (New York: Macmillan, 1982).
62. Hendy, *Studies*, 329–333, 364–366; P. Guest, "Roman Gold and Hun Kings: The Use and Hoarding of Solidi in the Late Fourth and Fifth Centuries," in *Roman Coins outside the Empire: Ways and Phases, Contexts and Functions*, eds. A. Bursche, R. Ciołek and R. Wolters. Collection Moneta, 82 (Wetteren: Moneta, 2008), 300.
63. C. Morrisson, "Imperial Generosity and Its Monetary Expression: The Rise and Decline of the 'Largesses'," in *Donation et donateurs dans le monde byzantin*, eds. J.-M. Spieser and É. Yota. Réalités Byzantines, 14 (Paris: Desclée de Brouwer, 2012), 25–27; Guest, "Roman Gold," 299–300. On the functions of the *comes sacrarum largitionum*, see also Jones, *The Later Roman Empire*, vol. 1, 369–370, 427–438; vol. 2, 624–625, 835.
64. *CTh* 15.9.1.
65. *CJ* 12.3.2.
66. Hendy, *Studies*, 193–195; Morrisson, "Imperial Generosity," 30–32.
67. Guest, "Roman Gold," 299; Moorhead, "Coinage," 605.

68. John Lydus, *De magistratibus populi romani libri tres* 3.43 (ed. A. C. Bandy, *Ioannes Lydus, On Powers, or, The Magistracies of the Roman State*. Memoirs of the American Philosophical Society, 149 [Philadelphia, PA: The American Philosophical Society, 1983], 200).
69. Harl, *Coinage*, 310; Moorhead, "Coinage," 607–608.
70. Burnett, *Coinage*, 152; Moorhead, "Coinage," 607.
71. Hendy, *Studies*, 221, 226; Harl, *Coinage*, 176; Moorhead, "Coinage," 611.
72. Hendy, *Studies*, 226–227.
73. Procopius, *Historia arcana* 19.7–8 (ed. J. Haury and G. Wirth, *Procopii Caesariensis opera omnia*, 4 vols. BSGRT [Leipzig: B.G. Teubner, 1962–1964], vol. 3, 121). Cf. Hendy, *Studies*, 224, 226; Harl, *Coinage*, 176 and 433 (n. 46).
74. Banaji, "Precious Metal Coinages," 116–117 and n. 34.
75. *NVal* 16.1; Eng. trans. C. Pharr, *The Theodosian Code and Novels, and the Sirmondian Constitutions*. Corpus of Roman Law, 1 (Princeton, NJ: Princeton University Press, 1952), 530: "never shall a solidus be sold for less than seven thousand nummi if it was bought from a money changer for seven thousand two hundred nummi. For uniformity of price shall protect both the welfare of the seller and the established prices of all salable goods." See Burnett, *Coinage*, 151; also Hendy, *Studies*, 364–366, 477; Moorhead, "Coinage," 621; S. Cosentino, "Banking in Early Byzantine Ravenna," *Cahiers de Recherches Médiévales et Humanistes* 28.2 (2014): 244. On the *collectarii/kollektarioi*, see R. Bogaert, "La banque en Égypte byzantine," *Zeitschrift für Papyrologie und Epigraphik* 116 (1997): 93–95, 127–128; D. Gofas, "La banque lieu de rencontre et instrument d'échange à Byzance," *Cahiers du Centre Gustave Glotz* 7 (1996): 146–147.
76. Banaji, "Economic Trajectories," 598–599 (= *idem*, "Economic Trajectories of Late Antiquity," 62–63).
77. P. Sarris, "The Early Byzantine Economy in Context: Aristocratic Property and Economic Growth Reconsidered," *Early Medieval Europe* 19.3 (2011): 257; Banaji, *Agrarian Change*, 129. On the formation of early Byzantine aristocracy, the various regional groups that constituted it and their particularities, see Banaji, *Agrarian Change*, 127–170.
78. M. Whittow, "Ruling the Late Roman and Early Byzantine City: A Continuous History," *Past & Present* 129 (1990): 3–29, has argued that the history of the elites that ruled the Roman cities in Syro-Palestine, Asia Minor and Greece between the fourth and the early seventh century was continuous. They had the ability to adapt to new circumstances and therefore to survive with their power rather intact. See also *idem*, "Early Medieval Byzantium and the End of the Ancient World," *Journal of Agrarian Change* 9.1 (2009): 140–141.

79. P. Sarris, "Social Relations and the Land: The Early Period," in *The Social History of Byzantium*, ed. J. Haldon (Chichester: Wiley-Blackwell, 2009), 101, 108–109.
80. Banaji, "Precious Metal Coinages," 114–115.
81. On the structure of elite landholding and its socio-economic implications, with reference to the related legal evidence, see P. Sarris, "Rehabilitating the Great Estate: Aristocratic Property and Economic Growth in the Late Antique East," in *Recent Research on the Late Antique Countryside*, eds. W. Bowden, L. Lavan and C. Machado. Late Antique Archaeology, 2 (Leiden and Boston, MA: Brill, 2004), 64–68; *idem*, "The Origins of the Manorial Economy: New Insights from Late Antiquity," *English Historical Review* 119 (2004): 279–311 (repr. in *Late Antiquity on the Eve of Islam*, ed. A. Cameron. The Formation of the Classical Islamic World, 1 [Farnham: Ashgate, 2013], 109–141); *idem*, *Economy and Society in the Age of Justinian* (Cambridge: Cambridge University Press, 2006), 29–49; *idem*, "Social Relations," 99–104; *idem*, "Early Byzantine Economy in Context," 255–284. Cf. T. M. Hickey, "Aristocratic Landholding and the Economy of Byzantine Egypt," in *Egypt in the Byzantine World, 300–700*, ed. R. S. Bagnall (Cambridge: Cambridge University Press, 2007), 288–308. On the Apions, see the overview in C. Wickham, *Framing the Early Middle Ages: Europe and the Mediterranean, 400–800* (Oxford: Oxford University Press, 2005), 242–249.
82. Sarris, *Economy and Society*, 129.
83. Banaji, "Economic Trajectories," 607 (= *idem*, "Economic Trajectories of Late Antiquity," 75–76).
84. A. Čekalova, "Fortune des sénateurs de Constantinople du IVe au début du VIIe siècle," in *EYΨYXIA: Mélanges offerts à Hélène Ahrweiler*, 2 vols. Byzantina Sorbonensia, 16 (Paris: Publications de la Sorbonne, 1998), vol. 1, 119–130.
85. Banaji, "Economic Trajectories," 597–624 (= *idem*, "Economic Trajectories of Late Antiquity," 61–88).
86. Greg. Naz., *Or.* 6.5: *De pace* 1 (ed. M.-A. Calvet-Sebasti, *Grégoire de Nazianze, Discours 6–12*. SC, 405 [Paris: Les Éditions du Cerf, 1995], 132); *Or.* 19: *Ad Julianum tributorum exaequatorem* (PG 35, 1045). See G. Merianos, "Literary Allusions to Trade and Merchants: The 'Great Merchant' in Late Twelfth-Century Byzantium," in *Byzantium, 1180–1204: 'The Sad Quarter of a Century'?* ed. A. Simpson. International Symposium, 22 (Athens: National Hellenic Research Foundation, Institute of Historical Research, 2015), 230–231. On the term μεγαλέμπορος (*megalemporos*), see LSJ; Lampe; Sophocles.
87. Eng. trans. NRSV: "Again, the kingdom of heaven is like a merchant in search of fine pearls; on finding one pearl of great value, he went and sold all that he had and bought it."

88. Greg. Naz., *Carmina dogmatica* 27 (PG 37, 500).
89. *De rebus bellicis*, Praef. 9 (Giardina, *Anonimo, Le cose della guerra*, 6). Cf. J. Banaji, "Mass Production, Monetary Economy and the Commercial Vitality of the Mediterranean," in idem, *Exploring the Economy of Late Antiquity*, 4–5.
90. R. Bogaert, "Changeurs et banquiers chez les Pères de l'Église," *Ancient Society* 4 (1973): 269; S. Cosentino, "Banking," 243. For a bibliography on banking activities in late antiquity and the early Byzantine period, see Cosentino, "Banking," 245 n. 1.
91. Basil, *Regulae brevius tractatae* 254 (PG 31, 1252). Cf. Bogaert, "Changeurs et banquiers," 256; idem, "La banque en Égypte byzantine," 97, 123.
92. Chrysostom, *Princ. Act. hom.* 4.2 (PG 51, 99). Cf. Bogaert, "Changeurs et banquiers," 257–258; C. Rapp, "Spiritual Guarantors at Penance, Baptism, and Ordination in the Late Antique East," in *A New History of Penance*, ed. A. Firey. Brill's Companions to the Christian Tradition, 14 (Leiden and Boston, MA: Brill, 2008), 132 n. 36.
93. D. Janes, *God and Gold in Late Antiquity* (Cambridge: Cambridge University Press, 1998), 18; L. James, *Light and Colour in Byzantine Art*. Clarendon Studies in the History of Art, 15 (Oxford: Clarendon Press, 1996), 107.
94. Cf. Brown, *Eye of a Needle*, 16.
95. Asterius of Amasea, *Serm.* 3.12.2 (ed. C. Datema, *Asterius of Amasea, Homilies I-XIV* [Leiden: Brill, 1970], 35).
96. Janes, *God and Gold*, 91.
97. Janes, *God and Gold*, 91–92.
98. H. Rhee, *Loving the Poor, Saving the Rich: Wealth, Poverty, and Early Christianity* (Grand Rapids, MI: Baker Academic, 2012), Chap. 5.
99. *CTh* 12.7.1; Eng. trans. Pharr, *Theodosian Code*, 377: "The same ratio must be observed also if any person should pay gold bullion, so that he shall appear to have paid solidi." For an interpretation, see Hendy, *Studies*, 330.
100. *SH, Vis.* 4.1.10 [22], 4.3.4 [24]. Two of the references are to the colour of gold and two to the metal.
101. On the Western senatorial aristocracy, see Wickham, *Framing the Early Middle Ages*, 156–166. He stresses, of course, that the wealthiest senatorial families were all based in Rome (ibid., 163).
102. *VitMelGr* 17 (p. 160); Eng. trans. E. A. Clark, *The Life of Melania the Younger*. Studies in Women and Religion, 14 (New York: The Edwin Mellen Press, 1984), 39–40. Cf. *VitMelL* 17.1-3 (pp. 186–188). See Brown, *Eye of a Needle*, 17. On the ascetic couple, see *PLRE* 1, 593 (Melania 2), 702 (Valerius Pinianus 2).
103. *VitMelGr* 12 (p. 148); Eng. trans. Clark, *Life of Melania*, 35. Cf. *VitMelL* 12.1 (p. 176). On various aspects of this meeting, see Janes,

God and Gold, 159; J. E. Salisbury, *Rome's Christian Empress: Galla Placidia Rules at the Twilight of the Empire* (Baltimore, MD: Johns Hopkins University Press, 2015), 57–58.

104. On the two versions, see M. Detoraki, "Copie sous dictée et bains monastique. Deux renseignements propres à la *Vie* latine de sainte Mélanie la Jeune," *Jahrbuch für Antike und Christentum* 47 (2004): 98–107.

105. See B. Flusin, "Palestinian Hagiography (Fourth–Eighth Centuries)," in *The Ashgate Research Companion to Byzantine Hagiography*, vol. 1: *Periods and Places*, ed. S. Efthymiadis (Farnham: Ashgate, 2011), 204–205.

106. *VitMelGr* 1 (p. 132); 5, 6 (p. 136). Cf. *VitMelL* 1.4 (p. 158); 5.3, 6.5 (p. 164).

107. It is noteworthy that attitudes favouring total renunciation of possessions, like those epitomized in the *Life* of Melania the Younger, represented a deliberate personal choice. In an Origenian-Evagrian line of reasoning, on which Melania's spirituality was seemingly grounded, reducing one's wealth was an intrinsically just and good act, since excess wealth was tantamount to theft from the poor. Yet this stance was considered potentially subversive in late Roman society; see I. L. E. Ramelli, *Social Justice and the Legitimacy of Slavery: The Role of Philosophical Asceticism from Ancient Judaism to Late Antiquity*. OECS (Oxford: Oxford University Press, 2016), 223. Total renunciation of wealth was far from being uncontroversial, and it did not dominate fifth-century Christian discourse on proper management of financial resources. Leo the Great, for instance, did not consider total divestment as a prerequisite for attaining spiritual perfection. In Leo's traditional view, the wealthy were socially beneficial if they could turn their surplus money into a source of charitable donations to a network of church institutions mediating the distribution of humanitarian care for the needy; see S. Wessel, *Passion and Compassion in Early Christianity* (New York: Cambridge University Press, 2016), 144. Hoarding could not be countenanced, because it contravened the primary purpose of wealth: excess wealth was perceived as stemming from divine largesse and it "was thereby construed as the instrument through which God enabled virtuous Christians to perform charitable deeds"; see S. Wessel, *Leo the Great and the Spiritual Rebuilding of a Universal Rome*. SupVC, 93 (Leiden: Brill, 2008), 201.

108. *VitMelGr* 15 (pp. 156–158). Cf. *VitMelL* 15.1 (p. 184). See Hendy, *Studies*, 202; Brown, *Eye of a Needle*, 295.

109. On all three aspects, see Clark, *Life of Melania*, 95–100.

110. See, for instance, L. L. Coon, *Sacred Fictions: Holy Women and Hagiography in Late Antiquity*. The Middle Ages Series (Philadelphia,

PA: University of Pennsylvania Press, 1997), 109–119; K. Cooper, "Gender and the Fall of Rome," in *A Companion to Late Antiquity*, ed. P. Rousseau (with the assistance of J. Raithel). Blackwell Companions to the Ancient World (Chichester: Wiley-Blackwell, 2009), 187, 198–199; J. Evans-Grubbs, "Marriage and Family Relationships in the Late Roman West," in *Companion to Late Antiquity*, ed. Rousseau, 207–212.

111. Eng. trans. NRSV: "If you wish to be perfect, go, sell your possessions, and give the money to the poor, and you will have treasure in heaven; then come, follow me."

112. *VitMelGr* 8 (p. 140) [on the couple's age]; 9 (p. 144) [on the evangelical precept]. Cf. *VitMelL* 8.1 (p. 168); 9.2 (p. 172) respectively.

113. *VitMelGr* 10 (pp. 144–146); cf. *VitMelL* 10.1 (p. 172); Palladius, *Historia Lausiaca* 61.5 (ed. G. J. M. Bartelink, trans. M. Barchiesi, *Palladio, La Storia Lausiaca*. Scrittori Greci e Latini; Vite dei Santi, 2. [(Milan): Fondazione Lorenzo Valla and A. Mondadori, 1974], 266). On various implications of the couple's decision to sell or manumit their slaves in Rome, such as Pinianus' failure to meet his obligations to his dependents, see A. Giardina, "Carità eversiva: le donazioni di Melania la giovane e gli equilibri della società tardoromana," *Studi Storici* 29.1 (1988): 136–140; C. Lepelley, "Mélanie la Jeune, entre Rome, la Sicile et l'Afrique: les effets socialement pernicieux d'une forme extrême de l'ascétisme," *ΚΩΚΑΛΟΣ: Studi pubblicati dall'Istituto di Storia Antica dell'Università di Pallermo* 43–44.1.1 (1997–1998): 21–23; K. Cooper, "Poverty, Obligation, and Inheritance: Roman Heiresses and the Varieties of Senatorial Christianity in Fifth-Century Rome," in *Religion, Dynasty, and Patronage in Early Christian Rome, 300–900*, eds. K. Cooper and J. Hillner (Cambridge: Cambridge University Press, 2007), 165–166; eadem, *The Fall of the Roman Household* (Cambridge: Cambridge University Press, 2007), 116–117; Brown, *Eye of a Needle*, 296–297.

114. On Serena and Stilicho, see *PLRE* 1, 824 (Serena), 853–858 (Flavius Stilicho).

115. *VitMelGr* 11–12 (pp. 146–152).

116. *VitMelGr* 12 (p. 152); Eng. trans. Clark, *Life of Melania*, 37. Cf. *VitMelL* 12.9 (p. 180).

117. Brown, *Eye of a Needle*, 297–298.

118. According to *VitMelL* 15.5 (p. 184), the sales involved different means of exchange: *aurum* (gold), *argentum* (silver) and *cautiones* (bonds). See Hendy, *Studies*, 202.

119. *PLRE* 2, 897–898 (Gabinius Barbarus Pompeianus 2).

120. *VitMelGr* 19 (p. 166). G. D. Dunn, "The Poverty of Melania the Younger and Pinianus," *Augustinianum* 54.1 (2014): 105–106, speculates on the reason behind Pompeianus' attempt to confiscate the couple's property.

121. *VitMelGr* 19 (p. 164). Cf. *VitMelL* 19.6 (p. 192); Palladius, *Historia Lausiaca* 61.5 (ed. Bartelink, *Palladio, La Storia Lausiaca*, 266).
122. R. Alciati and M. Giorda, "Possessions and Asceticism: Melania the Younger and Her Slow Way to Jerusalem," *ZAC* 14 (2010): 426, 432–433; also Evans-Grubbs, "Marriage," 210.
123. See Dunn, "Poverty of Melania," 93–115.
124. *VitMelGr* 30 (p. 184). Cf. *VitMelL* 30.2 (p. 208). See Coon, *Sacred Fictions*, 117–118.
125. *PLRE* 2, 1206–1207 (Zoticus).
126. John Lydus, *De magistratibus populi romani libri tres* 3.27 (ed. Bandy, *Ioannes Lydus, On Powers*, 174). Cf. Banaji, "Economic Trajectories," 608 (= *idem*, "Economic Trajectories of Late Antiquity," 76). On the office of *chartoularios*, see A. Kazhdan, "Chartoularios," in *ODB*, vol. 1, 416.
127. See *Vita Olympiadis* (ed. A.-M. Malingrey, *Jean Chrysostome, Lettres à Olympias. Seconde édition augmentée de la Vie anonyme d'Olympias*. SC, 13bis [Paris: Les Éditions du Cerf, 1968], 406–448).
128. W. Mayer, "Poverty and Generosity toward the Poor in the Time of John Chrysostom," in *Wealth and Poverty in Early Church and Society*, ed. S. R. Holman. Holy Cross Studies in Patristic Theology and History (Grand Rapids, MI: Baker Academic, 2008), 143–146. On Olympias, see also *PLRE* 1, 642–643 (Olympias 2); G. Dagron, *Naissance d'une capitale. Constantinople et ses institutions de 330 à 451*. Bibliothèque Byzantine, Études, 7 (Paris: Presses Universitaires de France, 1974), 501–506; W. Mayer and P. Allen, *John Chrysostom*. ECF (London: Routledge, 2000), 49.
129. Palladius, *Historia Lausiaca* 61.3 (ed. Bartelink, *Palladio, La Storia Lausiaca*, 266). On the dispersal of Olympias' riches to the poor, see Palladius, *Historia Lausiaca* 56.2 (ibid., 252).
130. *VitMelGr* 29 (p. 182); Eng. trans. Clark, *Life of Melania*, 47. Cf. *VitMelL* 29.1 (p. 206). See Coon, *Sacred Fictions*, 116.
131. *VitMelGr* 37–38 (pp. 196–198). Cf. *VitMelL* 37.5–38.8 (pp. 226–230). See Giardina, "Carità eversiva," 136; Coon, *Sacred Fictions*, 117.
132. *VitMelGr* 21 (p. 172). Cf. *VitMelL* 21.3 (p. 194).
133. Cf. Coon, *Sacred Fictions*, 117.
134. Cf. Brown, *Eye of a Needle*, 26, 170.
135. *VitMelGr* 21 (p. 172). Cf. *VitMelL* 21.3 (p. 194).
136. On the incident and its analysis, see G. A. Cecconi, "Un evergete mancato: Piniano a Ippona," *Athenaeum* 66 (1988): 371–389; Lepelley, "Mélanie," 24–27; P. Brown, *Poverty and Leadership in the Later Roman Empire*. The Menahem Stern Jerusalem Lectures (Hanover, NH: University Press of New England, 2002), 55–56; *idem*, *Eye of a Needle*, 323–325; Dunn, "Poverty of Melania," 109–112.

137. Brown, *Eye of a Needle*, 365–366.
138. Alciati and Giorda, "Possessions and Asceticism," 425–444.
139. *VitMelGr* 20 (pp. 168–170); Eng. trans. Clark, *Life of Melania*, 43. Cf. *VitMelL* 20.1–2 (pp. 192–194).
140. Brown, *Eye of a Needle*, 170. Theoretically, the abandonment of property was considered, after the fourth century, a prerequisite for one to become priest or bishop. Donating property to the Church, or naming the Church as the administrator and recipient of the revenue deriving from it, were some of the ways to give up property for Christian causes; see C. Rapp, *Holy Bishops in Late Antiquity: The Nature of Christian Leadership in an Age of Transition*. TCH, 37 (Berkeley, CA: University of California Press, 2005), 212–213.
141. Lepelley, "Mélanie," 27–31; Cooper, "Poverty, Obligation, and Inheritance," 167–169; J. Hillner, "Families, Patronage, and the Titular Churches of Rome, *c.* 300-*c.* 600," in *Religion, Dynasty, and Patronage in Early Christian Rome*, eds. Cooper and Hillner, 242–243; Alciati and Giorda, "Possessions and Asceticism," 433–434. The prospect of the wealthy defining their social status and individual virtue in accordance with the traditional ideals of patronage and civic euergetism was in certain instances objected to: monetary surplus was no longer deemed as a means of acquiring social praise as in Graeco-Roman benefaction, but rather as an instrument for the spiritual transformation of both donors and recipients (Wessel, *Passion and Compassion*, 145). However, the established Christian transformation of euergetism helped to shape the figure of the aristocratic and influential patron as a conduit for enacting generosity toward the destitute. "The model favored by the majority in the west involved minimal self-sacrifice, and respected the traditional need of donors for positive publicity for acts of euergetism"; see B. Neil, "Models of Gift Giving in the Preaching of Leo the Great," *JECS* 18.2 (2010): 258.
142. *VitMelGr* 22 (p. 172). Cf. *VitMelL* 22.1 (p. 196). See J. P. Thomas, *Private Religious Foundations in the Byzantine Empire*. Dumbarton Oaks Studies, 24 (Washington, D.C.: Dumbarton Oaks Research Library and Collection, 1987), 18; Alciati and Giorda, "Possessions and Asceticism," 434–435.
143. See Alciati and Giorda, "Possessions and Asceticism," 435–443. On private religious foundations, see Thomas, *Private Religious Foundations*.
144. *Concilium universale Chalcedonense*, cann. 4 and 8 (ACO 2.1.2, 159–160 [355–356]). See Thomas, *Private Religious Foundations*, 37–40.
145. C. M. Chin, "Apostles and Aristocrats," in *Melania: Early Christianity through the Life of One Family*, eds. C. M. Chin and C. T. Schroeder. Christianity in Late Antiquity, 2 (Oakland, CA: University of California

Press, 2017), 29–30. Cf. C. Luckritz Marquis, "Namesake and Inheritance," in *Melania*, eds. Chin and Schroeder, 44–45, who argues that Melania did not found monasteries in Jerusalem but only renovated those of her grandmother, Melania the Elder.

146. Cf., for instance, F. Vasileiou, "For the Poor, the Family, the Friends: Gregory of Nazianzus' Testament in the Context of Early Christian Literature," in *Inheritance, Law and Religions in the Ancient and Mediaeval Worlds*, eds. B. Caseau and S. R. Huebner. Centre de Recherche d'Histoire et Civilisation de Byzance, Monographies, 45 (Paris: ACHCByz, 2014), 146.

147. *VitMelGr* 68 (p. 266); Eng. trans. Clark, *Life of Melania*, 80. Cf. *VitMelL* 68.2 (p. 294).

148. P. Brown, *The Ransom of the Soul: Afterlife and Wealth in Early Western Christianity* (Cambridge, MA: Harvard University Press, 2015).

149. D. Hunt, "The Church as a Public Institution," in *The Cambridge Ancient History*, vol. 13: *The Late Empire, AD 337–425*, eds. A. Cameron and P. Garnsey (Cambridge: Cambridge University Press, 1998), 258.

150. Palladius, *Historia Lausiaca* 61.4 (ed. Bartelink, *Palladio, La Storia Lausiaca*, 266).

151. W. E. Kaegi, Jr., *Byzantium and the Decline of Rome* (Princeton, NJ: Princeton University Press, 1968), 250–251.

152. Brown, *Eye of a Needle*, 299; cf. Dunn, "Poverty of Melania," 108.

153. *VitMelGr* 19 (p. 164). Cf. *VitMelL* 19.3 (p. 190).

154. Brown, *Eye of a Needle*, 299.

155. Clark, *Life of Melania*, 137–138; Brown, *Eye of a Needle*, 299–300.

CHAPTER 7

Conclusions

What has the examination of Greek Fathers' views on hoarding and savings offered, or, in other words, what was the purpose of focusing on these particular practices concerning the management of financial resources, since Greek and Latin patristic views on wealth have already received due attention? As we have seen—although there was not a single or uniform attitude—material possessions, gold and money were considered more or less as "instruments." One cannot blame an instrument but rather its licit or illicit use, and the temporal holder of wealth should act as its steward rather than its owner. Since wealth has an inherent neutral meaning, which has been long pointed out, then it is not wealth per se but rather the conceptualization of its management that assists us to better understand patristic stances toward contemporary economic phenomena and practices.

Hoarding wealth, in particular, denoted an economic process that roughly embodied two distinct aspects: on the one hand, hoarding of possessions that enabled higher social status or monetary surplus which secured enhanced purchasing power; and on the other hand, storing of commodities destined for market exchanges or required for daily needs. Although hoarding was a feature of all social groups, especially those who were in a position to generate material surplus, it mostly affected social welfare as a practice pertaining to prosperous elites who could significantly influence social outcomes. More specifically, the landowning elite performed its social role, which encompassed acts of benefaction and conspicuous consumption, as well as its economic role, through generating income flows and revenues (mainly by selling income in kind to local markets or exporting it to distant ones) to purchase luxuries, to finance acts of beneficence and to support an entire network of dependents.[1] Concomitantly, hoarding by the elite was deemed a self-interested practice intended to increase individualized consumption: extravagance and ostentation implied that more economic resources were diverted from productive engagements. In accordance with the Christian view of the era, these lifestyles, centred on conspicuous consumption, were thought to make the wealthy succumb to the enticements of dissipation, thus violating the precepts of virtuous self-sufficiency.

It is equally important that hoarding material surplus in the form of commodities necessary for sustenance (such as grain and food supply) often served lucrative purposes that aimed at personal enrichment through manipulation of market prices. The profit motive was salient to prosperous market participants who, because of their superfluous wealth, were afforded the opportunity to delay their entry into the marketplace until the prices rose. Such a practice was vehemently denounced by Church Fathers, who considered such hoarding behaviours not simply opportunistic but blatantly anti-social. It was taken for granted that seeking individual enrichment impeded efforts to meet the needs of others who were devoid of negotiating power in the market transactions. Lower strata, in their turn, could hoard food in times of emergency, but this was only a temporary response to a shortage of marketable goods, not the by-product of seeking to benefit from, or to intentionally induce, a price rise.

Beyond hoarding, early Christians strongly opposed luxury spending, because, in their view, the opportunity cost of spending excess wealth on a particular luxury item was extremely high: in fact, it amounted to increasing the suffering of the sick and the poor.[2] All three practices, speculative hoarding, hoarding of financial assets and luxury spending, were perceived to be "zero-sum games," in which the enhanced prosperity of the hoarders and luxury consumers presupposed the considerable economic deprivation of the more vulnerable social groups. As we have seen, to mitigate social tensions, but also to foster "positive-sum games," Church Fathers intended to shape a redistributive network that would benefit not only the less privileged members of society, but also the more powerful. In so doing, they defined moral responsibilities for all interacting social partners in a new and promising religious "marketplace," that of Christian philanthropy. In this kind of balanced reciprocity, the prosperous could exchange their excess wealth for a heavenly reward, while the poor, receiving temporal relief from their suffering, would mediate between the generous wealthy and God. Accordingly, a highly inclusive system emerged that placed an emphasis on common humanity in anticipating the needs of all, not excluding the distant and marginalized others.[3]

The development of patristic attitudes toward hoarding was gradual and it was influenced by various traditions. New Testament rhetoric on refraining from hoarding stressed that this practice undermines personal and communal integrity, diminishes possibilities of charity, distorts primary human allegiances and promotes mundane pursuits reflecting a complete attachment to material possessions. These commonalities, evidenced in almost all discourses referring to hoarding, were assimilated into, or slightly modified by, patristic developments in wealth ethics.

In patristic thinking, hoarding unequivocally occupies the extreme negative end of an alleged "proper management of resources scale." Accumulating riches and letting them be buried or "imprisoned" was thought of as a reproachable activity by Graeco-Roman moralists too, who saw in it a manifestation of greed. Social justification was a prerequisite for the ethical justification of wealth: one of the keys to understanding both Graeco-Roman and Christian attitudes toward hoarding as an anti-social practice is the requirement for the interests of the individual and the community to be in concord. From a Christian perspective, the rich man who manages his resources properly relieves those in need and saves his soul; from a Graeco-Roman perspective, he engages in civic benefaction and competes with his peers to exceed them in reputation and honour. As Christianity was gradually integrated into and ultimately identified with the Empire, the Christian and Graeco-Roman notions of proper management of wealth coincided to an extent.

An aim of this study is to show that the notion of the Christian rich, as presented in patristic texts of different eras, should be relativized. The rich to whom the *Shepherd of Hermas* refers do not correspond socioeconomically to the rich that Theodoret of Cyrrhus addresses: the former were probably members of middling groups, while the latter were members of the elite. Isidore of Pelusium even addresses the emperor himself, the literal "lord of the gold." The volume of wealth implied in these indicative cases is incomparable, but this difference reflects the progressive widening of the composition of Christian communities and the respective socio-economic status of their wealthiest members. The departure from the imminent eschatological perspective rendered adaptation to Graeco-Roman environments inevitable.[4] This was also reflected in the negotiation of the role of the rich and their activities in the congregations. The communal utility of the capital resources of the richer Christians, and to a degree of their financial activities, was recognized in sustaining expanding Christian communities.

The views toward the utility and proper management of financial surplus were not identical, and these differences reflected in part the milieu in which they had been cultivated. In the late first and second centuries, the so-called "Apostolic Fathers" elaborated on views that acknowledged the existence of both material and financial surpluses within the faith community, thus providing new opportunities for prosperous Christians to renegotiate their identities as members of the congregations. This is more evident in the *Shepherd of Hermas*, in the context of which believers were mandated to channel their financial surplus created from business activities into charitable practices. This exhortation implied that investment of capital through the pursuit of larger-scale business agendas was not countenanced. Other texts such as the *Didache* and the *Epistle of Barnabas* adopted a more radical strategy of liquidating financial surplus, epitomized in their strong call for sharing resources, typical of faith communities that claimed their distinctive identity in the wider socio-cultural milieu. However, in major urban centres such as those of late-second/early-third-century Alexandria, the financial prosperity of the Christian wealthy increasingly embodied a new spiritual dimension. Clement of Alexandria addressed from an elite standpoint the salvific perspectives of social groups differing in access to resources and status. He promoted the beneficial aspect of wealth, which could help the rich to be properly situated in the faith community. Divestment of at least a part of material and financial surpluses were strongly encouraged as being beneficial not only to the community but also to the wealthy as a prerequisite for salvation.

The episcopal organization of the Church had been a key development, influenced by the Graeco-Roman socio-cultural milieu. It is notable that the qualifications for the episcopate from a relatively early point were not pertinent to spiritual accomplishments but rather to the general moral requirements of offices in the Graeco-Roman world.[5] From the fourth century, as the identification of Christianity with the Empire progressed, the bishops of curial and senatorial status increased in number, although bishops of low or middling origins did not disappear. The Fathers of the classical period of patristic thinking were often bishops themselves, and not infrequently when they advised the "wealthy" they in fact addressed their peers.

After Constantine, the Fathers faced a novel situation, in which the realization of the ideal of an equitable society seemed to be at hand. But their idealism and good intentions were soon to be checked by reality. It was one thing trying to persuade freedmen to share their surplus with their fellow Christians in local congregations, and yet another attempting to persuade senators and curials to act in the same manner concerning entire cities. The resignification of resource management with a view to alleviating the needy was not so easy to ask of property-conscious elites, whose status was bequeathed to their heirs along with their property. As we have seen, holding significant cash reserves, mainly in gold, facilitated the bequest and allocation of assets to multiple heirs, as well as the offering of dowries. Christian tenets on hoarding, saving and virtuous management of resources contradicted dominant familial and societal norms. Furthermore, in comparison with the previous era of economic crisis, the increasing monetization of the economy further promoted productive investment of savings, for instance, into entrepreneurial ventures and loans at interest. The opportunities for profit making that the favourable conditions of growing monetization and increased liquidity presented in the urban centres of the Eastern Mediterranean were too appealing to be disregarded by both elite and middling groups. However, not all of them shared the economic euphoria: for instance, a large number of wage earners in the cities were casually employed.

The economic and monetary expansion had social consequences, one of them being the rise and consolidation of a new elite in the early Byzantine world, which prospered in great part at the expense of the poor, and contributed to the aforementioned monetization. Its members would also place their assets, apart from productive investment, into non-productive activities such as luxury consumption, conspicuous building, gift giving (e.g., upon assumption of office) and bribery, which were traditional practices for exhibiting, maintaining and further strengthening their status. Even if wealth was not hoarded, and thus withdrawn from circulation, the aforementioned vainglorious or exploitative activities were usually censured by the Fathers. A patristic strategy, employed to accommodate the mentalities of relatively recently converted elite members, was the transformation of the objective of traditional patronage from civic to ecclesiastical benefaction. Charity, the foundation and patronage of monastic institutions, donations made on one's deathbed, *et cetera*, were virtuous activities through which wealth was spiritually legitimized.

The Cappadocians and John Chrysostom advanced new rationales for sharing financial resources through benevolent practices in religiously pluralistic environments. Basil of Caesarea in particular, censuring the grain hoarders during the famine of 368/9 in Cappadocia, elaborated his views on property and wealth. John Chrysostom, serving the Church in the great urban centres of Antioch and Constantinople, witnessed severe inequality and prompted the rich to assume their social responsibilities. Apart from hoarding, both condemned other practices of mismanaging resources, such as luxury and conspicuous consumption, but above all usury. Although they often express radical views, their aim was not to undermine the extant socio-economic structure but rather to mitigate social injustice.

In an era of sharp socio-economic divisions, hoarding of surplus was considered detrimental to social cohesion, insofar as amassing wealth for its own sake impeded the circulation of resources and contravened the principles of a just society. These Fathers offered a more integrated view on the very process of accumulation. Hoarding of both financial and material wealth was strongly denounced, whereas the act of saving in the form of excess income beyond virtuous self-sufficiency was prompted to be transformed into a form of spiritual saving, a deposit made in heaven through charity. This salvific and ultimately eschatological dimension of saving was employed in patristic rhetoric, now taking precedence over the realistic view of savings as a pool of resources destined to meet future needs. In the Fathers' moral reasoning, the unpredictability of life rendered future planning redundant and inefficient, even potentially perilous, thus the only safe solution was to entrust one's self into God's care. On the other hand, investing the surplus in profitable pursuits was reflective of an economic reality with which the Fathers were familiar, yet in their symbolic depiction of the operation of markets, moral and eschatological discourses were entwined with more pragmatic ones.

The fourth-century Fathers experimented with the new possibilities that opened before them. Their fifth-century counterparts would experience the obstacles to and limitations of these experimentations. An evolving society required the Church Fathers to revise, update and adapt their views so as to correspond to contemporary needs and to respond to pressing questions. For instance, a long-observed antinomy concerning ecclesiastical wealth was manifest. The Church owned significant property acquired mainly by imperial donations but also augmented by offerings from members of all social strata. Although total divestment with a view to redistributing wealth to the needy was no longer expected from the prosperous, their donations, as well as those of the less prosperous, supported the poor-relief programme of the Church. In order for the clergy to convince the wealthy to partially redistribute their riches through charitable donations, it was imperative that the finances of the Church—being the institution that managed donations and offerings—be properly administrated. It is no coincidence that the Fathers sometimes admitted that the mismanagement of ecclesiastical property made the upper social strata less enthusiastic about sharing their surplus with the poor, scandalized the other social groups, and, what is more, offered an excuse to pagans to reproach the Christian Church. In this respect, the vivid depiction in the epistles of Isidore of Pelusium of a corrupt band of clerics who ravaged the property of the Church of Pelusium, including among them a bishop and two *oikonomoi* (stewards), offers us a glance at the very practices of mismanagement. A main goal of the book is to show through Isidore that the tenets of the proper administration of resources concerned not only lay but also ecclesiastical wealth.

If Isidore of Pelusium does not depart from the fourth-century "classical" patristic stance toward hoarding and saving, his younger contemporary Theodoret of Cyrrhus chooses to adapt patristic vindication of wealth to the socio-economic reality of Antioch. The social situation, the way it is depicted in his *On Providence*, was characterized by sharp inequalities. He was aware that many city dwellers were contented neither with the socio-economic situation nor with basic Christian concepts, such as divine providence, that seemed to ignore reality. Moreover, the economic and monetary expansion of the period benefitted wealthy members of middling groups who sought to complement their economic advancement with social elevation. A kind of vertical social mobility in the fifth century is also affirmed by Isidore of Pelusium, as he refers to people of low social origin who managed to climb the ladder of ecclesiastical hierarchy.

Our study of Theodoret shows that he attempted, as a proven broker, to reconcile the poor with the rich, and at the same time to demonstrate that any attempt to surpass one's status defies providence. The crafts–money circuit, which he presents as the core of the providential structure of society, assumes the full engagement of the rich in the purchase and consumption of a diversity of services and goods produced by the poor. The notion of reciprocities, which was fundamental for the development of views of social cohesion since early patristic thinking, has been transformed here into economic exchange conducted in the context of the marketplace. The favourable economic conditions in the major urban centres of the Eastern Mediterranean permitted Theodoret to promote his contemporary economic reality as a solution to the economic problem.

An economic exchange, not a trade of donations with prayers, promises for salvation or honour, was his proposal for the achievement of social cohesion. Theodoret's solution seems also to imply that the answer to poverty is labour: if one works then someone will purchase the products of one's toil. Full engagement of the rich in consumption meant that even luxurious and conspicuous consumption was permitted, another point with which Theodoret distances himself from the traditional patristic teachings. This attitude is vital to construe his view on the management of financial resources, which encourages savings to be channelled into the market. Thus, we assume that for Theodoret the purpose of transactions is less important than the transactions themselves and the sustenance of his model of social cooperation. Yet we do not intend to exaggerate Theodoret's rationality; he offers the crafts–money circuit to his audience, but he is not willing to justify aspirations for social improvement. The positions in which he places the givers of money and the givers of services are fixed.

A basic aim of this book is to show the need for contextualization in studying patristic views on the management of financial resources. In the sixth chapter, although we did not provide the particular context for every Father we examined, we attempted to sketch out an overview of economic, monetary and social developments in which the differences in patristic teachings acquired a more pragmatic meaning. For instance, views on hoarding can be evaluated diversely if they are expressed in a time of debasement and rampant inflation. In the same manner, a censure of conspicuous consumption tells a different story if it is set before or after the introduction of the *solidus*. Our effort was to demonstrate that indifference to the socio-economic setting in which patristic views on various issues were embedded inevitably leads to their treatment just as a kind of religio-ethical discourse.

The book closes with a saint, Melania the Younger, a choice that is not without symbolic meaning as it implies the emerging significance of hagiography to the views on hoarding and saving. Our aim was to show, after having outlined the socio-economic conditions, how a super-rich person would have tried to respond to the call for ethical perfection and redistribution. Although Melania's case is atypical in terms of origin and wealth, her divestment had a "universal" impact in the late Roman world (Eastern and Western), whereas her *Life* allows glimpses into ecclesiastical views and practices all over the Mediterranean. What is striking is the adaptation of Christian and patristic precepts to the notions of the elite: as a result, divestment could not be absolute and benefaction remained a kind of aristocratic euergetism. The *Life* of Melania—like that of her Eastern counterpart, Olympias—shows that no matter how an aristocrat embraced ideals of asceticism, the preservation of a part of his/her assets was not considered a contradiction. Would not it be plausible to assume that this wealth was sometimes "invested" and "deposited" in their private foundations, usually but not exclusively in the form of endowments? It seems that the rich, even when they conformed to Christian tenets, wanted to have the last word on how to share their surplus; them, not the bishop.

The Greek Fathers' positions on hoarding, saving and the proper management of financial resources gradually lost their radical character, especially as Christianity was progressively identified with the Empire. Yet essential patristic views—such as the consideration of wealth as an instrument that is good when it is not abused, but becomes bad when it is idle, stored up and not spread to the needy—never ceased to be referred to in Byzantium, forming a fundamental part of its economic ideology.

Notes

1. P. Erdkamp, "Urbanism," in *The Cambridge Companion to the Roman Economy*, ed. W. Scheidel (Cambridge: Cambridge University Press, 2012), 258.
2. B. J. Matz, "Early Christian Philanthropy as a 'Marketplace' and the Moral Responsibility of Market Participants," in *Distant Markets, Distant Harms: Economic Complicity and Christian Ethics*, ed. D. K. Finn (Oxford: Oxford University Press, 2014), 131–132.
3. Matz, "Early Christian Philanthropy," 133.
4. H. Koester, "The Apostolic Fathers and the Struggle for Christian Identity," in *The Writings of the Apostolic Fathers*, ed. P. Foster (London: T & T Clark, 2007), 12.
5. Koester, "Apostolic Fathers," 11; cf. C. Rapp, *Holy Bishops in Late Antiquity: The Nature of Christian Leadership in an Age of Transition*. TCH, 37 (Berkeley, CA: University of California Press, 2005), 200.

BIBLIOGRAPHY

Editions and Translations of Primary Sources

We cite editions and translations of primary sources, with the exception of standard editions of classical and Christian texts as well as patristic works included in the Patrologia Graeca.

Ammianus Marcellinus
  Rolfe, J. C., trans., *Ammianus Marcellinus*, 3 vols. LCL, 300, 315, 331. Cambridge, MA: Harvard University Press, 1935–1939.
  Seyfarth, W., ed. and trans., *Ammianus Marcellinus, Römische Geschichte. Lateinisch und Deutsch und mit einem Kommentar*, 4 vols. Schriften und Quellen der Alten Welt, 21.1–4. Berlin: Akademie-Verlag, 1968–1971.
Apostolic Fathers
  Ehrman, B. D., ed. and trans., *The Apostolic Fathers*, 2 vols. LCL, 24–25. Cambridge, MA: Harvard University Press, 2003.
Asterius of Amasea
  Datema, C., ed., *Asterius of Amasea, Homilies I–XIV*. Leiden: Brill, 1970.
Clement of Alexandria
  Stählin, O., and Früchtel, L., ed., *Clemens Alexandrinus*, vol. 3: *Stromata Buch VII und VIII; Excerpta ex Theodoto; Eclogae propheticae; Quis dives salvetur; Fragmente*. GCS, 17. 2nd edn. Berlin: Akademie-Verlag, 1970.
  Stählin, O., Früchtel, L., and Treu, U., ed., *Clemens Alexandrinus*, vol. 2: *Stromata Buch I–VI*. GCS, 52. 4th edn. Berlin: Akademie-Verlag, 1985.
Codex Justinianus
  Krüger, P., ed., *Corpus iuris civilis*, vol. 2: *Codex Justinianus*. Berlin: Weidmann, 1877.

Codex Theodosianus
Krüger, P., and Mommsen, Th., ed., *Theodosiani libri XVI cum constitutionibus Sirmondianis*, vol. 1.2. Berlin: Weidmann, 1905.
Pharr, C., trans., *The Theodosian Code and Novels, and the Sirmondian Constitutions*. Corpus of Roman Law, 1. Princeton, NJ: Princeton University Press, 1952.

De rebus bellicis
Giardina, A., ed. and trans., *Anonimo, Le cose della guerra*. Scrittori Greci e Latini. Milan: A. Mondadori, 1989.
Thompson, E. A., trans., *A Roman Reformer and Inventor, Being a New Text of the Treatise* De Rebus Bellicis. Oxford: Clarendon Press, 1952.

Gregory of Nazianzus
Beaucamp, J., ed. and trans., "Le testament de Grégoire de Nazianze," *Fontes Minores*, 10 (1998): 1–100.
Bernardi, J., ed. and trans., *Grégoire de Nazianze, Discours 42–43*. SC, 384. Paris: Les Éditions du Cerf, 1992.
Calvet-Sebasti, M.-A., ed. and trans., *Grégoire de Nazianze, Discours 6–12*. SC, 405. Paris: Les Éditions du Cerf, 1995.

Gregory of Nyssa
Jaeger W. et al., ed., *Gregorii Nysseni Opera*, vol. 1–. Leiden: Brill, 1952–.

Isidore of Pelusium
Évieux, P., ed. and trans., *Isidore de Péluse, Lettres*, 2 vols. SC, 422, 454. Paris: Les Éditions du Cerf, 1997–2000.

John Chrysostom
Malingrey, A.-M., ed. and trans., *Jean Chrysostome, Sur la providence de Dieu*. SC, 79. Paris: Les Éditions du Cerf, 1961.
Musurillo, H., ed., Grillet., B., trans., *Jean Chrysostome, La virginité*. SC, 125. Paris: Les Éditions du Cerf, 1966.

John Lydus
Bandy, A. C., ed. and trans., *Ioannes Lydus, On Powers, or, The Magistracies of the Roman State*. Memoirs of the American Philosophical Society, 149. Philadelphia, PA: The American Philosophical Society, 1983.

Julian
Bidez, J., ed. and trans., *L'empereur Julien, œuvres complètes*, vol. 1.2: *Lettres et fragments*. Collection des Universités de France. 2nd edn. Paris: Les Belles Lettres, 1960.
Lacombrade, C., ed. and trans., *L'empereur Julien, œuvres complètes*, vol. 2.2: *Discours de Julien empereur*. Collection des Universités de France. Paris: Les Belles Lettres, 1964.
Wright, W. C., trans., *The Works of Emperor Julian*, 3 vols. LCL, 13, 29, 157. London: W. Heinemann, 1913–1923.

Lactantius
Städele, A., ed., *Laktanz, De mortibus persecutorum / Die Todesarten der Verfolger*. Fontes Christiani, 43. Turnhout: Brepols, 2003.
Libanius
Foerster, R., ed., *Libanii opera*, 12 vols. in 13. BSGRT. Leipzig: B. G. Teubner, 1903-1923.
Life of Melania the Younger
Clark, E. A., trans., *The Life of Melania the Younger*. Studies in Women and Religion, 14. New York: The Edwin Mellen Press, 1984.
Gorce, D., ed. and trans., *Vie de sainte Mélanie*. SC, 90. Paris: Les Éditions du Cerf, 1962.
Laurence, P., ed. and trans., *Gérontius, La Vie latine de sainte Mélanie*. Studium Biblicum Franciscanum, Collectio Minor, 41. Jerusalem: Franciscan Printing Press, 2002.
Life of Olympias
Malingrey, A.-M., ed. and trans., *Jean Chrysostome, Lettres à Olympias. Seconde édition augmentée de la Vie anonyme d'Olympias*. SC, 13bis. Paris: Les Éditions du Cerf, 1968.
Nemesius of Emesa
Morani, M., ed., *Nemesii Emeseni, De natura hominis*. BSGRT. Leipzig: B. G. Teubner, 1987.
Origen
Klostermann, E., and Benz, E., ed., *Origenes Werke 10: Origenes Matthäuserklärung, 1: Die griechisch erhaltenen Tomoi*. GCS, 40 = Origenes, 10. Leipzig: J. C. Hinrichs'sche Buchhandlung, 1935.
Palladius
Bartelink, G. J. M., ed., Barchiesi, M., trans., *Palladio, La Storia Lausiaca*. Scrittori Greci e Latini; Vite dei Santi, 2. [Milan]: Fondazione Lorenzo Valla and A. Mondadori, 1974.
Malingrey, A.-M., with Leclercq, P., ed. and trans., *Palladios, Dialogue sur la vie de Jean Chrysostome*, 2 vols. SC, 341-342. Paris: Les Éditions du Cerf, 1988.
Priscus of Panium
Carolla, P., ed., *Priscus Panita, Excerpta et fragmenta*. BSGRT. Berlin: W. de Gruyter, 2008.
Given, J., trans., *The Fragmentary History of Priscus: Attila, the Huns and the Roman Empire, AD 430–476*. Christian Roman Empire Series, 11. Merchantville, NJ: Evolution Publishing, 2014.
Procopius
Haury, J., and Wirth, G., ed., *Procopii Caesariensis opera omnia*, 4 vols. BSGRT. Leipzig: B. G. Teubner, 1962-1964.

Sozomen
  Bidez, J., and Hansen, G. C., ed., *Sozomenus, Kirchengeschichte*. GCS NF, 4. 2nd edn. Berlin: Akademie-Verlag, 1995.
Themistius
  Schenkl, H. (vols. 1–3), Downey, G. (vols. 1–3), and Norman, A. F. (vols. 2–3), ed., *Themistii orationes quae supersunt*, 3 vols. BSGRT. Leipzig: B. G. Teubner, 1965–1974.
Theodoret of Cyrrhus
  Azéma, Y., trans., *Théodoret de Cyr, Discours sur la Providence*. Paris: Les Belles Lettres, 1954.
  Azéma, Y., ed. and trans., *Théodoret de Cyr, Correspondance*, 4 vols. SC, 40, 98, 111, 429. Paris: Les Éditions du Cerf, 1955–1998.
  Canivet, P., ed. and trans., *Théodoret de Cyr, Thérapeutique des maladies helléniques*, 2 vols. SC, 57. Paris: Les Éditions du Cerf, 1958.
  Halton, T., trans., *Theodoret of Cyrus, On Divine Providence*. Ancient Christian Writers, 49. New York: Newman Press, 1988.
Theophanes the Confessor
  de Boor, C., ed., *Theophanis Chronographia*, vol. 1. Leipzig: B. G. Teubner, 1883.
  Mango, C., and Scott, R., trans., *The Chronicle of Theophanes the Confessor. Byzantine and Near Eastern History, AD 284–813*. Oxford: Clarendon Press, 1997.

Secondary Literature

Abdy, R. "Tetrarchy and the House of Constantine," in *The Oxford Handbook of Greek and Roman Coinage*, ed. W. E. Metcalf. Oxford: Oxford University Press, 2012, 584–600.

Aizenman, J., Cheung, Y.-W., and Ito, H. "International Reserves Before and After the Global Crisis: Is There no End to Hoarding?" *Journal of International Money and Finance* 52 (2015): 102–126.

Alciati, R., and Giorda, M. "Possessions and Asceticism: Melania the Younger and Her Slow Way to Jerusalem," *ZAC* 14 (2010): 425–444.

Allen, P., and Neil, B. *Crisis Management in Late Antiquity (410–590 CE): A Survey of the Evidence from Episcopal Letters*. SupVC, 121. Leiden and Boston, MA: Brill, 2013.

Allen, P., Neil, B., and Mayer, W., eds., *Preaching Poverty in Late Antiquity: Perceptions and Realities*. Arbeiten zur Kirchen- und Theologiegeschichte, 28. Leipzig: Evangelische Verlagsanstalt, 2009.

Allen, R. C. "How Prosperous Were the Romans? Evidence from Diocletian's Price Edict (AD 301)," in *Quantifying the Roman Economy: Methods and*

Problems, eds. A. Bowman and A. Wilson. Oxford Studies on the Roman Economy. Oxford: Oxford University Press, 2009, 327–345.

Amemiya, T. *Economy and Economics of Ancient Greece*. Routledge Explorations in Economic History, 33. London: Routledge, 2007.

Anderson, G. A. *Charity: The Place of the Poor in the Biblical Tradition*. New Haven, CT: Yale University Press, 2013.

Andreau, J. *Banking and Business in the Roman World*. Translated by J. Lloyd. Key Themes in Ancient History. Cambridge: Cambridge University Press, 1999.

Andresen, T. "A Critique of a Post Keynesian Model of Hoarding, and an Alternative Model," *Journal of Economic Behavior and Organization* 60.2 (2006): 230–251.

Arruñada, B. "How Rome Enabled Impersonal Markets," *Explorations in Economic History* 61 (2016): 68–84.

Asolati, M., and Gorini, G., eds., *I ritrovamenti monetali e la legge di Gresham*. Numismatica Patavina, 8. Padua: Esedra, 2006.

Bagnall, R. S. *Currency and Inflation in Fourth Century Egypt*. Bulletin of the American Society of Papyrologists, Supplements, 5. [Chico, CA]: Scholars Press, 1985.

Bagus, P. *In Defense of Deflation*. Financial and Monetary Policy Studies, 41. Cham: Springer, 2015.

Ballan, J. "Basil of Caesarea on the Ascetic Craft: The Invention of Ascetic Community and the Spiritualization of Work in the *Asketikon*," *Heythrop Journal* 52.4 (2011): 559–568.

Banaji, J. *Agrarian Change in Late Antiquity: Gold, Labour, and Aristocratic Dominance*. Oxford Classical Monographs. 2nd edn. Oxford: Oxford University Press, 2007.

Banaji, J. "Economic Trajectories," in *The Oxford Handbook of Late Antiquity*, ed. S. F. Johnson. Oxford: Oxford University Press, 2012, 597–624.

Banaji, J. "The Economic Trajectories of Late Antiquity," in *idem, Exploring the Economy of Late Antiquity: Selected Essays*. Cambridge: Cambridge University Press, 2016, 61–88.

Banaji, J. "Mass Production, Monetary Economy and the Commercial Vitality of the Mediterranean," in *idem, Exploring the Economy of Late Antiquity: Selected Essays*. Cambridge: Cambridge University Press, 2016, 1–34.

Banaji, J. "Precious Metal Coinages and Monetary Expansion in Late Antiquity," in *idem, Exploring the Economy of Late Antiquity: Selected Essays*. Cambridge: Cambridge University Press, 2016, 110–140 [originally published in *Dal denarius al dinar: l'Oriente e la moneta romana*, eds. F. De Romanis and S. Sorda. Studi e Materiali, 12. Rome: Istituto Italiano di Numismatica, 2006, 265–303].

Bang, P. F. "Imperial Bazaar: Towards a Comparative Understanding of Markets in the Roman Empire," in *Ancient Economies, Modern Methodologies: Archaeology, Comparative History, Models and Institutions*, eds. P. F. Bang, M. Ikeguchi and H. G. Ziche. Pragmateiai, 12. Bari: Edipuglia, 2006, 51–88.

Bang, P. F. "Trade and Empire—In Search of Organizing Concepts for the Roman Economy," *Past & Present* 195.1 (2007): 3–54.

Baratte, F. "Les objets précieux dans la vie économique et sociale du monde romain à la fin de l'Antiquité," *Revue Numismatique* 159 (2003): 205–216.

Bar-Ilan, M. "Wealth in the World of the Sages: Why Were Korach and Moses Rich People?" in *Wealth and Poverty in Jewish Tradition*, ed. L. J. Greenspoon. Studies in Jewish Civilization, 26. West Lafayette, IN: Purdue University Press, 2015, 1–12.

Bassett, S. *The Urban Image of Late Antique Constantinople*. Cambridge: Cambridge University Press, 2004.

Batiffol, P. "Les présents de Saint Cyrille à la cour de Constantinople," in idem, *Études de liturgie et d'archéologie chrétienne*. Paris: J. Gabalda, 1919, 159–173.

Batten, A. J. "Neither Gold nor Braided Hair (1 Timothy 2.9; 1 Peter 3.3): Adornment, Gender and Honour in Antiquity," *NTS* 55.4 (2009): 484–501.

Batten, A. J. "The Urban and the Agrarian in the Letter of James," *Journal of Early Christian History* 3.2 (2013): 4–20.

Beeley, C. A. *Gregory of Nazianzus on the Trinity and the Knowledge of God: In Your Light We Shall See Light*. Oxford Studies in Historical Theology. Oxford: Oxford University Press, 2008.

Beers, W. F. "'Furnish Whatever is Lacking to Their Avarice': The Payment Programme of Cyril of Alexandria," in *From Constantinople to the Frontier: The City and the Cities*, eds. N. S. M. Matheou, T. Kampianaki and L. M. Bondioli. The Medieval Mediterranean, 106. Leiden and Boston, MA: Brill, 2016, 67–83.

Biddle, M. E. "The Biblical Prohibition Against Usury," *Interpretation: A Journal of Bible and Theology* 65.2 (2011): 117–127.

Bingham, D. J. "Heresy and Catholicity in Economic Perspective: Irenaeus on Wealth," *Ephemerides Theologicae Lovanienses* 92.3 (2016): 381–405.

Binswanger, M. "The Finance Process on a Macroeconomic Level from a Flow Perspective: A New Interpretation of Hoarding," *International Review of Financial Analysis* 6.2 (1997): 107–131.

Blomberg, C. L. *Neither Poverty nor Riches: A Biblical Theology of Material Possessions*. New Studies in Biblical Theology, 7. Downers Grove, IL and Leicester: InterVarsity Press and Apollos, 1999.

Blosser, B. "Love and Equity: The Social Doctrine of Origen of Alexandria," *Studies in Christian Ethics* 27.4 (2014): 385–403.

Blowers, P. M. "2009 NAPS Presidential Address. Pity, Empathy, and the Tragic Spectacle of Human Suffering: Exploring the Emotional Culture of Compassion in Late Ancient Christianity," *JECS* 18.1 (2010): 1–27.
Boer, R. *The Sacred Economy of Ancient Israel.* Library of Ancient Israel. Louisville, KY: Westminster John Knox Press, 2015.
Boersma, H. *Embodiment and Virtue in Gregory of Nyssa: An Anagogical Approach.* OECS. Oxford: Oxford University Press, 2013.
Bogaert, R. *Banques et banquiers dans les cités grecques.* Leiden: A. W. Sijthoff, 1968.
Bogaert, R. "Changeurs et banquiers chez les Pères de l'Église," *Ancient Society* 4 (1973): 239–270.
Bogaert, R. "La banque en Égypte byzantine," *Zeitschrift für Papyrologie und Epigraphik* 116 (1997): 85–140.
Bouffartigue, J. "L'authenticité de la Lettre 84 de l'empereur Julien," *Revue de Philologie, de Littérature et d'Histoire Anciennes* 79.2 (2005): 231–242.
Brändle, R. "This Sweetest Passage: Matthew 25:31–46 and Assistance to the Poor in the Homilies of John Chrysostom," in *Wealth and Poverty in Early Church and Society*, ed. S. R. Holman. Holy Cross Studies in Patristic Theology and History. Grand Rapids, MI: Baker Academic, 2008, 127–139.
Bresson, A. *The Making of the Ancient Greek Economy: Institutions, Markets, and Growth in the City-States.* Translated by S. Rendall. Princeton, NJ: Princeton University Press, 2016.
Brewer, A. "Pre-Classical Economics in Britain," in *A Companion to the History of Economic Thought*, eds. W. J. Samuels, J. E. Biddle and J. B. Davis. Blackwell Companions to Contemporary Economics, 3. Malden, MA: Blackwell Publishing, 2003, 78–93.
Broekaert, W. "Freedmen and Agency in Roman Business," in *Urban Craftsmen and Traders in the Roman World*, eds. A. Wilson and M. Flohr. Oxford: Oxford University Press, 2016, 222–253.
Brookins, T. A. *Corinthian Wisdom, Stoic Philosophy, and the Ancient Economy.* SNTSMS, 159. Cambridge: Cambridge University Press, 2014.
Brown, P. *Power and Persuasion in Late Antiquity: Towards a Christian Empire.* Madison, WI: University of Wisconsin Press, 1992.
Brown, P. *Poverty and Leadership in the Later Roman Empire.* The Menahem Stern Jerusalem Lectures. Hanover, NH: University Press of New England, 2002.
Brown, P. *Through the Eye of a Needle: Wealth, the Fall of Rome, and the Making of Christianity in the West, 350–550 AD.* Princeton, NJ: Princeton University Press, 2012.
Brown, P. *The Ransom of the Soul: Afterlife and Wealth in Early Western Christianity.* Cambridge, MA: Harvard University Press, 2015.

Brown, P. *Treasure in Heaven: The Holy Poor in Early Christianity*. Page-Barbour and Richard Lectures Series, Richard Lectures, 2012. Charlottesville, VA: University of Virginia Press, 2016.

Brughmans, T., and Poblome, J. "Roman Bazaar or Market Economy? Explaining Tableware Distributions through Computational Modelling," *Antiquity* 90.350 (2016): 393–408.

Bruun, P. *Studies in Constantinian Chronology*. Numismatic Notes and Monographs, 146. New York: American Numismatic Society, 1961.

Buell, D. K. "'Be Not One Who Stretches Out Hands to Receive but Shuts Them when It Comes to Giving': Envisioning Christian Charity when Both Donors and Recipients Are Poor," in *Wealth and Poverty in Early Church and Society*, ed. S. R. Holman. Holy Cross Studies in Patristic Theology and History. Grand Rapids, MI: Baker Academic, 2008, 37–47.

Burnett, A. *Coinage in the Roman World*. London: Seaby, 1987.

Caner, D. *Wandering, Begging Monks: Spiritual Authority and the Promotion of Monasticism in Late Antiquity*. TCH, 33. Berkeley, CA: University of California Press, 2002.

Caner, D. "Towards a Miraculous Economy: Christian Gifts and Material 'Blessings' in Late Antiquity," *JECS* 14.3 (2006): 329–377.

Caner, D. "Wealth, Stewardship, and Charitable 'Blessings' in Early Byzantine Monasticism," in *Wealth and Poverty in Early Church and Society*, ed. S. R. Holman. Holy Cross Studies in Patristic Theology and History. Grand Rapids, MI: Baker Academic, 2008, 221–242.

Canivet, P. *Le monachisme syrien selon Théodoret de Cyr*. Théologie Historique, 42. Paris: Beauchesne, 1977.

Caprariello, P. A., and Reis, H. T. "To Do, to Have, or to Share? Valuing Experiences over Material Possessions Depends on the Involvement of Others," *Journal of Personality and Social Psychology* 104.2 (2013): 199–215.

Cardman, F. "Poverty and Wealth as Theater: John Chrysostom's Homilies on Lazarus and the Rich Man," in *Wealth and Poverty in Early Church and Society*, ed. S. R. Holman. Holy Cross Studies in Patristic Theology and History. Grand Rapids, MI: Baker Academic, 2008, 159–175.

Carrié, J.-M. "Were Late Roman and Byzantine Economies Market Economies? A Comparative Look at Historiography," in *Trade and Markets in Byzantium*, ed. C. Morrisson. Dumbarton Oaks Byzantine Symposia and Colloquia. Washington, DC: Dumbarton Oaks Research Library and Collection, 2012, 13–26.

Caseau, B. "Late Antique Paganism: Adaptation under Duress," in *The Archaeology of Late Antique 'Paganism'*, eds. L. Lavan and M. Mulryan. Late Antique Archaeology, 7. Leiden and Boston, MA: Brill, 2011: 111–134.

Caseau, B. "Autour de l'autel: le contrôle des donateurs et des donations alimentaires," in *Donation et donateurs dans le monde byzantin*, eds. J.-M. Spieser and É. Yota. Réalités Byzantines, 14. Paris: Desclée de Brouwer, 2012, 47–73.

Cecconi, G. A. "Un evergete mancato: Piniano a Ippona," *Athenaeum* 66 (1988): 371–389.

Čekalova, A. "Fortune des sénateurs de Constantinople du IVe au début du VIIe siècle," in *EYΨYXIA: Mélanges offerts à Hélène Ahrweiler*, 2 vols. Byzantina Sorbonensia, 16. Paris: Publications de la Sorbonne, 1998, vol. 1, 119–130.

Chadwick, H. *Early Christian Thought and the Classical Tradition: Studies in Justin, Clement, and Origen*. Oxford: Clarendon Press, 1966.

Cherrier, H., and Ponnor, T. "A Study of Hoarding Behavior and Attachment to Material Possessions," *Qualitative Market Research* 13.1 (2010): 8–23.

Chin, C. M. "Apostles and Aristocrats," in *Melania: Early Christianity through the Life of One Family*, eds. C. M. Chin and C. T. Schroeder. Christianity in Late Antiquity, 2. Oakland, CA: University of California Press, 2017, 19–33.

Claes, L., Müller, A., and Luyckx, K. "Compulsive Buying and Hoarding as Identity Substitutes: The Role of Materialistic Value Endorsement and Depression," *Comprehensive Psychiatry* 68 (2016): 65–71.

Clark, A. D. "'Do Not Judge Who Is Worthy and Unworthy': Clement's Warning Not to Speculate about the Rich Young Man's Response (Mark 10.17–31)," *JSNT* 31.4 (2009): 447–468.

Constantelos, D. J. *Byzantine Philanthropy and Social Welfare*. Rutgers Byzantine Series. New Brunswick, NJ: Rutgers University Press, 1968.

Conway-Jones, A. *Gregory of Nyssa's Tabernacle Imagery in Its Jewish and Christian Contexts*. OECS. Oxford: Oxford University Press, 2014.

Coomber, M. J. M. "Caught in the Crossfire? Economic Injustice and Prophetic Motivation in Eighth-Century Judah," *Biblical Interpretation* 19.4–5 (2011): 396–432.

Coon, L. L. *Sacred Fictions: Holy Women and Hagiography in Late Antiquity*. The Middle Ages Series. Philadelphia, PA: University of Pennsylvania Press, 1997.

Cooper, K. *The Fall of the Roman Household*. Cambridge: Cambridge University Press, 2007.

Cooper, K. "Poverty, Obligation, and Inheritance: Roman Heiresses and the Varieties of Senatorial Christianity in Fifth-Century Rome," in *Religion, Dynasty, and Patronage in Early Christian Rome, 300–900*, eds. K. Cooper and J. Hillner. Cambridge: Cambridge University Press, 2007, 165–189.

Cooper, K. "Gender and the Fall of Rome," in *A Companion to Late Antiquity*, ed. P. Rousseau (with the assistance of J. Raithel). Blackwell Companions to the Ancient World. Chichester: Wiley-Blackwell, 2009, 187–200.

Cooper, J. E., and Decker, M. J. *Life and Society in Byzantine Cappadocia*. Houndmills, Basingstoke: Palgrave Macmillan, 2012.
Cosentino, S. "Banking in Early Byzantine Ravenna," *Cahiers de Recherches Médiévales et Humanistes* 28.2 (2014): 243–254.
Coulie, B. *Les richesses dans l'œuvre de saint Grégoire de Nazianze. Étude littéraire et historique*. Publications de l'Institut Orientaliste de Louvain, 32. Louvain-la-Neuve: Institut Orientaliste, 1985.
Creed, R. P. "*Beowulf* and the Language of Hoarding," in *Medieval Archaeology: Papers of the Seventeenth Annual Conference of the Center for Medieval and Early Renaissance Studies*, ed. C. L. Redman. Medieval and Renaissance Texts and Studies, 60. Binghamton, NY: Center for Medieval and Early Renaissance Studies, 1989, 155–167.
Crislip, A. T. *From Monastery to Hospital: Christian Monasticism & the Transformation of Health Care in Late Antiquity*. Ann Arbor, MI: The University of Michigan Press, 2005.
Croke, B. "Anatolius and Nomus: Envoys to Attila," *Byzantinoslavica* 42.2 (1981): 159–170.
Croke, B. "Dating Theodoret's *Church History* and *Commentary on the Psalms*," *Byzantion* 54.1 (1984): 59–74.
Croke, B. *Christian Chronicles and Byzantine History, 5th–6th Centuries*. CS, 386. Aldershot: Variorum, 1992.
Dagron, G. *Naissance d'une capitale. Constantinople et ses institutions de 330 à 451*. Bibliothèque Byzantine, Études, 7. Paris: Presses Universitaires de France, 1974.
Daley, B. E. "1998 NAPS Presidential Address. Building a New City: The Cappadocian Fathers and the Rhetoric of Philanthropy," *JECS* 7.3 (1999): 431–461.
Daley, B. E. *Gregory of Nazianzus*. ECF. London: Routledge, 2006.
Dalrymple, W. *From the Holy Mountain: A Journey in the Shadow of Byzantium*. London: Harper Collins, 1997.
Dean, T. *Crime and Justice in Late Medieval Italy*. Cambridge: Cambridge University Press, 2007.
De Giorgi, A. U. *Ancient Antioch: From the Seleucid Era to the Islamic Conquest*. Cambridge: Cambridge University Press, 2016.
De Moor, T., and Zuijderduijn, J. "Preferences of the Poor: Market Participation and Asset Management of Poor Households in Sixteenth-Century Holland," *European Review of Economic History* 17.2 (2013): 233–249.
Detoraki, M. "Copie sous dictée et bains monastique. Deux renseignements propres à la *Vie* latine de sainte Mélanie la Jeune," *Jahrbuch für Antike und Christentum* 47 (2004): 98–107.

de Wet, C. L. "'No Small Counsel about Self-Control': *Enkrateia* and the Virtuous Body as Missional Performance in *2 Clement*," *HTSTS* 69.1 (2013). Art. #1340, 10 pp. (10.4102/hts.v69i1.1340).

de Wet, C. L. *Preaching Bondage: John Chrysostom and the Discourse of Slavery in Early Christianity.* Oakland, CA: University of California Press, 2015.

Dinan, A. "Manual Labor in the Life and Thought of St. Basil the Great," *Logos: A Journal of Catholic Thought and Culture* 12.4 (2009): 133–157.

Doran, R. *Stewards of the Poor: The Man of God, Rabbula, and Hiba in Fifth-Century Edessa.* Cistercian Studies Series, 208. Kalamazoo, MI: Cistercian Publications, 2006.

Doty, R. G. *The Macmillan Encyclopedic Dictionary of Numismatics.* New York: Macmillan, 1982.

Downey, G. *A History of Antioch in Syria: From Seleucus to the Arab Conquest.* Princeton, NJ: Princeton University Press, 1961.

Downs, D. J. *The Offering of the Gentiles: Paul's Collection for Jerusalem in Its Chronological, Cultural and Cultic Contexts.* WUNT, 2.248. Tübingen: Mohr Siebeck, 2008.

Downs, D. J. "Is God Paul's Patron? The Economy of Patronage in Pauline Theology," in *Engaging Economics: New Testament Scenarios and Early Christian Reception*, eds. B. W. Longenecker and K. D. Liebengood. Grand Rapids, MI: W. B. Eerdmans, 2009, 129–156.

Downs, D. J. "Redemptive Almsgiving and Economic Stratification in *2 Clement*," *JECS* 19.4 (2011): 493–517.

Downs, D. J. "'Love Covers a Multitude of Sins': Redemptive Almsgiving in 1 Peter 4:8 and Its Early Christian Reception," *Journal of Theological Studies* 65.2 (2014): 489–514.

Downs, D. J. *Alms: Charity, Reward, and Atonement in Early Christianity.* Waco, TX: Baylor University Press, 2016.

Draper, J. A. "Social Ambiguity and the Production of Text: Prophets, Teachers, Bishops, and Deacons and the Development of the Jesus Traditions in the Community of the *Didache*," in *The Didache in Context: Essays on Its Text, History, and Transmission*, ed. C. N. Jefford. SNT, 77. Leiden: Brill, 1995, 284–312.

Draper, J. A. "The *Didache*," in *The Writings of the Apostolic Fathers*, ed. P. Foster. London: T & T Clark, 2007, 13–20.

Draper, J. A. "The Moral Economy of the *Didache*," *HTSTS* 67.1 (2011). Art. #907, 10 pp. (10.4102/hts.v67i1.907).

Draper, J. A. "Children and Slaves in the Community of the *Didache* and the Two Ways Tradition," in *The Didache: A Missing Piece of the Puzzle in Early Christianity*, eds. J. A. Draper and C. N. Jefford. Early Christianity and Its Literature, 14. Atlanta, GA: SBL Press, 2015, 85–121.

Dunn, G. D. "The Poverty of Melania the Younger and Pinianus," *Augustinianum* 54.1 (2014): 93–115.
Dunning, B. H. *Aliens and Sojourners: Self as Other in Early Christianity*. Divinations: Rereading Ancient Religion. Philadelphia, PA: University of Pennsylvania Press, 2009.
Dyck, B. *Management and the Gospel: Luke's Radical Message for the First and Twenty-First Centuries*. New York: Palgrave Macmillan, 2013.
Dyck, B., Starke, F. A., and Weimer, J. B. "Toward Understanding Management in First Century Palestine," *Journal of Management History* 18.2 (2012): 137–165.
Elliott, M. W. *Providence Perceived: Divine Action from a Human Point of View*. Arbeiten zur Kirchengeschichte, 124. Berlin and Boston, MA: W. de Gruyter, 2015.
Ellis, S. "Middle Class Houses in Late Antiquity," in *Social and Political Life in Late Antiquity*, eds. W. Bowden, A. Gutteridge and C. Machado. Late Antique Archaeology, 3.1. Leiden and Boston, MA: Brill, 2006, 413–437.
Elm, S. *Sons of Hellenism, Fathers of the Church: Emperor Julian, Gregory of Nazianzus, and the Vision of Rome*. TCH, 49. Berkeley, CA: University of California Press, 2012.
Erdkamp, P. *The Grain Market in the Roman Empire: A Social, Political and Economic Study*. Cambridge: Cambridge University Press, 2005.
Erdkamp, P. "Urbanism," in *The Cambridge Companion to the Roman Economy*, ed. W. Scheidel. Cambridge: Cambridge University Press, 2012, 241–265.
Erdkamp, P. "Economic Growth in the Roman Mediterranean World: An Early Good-bye to Malthus?" *Explorations in Economic History* 60 (2016): 1–20.
Estiot, S. "The Later Third Century," in *The Oxford Handbook of Greek and Roman Coinage*, ed. W. E. Metcalf. Oxford: Oxford University Press, 2012, 538–560.
Eubank, N. "Almsgiving is 'The Commandment': A Note on 1 Timothy 6.6–19," *NTS* 58.1 (2012): 144–150.
Eubank, N. *Wages of Cross-Bearing and Debt of Sin: The Economy of Heaven in Matthew's Gospel*. Beihefte zur Zeitschrift für die neutestamentliche Wissenschaft und die Kunde der älteren Kirche, 196. Berlin and Boston, MA: W. de Gruyter, 2013.
Evans-Grubbs, J. "Marriage and Family Relationships in the Late Roman West," in *A Companion to Late Antiquity*, ed. P. Rousseau (with the assistance of J. Raithel). Blackwell Companions to the Ancient World. Chichester: Wiley-Blackwell, 2009, 201–219.
Évieux, P. *Isidore de Péluse*. Théologie Historique, 99. Paris: Beauchesne, 1995.
Évieux, P. "Isidore de Péluse, moine égyptien du Ve siècle," *SP* 29 (1997): 451–454.

Évieux, P., Burns, W. H., Arragon, L., Boulnois, M.-O., Forrat, M., and Meunier, B. *Cyrille d'Alexandrie, Lettres festales*, vol. 1: *I–VI*. SC, 372. Paris: Les Éditions du Cerf, 1991.

Ferrer-Maestro, J. J. "Speculation and Crisis: Some Examples in the Eastern Provinces of the Later Roman Empire," in *New Perspectives on Late Antiquity in the Eastern Roman Empire*, eds. A. de Francisco Heredero, D. Hernández de la Fuente and S. Torres Prieto. Newcastle upon Tyne: Cambridge Scholars Publishing, 2014, 245–257.

Fiensy, D. A. "Ancient Economy and the New Testament," in *Understanding the Social World of the New Testament*, eds. D. Neufeld and R. E. DeMaris. London: Routledge, 2010, 194–206.

Fiensy, D. A. "Did Large Estates Exist in Lower Galilee in the First Half of the First Century C.E.?" *Journal for the Study of the Historical Jesus* 10.2 (2012): 133–153.

Fiensy, D. A. *Christian Origins and the Ancient Economy*. Eugene, OR: Cascade Books, 2014.

Finn, R. *Almsgiving in the Later Roman Empire: Christian Promotion and Practice (313–450)*. Oxford Classical Monographs. Oxford: Oxford University Press, 2006.

Flusin, B. "Palestinian Hagiography (Fourth–Eighth Centuries)," in *The Ashgate Research Companion to Byzantine Hagiography*, vol. 1: *Periods and Places*, ed. S. Efthymiadis. Farnham: Ashgate, 2011, 199–226.

Foster, P. "The *Epistle to Diognetus*," in *The Writings of the Apostolic Fathers*, ed. P. Foster. London: T & T Clark, 2007, 147–156.

Foster, P. "The Epistles of Ignatius of Antioch," in *The Writings of the Apostolic Fathers*, ed. P. Foster. London: T & T Clark, 2007, 81–107.

Fouskas, C. M. *Saint Isidore of Pelusium: His Life and His Works*. Athens: n.p., 1970.

Freyne, S. "Herodian Economics in Galilee: Searching for a Suitable Model," in *Modelling Early Christianity: Social Scientific Studies of the New Testament in Its Context*, ed. P. F. Esler. London: Routledge, 1995, 23–46.

Freyne, S. "Galilee and Judea: The Social World of Jesus," in *The Face of New Testament Studies: A Survey of Recent Research*, eds. S. McKnight and G. R. Osborne. Grand Rapids, MI and Leicester: Baker Academic and Apollos, 2004, 21–35.

Friesen, S. J. "Poverty in Pauline Studies: Beyond the So-Called New Consensus," *JSNT* 26.3 (2004): 323–361.

Friesen, S. J. "Injustice or God's Will? Early Christian Explanations of Poverty," in *Wealth and Poverty in Early Church and Society*, ed. S. R. Holman. Holy Cross Studies in Patristic Theology and History. Grand Rapids, MI: Baker Academic, 2008, 17–36.

Frost, R. O., Tolin, D. F., Steketee, G., Fitch, K. E., and Selbo-Bruns, A. "Excessive Acquisition in Hoarding," *Journal of Anxiety Disorders* 23.5 (2009): 632–639.
Fuhrmann, C. J. *Policing the Roman Empire: Soldiers, Administration, and Public Order.* Oxford: Oxford University Press, 2012.
Gamauf, R. "Slaves Doing Business: The Role of Roman Law in the Economy of a Roman Household," *European Review of History* 16.3 (2009): 331–346.
Gardner, G. E. "Care for the Poor and the Origins of Charity in Early Rabbinic Literature," in *Wealth and Poverty in Jewish Tradition*, ed. L. J. Greenspoon. Studies in Jewish Civilization, 26. West Lafayette, IN: Purdue University Press, 2015, 13–32.
Gardner, G. E. *The Origins of Organized Charity in Rabbinic Judaism.* Cambridge: Cambridge University Press, 2015.
Garnsey, P. *Famine and Food Supply in the Graeco-Roman World: Responses to Risk and Crisis.* Cambridge: Cambridge University Press, 1988.
Garnsey, P. *Thinking about Property: From Antiquity to the Age of Revolution.* Ideas in Context, 90. Cambridge: Cambridge University Press, 2007.
Giambrone, A. "'According to the Commandment' (*Did.* 1.5): Lexical Reflections on Almsgiving as 'The Commandment'," *NTS* 60.4 (2014): 448–465.
Giannakopoulos, N. "Μορφές αποταμίευσης, διαχείρισης και αξιοποίησης του χρήματος στην Ελλάδα κατά τους αυτοκρατορικούς χρόνους (27 π.Χ.–περ. 280 μ.Χ.). Μια αποτίμηση των πηγών," in *Αποταμίευση και διαχείριση χρήματος στην ελληνική ιστορία*, eds. K. Bouraselis and K. Meidani. Athens: Tachydromiko Tamieutērio Hellados, 2011, 105–150.
Giardina, A. "Carità eversiva: le donazioni di Melania la giovane e gli equilibri della società tardoromana," *Studi Storici* 29.1 (1988): 127–142.
Girardi, M. "Basilio di Cesarea: le coordinate scritturistiche della 'Basiliade' in favore di poveri e indigenti," *Classica et Christiana* 9.2 (2014): 459–483.
Gofas, D. C. "La banque lieu de rencontre et instrument d'échange à Byzance," *Cahiers du Centre Gustave Glotz* 7 (1996): 145–161.
González, J. L. *Faith and Wealth: A History of Early Christian Ideas on the Origin, Significance, and Use of Money.* Eugene, OR: Wipf and Stock Publishers, 1990.
Goodrich, J. K. *Paul as an Administrator of God in 1 Corinthians.* SNTSMS, 152. Cambridge: Cambridge University Press, 2012.
Gordon, B. *The Economic Problem in Biblical and Patristic Thought.* SupVC, 9. Leiden: Brill, 1989.
Gotsis, G. "Socio-Economic Ideas in the Petrine Epistles of the New Testament," *Storia del Pensiero Economico* 4.2 (2007): 67–105.
Gotsis, G., and Drakopoulou-Dodd, S. "Economic Ideas in the Pauline Epistles of the New Testament," *History of Economics Review* 35.1 (2002): 13–34.

Gotsis, G. N., and Drakopoulou-Dodd, S. "Economic Ideas in the Epistle of James," *History of Economic Ideas* 12.1 (2004): 7–35.

Gotsis, G. N., and Merianos, G. A. "Wealth and Poverty in Theodoret of Cyrrhus' *On Providence*," *Journal of Eastern Christian Studies* 59.1–2 (2007): 11–48.

Gotsis, G. N., and Merianos, G. "Early Christian Representations of the Economy: Evidence from New Testament Texts," *History and Anthropology* 23.4 (2012): 467–505.

Gregory, A. "*1 Clement*: An Introduction," in *The Writings of the Apostolic Fathers*, ed. P. Foster. London: T & T Clark, 2007, 21–31.

Grierson, P. "The Roman Law of Counterfeiting," in *Essays in Roman Coinage Presented to Harold Mattingly*, eds. R. A. G. Carson and C. H. V. Sutherland. London: Oxford University Press, 1956, 240–261.

Grierson, P. *Numismatics*. London: Oxford University Press, 1975.

Grubaugh, C. "The Anonymous *De rebus bellicis* and the Ethics of Empire in Late Antiquity: A Problem in Intellectual History," *Clio's Scroll* 17.1 (2015): 3–25.

Grundeken, M. *Community Building in the Shepherd of Hermas: A Critical Study of Some Key Aspects*. SupVC, 131. Leiden and Boston, MA: Brill, 2015.

Gudeman, S. *The Anthropology of Economy: Community, Market, and Culture*. Oxford: Blackwell, 2001.

Guest, P. "Roman Gold and Hun Kings: The Use and Hoarding of Solidi in the Late Fourth and Fifth Centuries," in *Roman Coins outside the Empire: Ways and Phases, Contexts and Functions*, eds. A. Bursche, R. Ciołek and R. Wolters. Collection Moneta, 82. Wetteren: Moneta, 2008, 295–307.

Guillaume, P. *Land, Credit and Crisis: Agrarian Finance in the Hebrew Bible*. Sheffield: Equinox, 2012.

Gwynn, D. M. "The 'End' of Roman Senatorial Paganism," in *The Archaeology of Late Antique 'Paganism'*, eds. L. Lavan and M. Mulryan. Late Antique Archaeology, 7. Leiden and Boston, MA: Brill, 2011, 135–161.

Haas, C. *Alexandria in Late Antiquity: Topography and Social Conflict*. Baltimore, MD: Johns Hopkins University Press, 1997.

Hägg, H. F. *Clement of Alexandria and the Beginnings of Christian Apophaticism*. OECS. Oxford: Oxford University Press, 2006.

Hanson, K. C., and Oakman, D. E. *Palestine in the Time of Jesus: Social Structures and Social Conflicts*. Minneapolis, MN: Fortress Press, 1998.

Harl, K. W. *Coinage in the Roman Economy, 300 B.C. to A.D. 700*. Ancient Society and History. Baltimore, MD: Johns Hopkins University Press, 1996.

Harland, P. A. "The Economy of First-Century Palestine: State of the Scholarly Discussion," in *Handbook of Early Christianity: Social Science Approaches*, eds. A. J. Blasi, J. Duhaime and P.-A. Turcotte. Walnut Creek, CA: AltaMira Press, 2002, 511–527.

Harries, J. "'Pius princeps': Theodosius II and Fifth-Century Constantinople," in *New Constantines: The Rhythm of Imperial Renewal in Byzantium, 4th–13th Centuries*, ed. P. Magdalino. Society for the Promotion of Byzantine Studies, Publications, 2. Aldershot: Variorum, 1994, 35–44.

Harries, J. *Imperial Rome AD 284 to 363: The New Empire*. The Edinburgh History of Ancient Rome. Edinburgh: Edinburgh University Press, 2012.

Harries, J. "Men without Women: Theodosius' Consistory and the Business of Government," in *Theodosius II: Rethinking the Roman Empire in Late Antiquity*, ed. C. Kelly. CCS. Cambridge: Cambridge University Press, 2013, 67–89.

Hawk, B. E. *Law and Commerce in Pre-Industrial Societies*. Leiden: Brill, 2016.

Hays, C. M. "By Almsgiving and Faith Sins Are Purged? The Theological Underpinnings of Early Christian Care for the Poor," in *Engaging Economics: New Testament Scenarios and Early Christian Reception*, eds. B. W. Longenecker and K. D. Liebengood. Grand Rapids, MI: W. B. Eerdmans, 2009, 260–280.

Hays, C. M. *Luke's Wealth Ethics: A Study in Their Coherence and Character*. WUNT, 2.275. Tübingen: Mohr Siebeck, 2010.

Hays, C. M. "Resumptions of Radicalism: Christian Wealth Ethics in the Second and Third Centuries," *Zeitschrift für die Neutestamentliche Wissenschaft* 102.2 (2011): 261–282.

Hays, C. M. "Provision for the Poor and the Mission of the Church: Ancient Appeals and Contemporary Viability," *HTSTS* 68.1 (2012). Art. #1218, 7 pp. (10.4102/hts.v68i1.1218).

Hays, C. M. "Slaughtering Stewards and Incarcerating Debtors: Coercing Charity in Luke 12:35–13:9," *Neotestamentica* 46.1 (2012): 41–60.

Heather, P., and Matthews, J. *The Goths in the Fourth Century*. Translated Texts for Historians, 11. Liverpool: Liverpool University Press, 1991.

Helm, P. *The Providence of God*. Contours of Christian Theology. Downers Grove, IL: InterVarsity Press, 1994.

Hendy, M. F. *Studies in the Byzantine Monetary Economy, c. 300–1450*. Cambridge: Cambridge University Press, 1985.

Hickey, T. M. "Aristocratic Landholding and the Economy of Byzantine Egypt," in *Egypt in the Byzantine World, 300–700*, ed. R. S. Bagnall. Cambridge: Cambridge University Press, 2007, 288–308.

Hillner, J. "Families, Patronage, and the Titular Churches of Rome, c. 300–c. 600," in *Religion, Dynasty, and Patronage in Early Christian Rome, 300–900*, eds. K. Cooper and J. Hillner. Cambridge: Cambridge University Press, 2007, 225–261.

Hofer, A. *Christ in the Life and Teaching of Gregory of Nazianzus*. OECS. Oxford: Oxford University Press, 2013.

Hollerich, M. J. "The Alexandrian Bishops and the Grain Trade: Ecclesiastical Commerce in Late Roman Egypt," *Journal of the Economic and Social History of the Orient* 25.2 (1982): 187–207.

Holman, S. R. "The Hungry Body: Famine, Poverty, and Identity in Basil's *Hom.* 8," *JECS* 7.3 (1999): 337–363.

Holman, S. R. *The Hungry Are Dying: Beggars and Bishops in Roman Cappadocia.* Oxford Studies in Historical Theology. Oxford: Oxford University Press, 2001.

Holman, S. R. "Constructed and Consumed: The Everyday Life of the Poor in 4th c. Cappadocia," in *Social and Political Life in Late Antiquity*, eds. W. Bowden, A. Gutteridge and C. Machado. Late Antique Archaeology, 3.1. Leiden and Boston, MA: Brill, 2006, 441–464.

Holmes, M. "Polycarp of Smyrna, *Epistle to the Philippians*," in *The Writings of the Apostolic Fathers*, ed. P. Foster. London: T & T Clark, 2007, 108–125.

Holum, K. G. *Theodosian Empresses: Women and Imperial Dominion in Late Antiquity*. Berkeley, CA: University of California Press, 1982.

Hoppe, R. "'Nur sollten wir an die Armen denken ...' (Gal 2,10): Arm und Reich als ekklesiale Herausforderung," *Theologische Quartalschrift* 193.3 (2013): 197–208.

Horsley, R. A. *Covenant Economics: A Biblical Vision of Justice for All.* Louisville, KY: Westminster John Knox Press, 2009.

Howgego, C. *Ancient History from Coins*. Approaching the Ancient World. London: Routledge, 1995.

Hülsmann, J. G. "Cultural Consequences of Monetary Interventions," *Journal des Économistes et des Études Humaines* 22.1 (2016): 77–98.

Hume, D. A. *The Early Christian Community: A Narrative Analysis of Acts 2:41–47 and 4:32–35*. WUNT 2.298. Tübingen: Mohr Siebeck, 2011.

Hummer, H. J. *Politics and Power in Early Medieval Europe: Alsace and the Frankish Realm, 600–1000*. Cambridge Studies in Medieval Life and Thought, 4th ser., 65. Cambridge: Cambridge University Press, 2005.

Hunt, D. "The Church as a Public Institution," in *The Cambridge Ancient History*, vol. 13: *The Late Empire, AD 337–425*, eds. A. Cameron and P. Garnsey. Cambridge: Cambridge University Press, 1998, 238–276.

Hutchison, T. *Before Adam Smith: The Emergence of Political Economy, 1662–1776*. Oxford: Blackwell, 1988.

Ibrahim, A. A., Elatrash, R. J., and Farooq, M. O. "Hoarding versus Circulation of Wealth from the Perspective of *maqasid al-Shari'ah*," *International Journal of Islamic and Middle Eastern Finance and Management* 7.1 (2014): 6–21.

Ihssen, B. L. "Basil and Gregory's Sermons on Usury: Credit where Credit Is Due," *JECS* 16.3 (2008): 403–430.

Ihssen, B. L. "'That Which Has Been Wrung from Tears': Usury, the Greek Fathers, and Catholic Social Teaching," in *Reading Patristic Texts on Social Ethics: Issues and Challenges for Twenty-First-Century Christian Social Thought*, eds. J. Leemans, B. J. Matz and J. Verstraeten. CUA Studies in Early Christianity. Washington, DC: The Catholic University of America Press, 2011, 124–160.

Ihssen, B. L. *They Who Give from Evil: The Response of the Eastern Church to Moneylending in the Early Christian Era*. Eugene, OR: Pickwick Publications, 2012.

James, L. *Light and Colour in Byzantine Art*. Clarendon Studies in the History of Art, 15. Oxford: Clarendon Press, 1996.

Janes, D. *God and Gold in Late Antiquity*. Cambridge: Cambridge University Press, 1998.

Jefford, C. N. "The Milieu of Matthew, the *Didache*, and Ignatius of Antioch: Agreements and Differences," in *Matthew and the Didache: Two Documents from the Same Jewish-Christian Milieu?* ed. H. van de Sandt. Assen and Minneapolis, MN: Royal Van Gorcum and Fortress Press, 2005, 35–47.

Johnston, D. *The Roman Law of Trusts*. Oxford: Clarendon Press, 1988.

Jones, A. H. M. *The Later Roman Empire, 284–602: A Social, Economic and Administrative Survey*, 3 vols. Oxford: Blackwell, 1964.

Jones, A. H. M. *The Cities of the Eastern Roman Provinces*. 2nd edn. Oxford: Clarendon Press, 1971.

Jongman, W. "A Golden Age: Death, Money Supply and Social Succession in the Roman Empire," in *Credito e moneta nel mondo romano*, ed. E. Lo Cascio. Pragmateiai, 8. Bari: Edipuglia, 2003, 181–196.

Jongman, W. M. "Re-Constructing the Roman Economy," in *The Cambridge History of Capitalism*, vol. 1: *The Rise of Capitalism: From Ancient Origins to 1848*, eds. L. Neal and J. G. Williamson. Cambridge: Cambridge University Press, 2014, 75–100.

Kaegi, W. E., Jr. *Byzantium and the Decline of Rome*. Princeton, NJ: Princeton University Press, 1968.

Kamell, M. "The Economics of Humility: The Rich and the Humble in James," in *Engaging Economics: New Testament Scenarios and Early Christian Reception*, eds. B. W. Longenecker and K. D. Liebengood. Grand Rapids, MI: W. B. Eerdmans, 2009, 157–175.

Karayiannis, A. D., and Drakopoulou-Dodd, S. "The Greek Christian Fathers," in *Ancient and Medieval Economic Ideas and Concepts of Social Justice*, eds. S. Todd Lowry and B. Gordon. Leiden: Brill, 1998, 163–208.

Kazhdan, A. "Chartoularios," in *ODB*, vol. 1, 416.

Kehoe, D. P. "Law, Agency and Growth in the Roman Economy," in *New Frontiers: Law and Society in the Roman World*, ed. P. J. du Plessis. Edinburgh: Edinburgh University Press, 2013, 177–191.

Kelly, C. *Ruling the Later Roman Empire*. Revealing Antiquity, 15. Cambridge, MA: The Belknap Press of Harvard University Press, 2004.
Kelly, C. *Attila the Hun: Barbarian Terror and the Fall of the Roman Empire*. London: The Bodley Head, 2008.
Kelly, C., ed., *Theodosius II: Rethinking the Roman Empire in Late Antiquity*. CCS. Cambridge: Cambridge University Press, 2013.
Kelly, J. N. D. *Golden Mouth: The Story of John Chrysostom—Ascetic, Preacher, Bishop*. Ithaca, NY: Cornell University Press, 1995.
Kessler, D., and Temin, P. "Money and Prices in the Early Roman Empire," in *The Monetary Systems of the Greeks and the Romans*, ed. W. V. Harris. Oxford: Oxford University Press, 2008, 137–159.
Kloppenborg, J. S. "The Growth and Impact of Agricultural Tenancy in Jewish Palestine (III BCE–I CE)," *Journal of the Economic and Social History of the Orient* 51.1 (2008): 31–66.
Koester, H. "The Apostolic Fathers and the Struggle for Christian Identity," in *The Writings of the Apostolic Fathers*, ed. P. Foster. London: T & T Clark, 2007, 1–12.
Krautheimer, R. *Three Christian Capitals: Topography and Politics*. Una's Lectures, 4. Berkeley, CA: University of California Press, 1983.
Kraybill, D. B., and Sweetland, D. M. "Possessions in Luke-Acts: A Sociological Perspective," *Perspectives in Religious Studies* 10.3 (1983): 215–239.
Kraybill, J. N. *Imperial Cult and Commerce in John's Apocalypse*. JSNTSup, 132. Sheffield: Sheffield Academic Press, 1996.
Kress, V. E., Stargell, N. A., Zoldan, C. A., and Paylo, M. J. "Hoarding Disorder: Diagnosis, Assessment, and Treatment," *Journal of Counseling and Development* 94.1 (2016): 83–90.
Kuecker, A. J. "The Spirit and the 'Other,' Satan and the 'Self': Economic Ethics as a Consequence of Identity Transformation in Luke-Acts," in *Engaging Economics: New Testament Scenarios and Early Christian Reception*, eds. B. W. Longenecker and K. D. Liebengood. Grand Rapids, MI: W. B. Eerdmans, 2009, 81–103.
Laiou, A. E. "The Church, Economic Thought and Economic Practice," in *The Christian East, Its Institutions and Its Thought: A Critical Reflection*, ed. R. F. Taft. Orientalia Christiana Analecta, 251. Rome: Pontificio Istituto Orientale, 1996, 435–464.
Laiou, A. E. "Economic Thought and Ideology," in *The Economic History of Byzantium: From the Seventh through the Fifteenth Century*, 3 vols., ed. A. E. Laiou. Dumbarton Oaks Studies, 39. Washington, DC: Dumbarton Oaks Research Library and Collection, 2002, vol. 2, 1123–1144.
Laiou, A. E. "Trade, Profit, and Salvation in the Late Patristic and the Byzantine Period," in *Wealth and Poverty in Early Church and Society*, ed. S. R. Holman.

Holy Cross Studies in Patristic Theology and History. Grand Rapids, MI: Baker Academic, 2008, 243–264.
Laiou, A. E. *Economic Thought and Economic Life in Byzantium*. CS, 1033. Farnham: Ashgate, 2013.
La Matina, M. "Basilio di Cesarea, Gregorio di Nissa e le passioni dell'usura," *Pan* 15–16 (1998): 131–168.
Lampe, P. *From Paul to Valentinus: Christians at Rome in the First Two Centuries*. Translated by M. Steinhauser, edited by M. D. Johnson. London: Continuum, 2003.
Lastovicka, J. L., and Anderson, L. "Loneliness, Material Possession Love, and Consumers' Physical-Well-Being," in *Consumption and Well-Being in the Material World*, ed. M. Tatzel. Dordrecht: Springer, 2014, 63–72.
Lee, A. D. "The Eastern Empire: Theodosius to Anastasius," in *The Cambridge Ancient History*, vol. 14: *Late Antiquity: Empire and Successors, A.D. 425–600*, eds. A. Cameron, B. Ward-Perkins and M. Whitby. Cambridge: Cambridge University Press, 2000, 33–62.
Lee, D. "Theodosius and His Generals," in *Theodosius II: Rethinking the Roman Empire in Late Antiquity*, ed. C. Kelly. CCS. Cambridge: Cambridge University Press, 2013, 90–108.
Lenski, N. *Failure of Empire: Valens and the Roman State in the Fourth Century A.D.* TCH, 34. Berkeley, CA: University of California Press, 2002.
Leontaritou, V. A. Εκκλησιαστικά αξιώματα και υπηρεσίες στην πρώιμη και μέση βυζαντινή περίοδο. Forschungen zur byzantinischen Rechtsgeschichte, Athener Reihe, 8. Athens and Komotini: Ekdoseis Ant. N. Sakkoula, 1996.
Lepelley, C. "Mélanie la Jeune, entre Rome, la Sicile et l'Afrique: les effets socialement pernicieux d'une forme extrême de l'ascétisme," *KΩKAΛOΣ: Studi pubblicati dall'Istituto di Storia Antica dell'Università di Palermo* 43–44.1.1 (1997–1998): 15–32.
Leshem, D. "Oikonomia in the Age of Empires," *History of the Human Sciences* 26.1 (2013): 29–51.
Leshem, D. "Oikonomia Redefined," *Journal of the History of Economic Thought* 35.1 (2013): 43–61.
Leshem, D. "The Ancient Art of Economics," *European Journal of the History of Economic Thought* 21.2 (2014): 201–229.
Leshem, D. "What Did the Ancient Greeks Mean by *Oikonomia*?" *Journal of Economic Perspectives* 30.1 (2016): 225–238.
Liebeschuetz, J. H. W. G. *Antioch: City and Imperial Administration in the Later Roman Empire*, Oxford: Clarendon Press, 1972.
Liebeschuetz, J. H. W. G. *Ambrose and John Chrysostom: Clerics between Desert and Empire*. Oxford: Oxford University Press, 2011.
Lim, R. "Isidore of Pelusium on Roman Spectacles," *SP* 29 (1997): 66–74.

Lindemann, A. "Eigentum und Reich Gottes: Die Erzählung 'Jesus und der Reiche' im Neuen Testament und bei Clemens Alexandrinus," *Zeitschrift für Evangelische Ethik* 50.2 (2006): 89–109.
Little, L. K. *Religious Poverty and the Profit Economy in Medieval Europe.* Ithaca, NY: Cornell University Press, 1978.
Longenecker, B. W. "Exposing the Economic Middle: A Revised Economy Scale for the Study of Early Urban Christianity," *JSNT* 31.3 (2009): 243–278.
Longenecker, B. W. "Socio-Economic Profiling of the First Urban Christians," in *After the First Urban Christians: The Social-Scientific Study of Pauline Christianity Twenty-Five Years Later*, eds. T. D. Still and D. G. Horrell. London: T & T Clark, 2009, 36–59.
Longenecker, B. W. *Remember the Poor: Paul, Poverty, and the Greco-Roman World.* Grand Rapids, MI: W. B. Eerdmans, 2010.
López, A. G. *Shenoute of Atripe and the Uses of Poverty: Rural Patronage, Religious Conflict, and Monasticism in Late Antique Egypt.* TCH, 50. Berkeley, CA: University of California Press, 2013.
Luckritz Marquis, C. "Namesake and Inheritance," in *Melania: Early Christianity through the Life of One Family*, eds. C. M. Chin and C. T. Schroeder. Christianity in Late Antiquity, 2. Oakland, CA: University of California Press, 2017, 34–49.
Maas, M., ed., *The Cambridge Companion to the Age of Attila.* Cambridge Companions to the Ancient World. New York: Cambridge University Press, 2015.
MacDonald, M. Y. "Kinship and Family in the New Testament World," in *Understanding the Social World of the New Testament*, eds. D. Neufeld and R. E. DeMaris. London: Routledge, 2010, 29–43.
MacDonald, M. Y. "Beyond Identification of the Topos of Household Management: Reading the Household Codes in Light of Recent Methodologies and Theoretical Perspectives in the Study of the New Testament," *NTS* 57.1 (2011): 65–90.
Maier, H. O. "From Material Place to Imagined Space: Emergent Christian Community as Thirdspace in the *Shepherd of Hermas*," in *Early Christian Communities between Ideal and Reality*, eds. M. Grundeken and J. Verheyden. WUNT, 1.342. Tübingen: Mohr Siebeck, 2015, 143–160.
Malherbe, A. J. "Godliness, Self-Sufficiency, Greed, and the Enjoyment of Wealth: 1 Timothy 6:3–19, Part 2," in *idem*, *Light from the Gentiles: Hellenistic Philosophy and Early Christianity: Collected Essays, 1959–2012*, 2 vols. Edited by C. R. Holladay, J. T. Fitzgerald, J. W. Thompson and G. E. Sterling. SNT, 150. Leiden and Boston, MA: Brill, 2014, vol. 1, 535–557.
Malina, B. J. *The New Testament World: Insights from Cultural Anthropology.* 3rd edn. Louisville, KY: Westminster John Knox Press, 2001.

Malina, B. J. *The Social Gospel of Jesus: The Kingdom of God in Mediterranean Perspective*. Minneapolis, MN: Fortress Press, 2001.
Malina, B. J. "Collectivism in Mediterranean Culture," in *Understanding the Social World of the New Testament*, eds. D. Neufeld and R. E. DeMaris. London: Routledge, 2010, 17–28.
Malina, B. J., and Pilch, J. J. *Social-Science Commentary on the Book of Revelation*. Minneapolis, MN: Fortress Press, 2000.
Mango, C. *Le développement urbain de Constantinople, IVe–VIIe siècles*. Travaux et Mémoires, Monographies, 2. 2nd edn. Paris: De Boccard, 1990.
Mathews, M. D. *Riches, Poverty, and the Faithful: Perspectives on Wealth in the Second Temple Period and the Apocalypse of John*. SNTSMS, 154. Cambridge: Cambridge University Press, 2013.
Matz, B. "The Principle of Detachment from Private Property in Basil of Caesarea's *Homily* 6 and Its Context," in *Reading Patristic Texts on Social Ethics: Issues and Challenges for Twenty-First-Century Christian Social Thought*, eds. J. Leemans, B. J. Matz and J. Verstraeten. CUA Studies in Early Christianity. Washington, DC: The Catholic University of America Press, 2011, 161–184.
Matz, B. J. "Deciphering a Recipe for Biblical Preaching in *Oration* 14," in *Re-Reading Gregory of Nazianzus: Essays on History, Theology, and Culture*, ed. C. A. Beeley. CUA Studies in Early Christianity. Washington, DC: The Catholic University of America Press, 2012, 49–66.
Matz, B. J. "Early Christian Philanthropy as a 'Marketplace' and the Moral Responsibility of Market Participants," in *Distant Markets, Distant Harms: Economic Complicity and Christian Ethics*, ed. D. K. Finn. Oxford: Oxford University Press, 2014, 115–145.
Maxwell, J. L. *Christianization and Communication in Late Antiquity: John Chrysostom and His Congregation in Antioch*. Cambridge: Cambridge University Press, 2006.
Mayer, W. "John Chrysostom and His Audiences: Distinguishing Different Congregations at Antioch and Constantinople," *SP* 31 (1997): 70–75.
Mayer, W. "Poverty and Society in the World of John Chrysostom," in *Social and Political Life in Late Antiquity*, eds. W. Bowden, A. Gutteridge and C. Machado. Late Antique Archaeology, 3.1. Leiden and Boston, MA: Brill, 2006, 465–484.
Mayer, W. "John Chrysostom's Use of Luke 16:19–31," *Scrinium* 4 (2008): 45–59.
Mayer, W. "Poverty and Generosity toward the Poor in the Time of John Chrysostom," in *Wealth and Poverty in Early Church and Society*, ed. S. R. Holman. Holy Cross Studies in Patristic Theology and History. Grand Rapids, MI: Baker Academic, 2008, 140–158.

Mayer, W. "John Chrysostom on Poverty," in *Preaching Poverty in Late Antiquity: Perceptions and Realities*, eds. P. Allen, B. Neil and W. Mayer. Arbeiten zur Kirchen- und Theologiegeschichte, 28. Leipzig: Evangelische Verlagsanstalt, 2009, 69–118.

Mayer, W. "The Topography of Antioch Described in the Writings of John Chrysostom," in *Les sources de l'histoire du paysage urbain d'Antioche sur l'Oronte*, ed. C. Saliou. Paris: Université Paris 8, Vincennes-Saint-Denis, 2012, 81–100.

Mayer, W., and Allen, P. *John Chrysostom*. ECF. London: Routledge, 2000.

Mazzarino, S. *Aspetti sociali del quarto secolo. Ricerche di storia tardo-romana*. Problemi e Ricerche di Storia Antica, 1. Rome: "L'Erma" di Bretschneider, 1951.

McGuckin, J. A. *Saint Gregory of Nazianzus: An Intellectual Biography*. Crestwood, NY: St. Vladimir's Seminary Press, 2001.

McGuckin, J. A. "St. Gregory of Nazianzus on the Love of the Poor (Oration 14)," in *The Ecumenical Legacy of the Cappadocians*, ed. N. Dumitraşcu. Pathways for Ecumenical and Interreligious Dialogue. Houndmills, Basingstoke: Palgrave Macmillan, 2016, 139–157.

Medema, S. G. "The Economic Role of Government in the History of Economic Thought," in *A Companion to the History of Economic Thought*, eds. W. J. Samuels, J. E. Biddle and J. B. Davis. Blackwell Companions to Contemporary Economics, 3. Malden, MA: Blackwell Publishing, 2003, 428–444.

Meeks, M. D. "The Peril of Usury in the Christian Tradition," *Interpretation: A Journal of Bible and Theology* 65.2 (2011): 128–140.

Merianos, G. "Αντιλήψεις περί αποταμιεύσεως στο Βυζάντιο: Πατερικές διδαχές, ψυχωφελείς διηγήσεις και κοσμικές θεωρήσεις," in *Αποταμίευση και διαχείριση χρήματος στην ελληνική ιστορία*, eds. K. Bouraselis and K. Meidani. Athens: Tachydromiko Tamieutērio Hellados, 2011, 177–218.

Merianos, G. "Literary Allusions to Trade and Merchants: The 'Great Merchant' in Late Twelfth-Century Byzantium," in *Byzantium, 1180–1204: 'The Sad Quarter of a Century'?* ed. A. Simpson. International Symposium, 22. Athens: National Hellenic Research Foundation, Institute of Historical Research, 2015, 221–243.

Metzger, J. A. *Consumption and Wealth in Luke's Travel Narrative*. Biblical Interpretation Series, 88. Leiden and Boston, MA: Brill, 2007.

Milavec, A. *The Didache: Faith, Hope and Life of the Earliest Christian Communities, 50–70 C.E.* New York: Newman Press, 2003.

Millar, F. *A Greek Roman Empire: Power and Belief under Theodosius II, 408–450*. Sather Classical Lectures, 64. Berkeley, CA: University of California Press, 2006.

Miller, A. C. *Rumors of Resistance: Status Reversals and Hidden Transcripts in the Gospel of Luke*. Minneapolis, MN: Fortress Press, 2014.

Miller, T. S. *The Birth of the Hospital in the Byzantine Empire*. The Henry E. Sigerist Supplements to the Bulletin of the History of Medicine, new ser., 10. 2nd edn. Baltimore, MD: Johns Hopkins University Press, 1997.

Mitchell, M. M. "Silver Chamber Pots and Other Goods Which Are Not Good: John Chrysostom's Discourse against Wealth and Possessions," in *Having: Property and Possession in Religious and Social Life*, eds. W. Schweiker and C. Mathewes. Grand Rapids, MI: W. B. Eerdmans, 2004, 88–121.

Moore, E. "Wealth, Poverty, and the Value of the Person: Some Notes on the *Hymn of the Pearl* and Its Early Christian Context," in *Wealth and Poverty in Early Church and Society*, ed. S. R. Holman. Holy Cross Studies in Patristic Theology and History. Grand Rapids, MI: Baker Academic, 2008, 56–63.

Moorhead, S. "The Coinage of the Later Roman Empire, 364–498," in *The Oxford Handbook of Greek and Roman Coinage*, ed. W. E. Metcalf. Oxford: Oxford University Press, 2012, 601–632.

Moreschini, C. "Gregory Nazianzen and Philosophy, with Remarks on Gregory's Cynicism," in *Re-Reading Gregory of Nazianzus: Essays on History, Theology, and Culture*, ed. C. A. Beeley. CUA Studies in Early Christianity. Washington, DC: The Catholic University of America Press, 2012, 103–122.

Morrisson, C. "Imperial Generosity and Its Monetary Expression: The Rise and Decline of the 'Largesses'," in *Donation et donateurs dans le monde byzantin*, eds. J.-M. Spieser and É. Yota. Réalités Byzantines, 14. Paris: Desclée de Brouwer, 2012, 25–46.

Mouritsen, H. *The Freedman in the Roman World*. Cambridge: Cambridge University Press, 2011.

Müller, A. "'All das ist Zierde für den Ort …'. Das diakonisch-karitative Großprojekt des Basileios von Kaisareia," *ZAC* 13.3 (2010): 452–474.

Mundell, R. "Uses and Abuses of Gresham's Law in the History of Money," *Zagreb Journal of Economics* 2.2 (1998): 3–38 [repr. in *I ritrovamenti monetali e la legge di Gresham*, eds. M. Asolati and G. Gorini. Numismatica Patavina, 8. Padua: Esedra, 2006, 195–222].

Mundell Mango, M. "Cyrrhus," in *ODB*, vol. 1, 574.

Murphy, C. M. *Wealth in the Dead Sea Scrolls and in the Qumran Community*. Studies on the Texts of the Desert of Judah, 40. Leiden: Brill, 2002.

Murphy, E. "Cyprian, Paul, and Care for the Poor and Captive: Offering Sacrifices and Ransoming Temples," *ZAC* 20.3 (2016): 418–436.

Neil, B. "Models of Gift Giving in the Preaching of Leo the Great," *JECS* 18.2 (2010): 225–259.

Newhauser, R. *The Early History of Greed: The Sin of Avarice in Early Medieval Thought and Literature*. Cambridge Studies in Medieval Literature, 41. Cambridge: Cambridge University Press, 2000.

Niederwimmer, K. *The Didache: A Commentary*. Translated by L. M. Maloney, edited by H. W. Attridge. Hermeneia. Minneapolis, MN: Fortress Press, 1998.
Nielsen, R. "Storage and English Government Intervention in Early Modern Grain Markets," *Journal of Economic History* 57.1 (1997): 1–33.
Nigro, G. A. "L'esegesi di 2 Cor 8,9 nei Padri Cappadoci," *Vetera Christianorum* 51 (2014): 197–212.
Novic, T. "Charity and Reciprocity: Structures of Benevolence in Rabbinic Literature," *Harvard Theological Review* 105.1 (2012): 33–52.
Oakman, D. E. "The Ancient Economy and St. John's Apocalypse," *Listening: Journal of Religion and Culture* 28 (1993): 200–214.
Oakman, D. E. *Jesus, Debt, and the Lord's Prayer: First-Century Debt and Jesus' Intentions*. Eugene, OR: Cascade Books, 2014.
Ogereau, J. M. *Paul's Koinonia with the Philippians: A Socio-Historical Investigation of a Pauline Economic Partnership*. WUNT, 2.377. Tübingen: Mohr Siebeck, 2014.
Osborn, E. *Clement of Alexandria*. Cambridge: Cambridge University Press, 2005.
Osiek, C. *Shepherd of Hermas: A Commentary*. Hermeneia. Minneapolis, MN: Fortress Press, 1999.
Paganelli, M. P. "David Hume on Banking and Hoarding," *Southern Economic Journal* 80.4 (2014): 968–980.
Paget, J. C. "The *Epistle of Barnabas*," in *The Writings of the Apostolic Fathers*, ed. P. Foster. London: T & T Clark, 2007, 72–80.
Papadakis, A. "Synkellos," in *ODB*, vol. 3, 1993–1994.
Parvis, P. "*2 Clement* and the Meaning of the Christian Homily," in *The Writings of the Apostolic Fathers*, ed. P. Foster. London: T & T Clark, 2007, 32–41.
Pastor, J. *Land and Economy in Ancient Palestine*. London: Routledge, 1997.
Pásztori-Kupán, I. *Theodoret of Cyrus*. ECF. London: Routledge, 2006.
Patlagean, E. *Pauvreté économique et pauvreté sociale à Byzance, 4ᵉ–7ᵉ siècles*. Civilisations et Sociétés, 48. Paris: Mouton, 1977.
Patlagean, E. "The Poor," in *The Byzantines*, ed. G. Cavallo. Translated by T. Dunlap, T. L. Fagan and C. Lambert. Chicago, IL: The University of Chicago Press, 1997, 15–42.
Penna, V. "Βυζαντινό νόμισμα και παραχαράκτες," in Ἔγκλημα και τιμωρία στο Βυζάντιο, ed. S. N. Troianos. Athens: Idryma Goulandri-Horn, 1997, 273–294.
Penzel, F. "Hoarding in History," in *The Oxford Handbook of Hoarding and Acquiring*, eds. R. O. Frost and G. Steketee. Oxford Library of Psychology. Oxford: Oxford University Press, 2014, 6–16.

Perrotta, C. "The Legacy of the Past: Ancient Economic Thought on Wealth and Development," *European Journal of the History of Economic Though* 10.2 (2003): 177–229.

Phillips, T. E. "Revisiting Philo: Discussion of Wealth and Poverty in Philo's Ethical Discourse," *JSNT* 83 (2001): 111–121.

Phung, P. J., Moulding, R., Taylor, J. K., and Nedeljkovic, M. "Emotional Regulation, Attachment to Possessions and Hoarding Symptoms," *Scandinavian Journal of Psychology* 56.5 (2015): 573–581.

Ramelli, I. L. E. *Social Justice and the Legitimacy of Slavery: The Role of Philosophical Asceticism from Ancient Judaism to Late Antiquity*. OECS. Oxford: Oxford University Press, 2016.

Ramskold, L. "Constantine's Vicennalia and the Death of Crispus," *Niš & Byzantium* 11 (2013): 409–456.

Rapp, C. *Holy Bishops in Late Antiquity: The Nature of Christian Leadership in an Age of Transition*. TCH, 37. Berkeley, CA: University of California Press, 2005.

Rapp, C. "Spiritual Guarantors at Penance, Baptism, and Ordination in the Late Antique East," in *A New History of Penance*, ed. A. Firey. Brill's Companions to the Christian Tradition, 14. Leiden and Boston, MA: Brill, 2008, 121–148.

Reinstorf, D. H. "The Rich, the Poor, and the Law," *HTSTS* 60.1–2 (2004): 329–348.

Reinstorf, D. H. "The Parable of the Shrewd Manager (Lk 16:1–8): A Biography of Jesus and a Lesson on Mercy," *HTSTS* 69.1 (2013). Art. #1943, 7 pp. (10.4102/hts.v69i1.1943).

Rhee, H. "A Patristic View of Wealth and Possessions," *Ex Auditu: An International Journal of the Theological Interpretation of Scripture* 27 (2011): 51–77.

Rhee, H. "Wealth, Poverty, and Eschatology: Pre-Constantine Christian Social Thought and the Hope for the World to Come," in *Reading Patristic Texts on Social Ethics: Issues and Challenges for the Twenty-First Century*, eds. J. Leemans, B. J. Matz and J. Verstraeten. CUA Studies in Early Christianity. Washington, DC: The Catholic University of America Press, 2011, 64–84.

Rhee, H. *Loving the Poor, Saving the Rich: Wealth, Poverty, and Early Christianity*. Grand Rapids, MI: Baker Academic, 2012.

Rhee, H. "'Every Good and Perfect Gift Comes from Above': The Episcopal Control of Charity and Christian(-ized) Patronage," *Scrinium* 9.1 (2013): 165–181.

Rhee, H. "Wealth, Business Activities, and Blurring of Christian Identity," *SP* 62 (2013): 245–257.

Rodziewicz, E. "Ivory, Bone, Glass and Other Production at Alexandria, 5th–9th Centuries," in *Byzantine Trade, 4th–12th Centuries: The Archaeology of Local, Regional and International Exchange*, ed. M. Mundell Mango. Society for the

Promotion of Byzantine Studies, Publications, 14. Farnham: Ashgate, 2009, 83–95.
Rollens, S. E. *Framing Social Criticism in the Jesus Movement: The Ideological Project in the Sayings Gospel Q.* WUNT, 2.374. Tübingen: Mohr Siebeck, 2014.
Rordorf, W. "An Aspect of the Judeo-Christian Ethic: The Two Ways," in *The Didache in Modern Research*, ed. J. A. Draper. Leiden: Brill, 1996, 148–164.
Rosenfeld, B.-Z., and Menirav, J. *Markets and Marketing in Roman Palestine.* Translated by C. Cassel. Supplements to the Journal for the Study of Judaism, 99. Leiden: Brill, 2005.
Rosenfeld, B.-Z, and Perlmutter, H. "The Poor as a Stratum of Jewish Society in Roman Palestine 70–250 CE: An Analysis," *Historia: Zeitschrift für Alte Geschichte* 60.3 (2011): 273–300.
Rosner, B. S. *Greed as Idolatry: The Origin and Meaning of a Pauline Metaphor.* Grand Rapids, MI: W. B. Eerdmans, 2007.
Rössner, P. R. "Luther – Ein tüchtiger Ökonom? Über die monetären Ursprünge der Deutschen Reformation," *Zeitschrift für Historische Forschung* 42.1 (2015): 37–74.
Rössner, P. "Burying Money? Monetary Origins and Afterlives of Luther's Reformation," *History of Political Economy* 48.2 (2016): 225–263.
Rousseau, P. "The Pious Household and the Virgin Chorus: Reflections on Gregory of Nyssa's *Life of Macrina*," *JECS* 13.2 (2005): 165–186.
Rowe, N. "Keynesian Parables of Thrift and Hoarding," *Review of Keynesian Economics* 4.1 (2016): 50–55.
Russell, N. *Cyril of Alexandria.* ECF. London: Routledge, 2000.
Russell, N. *Theophilus of Alexandria.* ECF. London: Routledge, 2007.
Safrai, Z. *The Economy of Roman Palestine.* London: Routledge, 1994.
Salisbury, J. E. *Rome's Christian Empress: Galla Placidia Rules at the Twilight of the Empire.* Baltimore, MD: Johns Hopkins University Press, 2015.
Samellas, A. "Public Aspects of Pain in Late Antiquity: The Testimony of Chrysostom and the Cappadocians in their Graeco-Roman Context," *ZAC* 19.2 (2015): 260–296.
Samellas, A. "The Anti-Usury Arguments of the Church Fathers of the East in Their Historical Context and the Accommodation of the Church to the Prevailing 'Credit Economy' in Late Antiquity," *Journal of Ancient History* 5.1 (2017): 134–178.
Sanders, J. *The God Who Risks: A Theology of Providence.* 2nd edn. Downers Grove, IL: IVP Academic, 2007.
Sargent, T. J., and Smith, B. D. "Coinage, Debasements, and Gresham's Laws," *Economic Theory* 10.2 (1997): 197–226.
Sarris, P. "The Origins of the Manorial Economy: New Insights from Late Antiquity," *English Historical Review* 119 (2004): 279–311 [repr. in *Late*

Antiquity on the Eve of Islam, ed. A. Cameron. The Formation of the Classical Islamic World, 1. Farnham: Ashgate, 2013, 109–141].

Sarris, P. "Rehabilitating the Great Estate: Aristocratic Property and Economic Growth in the Late Antique East," in *Recent Research on the Late Antique Countryside*, eds. W. Bowden, L. Lavan and C. Machado. Late Antique Archaeology, 2. Leiden and Boston, MA: Brill, 2004, 55–71.

Sarris, P. *Economy and Society in the Age of Justinian*. Cambridge: Cambridge University Press, 2006.

Sarris, P. "Social Relations and the Land: The Early Period," in *The Social History of Byzantium*, ed. J. Haldon. Chichester: Wiley-Blackwell, 2009.

Sarris, P. "The Early Byzantine Economy in Context: Aristocratic Property and Economic Growth Reconsidered," *Early Medieval Europe* 19.3 (2011): 255–284.

Sarris, P. "Integration and Disintegration in the Late Roman Economy: The Role of Markets, Emperors, and Aristocrats," in *Local Economies? Production and Exchange of Inland Regions in Late Antiquity*, ed. L. Lavan. Late Antique Archaeology, 10. Leiden and Boston, MA: Brill, 2015, 167–188.

Schervish, P. G., and Whitaker, K. *Wealth and the Will of God: Discerning the Use of Riches in the Service of Ultimate Purpose*. Bloomington, IN: Indiana University Press, 2010.

Schor, A. M. *Theodoret's People: Social Networks and Religious Conflict in Late Roman Syria*. TCH, 48. Berkeley, CA: University of California Press, 2011.

Seiler, S. "Die theologische Dimension von Armut und Reichtum im Horizont alttestamentlicher Prophetie und Weisheit," *Zeitschrift für die Alttestamentliche Wissenschaft* 123.4 (2011): 580–595.

Seow, C.-L. "The Social World of Ecclesiastes," in *Money as God? The Monetization of the Market and Its Impact on Religion, Politics, Law, and Ethics*, eds. J. von Hagen and M. Welker. Cambridge: Cambridge University Press, 2014, 137–158.

Sharp, B. "Royal Paternalism and the Moral Economy in the Reign of Edward II: The Response to the Great Famine," *Economic History Review* 66.2 (2013): 628–647.

Sharples, R. W. "Nemesius of Emesa and Some Theories of Divine Providence," *VC* 37 (1983): 141–156.

Siecienski, A. E. "Gilding the Lily: A Patristic Defense of Liturgical Splendor," in *Wealth and Poverty in Early Church and Society*, ed. S. R. Holman. Holy Cross Studies in Patristic Theology and History. Grand Rapids, MI: Baker Academic, 2008, 211–220.

Silver, M. "The Plague under Commodus as an Unintended Consequence of Roman Grain Market Regulation," *Classical World* 105.2 (2012): 199–225.

Silver, M. "The Business Model of the Early Christian Church and Its Implications for Labor Force Participation in the Roman Empire," *Marburger*

Beiträge zur Antiken Handels-, Wirtschafts- und Sozialgeschichte 32 (2014): 71–116.

Siniossoglou, N. *Plato and Theodoret: The Christian Appropriation of Platonic Philosophy and the Hellenic Intellectual Resistance*. CCS. Cambridge: Cambridge University Press, 2008.

Sitzler, S. "Identity: The Indigent and the Wealthy in the Homilies of John Chrysostom," *VC* 63.5 (2009): 468–479.

Sivertsev, A. "The Household Economy," in *The Oxford Handbook of Jewish Daily Life in Roman Palestine*, ed. C. Hezser. Oxford: Oxford University Press, 2010, 229–245.

Smith, J. C. H. "The *Epistle of Barnabas* and the Two Ways of Teaching Authority," *VC* 68.5 (2014): 465–497.

Smith, R. *Julian's Gods: Religion and Philosophy in the Thought and Action of Julian the Apostate*. London: Routledge, 1995.

Stambaugh, J. E., and Balch, D. L. *The New Testament in Its Social Environment*. Library of Early Christianity, 2. Philadelphia, PA: The Westminster Press, 1986.

Stander, H. "Chrysostom on Hunger and Famine," *HTSTS* 67.1 (2011). Art. #880, 7 pp. (10.4102/hts.v67i1.880).

Stander, H. "Economics in the Church Fathers," in *The Oxford Handbook of Christianity and Economics*, ed. P. Oslington. Oxford: Oxford University Press, 2014, 22–43.

Stathakopoulos, D. C. *Famine and Pestilence in the Late Roman and Early Byzantine Empire: A Systematic Survey of Subsistence Crises and Epidemics*. Birmingham Byzantine and Ottoman Monographs, 9. Aldershot: Ashgate, 2004.

Stenger, J. R. "Where to Find Christian Philosophy? Spatiality in John Chrysostom's Counter to Greek *Paideia*," *JECS* 24.2 (2016): 173–198.

Stoyas, Y. "Πρακτικές αποταμίευσης και νομισματικοί «θησαυροί», 4ος–15ος αι.," in *Αποταμίευση και διαχείριση χρήματος στην ελληνική ιστορία*, eds. K. Bouraselis and K. Meidani. Athens: Tachydromiko Tamieutērio Hellados, 2011, 359–395.

Stoyas, Y. "Φαινόμενα αποταμίευσης από τους υστερορωμαϊκούς στους βυζαντινούς χρόνους, περ. 301–650," in *Αποταμίευση και διαχείριση χρήματος στην ελληνική ιστορία*, eds. K. Bouraselis and K. Meidani. Athens: Tachydromiko Tamieutērio Hellados, 2011, 219–246.

Telelis, I. G. *Μετεωρολογικά φαινόμενα και κλίμα στο Βυζάντιο*, 2 vols. Πονήματα, 5.1–2. Athens: Akadēmia Athēnōn, Kentron Ereunēs tēs Hellēnikēs kai Latinikēs Grammateias, 2004.

Temin, P. *The Roman Market Economy*. The Princeton Economic History of the Western World. Princeton, NJ: Princeton University Press, 2013.

Thomas, J. P. *Private Religious Foundations in the Byzantine Empire*. Dumbarton Oaks Studies, 24. Washington, DC: Dumbarton Oaks Research Library and Collection, 1987.

Timm, S. *Das christlich-koptische Ägypten in arabischer Zeit*, vol. 2. Wiesbaden: Reichert, 1984.

Toca, M. "Isidore of Pelusium's Letters to Didymus the Blind," *SP* 96 (2017) (forthcoming).

Tolin, D. F., Frost, R. O., Steketee, G., Gray, K. D., and Fitch, K. E. "The Economic and Social Burden of Compulsive Hoarding," *Psychiatry Research* 160.2 (2008): 200–211.

Tompkins, I. G. "Problems of Dating and Pertinence in Some Letters of Theodoret of Cyrrhus," *Byzantion* 65.1 (1995): 176–195.

Tull, P. K. "Consumerism, Idolatry, and Environmental Limits in Isaiah," in *The Book of Isaiah: Enduring Questions Answered anew: Essays Honoring Joseph Blenkinsopp and His Contribution to the Study of Isaiah*, eds. R. J. Bautch and J. T. Hibbard. Grand Rapids, MI: W. B. Eerdmans, 2014, 196–213.

Urbainczyk, T. *Theodoret of Cyrrhus: The Bishop and the Holy Man*. Ann Arbor, MI: The University of Michigan Press, 2002.

Van Dam, R. "Self-Representation in the Will of Gregory of Nazianzus," *Journal of Theological Studies* 46.1 (1995): 118–148.

Van Dam, R. *Kingdom of Snow: Roman Rule and Greek Culture in Cappadocia*. Philadelphia, PA: University of Pennsylvania Press, 2002.

Van Dam, R. *Families and Friends in Late Roman Cappadocia*. Philadelphia, PA: University of Pennsylvania Press, 2003.

van den Hoek, A. "Widening the Eye of the Needle: Wealth and Poverty in the Works of Clement of Alexandria," in *Wealth and Poverty in Early Church and Society*, ed. S. R. Holman. Holy Cross Studies in Patristic Theology and History. Grand Rapids, MI: Baker Academic, 2008, 67–75.

van der Bergh, R. H. "Chrysostom's Reception of Luke 19:8b (the Declaration of Zacchaeus)," *HTSTS* 70.1 (2014). Art. #2730, 6 pp. (10.4102/hts.v70i1.2730).

Vanderspoel, J. *Themistius and the Imperial Court: Oratory, Civic Duty, and Paideia from Constantius to Theodosius*. Ann Arbor, MI: The University of Michigan Press, 1995.

van de Sandt, H., and Flusser, D. *The Didache: Its Jewish Sources and Its Place in Early Judaism and Christianity*. Compendia Rerum Iudaicarum ad Novum Testamentum, Section 3, Jewish Traditions in Early Christian Literature, 5. Assen and Minneapolis, MN: Royal Van Gorcum and Fortress Press, 2002.

van Eck, E. "When Patrons are Patrons: A Social-Scientific and Realistic Reading of the Parable of the Feast (Lk 14:16b–23)," *HTSTS* 69.1 (2013). Art. #1375, 14 pp. (10.4102/hts.v69i1.1375).

van Eck, E. "The Harvest and the Kingdom: An Interpretation of the Sower (Mk 4:3b–8) as a Parable of Jesus the Galilean," *HTSTS* 70.1 (2014). Art. #2715, 10 pp. (10.4102/hts.v70i1.2715).

van Eck, E. "Honour and Debt Release in the Parable of the Unmerciful Servant (Mt 18:23–33): A Social-Scientific and Realistic Reading," *HTSTS* 71.1 (2015). Art. #2838, 11 pp. (10.4102/hts.v71i1.2838).

van Eck, E. "When an Outsider Becomes an Insider: A Social-Scientific and Realistic Reading of the Merchant (Mt 13:45–46)," *HTSTS* 71.1 (2015). Art. #2859, 8 pp. (10.4102/hts.v71i1.2859).

van Eck, E., and Kloppenborg, J. S. "An Unexpected Patron: A Social-Scientific and Realistic Reading of the Parable of the Vineyard Labourers (Mt 20:1–15)," *HTSTS* 71.1 (2015). Art. #2883, 11 pp. (10.4102/hts.v71i1.2883).

Van Nuffelen, P. "Deux fausses lettres de Julien l'Apostat (la lettre aux Juifs, *Ep.* 51 [Wright], et la lettre à Arsacius, *Ep.* 84 [Bidez])," *VC* 56.2 (2002): 131–150.

Van Nuffelen, P., and Leemans, J. "Episcopal Elections in Late Antiquity: Structures and Perspectives," in *Episcopal Elections in Late Antiquity*, eds. J. Leemans, P. Van Nuffelen, S. W. J. Keough and C. Nicolaye. Arbeiten zur Kirchengeschichte, 119. Berlin and Boston, MA: W. de Gruyter, 2011, 1–19.

Vasileiou, F. "For the Poor, the Family, the Friends: Gregory of Nazianzus' Testament in the Context of Early Christian Literature," in *Inheritance, Law and Religions in the Ancient and Mediaeval Worlds*, eds. B. Caseau and S. R. Huebner. Centre de Recherche d'Histoire et Civilisation de Byzance, Monographies, 45. Paris: ACHCByz, 2014, 141–157.

Vearncombe, E. K. "Redistribution and Reciprocity: A Socio-Economic Interpretation of the Parable of the Labourers in the Vineyard (Matthew 20.1–15)," *Journal for the Study of the Historical Jesus* 8.3 (2010): 199–236.

Verheyden, J. "The *Shepherd of Hermas*," in *The Writings of the Apostolic Fathers*, ed. P. Foster. London: T & T Clark, 2007, 63–71.

Verheyden, J. "Matthew and the Didache: Some Comments on the Comments," in *The Didache: A Missing Piece of the Puzzle in Early Christianity*, eds. J. A. Draper and C. N. Jefford. Early Christianity and Its Literature, 14. Atlanta, GA: SBL Press, 2015, 409–426.

Verhoeff, M. "A Genuine Friend Wishes to be a Debtor: John Chrysostom's Discourse on Almsgiving Reinterpreted," *Sacris Erudiri* 52 (2013): 47–66.

Viner, J. "The Economic Doctrines of the Christian Fathers," *History of Political Economy* 10 (1978): 9–45.

Vlachou-Mogire, C., Stern, B., and McDonnell, J. G. "The Application of LA-ICP-MS in the Examination of the Thin Plating Layers Found in Late Roman Coins," *Nuclear Instruments and Methods in Physics Research B* 265 (2007): 558–568.

Vrolijk, P. D. *Jacob's Wealth: An Examination into the Nature and Role of Material Possessions in the Jacob-Cycle (Gen 25:19–35:29)*. Supplements to Vetus Testamentum, 146. Leiden and Boston, MA: Brill, 2011.

Wärneryd, K.-E. *The Psychology of Saving: A Study on Economic Psychology*. Cheltenham: E. Elgar, 1999.

Watson, M. "Desperately Seeking Social Approval: Adam Smith, Thorstein Veblen and the Moral Limits of Capitalist Culture," *The British Journal of Sociology* 63.3 (2012): 491–512.

Wessel, S. *Cyril of Alexandria and the Nestorian Controversy: The Making of a Saint and of a Heretic*. OECS. Oxford: Oxford University Press, 2004.

Wessel, S. *Leo the Great and the Spiritual Rebuilding of a Universal Rome*. SupVC, 93. Leiden: Brill, 2008.

Wessel, S. *Passion and Compassion in Early Christianity*. New York: Cambridge University Press, 2016.

Westfall, C. L. "Running the Gamut: The Varied Responses to Empire in Jewish Christianity," in *Empire in the New Testament*, eds. S. E. Porter and C. L. Westfall. New Testament Study Series, 10. Eugene, OR: Pickwick Publications, 2011, 230–258.

Wheaton, M. G. "Understanding and Treating Hoarding Disorder: A Review of Cognitive-Behavioral Models and Treatment," *Journal of Obsessive-Compulsive and Related Disorders* 9 (2016): 43–50.

Whitby, M. "The Balkans and Greece, 420–602," in *The Cambridge Ancient History*, vol. 14: *Late Antiquity: Empire and Successors, A.D. 425–600*, eds. A. Cameron, B. Ward-Perkins and M. Whitby. Cambridge: Cambridge University Press, 2000, 701–730.

Whittow, M. "Ruling the Late Roman and Early Byzantine City: A Continuous History," *Past & Present* 129 (1990): 3–29.

Whittow, M. "Early Medieval Byzantium and the End of the Ancient World," *Journal of Agrarian Change* 9.1 (2009): 134–153.

Wickham, C. *Framing the Early Middle Ages: Europe and the Mediterranean, 400–800*. Oxford: Oxford University Press, 2005.

Wickham, L. R. *Cyril of Alexandria: Select Letters*. OECS. Oxford: Clarendon Press, 1983.

Winters, R. M. *The Hoarding Impulse: Suffocation of the Soul*. Hove, East Sussex: Routledge, 2015.

Wipszycka, E. *Les ressources et les activités économiques des églises en Égypte du IVe au VIIIe siècle*. Papyrologica Bruxellensia, 10. Brussels: Fondation Égyptologique Reine Élisabeth, 1972.

Wipszycka, E. "Le istituzioni ecclesiastiche in Egitto dalla fine del III all'inizio dell'VIII secolo," in *L'Egitto cristiano. Aspetti e problemi in età tardo-antica*, ed. A. Camplani. Studia Ephemeridis Augustinianum, 56. Rome: Institutum Patristicum Augustinianum, 1997, 219–271.

Wipszycka, E. "The Institutional Church," in *Egypt in the Byzantine World, 300–700*, ed. R. S. Bagnall. Cambridge: Cambridge University Press, 2007, 331–349.

Wipszycka, E. "Les élections épiscopales en Égypte aux VIᶜ–VIIᶜ siècles," in *Episcopal Elections in Late Antiquity*, eds. J. Leemans, P. Van Nuffelen, S. W. J. Keough and C. Nicolaye. Arbeiten zur Kirchengeschichte, 119. Berlin and Boston, MA: W. de Gruyter, 2011, 259–291.

Wood, D. *Medieval Economic Thought*. Cambridge Medieval Textbooks. Cambridge: Cambridge University Press, 2002.

Wood, P. "Social Heresy in Theodoret of Cyrrhus: The Sermon *On Divine Providence*," in *Hérésies: une construction d'identités religieuses*, eds. C. Brouwer, G. Dye and A. van Rompaey. Problèmes d'Histoire des Religions, 22. Brussels: Éditions de l'Université de Bruxelles, 2015, 43–54.

Wright, B. D., and Williams, J. C. "Anti-Hoarding Laws: A Stock Condemnation Reconsidered," *American Journal of Agricultural Economics* 66.4 (1984): 447–455.

Yan, Y. "The Gift and Gift Economy," in *A Handbook of Economic Anthropology, Second Edition*, ed. J. G. Carrier. Cheltenham: E. Elgar, 2012, 275–290.

Zanini, E. "Artisans and Traders in the Early Byzantine City: Exploring the Limits of Archaeological Evidence," in *Social and Political Life in Late Antiquity*, eds. W. Bowden, A. Gutteridge and C. Machado. Late Antique Archaeology, 3.1. Leiden and Boston, MA: Brill, 2006, 373–411.

Zuckerman, C. "L'Empire d'Orient et les Huns. Notes sur Priscus," *Travaux et Mémoires* 12 (1994): 159–182.

Zuiderhoek, A. *The Politics of Munificence in the Roman Empire: Citizens, Elites, and Benefactors in Asia Minor*. Greek Culture in the Roman World. Cambridge: Cambridge University Press, 2009.

Zuijderduijn, J., and De Moor, T. "Spending, Saving, or Investing? Risk Management in Sixteenth-Century Dutch Households," *Economic History Review* 66.1 (2013): 38–56.

INDEX

A
Achilles, 149n58
Acts, 23, 25, 89. *See also* Luke–Acts
Acts of Peter and the Twelve Apostles, 62n1
Acts of Thomas, 62n1
Adiaphoron, 54, 55, 68n68, 109n88, 137
Africa, North, 168, 174, 177
Agamemnon, 149n58
Agriculture, 17, 77, 169
Alaric, 175–177
Albina, mother of Melania the Younger, 177, 181
Alexandria, 2, 48, 53, 54, 55, 118, 128, 151n86, 171, 200. *See also* Church: of Alexandria
 coinage of, 184n10
 private bankers of, 171
Allen, Pauline, 134
Alms. *See* almsgiving
Almsgiving, 4, 8, 51, 58–61, 64n25, 70n92, 70n98, 71n104, 71n105, 80, 82, 100n14, 110n107, 120, 121, 123, 126, 142, 143, 148n38, 148n40, 148n41, 157n167, 183. *See also* charity

 as deposit in heaven, 93
 in *2 Clement*, 58, 59
 in Clement of Alexandria, 58, 59, 61
 in Origen, 55, 56
 in the *Shepherd of Hermas*, 51
 John Chrysostom on the benefit of, 86, 87, 91, 92–95, 98, 112n132, 115n179
 mismanagement of, 123, 130
 models of, 59, 95
 redemptive, 59, 61
Alypius of Thagaste, 178–179, 180
Ammianus Marcellinus, 165–166
Ammonius of Pelusium, 127
Amos, 106n64
Anastasius I, emperor, 3, 163, 168
Anatolius, patrician, 132–133
Anchorites. *See* Egypt: anchorites
Anderson, Gary A., 61
Anthemius, emperor, 168
Antioch, 2, 46, 76, 80, 85–86, 88, 93, 94, 103n47, 108n87, 132, 135, 136, 143, 144, 182, 202, 203
Antoninianus, 159–160
Apion
 estates, 170

© The Editor(s) (if applicable) and The Author(s) 2017 241
G. Merianos and G. Gotsis, *Managing Financial Resources in Late Antiquity*, New Approaches to Byzantine History and Culture, DOI 10.1057/978-1-137-56409-2

242 INDEX

family, 170
Apion (correspondent), 163
Apuleius
 Metamorphoses, 45
Areobindus, *magister utriusque militiae*, 135
Argenteus, 161, 166
Argentum, 192n118
Arianzus, 84
Aristocracy/aristocrats, 85, 110n104, 165, 167, 169, 182, 205. *See also* elite
 and business, 170–171
 early Byzantine, 188n77
 landed, 25, 103n47
 local, 169
 municipal, 169
 of service, 169
 provincial, 165
 Roman, 17
 senatorial, 182, 190n101; of Constantinople, 170
Aristotle
 Politics, 18
Arruñada, Benito, 40n95
Arsacius, high priest of Galatia, 75
Artisans, 16, 21, 43, 60, 92, 143
Asterius of Amasea
 Against Avarice, 172
Attila, 122, 168
Augustamnica Prima, province, 118
Augustine of Hippo, 179, 180
Aurelian, emperor
 Reform of, 161
Aurelianianus, 161
Aurelius of Carthage, 180
Aureus, 160, 161, 164
Aurum, 192n118
Autarkeia, 24, 26, 55, 81, 105n57
Autourgia, 170
Avarice, 32n25, 120, 122, 126, 131, 156n143, 161. *See also avaritia*; love of money
Avaritia, 5

B

Balch, David L., 30n3
Banaji, Jairus, 164–165, 170
Bankers, 45, 60, 170, 171
 private b. of Alexandria. *See* Alexandria
Banking activities, 171
Banks, 45
Banquet tradition, Graeco-Roman, 23
Basileias. *See* Basil of Caesarea: *ptōchotropheion*
Basil of Caesarea, 9, 73, 77, 79–83, 84, 85, 88, 89, 96–98, 104n50, 105n59, 106n68, 171, 202.
 See also under hoarding; luxury; patron; poor; property; rich; self-sufficiency; usury; wealth
 on the famine in Cappadocia, 77, 104
ptōchotropheion, 80, 82–83, 84, 85
Batiffol, Pierre, 152n89
Batten, Alicia, 38n77
Beggars, 86, 89, 97, 98, 108n87, 143
Benedictiones, 129. *See also eulogiai*
Benefaction, 29, 37n60, 55, 76, 78, 83, 85, 121, 131, 173, 180, 197, 201. *See also under* Melania the Younger; patronage
 Graeco-Roman, 194n141, 199
 in elite asceticism, 178, 205
 in Paul, 76
 Theodoret's b. to Cyrrhus, 133–134
Beowulf, 1
Bipartitism, 170
Bishop(s), 9, 64n21, 73, 83, 85, 110n104, 118, 123–124, 125–126, 128, 129, 130, 131, 132–134, 178, 179, 180, 181, 194n140, 200, 203, 205
 African, 180–181
 as manager, 24, 134, 180
 as patron. *See under* patron
 Egyptian, 150n76

INDEX 243

Blowers, Paul M., 110n106
Boer, Roland, 31n11
Bonus, *nauklēros*, 119
Bouffartigue, Jean, 75
Bronzesmiths, 98
Brookins, Timothy A., 25
Brown, Peter, 79, 83, 117, 121, 153n113, 157n167
Bryson, 18
Buell, Denise Kimber, 70n98
Bullion. *See* gold; silver
Burnett, Andrew, 160
Business activities, 19, 27, 34n37, 35n45, 40n91, 44, 45, 53, 54, 66n43, 170, 171. *See also under* aristocracy; elite
  in the Revelation, 29
  in the *Shepherd of Hermas*, 48–49, 50, 51, 200
Businessmen. *See* entrepreneurs
Byzantium, 105n57, 169, 205

C
Caesarea, 77, 79, 83, 103n39
Callicratidas, 18
Campania, 177
Caner, Daniel, 151n85
Capital, 7, 8, 20, 23, 54, 67n54, 78, 88, 90, 129, 170, 200
  accumulation, 7, 28, 39n82, 165
  financial, 29, 44, 96
  monetary, 26, 96
Cappadocia, 77, 202
Caracalla, emperor, 159
Cardman, Francine, 109n97
Cautiones, 192n118
Čekalova, Alexandra, 170
Centenarium, 168
Charity, 27, 33n33, 46, 53, 55, 56–58, 61, 64n25, 66n43, 71n105, 75, 92, 142, 143, 157n167, 173, 199, 201, 202. *See also* almsgiving

Chartoularios, 177
Chōria, 170
Christianization of space, 125
Chrysion, 173
Chrysolatrēs, 125
Church
  allowance, 93
  -building activity, 126, 173; Isidore of Pelusium on excessive, 125–126, 130
  finances, 124, 127, 128, 131, 134, 203
  in Corinth, 47
  Jerusalem. *See* Jerusalem: Church
  of Alexandria, 128, 130
  of Hierapolis, 135
  of Nazianzus, 84–85
  of Pelusium, 122, 127, 128, 203
  of Thagaste, 179
  property. *See* property: church
Cicero, 80. *See also* Stoic/Stoicism: image of the public theatre
City council, 169. *See also curia*
Claudius II Gothicus, emperor, 160
1 Clement, 47, 48, 53, 56, 70n90, 70n98. *See also under* organicist view of society; social harmony
2 Clement, 48, 49, 58, 59, 61, 70n90. *See also under* almsgiving; commerce; merchants
Clement of Alexandria, 2, 9, 53–54, 55–56, 58, 59, 61, 70n90, 94, 119, 137, 142, 200. *See also under* almsgiving; rich; Stoic/Stoicism; wealth
Stromateis, 54
Who Is the Rich Man Who Can Be Saved? 53
Coinage, 5, 162, 187n61. *See also antoninianus, argenteus, aurelianianus, aureus, chrysion, denarius, follis, miliarense, nomisma, nummus, solidus, tremissis*

billon, 160, 161, 162
bronze/copper, 3, 160–161, 162, 163–164, 165, 167
gold, 5, 74, 160–161, 162–166, 169, 173, 184n14
Roman Provincial. *See* Roman Provincial coinages
silver, 159–162, 166–167; Italian s., 163
Collectarii, 168, 188n75. *See also kollektarioi*
Comes Orientis, 133
Comes sacrarum largitionum, 167
Comitatus, 166
Commerce, 5, 34n37, 158n170, 171. *See also* trade
in *2 Clement*, 48
Communis aestimatio, 92
Community
Christian, 15, 25, 43, 50, 55, 60, 80, 86, 89, 112n132, 199, 200
Jewish, 76–77
COMOB, 166
Conspicuous consumption, 5, 8, 30n6, 32n25, 45, 81, 87, 89, 91, 93, 95, 97, 106n64, 129, 144, 172, 197, 198, 202, 204
Constantine I, emperor, 74, 162, 164–165, 169, 173, 186n45, 201. *See also under* market
gold coin of. *See solidus*
Constantinople, 2, 85, 86, 108n87, 118, 129, 167, 178, 183, 202
Great Church of, 178
Constantinus, *praefectus praetorio per Orientem*, 135
Constantius II, emperor, 164, 165
Coomber, Matthew J. M., 4
Corinth, 23, 47. *See also* Church: in Corinth
Corrector, 120
Council of Chalcedon, 123, 181
Council of Ephesus, 136

Crafts, 97, 139, 140
interdependence of the c. in Theodoret of Cyrrhus, 156n151
-money circuit in Theodoret of Cyrrhus, 144, 203–204
Craftsmen, 143
Creditor. *See* Usurer
Cult
imperial Roman, 41n98
pagan, 74
Curia, 169
Curialis, 120, 169
Cyprian of Carthage, 69n88, 70n92
Cyrenius, *corrector* of Augustamnica, 120
Cyril of Alexandria, 117, 127–128, 129–131, 151n85, 152n91
Cyrrhus, 132–136, 154n121, 154n125

D
Danube, 102n37
Debasement, 4, 159, 160, 162, 164, 204
Debt, 4, 21, 22, 36n51, 93, 97, 127
Debtor, 96–98
Dekatēlogoi, 96
Dēmoboros, 125, 149n58
De Moor, Tine, 4
Denarius, 159, 160
Denarius communis, 162–163
De rebus bellicis, 74, 164–165, 171
Despoteia, 92
de Wet, Chris L., 66n40, 112n142
Diakonia, 51
Didache, 46–47, 57, 59, 60, 63n21, 64n25, 70n98, 71n101, 200. *See also under* economic safety network; self-sufficiency; Two Ways doctrine
work ethic in, 46–47

INDEX   245

Didascalia Apostolorum, 70n90
Dignōmōn, 47
Dio Chrysostom, 45, 78, 102n32. *See also under* hoarding
Diocletian, emperor, 161, 164, 184n10
  Monetary Edict, 162
  Price Edict, 161, 162, 184n18
Dionysius (correspondent), 163
Dioscorus of Alexandria, 118, 130
Dipsychos, 47
Division of labour, 2, 137, 157n153
  in Theodoret of Cyrrhus, 139, 142
Domesticus, 119
Dominus, 175
Donations, 70n98, 82–84, 85, 95, 123, 131, 173, 177, 178, 180, 182, 191n107, 201, 203, 204
Donativum, 160
Downs, David J., 38n69, 59, 60, 70n90, 95
Dunn, Geoffrey D., 192n120

E
Economic growth, 2, 5, 12n24, 28, 31n14, 40n95
Economic inequality, 2, 81, 202
  in John Chrysostom, 88–89
  in Theodoret of Cyrrhus, 137, 139
Economics, 5, 16, 18
  classical, 7
  Keynesian, 5, 7
  mercantilist, 5, 6, 12n24
  modern, 1, 12n16, 16
  neoclassical, 7
  post-Keynesian, 7
Economic safety network
  in the *Didache*, 64n21
  in Gregory of Nyssa, 95
  in Paul, 24
Economy. *See also under* subsistence
  agrarian, 20, 88
  ancient, 15–17, 18, 25, 30n3
  divine, 59
  domestic, 16
  embedded, 16
  Herodian, 16
  market. *See* market: economy
  miraculous, 100, 101n20
  Roman, 15, 17, 31n14, 164
Edward II, king of England, 4
Edward III, king of England, 4
Egypt, 103n47, 117, 118, 125, 128, 157n167, 182
  anchorites, 178
Ekatostologoi, 96
Ekklēsia, 125
Ekklēsiastērion, 125
Elaphius, notary of Gregory of Nazianzus, 84
Elite, 6, 9, 15–18, 20, 21, 30n6, 32n19, 35n39, 40n95, 45, 51, 53, 59, 74, 78, 81, 85, 91, 97, 106n64, 117, 129, 130, 134, 136, 137, 144, 169–173, 174, 176, 178, 180–181, 188n78, 197, 199, 200, 205. *See also* aristocracy
  and business, 170–171
  and hoarding, 4, 6, 8, 79–80, 198
  and patronage, 174, 179–180, 201
  and trade, 15, 17, 20
  Antiochene, 103n47
  bequeathing of assets, 45, 201
  cash reserves of, 45, 201
  Constantinian, 165, 169
  dowries, 45, 201
  early Byzantine, 134, 201
  East Roman, 166
  financiers, 45
  landholding, 170, 189n81
  Roman, 29, 174
Elm, Susanna, 75
Emon, 89

Emporoi, 171
Enkrateia, 24
Enochic traditions, 41n98
Entrepreneurs, 45, 52, 170
Eparchos, 118
Epiphanius, archdeacon and *syncellus* of Cyril of Alexandria, 129
Epistle of Barnabas, 48, 57, 60, 64n26, 71n101, 200
Epistle of James, 27–28, 40n88, 40n93. *See also under* landowners; traders
Epistle to Diognetus, 57
Epitropos, 128
Epoikia, 170
Erdkamp, Paul, 31n14
Eschaton, 66
Essenes, 45
Eubank, Nathan, 36n51
Eucharist, 23
Euergetai, 79
Euergetism, 37n60, 45, 115n79, 134, 181, 194n141, 205
Eulogiai, 151n85
Euphratensis, province, 132
Eupraxius, servant of Gregory of Nazianzus, 84
Eusebius of Pelusium, 124–125, 126, 127–128, 129, 131
Eustathius, monk, 84
Eutrechius, *hyparchos* (*praefectus urbi Constantinopolis*), 153n112
Eutyches, archimandrite, 118
Evagrius, deacon, 84
Evagrius Ponticus, 56
Évieux, Pierre, 124

F
Fafnir, dragon (*Nibelungenlied*), 1
Famine, 102n37
  in Antioch, 80
  in Cappadocia, 77–79, 83, 103n39, 104n50, 202. *See also under* Basil of Caesarea; Gregory of Nazianzus
  in medieval England, 4
Farmers, 16, 78, 135, 170
Fideicommissum, 84
Fiensy, David A., 15, 35n39
Financial resources, 1, 2, 8, 37n60, 59, 96, 126, 130, 202
  management of, 9, 93, 98, 130, 131, 191n107, 197, 204, 205
Finley, Moses I., 16
Finn, Richard, 100n14
Follis (coin), 163
Follis (purse), 163
Formalist. *See* substantivist–formalist debate
Freedmen, 34n37, 51, 52, 67n54, 84, 85, 201
Freyne, Seán, 16
Friesen, Steven J., 24

G
Galatia, 75
Galilee, 15, 21, 34n38, 35n39
Gallienus, emperor, 160
Gallo-Roman Empire, 161
Garnsey, Peter, 103n39
Germany, 5
Gerontius, monk, author of the *Life of Melania the Younger*, 174, 181
Gold, 45, 76, 81, 86, 87, 88, 93, 95, 97, 110n104, 125, 130, 148n35, 162, 164–168, 171–174, 176, 178, 182, 186n45, 190n99, 192n118, 197, 199, 201. *See also aurum*
  spiritual, 173
Goldsmiths, 98
Gordon, Barry, 81
Grain hoarding. *See* hoarding: of grain

Greece/Greeks, 45, 75, 79, 188n78
Greed, 1, 26, 39n79, 48, 49, 56, 57, 64n23, 73, 76, 81, 87, 88, 91, 121, 138, 186n45, 199
Gregory, deacon and monk, legal heir of Gregory of Nazianzus, 84
Gregory of Nazianzus, 73, 77, 79, 83–84, 101n29, 105n59, 112n135, 171, 181
  bequest to the Church of Nazianzus, 84–85
  Funeral Oration for Basil of Caesarea, 77
  on the famine in Caesarea, 77–78
  On the Love of the Poor, 81
  testament of, 84–85
Gregory of Nyssa, 73, 95, 96, 98, 112n135, 113n151. *See also under* economic safety network; usury
Gresham's Law, 159, 161, 162, 183n4
Grierson, Philip, 7
Guillaume, Philippe, 33n30

H
Hanson, Kenneth C., 22
Hayek, Friedrich August, 6
Hays, Christopher M., 23, 36n57, 39n88, 60, 69n88
Hēgemōn, 120
Hellenism, 75
Henry VII, king of England, 5
Hephaestion, *abbas*, 178
Hermesandros, presbyter, 120
Herodes Atticus, 44
Hiba of Edessa, 126, 133
Hippo, 179
Hoarder, 3, 4, 6, 78–79, 81, 96, 98, 102n29, 198, 202
Hoarding, *passim*. *See also under* elite and manipulation of market prices, 198

and thrift, 6
commercial, 78
definition of, 7
in economic history, 3–5
in the history of economic thought, 5–6
in modern economic psychology, 3
of gold, 4, 5, 45, 88, 122, 167–168, 186n45
of grain, 4, 6, 78, 80, 102n36, 102n37, 198; and Basil of Caesarea, 78–80, 202; and Dio Chrysostom, 78, 102n32; and Emperor Julian, 80, 103n47
of money, 6, 7, 12n24, 44, 80
of wealth, 2, 5, 6, 15, 23, 26, 27, 45, 59, 80, 81, 85, 88, 92, 94, 197, 202
public, 5, 78
speculative, 4, 6, 79, 163, 198
Hoards, 6–7, 184n16
Holman, Susan R., 82, 96, 97, 100n9
Honorius, emperor, 176
Horsley, Richard, 33n33
Household, 17, 22, 25, 39n77, 44, 45, 57, 93, 110n107
  ascetic, 90
  management, 8, 17–18, 25, 26, 32n21. *See also* oikonomia
Hülsmann, Jörg Guido, 6
Hume, David, 5
Huns, 122, 147n35, 168
Hymn of the Pearl, 62n1
Hyparchos, 153n112
Hypatius, *politeuomenos* (*curialis*), 120
Hypatos, 132

I
Ibas of Edessa. *See* Hiba of Edessa
Ibrahim, Ahmad Asad, 4
Ignatius of Antioch

Epistle to the Smyrnaeans, 47
Imperial generosity, 121, 147n35, 167
  Isidore of Pelusium on, 121–122
Imperial largesse, 121, 159, 160, 166–167
Imperial reserves, 122, 167–168
Imperial Roman cult. *See* cult: imperial Roman
Imperial treasury. *See* treasury: imperial
Income
  annual, 175
  from manual labour, 46
  from productive occupations, 48
  surplus, 2, 24, 29, 60, 82
Indebtedness, 33n33, 50, 98, 143. *See also* debt
  in Roman Palestine, 20, 22
Indifferent. *See adiaphoron*
Inflation, 159–163, 204
Instrument. *See organon*
Interest (on money), 96–98. *See also* lending; loans; *tokos*
Investing, 8, 202
  definition of, 7
Investment. *See* money: investment
Irenaeus of Lyons, 65n31
Irenaeus of Tyre, 133, 134
Isidore of Pelusium, 2, 9, 117–132, 137, 167, 199, 203. *See also under* church; imperial generosity; luxury; property; self-sufficiency
Isidorus, *eparchos* (*praefectus praetorio per Orientem*), 118–119
Israelites, 95
Italy, 80, 168, 177

J

Janes, Dominic, 172
Jerusalem, 23, 174, 180
  Church, 37n60, 89–90
foundation of monasteries by Melania the Younger. *See under* Melania the Younger
Jesus Christ, 15–16, 20, 21, 22, 23, 25, 29, 33n33, 35n41, 41n100, 46, 53, 54, 58, 68n67, 70n90, 71n105, 88, 98–99, 115n179, 120, 121
  as guarantor, 98
  Second Coming of, 25, 61. *See also* Parousia
Jewellery, 5, 87, 124
Johannites, 183
John
  1 Epistle of, 29
  Revelation. *See* Revelation, book of
John Chrysostom, 2, 9, 73–74, 76, 85–96, 98, 109n97, 110n106, 111n120, 111n128, 112n132, 112n135, 112n142, 115n179, 135, 136, 139, 143, 149n56, 156n151, 171, 178, 202. *See also under* almsgiving; economic inequality; luxury; poor; poverty; property; rich; self-sufficiency; social cooperation; social justice; stewardship; stratification; usury; wealth
  adherents of. *See* Johannites
  Homily 7 on Colossians, 88
  Homily 21 on 1 Corinthians, 93, 123
  on common ownership, 89
  on the value of goods, 92
John Lydus, 122, 168, 177
Julian, emperor, 74–76, 79, 80, 81, 100n14, 103n47. *See also under* hoarding; philanthropy
Justinian I, emperor, 3, 154n125, 168

INDEX 249

K
Kehoe, Dennis, 34n37
Kelly, Christopher, 152n89
Keynes, John Maynard, 6
Koinōnia (Christian fellowship), 60
Koinōnia (economic partnership), 37n61. *See also societas*
Kollektarioi, 188n75
Kōmai, 170
Ktēmata, 170

L
Labour, 20, 24, 31n14, 37, 46, 47, 126, 139, 141, 143, 157n167, 170, 204
Labourers, 16, 20, 43, 60, 170, 184n18
Lactantius, 162
Landowners, 23, 170
  great, 78, 79
  wealthy l. in the Epistle of James, 27
Lending, 1, 17, 20, 45, 46, 95, 96–99, 115n179
Leo I, emperor, 168
Leo I (the Great), bishop of Rome, 132, 133, 191n107
Leshem, Dotan, 18
Libanius, 76, 85
Libra (Roman pound), 161. *See also litra*
Licinius, emperor, 163
Limited good, 19, 32n28, 108n87
  economy, 19
Lithomanēs, 125
Lithomania, 125–126
Litra (Roman pound), 161
Loans, 20, 21, 45, 71n105, 96–98, 201
Longenecker, Bruce W., 24, 25, 38n69

Lord's Prayer, 22
Luke
  Gospel of, 21, 22–23, 36n53, 36n55, 87, 94
Luke–Acts, 25, 27
Luther, Martin, 5
Luxury, 28, 125, 126, 129, 137, 142, 144
  consumption, 4, 5, 12n24, 74, 144, 172, 198, 201, 202; in Basil of Caesarea, 81, 97; in Isidore of Pelusium, 120; in John Chrysostom, 87, 95, 98; in Theodoret of Cyrrhus, 144, 172
  gifts, 130
  goods/items/products, 12n24, 28, 129, 144, 198

M
Magister militum, 176
Magister utriusque militiae, 135
Maier, Harry O., 52
Malina, Bruce J., 16, 30n3
Mammon, 23, 39n79, 49
Marcellus, deacon and monk, 84
Marcian, emperor, 118, 122, 167–168
Marcus Aurelius, emperor, 68n68, 159
Market, 4, 12n16, 16–18, 28, 32n19, 77, 78, 79, 85, 92, 93, 102n36, 103n47, 139, 144, 160, 162, 163, 168, 197, 198, 202, 204
  economy, 16
  flooded with *solidi* by Constantine I, 164–165
  mechanisms, 12n16, 17, 80, 104n47
  prices, 79, 103n47, 198
  speculation, 79
Maron, *oikonomos*, 129
Martinianus, *oikonomos*, 127–129, 131
Martyria, 125
Mary's Magnificat, 36n53

Mathews, Mark D., 41n98
Matthew
  Gospel of, 56, 171, 175
Mauretania, 180
Maximianus of Constantinople, 129
Maximus of Tyre, 44
Mayer, Wendy, 86, 108n87, 134
Mazzarino, Santo, 165
McGuckin, John A., 105n59
Mediterranean, 1, 2, 9, 28, 35n40, 53, 77, 85, 130, 169, 170, 182, 201, 204, 205
Megalemporos, 171
Megas emporos, 171
Melania the Elder, St., 174, 195n145
Melania the Younger, St., 83, 85, 173–183, 204–205
  and money, 174, 176, 177–178, 179, 180–181, 182
  benefaction of, 177, 182
  divestment of, 175, 177, 183, 205
  foundation of monasteries, 177; in Jerusalem, 180, 181, 195n145; in Rome (villa-monastery), 180; in Thagaste, 180, 181
  Life of, 9, 173, 174, 177, 179, 183, 191n107, 205
  poverty of, 177–178
Mercantile economic system, 87
Merchants, 7, 41n99, 43, 103, 118, 165, 170, 171, 189n87. *See also emporoi*; traders
  in *2 Clement*, 60
  in the Revelation, 28
  in the *Shepherd of Hermas*, 49, 52
  silk, 170
Middle class. *See* middling groups
Middle social strata. *See* middling groups
Middling groups, 4, 21, 24, 35n41, 43, 51, 52, 73, 85, 94, 95, 96, 98, 170, 173, 199, 201, 203

Midrash, rabbinic, 71
Miliarense, 166
Militares, 165–166
Miller, Amanda C., 36n53
Mint(s), 167
  comitatensian, 166
Mitchell, Margaret M., 111n120
Modernist. *See* primitivist–modernist controversy
Monasteries/monastic institutions, 2, 85, 90, 91, 125, 132, 181, 182. *See also under* Melania the Younger
  patronage of, 173, 201
Monasticism, 73
  coenobitic, 90
Money, 12n24, 13n36, 39n78, 45, 47, 54, 58, 59, 76, 84, 93, 120, 121, 124, 125, 126, 127, 128, 129, 130, 134, 138, 139–140, 144, 147n35, 159, 162, 164, 169, 171, 174, 176, 177, 178, 179, 180, 181, 182, 183n4, 191n107, 192n111, 197, 203, 204. *See also* crafts: -money circuit in Theodoret of Cyrrhus
  -changer, 161, 168, 171, 188n75. *See also collectarii*; *kollektarioi*
  demand, 6
  hoarding of. *See* hoarding: of money
  investment, 1, 6, 7, 13n36, 17, 50, 129, 171, 177, 180, 200, 201
  -lending. *See* lending
  love of, 46, 47, 65n31, 120, 124
  supply, 5, 6
Moral literature/moralists
  Graeco-Roman, 28, 199
  Hellenistic, 24, 40n90, 91
  Jewish, 21, 24, 29, 40n90, 106n64
Mundell, Robert, 183n4
Musonius Rufus, 44

INDEX 251

N
Nahum, 41n99
Nauklēros, 119
Nazianzus, 83–84. *See also* Church: of Nazianzus
Negotiatores, 171
Neil, Bronwen, 134
Nestorianism, 133
Nestorius of Constantinople, 129–130
Nibelungenlied, 1
Nicomachus Flavianus, 78
Niederwimmer, Kurt, 46
Nielsen, Randall, 4
Nile, 118
Nineveh, 41n99
Nomisma, 164. *See also solidus*
Nomus, *hypatos*, 132, 133
Numidia, 180
Nummus
  Constantian, 162, 163
  Diocletianic, 161, 163
  of Licinius, 163

O
Oakman, Douglas E., 15, 22
Obol, 132, 133
Obryzum, 166
Obsequium, 51
Ogereau, Julien M., 37n61
Oikeiōsis, 75
Oikonomia, 18
Oikonomos, 123–124, 127–128, 129, 131, 203
Olympias, St., 178, 205
Operae, 51
Organicist view of society
  in *1 Clement*, 53
  in the *Shepherd of Hermas*, 51–53, 82
  in Theodoret of Cyrrhus, 142

Organon, 54, 58, 119, 137–138, 141, 142, 191n107, 197, 205
Origen, 55–56, 70n90. *See also under* almsgiving; rich; self-sufficiency; wealth
Orphans, 50, 76, 143
Osiek, Carolyn, 51
Ostrogoths, 168
Oxyrhynchus, 170

P
Palestine, 20, 22, 32n28, 33n30, 35n40, 118, 180, 182
Palladius, 125
  Lausiac History, 178, 182
Palmyrene Empire, 161
Pannonia, 168
Panopolis, 145n6
Papyri
  P. Oslo 3 83, 185n29
  P. Ryl. 4 607, 163, 185n29
Parable(s), 19, 20
  of the Feast, 34n38
  of the Pearl, 34n38, 171
  of the Rich Fool, 23
  of the Rich Man and Lazarus, 87, 109n97
  of the Rich Young Man, 68n66, 81
  of the Shrewd Manager, 34n38
  of the Sower, 34n38
  of the Unmerciful Servant, 34n38
  of the Vineyard Labourers, 34n38
Paraenesis, 37n57, 61
Parousia, 25, 66n41
Parrhēsia, 118, 121, 128
Pastoral Epistles, 26
  1 Timothy, 26, 91
  Titus, 26
Patlagean, Évelyne, 153n113
Patrimony, 80, 85, 97

Patron, 26, 51, 55, 60, 79, 85, 135, 178, 179, 182, 194n141
  bishop as; Basil of Caesarea, 83; Theodoret of Cyrrhus, 132–135, 136
  -client relationships, 21, 33n36, 64n21, 140
Patronage, 33n30, 33n33, 37n60, 37n61, 38n69, 51, 52, 60, 70n92, 74, 94, 97, 117, 126, 132–134, 148, 172, 173, 174, 179–180, 194n141, 203. *See also under* elite
  and benefaction, 55, 90
Paul, 23–25, 37n60, 37n61, 70n92, 76, 101n20, 138. *See also under* benefaction; self-sufficiency
2 Corinthians, 59
Pastoral Epistles. *See* Pastoral Epistles
2 Thessalonians, 24
Pelusium, 2, 117–118, 127–128, 145n6. *See also* Church: of Pelusium
1 Peter, 26
2 Peter, 27
Pharaōnios, 125
Philanthrōpia, 75, 100n9
Philanthropy, 59, 75, 76, 95, 123, 179, 198. *See also philanthrōpia*
  pagan ph. and Emperor Julian, 75–76, 79, 100n9
Philippians, 37n61
Philodemus of Gadara, 18
Philo of Alexandria, 21–22, 45
Philosophy, 18, 19, 46, 91, 100n14, 136
  classical, 9
  Hellenistic, 9
Pinianus, 173–183. *See also* Melania the Younger
  slaves of, 175–176, 192n113

Pinianus, *praefectus urbi Romae*, 78
Plato
  Republic, 139
Ploutou desmōtēria, 44
Plutarch, 45
Polanyi, Karl, 63n21
Polis, 91
Politeuomenos, 120
Polycarp of Smyrna
  Epistle to the Philippians, 47
Pompeianus, *praefectus urbi Romae*, 177
Poor, 21, 23, 27, 35n40, 37n60, 39n79, 40n93, 41n98, 51–53, 56, 58, 60, 64n25, 71n104, 75, 76, 77, 84–85, 93, 95, 98, 99, 110n106, 119, 120, 123, 124, 125, 126, 127, 129, 130, 133–134, 137–139, 141, 143, 148n38, 157n167, 165, 173, 178, 180, 182, 186n45, 191n107, 192n111, 198, 199, 201, 203, 204
  and rich. *See* rich: and poor
  in Basil of Caesarea, 79, 80, 81, 83, 96
  in John Chrysostom, 86, 89, 93–96, 98, 109n87
Possessions, *passim*
  attachment to, 3, 38n72
Poverty, 2, 15, 22, 32n28, 35, 37, 40n88, 52, 56, 61, 76, 81, 98, 100n9, 119, 126, 127, 137, 172, 178. *See also under* Melania the Younger
  as indifferent. *See adiaphoron*
  as instrument. *See organon*
  John Chrysostom on, 86–87, 90, 94, 95
  moral value of, 27, 55
  origins of, 90
  relief, 40n88, 64n25, 73, 75, 77, 83, 87, 96, 106n68, 125
  socio-economic, 86

INDEX   253

spiritual, 86
structural, 94, 143
Theodoret of Cyrrhus on, 132,
    136–140, 142–143, 156n144,
    204
voluntary, 84, 86
Praefectus praetorio per Orientem, 119,
    135, 177
Praefectus urbi Constantinopolis,
    145n9, 153n112
Primitivist. *See* primitivist–modernist
    controversy
Primitivist–modernist controversy, 16–17
Priscus of Panium, 122
Procopius of Caesarea, 154n125
Profit, 6, 7, 26, 28, 40n91, 40n93, 48,
    77–80, 96, 102n36, 103n47, 126,
    129, 158n170, 165, 170, 198, 201
    business, 44
    commercial, 19
    from a deposit, 171
    maximization, 17
    spiritual, 99
Profiteering, 80, 96, 102n32, 102n36,
    103n47, 163, 166
Property, 45, 50, 68, 76, 81, 84, 94,
    97, 120, 126, 132, 133, 134,
    138, 143, 170, 175–177, 180,
    181, 194n140, 201, 202, 203
    church, 24, 85, 123, 130, 132, 133,
    180; Isidore of Pelusium on the
    mismanagement of, 122–123,
    127, 129, 130, 131, 203
    common, 80, 90, 141
    landed, 19, 130
    management of, 134, 173
    private, 46, 132, 141; in Basil of
    Caesarea, 80–81, 104n50; in
    John Chrysostom, 87, 89–90
Proterius of Alexandria, 118
Proverbs, 61, 106n64

Providence, divine, 21, 90, 94,
    110n107, 155n138, 177
Theodoret of Cyrrhus on, 136–137,
    139, 141, 142, 203
Prusa, 78
Ptōchotropheion. *See* Basil of Caesarea:
    ptōchotropheion
Ptōchotrophoi, 84, 85
Pulcheria, Augusta, 154n126
Pusulatum, 166
Pythagorean School, 18

Q
Qumran community, 25

R
Rabbinic Judaism, 35n45, 71n104
Reciprocities, 16, 19, 33n33, 137,
    204
    balanced, 22, 23, 24, 51–53, 55,
    82, 93, 198
    generalized, 22, 64n21, 82, 93
Rents, 15, 21, 170
    in Roman Palestine, 20, 28
Revelation, book of, 28–29. *See
    also under* business activities;
    merchants; trade
Rhee, Helen, 43, 50
Rich, *passim*. *See also* wealthy
    and poor, 29, 95, 179, 203; in
    Clement of Alexandria, 55,
    59; in Origen, 55, 56; in the
    Shepherd of Hermas, 51–52,
    59; in Theodoret of Cyrrhus,
    135–136, 139, 142, 143
    in Basil of Caesarea, 79, 80, 82, 83,
    96
    in John Chrysostom, 86, 88–89, 90,
    92, 93, 94–95

Riches, 1, 4, 8, 15, 19, 21, 26, 27,
  33n30, 39n82, 40n93, 44, 46,
  50, 52, 54, 55, 58, 61, 62n1, 83,
  88, 91, 92, 109n97, 110n103,
  111n128, 120, 123, 124, 127,
  128, 131, 137–138, 140, 141,
  142, 172–173, 177, 179, 199,
  203. *See also* wealth
Rollens, Sarah E., 35n41
Roman Provincial coinages, 184n10
Rome, 28, 48, 167, 174, 175, 176,
  177, 180, 181, 190n101,
  192n113
  suburbium of, 175
  villa-monastery of Melania the
  Younger. *See under* Melania the
  Younger
Rosner, Brian S., 39n79
Rössner, Philipp Robinson, 5
Roussiane, relative of Gregory of
  Nazianzus, 84
Rowe, Nicholas, 6
Rufinus of Aquileia, 56

S
Sacrae largitiones, 166
Sarris, Peter, 31n19, 170
Saving, 2, 3, 8, 9, 13n36, 35n43, 44,
  134, 201–205
  definition of, 7
Savings, 2, 4, 6–7, 8, 45, 84, 93, 131,
  144, 197, 201–202, 204
Sayings Gospel Q, 21
Scarcity, 27, 78, 81, 126, 136, 172
Schor, Adam M., 133
Second Temple literature, 61
Self-sufficiency, 4, 17, 19, 26, 46, 73,
  102n36, 138, 198, 202. *See also*
  autarkeia
  in Basil of Caesarea, 81, 97
  in the *Didache*, 46

  in Isidore of Pelusium, 119, 126
  in John Chrysostom, 73, 87–88,
    90, 94
  in Origen, 55
  in Paul, 24
Septimius Severus, emperor, 169
Serena, wife of Stilicho, 174, 176–177
Severinus of Noricum, 102n37
Severus, Pinianus' brother, 175
Sharp, Buchanan, 4
Shenoute of Atripe, 145n5, 145n6
Shepherd of Hermas, 47, 48, 49–53,
  55, 58, 59, 61, 67n54, 67n57,
  70n98, 82, 142, 173, 199, 200.
  See also under almsgiving; business
  activities; merchants; organicist
  view of society; rich; social
  cooperation; stewardship; traders
  elm and vine parable, 51
  moderate prosperity, 50–52
Sicily, 177
Silver, 5, 45, 81, 87, 88–89, 93, 95,
  110n104, 160, 162, 166–167,
  178, 186n45, 192n118. *See also*
  argentum
  Italian. *See* coinage: silver
Silver, Morris, 102n36
Silversmiths, 98, 170
Simony, 129, 130
Sirach, 40n91, 61, 64n25, 71n104
Sitzler, Silke, 112n132
Social cooperation, 77
  in John Chrysostom, 89
  in the *Shepherd of Hermas*, 52
  in Theodoret of Cyrrhus, 135, 143,
    204
Social harmony, 21
  in *1 Clement*, 56
  in Theodoret of Cyrrhus, 135, 140,
    141, 144
Social justice
  in John Chrysostom, 88

Societas, 37n61
Society
　early Byzantine, 167
　Graeco-Roman, 25, 44
　late antique, 82, 131
　Roman/late Roman, 43, 52, 73, 130, 171, 191n107
Solidus, 74, 84, 122, 162–164, 166, 168, 169, 171, 173, 175, 182, 184n14, 188n75, 190n99, 204. *See also nomisma*
Son ("yours"), 89
Sozomen, 125
Sozomenus, *domesticus* of the *praefectus praetorio per Orientem*, 119
Spain, 177
Stambaugh, John, 30n3
Stenger, Jan R., 91
Steuart, Sir James, 5
Steward, 21, 34n37, 45, 58, 94, 197
　ecclesiastical. *See oikonomos*
　estate, 20, 33n36
Stewardship, 24, 26, 54, 58, 80, 110n107, 144
　monastic paradigm of, 89–90
　of wealth, 8, 18, 85, 95; John Chrysostom on, 89–90, 92; *Shepherd of Hermas* on, 50
Stilicho, *magister militum*, 176–177
Stoic/Stoicism, 68n68, 70, 79, 87, 91
　concept of *adiaphoron*. *See adiaphoron*
　concept of the wise man, 54
　image of the public theatre, 80
　influences on Clement of Alexandria, 54, 55, 119
Stratification
　Graeco-Roman economic, 24
　social, 16, 50, 52, 59, 95; of Antioch according to John Chrysostom, 94
Subjective theory of value, 92

Subsistence
　economy, 16, 30n6
　level, 19, 24, 60, 86, 143
Substantivist. *See* substantivist-formalist debate
Substantivist–formalist debate, 16–17
Surplus
　distribution of, 29, 55
　generation of, 18, 87
　income, 2, 24, 29, 60, 82
　moderate, 24, 51, 60, 143
　sharing of, 57, 70n92
Symmachus, 78
Synagogues, 37n60
Syncellus, 129, 151n84
Synkellos, 151n84
Syria, 46, 132, 135

T
Tabernacle, 95
Tamieion, 45
Taxation/taxes, 15, 16, 19, 20, 30n6, 121–122, 135, 147n35, 160, 162, 166, 168, 173
　commutation of, 165–166, 168
Temples, 44, 74, 76, 125, 165, 186n45
Tetrarchs, 161
Thagaste, 178, 179, 181
　church of. *See* Church: of Thagaste
　monasteries founded by Melania and Pinianus in. *See under* Melania the Younger
Thebaid, 182
Themistius, 121
Theodoret of Cyrrhus, 9, 57, 117, 119, 132–144, 156n144, 172, 199, 203–204. *See also under* benefaction; crafts; division of labour; economic inequality; luxury; organicist view of society; patron; poverty; providence;

social cooperation; social harmony; wealth
The Cure of Pagan Maladies, 136
On Providence, 136, 138, 142–144, 155n133, 156n151, 203
Theodosius I, emperor, 74, 176
Theodosius II, emperor, 75, 117, 121–122, 167–168
Theodosius, notary of Gregory of Nazianzus, 84
Theodoulus, deacon, 84
Theophanes the Confessor
Chronicle, 118
Theophilus, freed slave of Gregory of Nazianzus, 84
Theophilus, *nauklēros*, 119
Theophilus of Alexandria, 125
Thēsauros argos, 44
Thrift, 18
 in modern economics, 6
Tobit, 61, 64n25, 71n104
Tokos, 96
Trade, 16, 28, 34n37, 40n95, 45, 46, 48, 54, 85, 130, 165, 169, 170. *See also* commerce
 disdain toward, 44
 maritime t. in the Revelation, 28
 Roman, 28
Traders, 78, 79. *See also* merchants
 in the Epistle of James, 27
 in the *Shepherd of Hermas*, 52
 jewel, 170
Trapezitai, 171
Treasure, 1, 44, 45, 65n31, 74, 81, 120, 141. *See also thēsauros argos*
 chambers, 44. *See also ploutou desmōtēria*
 in heaven, 120, 157n167, 192n111
Treasury, 5, 130, 152n89, 177
 heavenly, 61, 71n105, 99, 169, 173

 imperial, 121, 166, 169, 173. *See also sacrae largitiones*
Tremissis, 163
Triclinium, 173
Tropheus, 79
Two Ways doctrine
 in the *Didache*, 47

U

Urbainczyk, Theresa, 135, 153n101
Usurer, 96–98
Usury, 74
 Basil of Caesarea on, 79, 96–98, 202
 Gregory of Nyssa on, 96, 98
 heavenly, 98
 John Chrysostom on, 96, 98, 202

V

Valens, emperor, 166
Valentinian I, emperor, 74, 165, 166
Valentinian III, emperor, 168
Vandals, 168
Van Nuffelen, Peter, 75
Veblen, Thorstein, 5
Verhoeff, Maria, 115n179
Vrolijk, Paul D., 33n30

W

Wealth, *passim*. *See also* riches
 accumulation of, 1, 4, 19, 20, 32n28, 41n98, 46, 50, 52, 59, 61, 73, 88, 92, 165, 169, 199
 as *adiaphoron*. *See adiaphoron*
 as false happiness, 21, 57–58, 62n1, 142
 as instrument. *See organon*

INDEX   257

circulation of, 4, 7, 24, 93, 201, 202
distribution of, 1, 2, 15, 19, 25, 49, 58, 59, 120, 139, 143–144, 167
ecclesiastical, 123, 131, 202
ethics, 36n57, 56, 69n88, 199
excess, 35n43, 35n45, 61, 62, 68n67, 88, 94, 104n50, 112n142, 121, 136, 191n107, 198, 199; in Origen, 55
functional definition by John Chrysostom, 87
Graeco-Roman attitudes toward, 28, 38n72, 44–46, 112n132, 194n141, 199
hoarding of. *See* hoarding: of wealth
inherited, 88, 141
justification of, 58, 173, 199, 202; in Clement of Alexandria, 54–55, 119, 137; in the *Shepherd of Hermas*, 50; in Theodoret of Cyrrhus, 137–138, 140, 142, 203
liquidation of, 51, 173, 175, 179, 181, 182, 200
mobility of, 92, 138
precarious nature of, 8, 26, 27, 58, 111n128, 138, 182, 197
redistribution of, 54, 55, 58, 64n21, 74, 82, 86, 90, 92, 94, 123, 131, 144, 183, 198, 203, 205

renunciation of, 9, 23, 51, 54, 55, 94, 112n142, 173–175, 177, 191n107
sharing of, 23, 29, 46, 51, 57, 60, 70n92, 76, 83, 87, 94, 120, 123, 140, 201, 203, 205
spiritual, 173
stewardship of. *See* stewardship: of wealth
stored, 2, 21, 35n45, 40, 50, 91, 92, 119, 121, 123, 130, 173, 205; Basil of Caesarea on, 82
true, 21, 61, 62n1
Wealthy, *passim*. *See also* rich
social obligations of, 51, 53, 55, 82, 148n38
Whittow, Mark, 188n78
Wickham, Lionel R., 152n91
Widows, 25, 49, 76, 143

X
Xenophon
  Oeconomicus, 18

Z
Zacchaeus, 23, 94
Zero-sum game, 19, 89, 198
Zosimus, presbyter, 126–127, 131
Zoticus, *praefectus praetorio per Orientem*, 177
Zuijderduijn, Jaco, 4

Printed in the United States
By Bookmasters